# My Story

# My Story

STEVEN GERRARD

*with* DONALD McRAE

MICHAEL JOSEPH
*an imprint of*
PENGUIN BOOKS

MICHAEL JOSEPH

UK | USA | Canada | Ireland | Australia
India | New Zealand | South Africa

Michael Joseph is part of the Penguin Random House group of companies
whose addresses can be found at global.penguinrandomhouse.com.

First published 2015
003

Picture permissions can be found on pages 459–60

The moral right of the author has been asserted

Set in 13/15.5 pt Garamond MT Std
Typeset by Jouve (UK), Milton Keynes
Printed in Great Britain by Clays Ltd, St Ives plc

A CIP catalogue record for this book is available from the British Library

HARDBACK ISBN: 978–1–405–92338–5
OM PAPERBACK ISBN: 978–1–405–92339–2

www.greenpenguin.co.uk

Penguin Random House is committed to a
sustainable future for our business, our readers
and our planet. This book is made from Forest
Stewardship Council® certified paper.

For My Family and Friends

# Author's Note

My first book, *Gerrard*, was published in 2006. This new book concentrates on recent events and offers further reflections on my twenty-seven-year career with Liverpool, and fourteen years with England, alongside a more personal analysis of some of the high and low points that have shaped my life.

# Contents

# Prologue: Slipping Away

*Liverpool, Sunday, 27 April 2014*

I sat in the back of the car and felt the tears rolling down my face. I hadn't cried for years but, on the way home, I couldn't stop. The tears kept coming on a sunlit evening in Liverpool. It was very quiet as we moved further and further away from Anfield. I can't remember now how long that journey lasted. I can't even tell you if the streets were thick with traffic or as empty as I was on the inside. It was killing me.

An hour earlier, after the Chelsea game, I'd wanted to disappear down a dark hole. Our second-last home match of the season was meant to have been the title-clincher. We had beaten our closest rivals, Manchester City, in the previous game at Anfield. We had just reeled off our eleventh straight win. One more victory and we would be almost certain to win the league for the first time since May 1990.

Twenty-four years earlier, in the month I turned ten, that team of me and my dad's dreams had been managed by Kenny Dalglish and captained by Alan Hansen. It was also the team of McMahon and Molby, of Beardsley and Rush, of Whelan and Barnes.

I was dreaming of today even then, as a boy who had joined the Liverpool Academy at the age of eight and wished and prayed that, one day, he might also win the league in front of the Kop. My first-team debut came in 1998, when I was eighteen and I had no idea how it might feel to be a thirty-three-year-old man crying in the back of a car.

I felt numb, like I had lost someone in my family.

It was as if my whole quarter of a century at this football club poured out of me. I did not even try to stem the silent tears as the events of the afternoon played over and over again in my head.

In the last minute of the first half against a cagey Chelsea, set up to stop our rush to glory by José Mourinho, it happened. A simple pass rolled towards me near the halfway line. It was a nothing moment, a lull in our surge to the title. I moved to meet the ball. It slid under my foot.

The twist came then. I slipped. I fell to the ground.

The ball was swept away and the devastating Chelsea attack began. I clambered to my feet and ran with all my heart. I chased Demba Ba as though my life depended on it. I knew the outcome if I couldn't catch him. But it was hopeless. I couldn't stop him.

Ba scored. It was over. My slip had been costly.

I was in the car with Alex, my wife, and Gratty, Paul McGratten, one of my closest friends. Alex and Gratty were trying hard to help me, to console me. They were saying words like, 'Look, it can still change, there're still a few games to go . . .'

But I knew. The fate of the title was now in Manchester City's hands and they would not blow it. There would be no comeback for Liverpool. There would be no Miracle of Istanbul – a repeat of that Champions League final when, in 2005, we were 3–0 down at half-time against AC Milan, the Italian masters of defence, and yet we fought back and won the game on penalties. I had been at the heart of that team. I was already Liverpool captain all those years ago. I scored the first goal in our long climb back against Milan. I kissed and held the Champions League trophy, and kissed it again, before anyone else on that magical night in Istanbul.

I knew the glory of victory – just as I knew the despair of

defeat. I had lost another Champions League final, against Milan once more, two years later. I was the only player to have scored in the finals of the League Cup, the FA Cup, the UEFA Cup and the Champions League. I had played more than one hundred times for England in World Cups and European Championships. I was still captain of England. Soon, we would travel to Brazil for my last major tournament.

At Liverpool, meanwhile, the battle to win justice for the families of our ninety-six fans, including my ten-year-old cousin Jon-Paul Gilhooley, who had died so tragically at Hillsborough, continued. We had just marked the twenty-fifth anniversary of our loss – and yet big steps had been taken to expose the lies and cover-ups which had hidden the truth for so long.

The dark and the light, the elation and the misery, were familiar. They stood together, apart but inseparable, like two posts in an empty goal at Anfield.

The league was different. I had wanted to win it with Liverpool for so long that, now it had gone again, I could not hold my emotion in check. The tears trickled on; and the city I loved became a blur.

I beat myself up. My head was all over the place. It's a familiar trait with me; but I didn't feel I was being too harsh or self-critical then. I had lived through many great moments in my career and achieved success beyond my most fevered boyhood dreams. I had played and scored in games and tournaments which belonged to another world from the Bluebell Estate in Huyton, Liverpool 36, where I had grown up. I had done things that would have shocked me as a kid.

I had also given absolutely everything of myself to Liverpool FC: in training, in almost 700 games, off the pitch, around the squad and as part of the club, the community and the city. I could not have done any more. I had squeezed out every last ounce of ambition and desire and hope inside me. In the end, it had not been quite enough to help us win the title everyone at Liverpool craved.

Instead of hitting a long crossfield pass to set up a goal, making a decisive tackle or curling the ball into the back of Mark Schwarzer's net to seal our victory, I had fallen over. Chelsea scored a second goal in the final minute, but the killer moment was that simple change of luck.

Here comes the ball, a pass from Mamadou Sakho, and here comes the slip. I fall down.

The Kop, and the whole of Anfield, had sung 'You'll Never Walk Alone' but, in the car, I felt isolated. I felt very alone. The Liverpool anthem reminds you to hold your head up high when you walk through a storm. It reminds you not to be afraid of the dark. It reminds you to walk on through the wind and the rain, though your dreams be tossed and blown, and to walk on with hope in your heart.

I did not feel like I had much hope left. It seemed like I was heading for suicide watch instead.

Eventually, I spoke to Alex. I asked her to phone Struan Marshall, my agent, so that he could arrange a flight out of the country that night. I needed to get away. I couldn't allow my three girls to see me so distressed and down. It would upset them to see their dad so broken. I had to get out of Liverpool because I still felt as if I had let everyone down. I needed to find somewhere we could be alone, just me and Alex, somewhere that would feel like a ghost town. Maybe I could try and bury the pain then.

I heard Alex's voice, talking to Struan, but the daze settled over me. The car picked up speed and soon we were all silent again. I was lost in my thoughts and memories of a thrilling but painful season, of a career full of bliss and love, and how I had ended up here, in the back of a car with my cheeks still damp from the tears I had begun to wipe away. I knew that, somehow, I would never feel this alone again.

# 1. The Stand-Off

When I was a little boy, playing football every day on Ironside Road, outside our house on the Bluebell Estate, I became John Barnes. He might have been seventeen years older than me, with a different skin colour, but on the big stretch of concrete that led straight to our front door, Liverpool's most brilliant player and I were clones.

In our cul-de-sac I pretended to be exactly like Barnes – skilful and unplayable, a dribbling machine and a scorer of wonder goals against my big brother Paul and his mates who were between three and five years older than me. They tackled hard and sometimes brought me down, making my knees bleed. I just got up, refusing to cry, and became John Barnes all over again on a street that was more like a football pitch to me.

All the signs were there. John Barnes wore the number 10 shirt for Liverpool and we lived at number 10 Ironside. We both loved football. We both loved Liverpool – even if he came to Merseyside from Jamaica, via Watford, while I was born right here, in the city.

I was a skinny little kid. Almost as often I turned into John Aldridge, without the moustache but full of Scouse goals, or Peter Beardsley, trying the same little jinking runs and passes, if not his Geordie accent. I might become Ronnie Whelan, a calm leader in midfield, or Steve McMahon, a tough-tackling hard man and master of the dragback with the same Liverpool accent as me. I practised the McMahon trick where you over-run the ball but keep it moving along the touchline. I would do that again and again. Liverpool's stars all belonged to me, and I became them in my head and on Ironside Road in games where everyone else was so much bigger and stronger than me. But my determination matched them every time.

I was eight years old when I was accepted into the Liverpool Centre of Excellence. My dad would take me to the Vernon Sangster, a now-demolished sports centre in Stanley Park, and we both felt very proud. I would wear the red of Liverpool at the club's Centre of Excellence and it didn't matter that Dad and I had to catch two buses in the rain and the cold, travelling through ice and snow on winter days. It felt like I was playing in sunshine every day.

When I did get tired, because I was still so young, Dad was always there to lift me up. On the few days I arrived home from school and said I was too knackered for the two-bus trip to the Vernon Sangster, Dad sorted me out. 'You're never too tired for Liverpool,' he reminded me. 'Go on. Get changed, wet your hair, smarten up and we'll be off.' By the time we arrived at the sports centre I was raring to play again.

I never stopped loving Aldridge, Barnes, Beardsley, McMahon, Whelan and the rest but, as the years passed and I became a teenager, a different fantasy formed at Anfield. Whenever I saw Robbie Fowler playing up front for Liverpool, with him in the iconic number 9 shirt and me just another besotted fan, I dreamed of being in the same team as him. Robbie also came from Liverpool, and he was a hero to every single one of us. He was the Toxteth boy given the nickname of 'God'. I imagined my next defence-splitting pass setting up yet another Fowler goal. I was convinced that, together, we would be unstoppable.

The dream came true. I never played with Robbie at his peak, or mine, but we became teammates. We played together for Liverpool and even for England.

In August 2013, after twenty-five years at Liverpool, from a happy boyhood at the Academy to two years of joy as a YTS apprentice to becoming an ecstatic Champions League-winning captain, I felt the same burning intensity that had consumed me on Ironside Road and at Anfield. I was thirty-three years old but I remained a fan. I still loved Liverpool FC and players as special as John Barnes, Robbie Fowler and Luis Suárez.

Just as I had done with Barnes and Fowler, I saw something of myself in Suárez. Luis was also a street footballer, and the same obsession ran through him. It didn't matter if we were from Montevideo or Merseyside, we were marked in the same way. Football ruled our lives.

Luis joined Liverpool on 31 January 2011. On his first full day at Melwood, our training ground, his fixation with football was so obvious it took my breath away. Luis belonged to that rare breed who trained like he played. Melwood on a drizzly Tuesday morning was the same as Camp Nou on a crackling Saturday night. Luis played to win a five-a-side training session like he was chasing the Champions League or the World Cup. If his team lost a Melwood kickaround he went home angry. He always needed to win that badly.

I loved that intensity and passion – and I loved his ability and skill most of all. I've trained with some stunning footballers during my career, but I've always believed I'm up there as one of the best. You need that conviction. And so I always wanted the very best players in the world to join Liverpool. I wanted them to lift the club to the heights Liverpool had scaled when I was that kid in the 1980s on Ironside Road. More selfishly, I wanted to prove to those great footballers that I belonged alongside them.

Luis Suárez gave Liverpool and me those beautiful opportunities. He also gave us a chance to compete against the money and power of Manchester United, Chelsea and Manchester City.

In training, and in matches, Luis proved again and again that he was at a different level from everyone else. I tried harder than ever to match him – but Luis was a better footballer than me.

It's always difficult to pick out the very best teammates in a career stretching across seventeen seasons but, when I think about it, the answers soon become clear. Four players stand out in my time at Liverpool and with England.

The first three all helped me become a better player. They all speak Spanish. Each of them unleashes a wave of emotion in me and in every Liverpool supporter.

Fernando Torres. Xabi Alonso. Luis Suárez.

Wayne Rooney, another Scouser but a Bluenose, an Evertonian who moved in 2004 from Goodison Park to Old Trafford, deserves to be bracketed alongside them. There have been training sessions and games with England when Wayne has shown that same gift and desire.

Alonso. Torres. Suárez. Rooney.

Barcelona showcase Lionel Messi, Neymar and Suárez in an attacking front line. Maybe I can have my own fantasy football team of Alonso and Gerrard in midfield, in the heat of battle, with Suárez, Torres and Rooney up front.

Suárez was very real. He was not just a fantasy player in some imaginary team. He ran and pressed and fought for the ball and ran again – while producing extraordinary moves and sublime goals. There was a sustained period when playing with Luis was like being under a magical spell. He blew me away with his talent.

Fernando came the closest to matching Luis. I had two years with Fernando when he made me feel invincible. I always knew where he was, where he was going to move next. I'm not a natural number 10 but, for a couple of years, Fernando helped me become one. I had my best season then, as a number 10, and that was down to Fernando in 2007–08.

I had my most impressive set of stats during that campaign, with twenty-four goals and nine assists. Every time I went on to the pitch with Fernando I was sure either he would score or I would, and we'd win the game. I felt the same with Suárez – and sometimes with Rooney. I would step out on to the pitch with Rooney before some big international games and think, 'We've got every chance of winning today – because of him.'

Michael Owen was another special forward. We played together when we were so much younger, but Michael was an absolute dream for me as a midfielder.

But, ultimately, Luis stands out. I would have loved to have played with Luis when I was a lot younger, and peaking, as we could have been phenomenal together for years. That's my only tinge of regret with Suárez.

Here's an example of what he did for me. On 13 March 2012 I scored a hat-trick at Anfield against Everton. It was the first hat-trick in thirty years of Merseyside derbies, since Ian Rush scored three at Goodison Park in 1982. I was told it was the first derby hat-trick at Anfield since 1935. History has always been part of my love of football. But history is not as thrilling as the feeling I had playing football with Luis Suárez that night.

I got the goals that game, pretty good goals too, and I remember it as my favourite match at Anfield – and not just because we beat Everton. I love winning derbies because Everton fans have given me unbelievable stick over the years. Proper verbal abuse. So it was incredibly sweet to bang three past them. It was made even better by the selfless magic Suárez sprinkled over me that night. It's a rare combination, to be a miraculous footballer who is willing to use his gifts to assist and create goals for a teammate. Messi, for all his greatness, also has that humility.

Luis is no saint – and I'm not sure he would have done the same for Daniel Sturridge. There was always a little bit of needling rivalry between Sturridge and Suárez. But when it came to me, especially against Everton, Luis went out of his way. He helped Liverpool, and me, play like kings.

All the people who revile Luis Suárez, never having met him, might be surprised if they had the chance to benefit from his unselfish willingness to sacrifice himself for his team. He will run himself into the ground, like he did that night, glittering like an unbreakable diamond. I got the hat-trick but Suárez, buzzing and swarming and sparkling around me, set up two of my goals on a plate.

I've got other wonderful memories of watching him play, seeing him every day, the way he gives everything to football. He doesn't go into the treatment room. He's a proper warrior. Suárez edges ahead of Torres because of that mentality, that robustness which means he doesn't miss a session, or a game. He scores goals. He creates goals. He's hard and horrible to play against. He's right up for it. You've got a chance of beating anyone in the world with Luis Suárez in your team.

### *Melwood Training Ground, West Derby, Liverpool, August 2013*

Every time I looked across at Luis I felt hurt and frustrated all over again. It was doing my head in. It was torture for a few days. I would be training with the first-team squad while Luis was two pitches away from us. He had just a fitness coach for company. Sometimes he would only be allowed to come out to work after we'd finished training. The stand-off between Liverpool and Suárez had become bitter.

I was caught in the middle. On one side we had the club's American owners, Fenway, headed by John Henry and Tom Werner, and our manager, Brendan Rodgers. On the other side, at the far end of the line of training pitches at Melwood, we had Luis Suárez.

Luis was angry with Fenway. He was fuming with Brendan. He was so angry that, for a week in early August, he barely moved a muscle in training. Luis was trying to make a point. He was disappointed in Brendan because he was convinced that the manager, or someone higher up at Fenway, had lied to him.

Luis just wants to play football. And so for him not to try a leg in training for a week cut into me. The same thought kept going round and round in my head: 'Has someone told Luis to behave in this way?'

I don't know exactly whose choice it was to banish him but I think Brendan had the final say. He must have thought, 'Well, I can't have him training with the team if he's not getting out of first gear.' I understood the decision but I still felt I had to help.

The division between Luis and Brendan, between the player and the club, ran deep and wide. It was hard to see any way of bringing them together. The root of the conflict was that Arsenal, after a ludicrously low initial bid, had offered Liverpool a pound over £40m to buy Suárez.

I didn't know what was in Luis's contract, but the rumour suggested that any offer over £40m would trigger a release clause. The measly quid tacked on to Arsenal's offer still seemed insulting, and surprising, behaviour. I thought it was extremely cynical. Arsenal, usually, are very classy. They have a class manager in Arsène Wenger, with class players, and they play the game the right way. I have great respect for Arsenal because they do things properly – but not this time.

Their pursuit of Suárez infuriated our owners. And Luis was seriously pissed off because Fenway refused to sell him.

The situation had escalated over the previous four months. I didn't have the kind of relationship with Luis where I'd text him every day or have lunch with him outside the club, but once we were together at Melwood we bounced off each other. I liked his personality, it was infectious, and his English was improving all the time. Luis and I could talk man to man because of our mutual respect.

We sat together in the dressing room. The numbers of the training tops and shirts go from 1 to 37, and obviously his number 7 was next to my 8. I was close enough to him to say, face to face, 'Come on, Luis, what's going on?'

At first it was just casual chat. Luis said, 'Look, there are a few clubs sniffing around me,' or, 'I want to play in the Champions League.'

Months before the Arsenal chaos, I had been worried that we would lose Luis because I knew how well he was playing.

By the end of the 2012–13 season he had scored fifty-one goals in ninety-six appearances for Liverpool. Thirty of those goals had come that season and they had been a key factor in our improvement under Brendan in his first year as our manager – after he succeeded Kenny Dalglish in the summer of 2012. It was similar to the Torres situation. When your best player is in scorching form and scoring most weeks, then the biggest clubs in Europe are going to be circling and watching. And when you're not in the Champions League, and your star player is performing that well, you are vulnerable. It's not easy to fend off rivals willing to spend massive money to take players like Torres and Suárez away from us.

I knew what it felt like to be the subject of such attention as a player. In 2005, just months after I led Liverpool to victory in the Champions League, José Mourinho came close to persuading me to leave. I was on the brink of agreeing to sign for Chelsea when, feeling suddenly sick at the thought of turning my back on Liverpool, even after we'd had such needless difficulties over a new contract, I made a decision I've never regretted. I committed myself to Liverpool. The offers kept coming. When I was playing my best football, probably in 2006 and even in 2009, there were some big chances to leave: Chelsea again; Real Madrid twice – and the second time was more tempting because, once more, Mourinho wanted me. Playing for José in the white shirts of Real Madrid, at the Bernabéu? Only Liverpool could have made me say 'no' again.

Even after Euro 2012, when I had my most consistent tournament for England and was included in the team of the Championship in Poland and Ukraine, Bayern Munich were in touch with my agent. They wanted to know whether I'd be interested in joining them. This was the summer before the season where they went on, under Jupp Heynckes, to win the treble, beating Borussia Dortmund in the Champions League final at Wembley in May 2013. Maybe I could have been part of that team but my mind had been made up eight years before when I rejected Chelsea. I knew I could never leave Liverpool. I would remain a one-club man as long as I played football in Europe.

I still understood how it felt to be flattered and chased. Mourinho, whom I admired so much as a manager, had also spoken about trying to sign me for Inter Milan in the season they won the Champions League. Barcelona apparently sniffed and skirted around me but I'm not sure they were ever especially interested. I think they also knew how tightly I was bound to Liverpool.

Of course, if you are a South American player the lure of Barça and Madrid is almost impossible to resist. But Arsenal? It would have broken my heart if Luis had left Liverpool for Arsenal.

I had stayed out of the way at first, because Brendan was all over it. He and Luis were still talking. After everything I had been through with Fernando, trying so hard to keep him at Liverpool, I didn't want to get involved again. I had my own game to worry about, my own position as captain, my own responsibilities to the other thirty players in our first-team squad.

My long history at Liverpool meant that I was probably different from any other captain in the game – certainly in the Premier League. Liverpool's players had always felt able to approach me, and so they came to me with their concerns and doubts, and I tried to help everyone.

I felt the weight of my role. It would be wrong to call it a burden because, most of the time, it felt like an honour. Whenever I walked into Melwood I saw the quote from Bill Shankly, our greatest manager, carved into the wall. It summed up the spirit of Shankly, and everyone who had followed him, as we were reminded every day what he had once said:

> Above all, I would like to be remembered as a man who was selfless, who strove and worried so that others could share the glory, and who built up a family of people who could hold their heads up high and say, 'We are Liverpool'.

Bill Shankly transformed Liverpool from a Second Division club into a European giant. He instilled the values we cherish at this club. I have only been a player. But I understood what he meant in that quote. It was a belief, an ethos, that I tried hard to match in my smaller place at the heart of the club.

And so there was a heavy responsibility on me during my last decade and more at Liverpool. I felt the need to help our incredible fans – and a massive chunk of that meant, whether it was Torres or Suárez, trying to keep hold of our star man. I had to try to help the manager as well, while listening to the player, who was not just a teammate but often a friend asking me for support in his battle with the club. So it was difficult. It was stressful – even if it was nothing compared to the challenge Shankly had overcome in the 1960s.

I had to deal with a transfer saga twice in four years. I did my best on both occasions to keep Fernando and Luis, and not just because it was the right thing for Liverpool. From a selfish point of view I knew my job as a player and as captain would be a lot easier with them in the side.

I realized that, without Luis, we seemed certain to have another mediocre season in 2013–14. With him, I was convinced we could improve on our seventh place and chase a spot in the top four. We would be Champions League contenders, if not quite title-challengers, because I knew how much he brought to Liverpool.

I had lost the battle that had seen Torres leave for a London club; I could not afford a similar defeat with Suárez. And it really was my responsibility because, unlike with Brendan or Fenway, Luis saw me differently. He looked at me with an expression which made me believe I had something to work with, a sliver of hope. Luis would talk and listen to me.

Without that link, we would lose him. And without Suárez we would be back in the wilderness. There was no other option. I had to get involved. I had to try hard and find a solution. It was a mess.

Life used to be so much simpler. My happiest days as a footballer are still vivid. They happened more than half my lifetime ago, in 1996, when I was sixteen. I spent my first of two years as a Youth Training Scheme apprentice at Melwood, mopping floors, cleaning boots and pumping up balls, in between playing football, football, football.

It was heaven. If I could revisit any period in my career it would be those two years.

There was no responsibility or pressure then and we were crazy about football. The YTS placement also meant I could escape the boring old slog of school. I now know that I really should have applied myself because I had the potential and intelligence to have done so much better. But, back then, I wasn't much of a fan of school. I had a little go but I should have tried harder. I guess I had the promise of a contract to become a professional footballer. And those YTS days gave me such a sweet taste of playing football for a living. I went from dreading school every day to going into Melwood to work full-time for the club I love, surrounded by my heroes.

I caught the bus from Bluebell Lane to the Melwood training ground in West Derby each morning. But if I got up late, which hardly ever happened because I was so keen, I needed to make a change and get two buses. I couldn't afford a taxi on my wages of £47.50 a week.

I remembered that figure when, in 2014, I turned down an offer of €13.5m net to play football in Qatar for two years.

Sometimes Tommy Culshaw, a first year professional, would give me a lift to and from training in his Ford Escort. He always refused to take any petrol money from me. Tommy was a big help, and he is still a friend today.

At the Academy we only got paid once a month but my parents, Julie and Paul, were given an additional £40 a week from the club to help with my living expenses. Mum and Dad, who both supported me every step of the way, were typically big-hearted. If I was good at home they would give me all the £40 weekly allowance. Those small payments from Liverpool, and my mum and dad, probably meant more to me than the tens of thousands of pounds a gifted teenager can earn every week in the game today.

At the end of the month, on payday, I went into town to get myself a new tracky or a pair of trainers. I would then spoil myself with a McDonald's. It meant I'd be skint for three and a half weeks but I didn't care. Football would keep me going.

A couple of my closest friends were with me in those fantastic, crazy years. Bavo (Ian Dunbavin) and Boggo (John Boggan) have been my mates for a very long time. We don't see each other as much these days but Boggo was the best man at my wedding to Alex. Bavo and I are closer than ever. He had joined the Academy at twelve, four years after me, but we clicked straightaway. Bavo was our keeper back then.

He eventually kept goal at Accrington Stanley, and is now coaching the young keepers at the Liverpool Academy in Kirkby. I think it's a real shame that the Academy kids are so sheltered and kept apart from the first-team squad today. My view is that they should be based at Melwood, just like we were in our first year, so that they can see up close the training regimes Jordan Henderson and Philippe Coutinho go through every day as the new stars of Liverpool. A little bit of that dedication, and magic, can rub off and make the difference to an Academy kid.

I also feel sorry that, being much more pampered and not expected to do the kind of dirty jobs we did at Melwood, they miss out on all the mad times we had mopping and cleaning. Apart from Boggo and Bavo our group included Neil Gregson (Greggo), Matty Cass, Stephen Wright (Wrighty) and Michael Owen – the Boy Wonder who was only a few years away from World Cup glory with England. But Michael was always ready to muck in and have a laugh.

We were footballing tearaways who used to take the piss out of the mighty Don, the strapping and powerful caretaker of Melwood. At the time we thought we were making Don's life a misery, which seemed hilarious, but the truth was different. Don was solid. We'd play all kinds of practical jokes on him – from pouring water on his teabags to turning out all the lights and throwing stuff at him. We thought we were terrorizing him and driving him up the wall but Don still had us doing every menial job that needed tackling on a muddy and freezing winter's day. He made sure we did it well – even if we sometimes jumped on top of him and wrestled him, the strongest man in Liverpool, to the ground. We would be pissing ourselves but Don would just get up, rant a little more, and move us on to our next chore.

In those days, unlike now, every kid was British. We shared the same culture, language and piss-taking mentality. The banter would be flying and I loved all the practical jokes we played – whether we were cutting up the clothes of one of our mates or someone was getting his own back on us. It was just twenty lads in the dressing room, all picking up £250 a month. Everyone was totally skint but there was very little pressure or responsibility.

On the weekends we couldn't wait to run out again for Liverpool's youth team and play our socks off against Everton, Manchester United or one of our other rivals. As a YTS kid, without being too cocky, I could see that, alongside Michael, I was the best in the group. Michael was six months older than me and when he started playing in the first team I felt even more confident. I saw how successful Michael was from the very start and that made me sure my turn would come. That certainty allowed me to relax and really enjoy the learning process. I could dream of playing football for ever while doing our jobs and having a laugh.

Steve Heighway, a Liverpool legend as a player, Dave Shannon and Hugh McAuley were three football coaches who transformed me. They showed me the Liverpool way and, at the Academy, they gave me the belief I could become a professional player. Under their guidance, Wrighty and I were invited to start training with the first-team squad.

John Barnes, my Ironside idol, was still there as he neared the end of his ten-year career with Liverpool. Where I had once imagined I was John Barnes, I was now actually trying to get the ball off him. But Digger, as everyone called him, skinned me every time. I could never shut John Barnes down, or stop him. My adoration turned into appreciation of his incredible skill.

I had no more luck against Jamie Redknapp. He was too good. Jamie was also kind, and he often took me aside either to praise me or to suggest ways in which I could improve as a young midfielder. Sometimes he would slip me a spare pair of brand-new Mizuno boots.

Robbie Fowler was another hero who became very real. I was in awe of Robbie and Steve McManaman, of their ability and achievements, and also because they came from Liverpool. One of my tasks was to wait for them outside the first-team dressing room so that they could sign the posters and shirts and footballs which could then be sent to local hospitals and schools – or auctioned for charity.

I might have been a real prankster around the Academy but I made sure I never looked a tit in front of Fowler or McManaman. I revered them and hoped that, one day, I might be the same as them – a Liverpool boy making and scoring goals in front of the Kop.

Dominic Matteo, a Scot who was six years older than me, had arrived at Liverpool from Dumfries in 1992. Four years later he had made the first team as a defender and at Christmas in 1996 he amazed me with a £200 bonus. All those established Liverpool players taught me a lot about being generous to young kids coming through.

The football, the first-team stars and the joking around always mattered more than the money to me. Even a boring and stinky job would be turned into a riot. How else could we react every morning when it was our task to pump up the balls at Melwood? Ronnie Moran, that great old Liverpool coach, would fine us if we failed to inflate every single ball to perfection. So we pumped and pumped and pumped in the ball room, and yelped with laughter because, every time, we had to battle through one of Joe Corrigan's shites. It was the time of morning when Big Joe settled down on the toilet. His favourite cubicle was right next door to the ball room.

Joe, the goalkeeping coach who had been a famous shot-stopper for Manchester City and England in the 1970s, must have loved his bran flakes. He was as regular as our attempts to come up with the funniest one-liner. While we pumped the footballs we had to listen to Joe's clockwork rituals in the khazi and, even more disturbingly, risk being suffocated by the powerful fumes he generated. There were six staff in the same room and so Joe might not have been the only one doing his morning drop-offs. We didn't try to find out by going any closer. We just kept laughing and pumping, pumping and laughing, as a very smelly fog descended on the Melwood staffroom.

A different kind of fog clogged football in the summer of 2013. Without a World Cup or European Championship to divert anyone in the long weeks of the off-season, the tedious transfer speculation whirred round and round. You could not pick up a paper, switch on the television or listen to the radio without being swamped by the latest gossip and rumour.

It was the summer of Gareth Bale, Wayne Rooney and, distressingly for me, Luis Suárez.

Bale, who had just enjoyed an outstanding season for Spurs, was being stalked by Real Madrid. Everyone knew he would eventually go to Madrid for over £85m but, to get that sort of transfer fee, Spurs were ready to drag it out for as many months as it took to reach that crazy amount.

Rooney was caught up in the kind of saga I remembered from the days when I was torn between Liverpool and a

Mourinho-led Chelsea. After his years away from England, coaching Inter and Real Madrid, Mourinho had returned to Stamford Bridge that summer. Rooney, like me, was enticed by the idea of playing for Mourinho at Chelsea. The situation was complicated by the fact that it seemed as if he wasn't getting on with Sir Alex Ferguson at Manchester United.

Ferguson's retirement at the end of the previous season added to the uncertainty. David Moyes had left Everton to attempt the impossible job of being Ferguson's replacement at United. Moyes, who had managed Rooney at Everton, had to try to hold on to England's best player.

I was consumed, instead, by the Suárez saga. It was far more tangled and bruising than the Bale and Rooney sideshows.

Luis Suárez, as we had all learnt by then, came with baggage. Trouble followed him wherever he went. Suárez had been banned for eight games for racially abusing Patrice Evra in the midst of a game against Manchester United in October 2011. Luis still protested his innocence and he and Liverpool had expressed anger with the length of the ban.

We got over it, eventually. But just as Suárez was on fire, ramming home goals and playing with all his heart, he unleashed yet more mayhem.

On 21 April 2013, in a game against Chelsea at Anfield, he bit Branislav Ivanović on the shoulder. Suárez used both his hands to grip the arm of Chelsea's defender. He then sank his teeth into Ivanović's flesh. It was indefensible.

Liverpool protested again when he was suspended for ten games – the last four of the 2012–13 campaign and the first six matches of the new season which loomed over us. I left it to the club to help him with counselling – and hoped that Luis would one day learn to steer clear of trouble.

Of course if a player less gifted and important to us as a team had behaved so badly it's unlikely we would have been as supportive. I am not proud to admit that – but the reality of professional football is that clubs are more ready to help the players who can help them most. It can be a harsh business.

More personally, it had not taken me long to decide that I liked Luis as a man as well as a footballer. Luis lives for his family and football. He is crazy about Sofi, his first girlfriend and now his wife, and their kids. If Luis is not playing football he wants to be with his family. He lives his life as simply as that; and it struck a chord with me.

Family and football also define me. But I am different from Luis. I would remain with Liverpool from the age of eight to thirty-five. I have a rich emotional attachment to my hometown club he could never enjoy. Luis has moved from Uruguay to Holland to England to Spain. But I don't regard him as a mercenary. I just see a man who wants to play football, for himself and his family, at the very highest level.

We all went away on international duty and then had our summer break. Even from thousands of miles away it seemed obvious that Luis was agitating for a move. I could not avoid it because, like almost every other player, I read the newspapers. I search the internet for all the latest football news from around the world. It was impossible to miss Luis Suárez day after day, week after week.

It started with an interview Luis gave to a Uruguayan radio station, Sport 890, on 29 May 2013. 'I'm happy at Liverpool. I'm happy because of the fans,' Luis began, 'but I'm not prepared to continue to put up with the English press. I have a contract with Liverpool, but it would be very difficult to say no to Real Madrid.'

Real Madrid's president, Florentino Pérez, was played that clip of the Suárez interview by a Spanish radio station. He stirred the pot a little more: 'Well, Suárez is a great player, like [Edinson] Cavani and [Robert] Lewandowski,' Pérez said. 'We can't talk about players from other clubs but . . . if you ask me if I like Luis Suárez then, yes.'

A day later I breathed more easily as Pérez switched his attention back to another Premier League target: 'Bale was born to play in Madrid,' he said as Spurs readied themselves for an all-out assault from Real on their most crucial player.

In June, ahead of Uruguay's friendly against France in Montevideo, Suárez addressed a press conference:

> It's a difficult moment for me. The English media don't treat me well. Because of the paparazzi I can't go in my garden or to the supermarket. My reason for leaving [England] is not the money. It's my family and image. I don't feel comfortable there any more. It's nothing against Liverpool but it's a good moment for a change of environment.

By early July, Arsenal had switched their attention from Gonzalo Higuaín, the Argentine striker who was on his way out of Real Madrid, to Suárez. They offered Liverpool £30m. It was a mockery of a bid compared to the £80–90m Spurs were demanding for Bale.

I heard the first serious alarm bell when Luis spoke again to Sport 890: 'I have to value that,' he said of Arsenal's offer. 'That makes me think that I can go back and do well over there. It's good that the top English clubs still want me.'

Cavani, his friend and striking partner for Uruguay, sank another little dagger into my heart. 'Luis has to be playing Champions League football. I can tell you his love for Liverpool is very real. If they were playing in the Champions League he would not consider leaving. But he knows he is now at the stage of his career that he needs to be playing at the top level.'

On 22 July, Arsenal made their insulting bid of £40m plus a pound. John Henry, our owner, was furious. 'What do you think they're smoking over there at the Emirates?' he asked.

We met up with Luis on our preseason tour of Australia and Indonesia. He clearly did not want to be there, even if the global power of Liverpool was obvious all over again. The sight and sound of 96,000 fans singing 'You'll Never Walk Alone' before a Liverpool friendly match in Melbourne was spine-tingling. We were mobbed and adored in Thailand – where I was invited to meet the king.

I carried out all my ceremonial duties but my head was swarming with Luis. He had spoken to me privately and said, 'Arsenal have met the release clause, Stevie. But the club won't let me go. Brendan and the owners lied to me.'

It was the first time he had come directly to me to discuss a contract issue or anything of real seriousness away from football. Until then I had only ever had banter with Luis, or conversations about the opposition team or individual players. I had never spoken to him about financial issues or our own contracts. Players don't really talk to each other about such details.

I was in an extremely tricky position. My loyalty to Liverpool, and my desire to keep Luis as a teammate, would always come first. But I had to accept that, in legal and moral terms, it might be wrong for us to refuse to sell him.

So I spoke instead about Fernando Torres. I said, 'Luis, look, Fernando was one of the best strikers Liverpool's ever had, goal-wise, and he was adored.'

The adoration for Fernando at Anfield was so fierce the whole ground used to rock with his own special song: *His armband proved he was a Red / Torres, Torres / You'll Never Walk Alone it read / Torres, Torres / We bought the lad from sunny Spain, he gets the ball and scores again / Fernando Torres is Liverpool's number 9!*

The Kopites embraced Torres as one of our own as soon as he arrived from Atlético Madrid in 2007. He scored thirty-three goals in his debut season at Liverpool and he was revered because it's an Anfield tradition to fall in love with the star forward. It's a chain that, in my lifetime as a fan, stretched from Dalglish to Rush to Aldridge to Fowler to Torres to Suárez. In the end Torres scored eighty-one goals in 142 games for the club.

Liverpool loved 'El Niño'; and for a long time Fernando loved them back. I felt the same because for a few seasons it seemed like we were unbeatable when Fernando was in the mood.

It then got complicated. We were no longer in the Champions League and Fernando began to press for a move to Chelsea. Liverpool didn't want to do any kind of deal with Chelsea. They were as desperate as I was to hold on to Torres.

But Fernando forced through the move. He came to me to ask for help to get him out of Liverpool so that he could play for Chelsea. I just said: 'No. Look, Fernando, I can't help you get out. I'm not in a position to do that – and I don't want to do it. I want you to stay because I'm a fan even before I'm a player and captain of this team. I'm not going to help you because I don't want you to go.'

He shook his head. 'Stevie, it's past that. I've got to go.'

I could see the lump in his throat. His agent, a woman I didn't really know, had been hanging around the club for days. So I knew that Fernando had been in and out of the manager's office, trying to force the move, and I could see he was frustrated that it wasn't happening. But as soon as he said those words to me I knew we'd lost him.

In January 2011 Fernando broke the heart of every Liverpool supporter, including me, by going to Chelsea for a British transfer record of £50m. He made it worse, on his arrival at Stamford Bridge, by saying, 'I'm really happy and I'm sure I am doing one big step forward in my career joining a club like Chelsea. This is a great club.'

It was a slap in the face of every Liverpool fan. Of course me and Fernando are fine. He's a good friend and I know he's had a tough time these past years. If he had that time again I think he would be a bit more careful. We've had many chats on the phone and I get the impression that, with hindsight, he regrets leaving Liverpool. He still has a real love for this club – but most Liverpool fans loathed him for a long time. They believed Torres had betrayed them. You always felt that when he came back here with Chelsea.

I said to Luis: 'Do you want that? After all you have given the fans – and everything that they have given you? You've got loads of time to win a few things here first. Then you can think about moving on. But don't ruin your relationship with the supporters like Fernando did.'

I explained to him the significance of the number 9 shirt at Anfield and why the striker always gets adulation from the Kop like no other player. They worship the star man, the goal-scorer, and the support they give you on a weekly basis is incredible.

Luis had felt that love for himself. But he was seething. It was touch-and-go but I still believed there was something there, something for me to work with as I fought so hard to keep him.

Other players helped as well – Lucas, Coutinho, José Enrique. We all tried to keep him. But as soon as the Arsenal situation escalated I had lost my hold. The rift between Luis and the club, and particularly between him and Brendan, became a chasm.

Apart from worrying about our best player I had another un-official role at the club. For the past ten years I had assumed more responsibility as captain and tried to persuade some great players to join Liverpool. It was the same ritual every summer.

The club would let me know which long-shot target they had in mind and then ask me to contact him. They thought that a request to consider moving to Liverpool would have more impact coming from me.

The latest player in our sights was Willian, the Brazilian midfielder, who had moved from Shakhtar Donetsk to the Russian club Anzhi Makhachkala. We had already lost one of our main targets of that preseason, the attacking midfielder Henrikh Mkhitaryan, who came from Armenia but played in the Ukraine for Shakhtar. Mkhitaryan decided to go to Borussia Dortmund instead of Liverpool – and I understood why. Dortmund had been Champions League finalists just a few weeks earlier and Liverpool were out of the frame in Europe.

The quest for Willian became more urgent. Brendan and the club hoped I could convince him. I also knew that if we got Willian, and the club were ready to spend £30m, it would show Luis we meant business.

I followed the usual routine when approaching a star player we wanted to sign. Instead of calling him directly I always sent a text. It seemed more respectful and allowed the player to read my message at a time when it suited him best. A cold call felt wrong.

I slipped into the groove with Willian. I said hello and hoped he didn't mind me contacting him directly. I stressed how much I admired him as a player and then, having mentioned the fact that I knew Liverpool were speaking to his agent, I used the standard line: 'If you need to chat or ask any questions I'm available at any time.'

It was the opening move in a familiar game. The reply came in and the same old conversation started. Willian thanked me and he said the usual, along the lines of, 'I'd love to play with you, Steven, blah-blah-blah, but there are other clubs who play in the Champions League I need to talk to as well.'

I knew Spurs and Chelsea were also very keen on Willian. So I answered him and said, of course, I understood the situation. But I then went in with my sales pitch. 'I think Liverpool would be a great move for you. The fans are amazing, the history is there and we're building a good team. You could do something great here – and we'd love to have you.'

I meant it, too, because the club only asked for my help if it was with a player I rated. But I always tried to persuade him with honesty and respect and I never mentioned anything about the player's financial situation or the contract he could expect from Liverpool.

The next text from Willian was so obvious I could have written it for him even before I read it. He again said that it would be great to play in the same team as me but 'I'm not sure Liverpool can give me the Champions League.'

There was no disputing it. I could not guarantee Champions League football with Liverpool to Willian or any of the other dozens of players I had contacted over the years. I could just stress that, with him joining us, we could do something special and he would love playing for our fans.

It was a game of texting ping-pong that had only small differences each time. Occasionally a player would say that his wife or girlfriend preferred the idea of living in London, Madrid or Paris than Liverpool. The clear message was that there were fancier shops and swankier restaurants in bigger cities than Liverpool. I knew then that the deal was dead.

Willian probably fancied London more than Liverpool too. We didn't get him and for a while it looked as if he was heading to Spurs. But the old Champions League lure, and José Mourinho, worked its magic because, in the end, Willian went to Chelsea.

At least I had my text patter ready for the next transfer window. This was how my life at Liverpool had turned out. It seemed a long way from mopping floors and having a laugh in those deliriously happy YTS days.

On Saturday, 3 August 2013, Liverpool staged my testimonial. The proceeds, which exceeded a million pounds, went to my foundation which aims to help disadvantaged children. We played against Olympiakos and they did not charge a penny for their appearance. Their generosity meant a lot.

I had scored my so-called 'wonder goal' in 2004 against the Greek champions when I volleyed home a twenty-five-yard screamer in the last few minutes of that Champions League group match. It meant we qualified for the knockout stages and so, as that was the season we actually won the Champions League, Olympiakos have always held a special place in my career.

Before my testimonial, much was made of the fact that I was one of the last, and perhaps the best-known, member of a dying breed – the one-club player. Before the 2013–14 season I had made 628 appearances for Liverpool and scored 159 goals. Beyond the Champions League I had won the UEFA Cup, two FA Cups and a couple of League Cups. I had become Liverpool captain ten years earlier – in 2003. I had also, in June 2013, signed a one-year extension to my existing contract. It meant that I would stay with the club until at least the summer of 2015, which would mark the end of my twenty-seventh year on Liverpool's books.

I felt proud but, secretly, I was stressing over Luis and the whole transfer nightmare. We spoke again in my testimonial week and Luis said, 'Look, I'm not going to come to the function after the game, but I'm playing in your testimonial. I want to be there for you, Stevie.'

I didn't mind him missing the evening bash. Luis doesn't go to any club do. He's such a family man that as soon as he finishes training or playing he wants to be back with them. So he never went to any team lunch or dinner. I respected him so much as a player that I accepted his ways. But he also admitted to me before the testimonial that he was hurt and confused. The Arsenal deal remained on the table.

Luis said to me: 'I understand the fans being a bit disappointed with me at the moment. But when I go out and put that shirt on I give the fans everything. I usually give everything in every session, but what I can't take is people lying to me.'

I didn't know whether that was true. I was just praying Luis would stay. He received a rapturous reception when he came on as a substitute against Olympiakos; and he was 'humbled' by the response.

Yet two days later, on the Monday, we had an open training session at Anfield and the ground was packed with supporters. Luis didn't try a leg. This was the start of him tossing off training for a week. He didn't want to know. He wasn't happy. He had spat out his dummy.

On Wednesday, 7 August, Luis gave an explosive interview in Spanish to the *Guardian*'s Sid Lowe – who would help write his autobiography:

Last year I had the opportunity to move to a big European club [Juventus] and I stayed on the understanding that if we failed to qualify for the Champions League the following season I'd be allowed to go. All I want is for Liverpool to honour our agreement. I have the club's word and we have the written contract and we are happy to take this to the Premier League for them to decide the case. But I do not want it to come to that.

I'm twenty-six. I need to be playing in the Champions League. I waited one year and no one can say that I did not give everything possible with my teammates last season to get us there. People say Liverpool deserve more from me but I have scored fifty goals in less than a hundred games and now they could double the money they paid for me.

I spoke with Brendan Rodgers several times last year and he told me: 'Stay another season, and you have my word if we don't make it then I will personally make sure that you can leave.' Now the story has changed. Liverpool is a club with a reputation for doing things the right way. I just want them to abide by the promises made last season.

Brendan and John Henry reiterated that Luis would not be sold – especially not to Arsenal. It was at that point Brendan banished Luis to the wilderness at Melwood. He would not be allowed to return to training until he apologized to the club, the supporters and the squad and agreed to remain at Liverpool. Luis looked as lost to me as Fernando had two and a half years earlier.

## Formby, Merseyside, Thursday, 8 August 2013

Alex had made my tea. She placed the salmon, pasta and salad in front of me. It was my favourite meal. But I stared at my food that early evening, feeling sick to my stomach. The three girls were running round the house, kicking up a racket, just being kids. My head seemed close to bursting. I could not pick up a knife and fork. My meal remained untouched.

'What's up?' Alex asked. 'Is there anything wrong with it?'

I shook my head. It felt as if I couldn't even talk, let alone eat.

'Is it football?' Alex asked after she tried to shush the girls a little. Alex doesn't even follow football closely, and neither do any of my daughters, but she has lived with me long enough to know that my good and bad moods are almost always connected to the game. I worried about Liverpool, the club and the team. I knew that some players just think about their own game, and keeping their place in the team, but decades at my hometown club had made me this way. I felt duty-bound to try and help us out of every problem we faced on or off the field.

I sometimes envied the way other players could seem so carefree. I also knew why my YTS days with the club stood out in such happy relief. Bring back the fog of Big Joe Corrigan any day. I was sick of the wheeling and dealing, the greedy manipulations of modern football.

Conflict twisted that 2013–14 preseason. It ripped up the idea that August should be the most optimistic month for any football fan. The time before a ball has even been kicked in a competitive match is meant to be one of hopeful dreaming. Will this be the season to make all the usual heartache of being a football fan seem really worth it?

But, gazing blankly at my dinner, I felt lost in despair.

We were ten days away from a new season. Our best player, already banned from playing for another six matches and banished from training by the club, was determined to leave us.

'I can't eat,' I thought to myself. 'It's doing my head in.'

I pushed my food away. I couldn't take it any longer. I reached for my phone. I had to call or text Luis.

I decided to send him a simple message:

Luis, what's going on here? We need to straighten this out.

He texted straight back:

Look mate, the manager's lying to me, the club's lying to me.

I pinged him another message:

I want to help sort this out for you and for the club.

A few texts flew in from Luis. He was upset and his English, even in text form, became more broken as he tried to express his frustration.

I sent him another message.

Can we have a chat tomorrow – and meet up early at Melwood?

I almost smiled when I saw his answer:

OK Stevie.

At Melwood, early that Friday morning, Liverpool's outcast and their captain were not really meant to be together. Luis had been told not to arrive at the training ground until the afternoon – once the rest of us had finished working. But it felt important that we should ignore that ban and talk openly to each other. I had informed the manager of my plan.

I spoke first. 'Look,' I said to Luis, 'I'm not going to help you get out of this club because I think you're making the wrong decision.'

Luis was very quiet.

'I'll be honest with you,' I said. 'You should stay for another year. If you keep performing like last season the clubs that you really want, the ones that can offer you what you really deserve, will come for you.'

'What if they don't?' Luis asked simply.

'Are they in for you now?'

'Well,' Luis said, 'they're sniffing around. Madrid have gone for Bale and we don't think Barcelona are ready. But they're interested in me.'

I told Luis that, from my own experience, when Madrid want you they always come back. Barcelona are the same. If they were interested in him now, they would be interested in him next season. He had to trust me. I had been in his position before – with Chelsea and Madrid.

I spoke more bluntly. 'All I'm interested in is that you don't go to Arsenal. I don't want to play against you. And I know Arsenal will be in a better situation than us if you go there. That's the honest truth. So I want you to be honest with me, Luis. Do you really want to leave Liverpool Football Club for Arsenal? Or do you want to leave Liverpool Football Club for a mega club?'

Luis hesitated. 'What do you mean by mega club?'

'Well,' I said, 'when you've got your relationship with these fans of ours, it's obvious. For me, putting myself in your shoes, I'm only leaving for two places. Real Madrid or Barça. I know that's what you want.'

Luis's silence told me I was making sense. I had hit the right spot. He was listening closely. 'I've had the opportunity to join Madrid and I turned it down,' I explained. 'But my situation is different. It means more to me to play in front of these supporters at Liverpool because they're my people . . .'

My teammate nodded. He understood. I pressed on. I said that if I had gone to Madrid or Barcelona it would have been a bigger risk for me because I had a young family. But I knew that, as a South American, it would feel like he was going home – especially if he went to Barça. His wife lived in Barcelona for years. His children speak Spanish.

I was closing the gap all the time. I pushed hard. 'And if you stay here one more season,' I said, 'I know we'll be a better team than Arsenal.'

Luis looked at me. 'Look, mate,' I said urgently. 'You just can't go to Arsenal. It doesn't make sense for Liverpool or for our fans. And it doesn't make sense for you either. I think you're getting the wrong advice if anyone is still telling you that you'll be better off at Arsenal.'

There was no protest from Luis. He wasn't saying to me, 'I love Arsenal – I want to go there' or 'I think they're a great club.'

Luis knew he could trust me. I laid out my plan. Forget Arsenal and stay with us one more season. Let's give the league a real crack. And then, definitely, we would all understand it was time for Liverpool to step aside when Madrid or, more likely, Barcelona came back in for him.

There was another small nod – but neither of us was smiling yet. I asked if I could arrange a meeting for him with Brendan.

Luis stretched out his hand to shake mine. 'OK, Stevie,' he said.

I texted Brendan:

> I've opened up to Luis. I've got a feeling we've got something
> to work with. But it has to be played right because he's angry.
> Can he meet you?

Brendan agreed and I set up a time for them to meet, but that night Luis messaged me. He would only meet Brendan if I was there.

'Luis wants me to come in with him,' I told Brendan.

'So do I,' he answered.

When the three of us met up we sat on the little leather couches in the manager's office. It was awkward. We were all smiling at each other – but Luis's smile to Brendan was more like a threat. I could tell that Brendan was not quite sure which way we were going at first. I was all set to play the role of peacemaker. It was a big moment.

Luis was ready to say words which Brendan might not like. He had told me often enough how he thought Brendan had lied to him.

But I had hope too. Brendan is understanding and a player's manager. He's the opposite of Rafa Benítez – my manager when we reached two Champions League finals in 2005 and 2007. Rafa is a brilliant tactician when it comes to winning football matches, but as a person he can be ice-cold. I liked the fact that Brendan was warm. I had also seen that, until they fell out over the transfer issue, Brendan treated Luis and I very well and showed us great respect. I was the club captain and Luis Suárez was our main man.

We started well, with Brendan catching the right mood, and quickly began to make progress. I was still worried that it could turn messy because I didn't know what had been said in their meetings with the owners. I didn't know all the ins and outs of Luis's contract. But the conversation in Brendan's office went as smoothly as I could have hoped. We agreed the same points that Luis and I had discussed. Brendan said he wanted Luis back in the team – and Luis responded by promising that he would train properly. We shook hands again after Brendan promised that, at the same time, he would speak to the owners and sort out the situation once and for all.

I felt great as I walked out of the office. It felt as if we had a chance of getting back on track.

The final test came in our first training session with Luis back in the squad after we all returned from international duty. Luis had just flown in from Japan, where he had played in a friendly for Uruguay. I had captained England to a 3–2 win over Scotland at Wembley that week.

I was worried again. There had been mixed messages in the media while Luis was away. At first I was relieved when Luis told the Uruguayan press that he'd had a change of heart: 'For now, due to all of the people's affection, I will be staying at Liverpool.' But a day later, after Uruguay won 4–2, Japan's Kyodo News ran a quote which suggested that Suárez had distanced himself from his earlier statement: 'I didn't say that . . . maybe someone else did.'

I could not bear the thought of seeing Luis again on his

own, two pitches away from the rest of us, the hurt written all over his face.

Everyone was happy to see him – especially the South American and Spanish players. Luis and Lucas Leiva, our Brazilian defensive midfielder, were the two pillars holding the Spaniards and South Americans together. They had all been hurting for Luis and they wanted him back in the group. I'd had the sense that they were looking to me to resolve the stand-off. But Lucas also played a big role in Luis staying. Lucas is a top lad and I love him to bits.

Training began early that Friday morning, 16 August 2013. I watched Luis carefully. After all the conflicting reports I was not 100 per cent convinced that he was committed to Liverpool.

But I was wrong. Luis tore into training like a man possessed. He ran and flew into tackles, and jinked and dazzled and ran some more, as if to remind us how much we had missed him. It was incredible to see his appetite and desire, with his talent even more obvious than his work rate.

Brendan and I kept shooting meaningful looks at each other. Sometimes we just grinned as we watched him.

Luis Suárez was back. And so were Liverpool and so was I. Suddenly, on the eve of a new season, we were surging with hope and happiness again.

# 2. Changing Seasons

Twenty-five years earlier, in August 1988, the landscape of English football was very different. When I joined their Academy as an eight-year-old, Liverpool were the reigning league champions. They had won the First Division for the seventeenth time the previous May, nine points clear of second-placed Manchester United. That season also saw Chelsea, having finished fourth from bottom, lose a relegation play-off against Middlesbrough. Chelsea tumbled out of the top flight on 28 May 1988.

It had been much more of a surprise exactly two weeks before when Liverpool lost the FA Cup final to Wimbledon. That 1–0 defeat ruined Liverpool's hopes of winning a second league and FA Cup double in the space of three seasons. It seems more incredible, now, to remember that Liverpool have won only one league championship since then, our eighteenth, in 1990.

The Premier League was set up in February 1992, and at that time there were no foreign club owners or managers at the highest level of English football. Ossie Ardiles became the first foreign manager in the breakaway league in the summer of 1993. The influx of overseas players and managers increased gradually. Five and a half years later I made my first-team debut for Liverpool when I came off the bench and replaced Vegard Heggem, the Norway international, in the unfamiliar position of right back.

Before that season began, Gérard Houllier, a former manager of the French national side, had joined Liverpool to work alongside Roy Evans, one of the old Boot Room stalwarts. By mid-November, Gérard was in sole charge and he gave me my chance. On 29 November 1998, Gérard, one of the nicest men I have met in football, said a few words while I stood trembling on the touchline in the eighty-fifth minute. Liverpool led Blackburn Rovers 2–0 after goals from Paul Ince and Michael Owen. 'Keep the ball for us,' Gérard instructed me calmly. 'Keep your position, see the game out.'

I managed one safe touch, a simple pass to a teammate, and then another. Then, in my only other moment of action, I tried to deliver a cross into the box after Incey set me up down the right. I overhit the ball so badly it almost sailed over the Centenary Stand. Incey looked like he wanted to murder me.

Under Gérard I made thirteen appearances in my debut season for Liverpool. Far more seismic events occurred elsewhere and by the end of that 1998–99 campaign Manchester United had won a unique treble – the league, FA Cup and Champions League. United, who had trailed Bayern Munich for eighty-five minutes, scored twice in injury time to become kings of Europe.

Over the next two seasons Man United completed a hat-trick of Premier League titles – with Arsenal second on each occasion. The battle between Alex Ferguson and Arsène Wenger was at its most intense but there were still faint rays of hope that Liverpool's quest to win the league again might succeed. Under Gérard we won our own treble in the 2000–01 season – with the League Cup, FA Cup and UEFA Cup giving me my first honours as a professional. We also finished third in the league that year.

Twelve months later we were runners-up – seven points behind Arsenal. United were champions again the following season, 2002–03, with Arsenal second and Liverpool sliding down to fifth. Chelsea had edged ahead of us to steal a Champions League qualification place.

It was then, in the summer of 2003, that everything changed

forever in the Premier League. Roman Abramovich, the Russian billionaire, bought Chelsea. The shock was horrible. But it was only the start of the overseas money-men coming in to seize control of the Premier League. It would soon get worse, far worse, both for Liverpool and for me.

When rival fans enjoy pointing out that, over seventeen seasons with Liverpool, I've never picked up a league winner's medal, I keep quiet. But I can say now that there are two major reasons why I didn't win at least one title with Liverpool: Roman Abramovich at Chelsea and Sheikh Mansour at Manchester City.

I also accept I have to look at myself and admit that if the team and I had played better, or done one or two things differently, and had a bit more luck, we might have done it. But the overseas ownership of clubs has had a massive impact on the Premier League over the last dozen years.

The memory of Abramovich arriving at Chelsea is still raw. I had just turned twenty-three and I knew enough about football and money to just swear out loud when the news filtered through. At first you think: 'How long will this last? Will he get bored or is it real?'

But the second season starts. Abramovich is still here. In May 2004 he appoints one of the best young managers in the world, José Mourinho, who has just won the Champions League with Porto. José swans into London, calling himself 'The Special One'. My heart drops a little more.

You could tell that Mourinho had the aura of a winner and he was backed by an owner with the deepest pockets in world football. It was hard not to be deflated.

If you're me, you're fucked as far as winning the league is concerned. I also knew that I'd almost certainly have to beat Chelsea, and Roman Abramovich, to win any trophy outside the Premier League as well.

I couldn't take it in. At Liverpool we'd been fighting as hard as we could to catch United. And we had Arsenal to deal with as well. When their team of Invincibles had already begun to take shape, we nicked the FA Cup final off them in 2001. We came from behind and Michael Owen scored two goals in the last seven minutes. Arsenal were a great team but we robbed them and went home with my fourth piece of silverware. English football still seemed more open then.

In 2003–04, Abramovich's first season, Arsenal gave him the best possible answer by winning the league without losing a single match. It was deeply impressive, with Chelsea second and United third. We were a disappointing fourth, an embarrassing thirty points behind Arsenal.

Houllier left the club in May 2004 and Rafa Benítez took charge. We clawed back real belief then because Rafa was a superb strategist. He had just led Valencia to a double of the UEFA Cup and the La Liga title, their second under Rafa, ahead of Real Madrid and Barcelona.

English football changed massively the next season. After a long duel between Ferguson and Wenger, Mourinho and Benítez turned it into an even more interesting and competitive battle. We won the Champions League in Rafa's first season, but we were not even the top team in our home city in the league. Chelsea were champions ahead of Arsenal, Manchester United and Everton, who were three points ahead of us in fourth place.

After getting over the initial hump of facing an Abramovich–Mourinho combination we felt ready to mix it with the rich boys. We had lost the Carling Cup final to Chelsea in February 2005, when I scored an own goal, but we were far from intimidated at the prospect of facing them in the Champions League semi-finals in Mourinho's first season. I had to have a painful pus-filled abscess removed from my mouth just hours before the first leg at Stamford Bridge, but I still played. It was a defensive match, which was hardly surprising when Mourinho and Benítez were in charge, and we were happy enough with a 0–0.

On 3 May 2005 the home leg at Anfield was billed as the Community Club versus the Billionaire's Club – and the support from the Liverpool fans created an unforgettable atmosphere. It was perhaps the loudest night of my career and, in the fourth minute, John Arne Riise nutmegged Frank Lampard and hared down the line. He whipped in a cross which I dinked cleverly towards Milan Baroš. Petr Cech, in Chelsea's goal, brought down his fellow Czech. As we howled for a penalty, Luis García nipped in and clipped the ball towards Chelsea's goal. William Gallas hoofed it out just as it seemed to cross the line. The whistle went and we were all confused. Finally, we realized that the referee, Luboš Michel, was pointing towards the halfway line. A goal had been awarded.

Chelsea were furious – Mourinho most of all. He raged against the 'ghost goal', returning to it repeatedly over the next ten years, but he could not change the result. Their protests overlooked the fact that Cech should have been sent off for the foul on Baroš. Chelsea would have been down to ten men – and we would have been awarded a penalty. All that really mattered was that we had beaten Chelsea 1–0 and sneaked through to the Champions League final. They made a record loss of £140m that year but it seemed meaningless when Abramovich could bail them out.

It might have been tough to match the money of Abramovich's Chelsea over the length of a season but we'd proved we could beat them over a fierce two-leg encounter. Rafa told the press that, before the game, 'I looked into Steven's eyes and saw the determination.' He was not wrong. I was burning with desire to beat Chelsea and win the Champions League for

Liverpool – where European football matters so much to every one of us who love the club. We were all ready.

The Champions League gave us hope that, even against Abramovich's billions, Rafa might create a team that could finish above Chelsea one season – even when they were spending £100m on new players every summer. Rafa did it and we finished ahead of the Londoners in May 2009. Manchester United still beat us to the title but at least we proved to ourselves that we could earn more points in a season than Chelsea.

But then, all of a sudden, here comes an Arab prince into the equation. Multi-billionaires all over again.

When the Abu Dhabi United Group takeover of Man City was announced on 1 September 2008 it was less of a gut-wrencher than the Abramovich jolt. Instead, I had a dark thought: 'Why couldn't they have just flown to Liverpool instead and touched down at Anfield?'

Our club had once been owned by a local family, with John Moores handing control to his nephew, David, in 1991. David Moores was a real gentleman whom I respected and liked. But, inevitably, he wasn't wealthy enough to compete with the likes of Abramovich, and he confirmed as much in 2004 when he put the club up for sale. David knew the club needed fresh investment to move to a new level. He was honest enough to admit it to me.

As Liverpool's captain it was part of my responsibility to talk to potential new owners. One company, Dubai International Capital, appeared seriously interested in buying the club, but they abandoned their bid in January 2007. Attention switched to two Americans, Tom Hicks and George Gillett, who eventually bought the club on 6 February 2007. I had numerous meetings with them and at first it seemed like an amazingly positive development. I allowed myself to dream that at last we might be able to mix it with Abramovich.

But within eighteen months Rafa was at war with them and soon Hicks and Gillett were at war with each other. The whole mess ended up in court. The dream had become a nightmare and I was mightily relieved when Fenway Sports Group, a company founded by a very different American pair, John Henry and Tom Werner, took over from the doomed duo of Hicks and Gillett in 2010.

At the start of the 2013–14 season, even after more than three years of stable ownership under Fenway, it was still immensely difficult to compete with Abramovich and Abu Dhabi. It's not easy trying to bring down a couple of oligarchs.

Manchester United had been the first to fall to an overseas takeover. Malcolm Glazer and his family had purchased their first shares in United, from their Tampa powerhouse, in early 2003. As the Glazers increased their stranglehold, eventually buying United outright while raising loans, there was anger amongst their supporters. I could understand why they were raging at the fact that the club had to pay the millions of pounds of interest stemming from the Glazers' loans, as they set up a flawed business model which Hicks and Gillett would copy. It was an insight into the way in which English football was being reshaped.

But I never really thought about the Glazers and Manchester United. I'm not interested in how they go about their business. I'm not interested in them at all. If I pick up a newspaper or go online to read about football I always skip any article that's about the Glazers or Abramovich or Sheikh Mansour. It doesn't interest me. I already know that they're making my life as a Liverpool player impossibly hard. I don't need to read how they gained control of a club. I am far more interested, and worried, about the game that is played out on the field, whether it's at Anfield or Old Trafford, Stamford Bridge or the more recently named Etihad and Emirates stadiums.

In August 2013, with the Suárez saga finally settled, I could look around me. There was an undercurrent of change, and uncertainty, everywhere. Mourinho was back at Chelsea but the previous season had been difficult at Stamford Bridge. Their fans hated the fact that Benítez had been the interim manager. Even winning the Europa League could not take the sour edge off the Chelsea supporters' reaction to Rafa. They loathed him because of his Liverpool past, and his spats with Mourinho. Chelsea only finished third in the league. Mourinho warned that he would need a season to regain control of the club.

Arsenal had missed out on Suárez and, weeks away from spending big money when they bought Mesut Özil from Real Madrid, their supporters railed against Wenger. They looked in store for their usual nervy battle for fourth place.

Manchester City were also unsettled. They had sacked Roberto Mancini and replaced him with Manuel Pellegrini, the Chilean who left Málaga for Manchester. Pellegrini was a very good manager but nothing was certain any longer. It's hard to know how a new man from a different league might adapt to the whirlwind of English football. And Sheikh Mansour and his cartel were surely impatient for sustained success, especially in Europe, after all the billions they had invested.

There was an even more intriguing situation at Old Trafford. It was the first summer in twenty-six years that Alex Ferguson would not be plotting and scheming over yet another league title for United. Ferguson was an undeniably great manager. His list of trophies told you everything you needed to know about his qualities. Even if we restricted his haul to my career between 1998 and 2013, he had won nine Premier League titles as United's manager. In that period he had also won the Champions League twice, the FA Cup twice and the League Cup twice. In total, Ferguson had led United to the league title thirteen times. It worked out at an average of one league championship every two years.

I knew David Moyes, his replacement, quite well. In his eleven years at Everton we had spoken a few times about football and I was always struck by his knowledge and insights into the game. But it was obvious that Moyes faced an immense task in replacing Ferguson. In mid-August he and the United board seemed to be thrashing around the transfer market with no impact.

I sensed a small opportunity amid all the unpredictability. I hoped that at least one of the four clubs which usually finished close to us might waver and fall.

My constant companion at Melwood for the previous fifteen seasons had gone. Jamie Carragher, my great friend and teammate, had retired. He played his last game for Liverpool on 19 May 2013. It coincided with Ferguson's final match in charge of United. Most of the attention flooded down on Fergie, of course, but I thought Carra won that last battle.

On the very last day for them both, Carra was happy with a 1–0 defeat of QPR at Anfield. He nearly scored an absolute peach of a goal too. I think he must have worn my boots to hit such a beauty. That same afternoon Ferguson watched United draw 5–5 at West Brom. Rack that up as a clear win for Carra, my mate and a monumental defender.

All summer I missed Carra. If he'd still been around at Melwood he would have shouldered some of the Suárez burden. He would have also been in my ear constantly, jabbering on about football, making complete sense with every intelligent and cutting observation.

Carra was second only to Ian Callaghan after he made his final and 737th appearance for Liverpool. I was third on the list of all-time appearances for the club but, being two years younger than Carra, I wouldn't move past the 700-game mark until February 2015. We were the last two of the old guard of Liverpool's one-club men.

While English football turned itself inside out, undergoing enormous upheaval, often fuelled by greed and selfishness, Carra and I kept on grinding away. Liverpool ran through the heart of both of us. We would not be moved until, finally, our time was up. Carra had gone first, aged thirty-five. I was thirty-three and the end was closing in on me. But I wanted to give it one last mighty tilt – for me and Carra and the whole of Liverpool.

I had roomed with Jamie for years. I had sat next to him on the bus before every game. We would talk unendingly about football, the games we faced and the teams and players we needed to beat. And then, suddenly, he was gone.

We had shared all the great moments and ecstatic victories. But we had helped each other survive the defeats. Only Carra would get nearly as low as I did when Liverpool lost. We went through the misery together on buses and planes as we headed home. No one else felt it as deeply – because we assumed the responsibility for the supporters and the club. Liverpool dominated our lives.

Carra had been in the group ahead of me at Melwood. We had some good players in my year but Carra's group was spoken about more than any other youth team. They won the FA Youth Cup and I remember them beating a very good West Ham side that included Frank Lampard and Rio Ferdinand. But Jamie was in a great team. I watched Stuey Quinn, Eddie Turkington, Jamie Cassidy, Lee Prior, David Thompson and Carra. For a long while I thought Thompson was the best young player I had ever seen at Liverpool. When we were both still in school I used to go and watch him play for the reserves. He was outstanding.

Thompson was part of Carra's gang. Carra, Thompson, Cassidy and Prior would rip into us younger lads mercilessly. Carra was the loudest and the sharpest of them all.

I remember the first time Carra really spoke to me. It was while I was mopping his floor at Melwood. He was on a first-year pro contract and he was a proper big-head. Ronnie Moran used to call every new pro at Liverpool a big-head. And that was Carra. He knew I was getting my £47.50 a week and he enjoyed the fact that I was still an apprentice and he was a pro. I was having to mop up all his sweat and the mud from his boots on the dressing-room floor. It was the same old Carra, though, dishing out the verbals.

He gave me loads of stick about my hair. He took the piss out of my fringe because, back then, I didn't use any products. I used to just get out of bed and throw my fringe forward. Who cared about my hair? I was obsessed with football and no one wanted a picture of me when I was seventeen. Carra would look at my fringe and he would say the same thing every time: 'Have you combed your hair from your arse again?'

I got plenty of verbal off Carra and all the older players in the first-team squad in my earliest years. It's part of football and I'll miss it when I'm gone. That's why I missed Carra so much in that miserable summer of 2013. No one is as aggressive or as sharp as Carra. I could have done with him by my side while I was fretting over Suárez.

When Danny Murphy left Liverpool in 2004 it coincided with Michael Owen's departure. Michael and Carra had been very close. They were a pair – just like me and Danny. The four of us often hung out together but I definitely spoke much more to Danny back then. Once he and Michael went, Carra and I were thrown together. He was from Bootle, and an Everton fan, and I was from Huyton. We were two football-mad Scousers and so it was obvious why we got on so well. I already knew Carra was very switched-on – but I came to appreciate his astute intelligence. He has a sharp tongue but his brain is even sharper.

Carra's memory and his fixation with football were quite scary. If he was not playing he would be watching a game or talking or reading about it. Carra's even more obsessed with the game than me. And he always wanted to win. In training he'd happily cheat to win a five-a-side. You saw it in matches too. He was always buzzing around the referee, trying to get an edge.

For some strange reason there were various rumours about the pair of us fighting on the training pitch. It was always bollocks. I would get more pissed off that they always had Carra winning our imaginary fights. I'll have to get the gloves on one night – especially now that Carra is sparring with Tony Bellew, one of our top boxers in Liverpool.

Jamie was a great footballer. It's incredible to think of all he achieved as a local boy just when money was pouring into football. At one stage, in those three years when we twice reached the Champions League final, Liverpool could have bought any defender in the world. But no one would have been able to take Carra's place at the heart of our defence.

Jamie became one of Europe's top defenders. In our Champions League runs we wouldn't have enjoyed such success without Carra. A lot of players, me included, get plaudits for the goals and the big moments, but Jamie shored us up at the back, game after game, season after season. He was consistently good for a decade or more but I think he had a couple of years where he was up there alongside Alessandro Nesta and John Terry. I've always believed Terry is the best defender of my generation. But Carra had a chunk of form when he was as great as Terry and Nesta.

The 120-minute Champions League final in Istanbul summed up Jamie Carragher and all he meant to Liverpool. He gave everything that night – blood, sweat, tears and cramp. It was last-ditch stuff, Carra's socks rolled down around his ankles, with heroic tackles to stop Kaká and Andriy Shevchenko. Carra said after the game that playing with cramp was worse than playing with a broken leg. Only Carra could have said that and really known what he meant. He once broke his leg against Blackburn and tried to keep playing. Of course, he didn't know the extent of his injury at the time and so he thought he could run off the pain. That was Carra. He was ready to give life and limb for the club.

His last season had been more difficult. I could see that, when he was out of the team until early in the New Year, it was killing him. Carra's just like me. His week would start on a Monday morning and he'd already be looking forward to the next game. He would do everything he needed to do. He would train hard, eat the right food, have the right massages, get his rest and make sure that he stuck to a regimen that would have him ready for the weekend. When a manager takes that away from you on a regular basis your life changes.

Brendan Rodgers, at the start of his career as Liverpool manager, made that call. Carra was no longer an automatic starter. It's very hard when you've had sixteen seasons playing virtually every weekend, knowing that you're needed and that the manager will pick you every time and back you to the hilt. When that changes, it hurts. I felt that a little in my own last season, when I was injured and then got banned for a few games, and it was harder than ever before.

It's even more difficult for a defender. When you're a sub as a defender you don't often get on the pitch and your confidence takes a hit. I know that, as a midfielder, if I'm rested as a sub I'm almost certainly going to play at some stage of the match. If things aren't going well for the team I might come on for the last thirty minutes. And if we're winning then I could be called in to help see the game out.

Yet neither Jamie nor I would ever be comfortable as a squad player. And that's why I was so happy when, after we lost to

Manchester United in January 2013 and Brendan said we needed more 'men' and 'leaders' in the team, Jamie came back into the side. We won our next game 5–0, against Norwich, and Carra stayed in the team for the rest of the season.

In that last year he was still fit and quick. And he obviously had vast experience. I thought we were always a much stronger team, and a better defensive unit, when Jamie was playing. His organization was incredible. He was still a pillar of the side. And every team needs its pillars, its spine and big personalities. Carra showed all of that in his final six months at the club. He remained an incredible defender.

He could have played in Liverpool's first team for another year but I think Carra went at the right time. People still wanted more of him – which is how you want to leave your only professional club. Paolo Maldini, one of the greatest defenders ever to play the game, and my opposition captain in those Champions League finals, spent all twenty-five of his years as a pro at AC Milan. He was booed, shamefully, by his own fans near the end.

Gary Neville was a great player, especially the way he committed himself to every game, but I remember watching him towards the end and it was painful. He was getting so many injuries and I could see he was struggling in one-on-one situations. That's hard to take when you've been a special player for so long. Gary was an unbelievable defender, and a force running up and down the wing, but I think he went on for six months too long. So I was really happy that Carra didn't go out like that for his sake. He timed his retirement just right.

We had finished Brendan's first season in charge in seventh place, which was one spot better than a year before under Kenny Dalglish. Tom Werner, the club chairman, had sounded hopeful in late May 2013 when he spoke to the *Liverpool Echo*:

Brendan has made remarkable progress. He's a great strategist and has shown strong leadership. Obviously there is disappointment that we didn't finish higher in the table but the team has certainly improved. To see the new additions in January, Daniel Sturridge and Philippe Coutinho, perform so well has been very positive. We scored a lot more goals than last season. The club is definitely moving in the right direction under Brendan. Our intention is to strengthen the squad further this summer.

On the brink of a new season, having held on to Suárez, we had some youthful punch to offset the loss of Carra's experience. I also had great faith in Brendan as a manager and I was invigorated by the arrival of young players as talented as Sturridge and Coutinho. But I was not convinced that we had brought in the right new players that summer – even though the transfer merry-go-round still had weeks to run before the window closed. Andy Carroll and Stewart Downing had both completed their moves to West Ham while Jonjo Shelvey had gone to Swansea and Jay Spearing had signed for Bolton.

Mamadou Sakho would join us on 1 September 2013 for £12m from Paris Saint-Germain alongside six other new players. Iago Aspas (Celta Vigo, £9m), Simon Mignolet (Sunderland, £9m), Luis Alberto (Sevilla, £6.8m), Tiago Ilori (Sporting Lisbon, £6.8m), Kolo Touré (Manchester City, free) and Victor Moses (Chelsea, loan) eventually completed the set.

Alberto and Aspas were two really nice boys who, technically, were very good footballers. They could play a one-two, they could see a pass. Both of them looked great at times in five-a-side and seven-a-side games. It was obvious why they had proved themselves to be decent players in a much more technical league in Spain.

But straightaway, as soon as I saw them in the dressing room, I knew they weren't going to make it in the Premier League. It boiled down to physique. They had the bodies of little boys – and looked about fifteen. I thought, 'Jesus, how are you going to cope against John Terry, Ashley Williams and Ryan Shawcross?'

I immediately knew that Aspas would never be able to play up front on his own. Could he play in a two? Maybe. He's quite clever but we hardly ever play with two up front. Nine million pounds could have been wasted. I was not wrong. Aspas went out on loan to Sevilla the following June – with the option of a three-year deal to stay in La Liga.

On the whole you know after two training sessions if a new player is going to cut it. I think my gut instinct, more often than not, proves I'm right. After a week's training, certainly, it's pretty clear. Everyone can have a bad session or two, but it's very rare for someone to have five or six in a row. You can look at someone's physique, their athleticism and power, and judge it pretty quickly.

Some players proved me wrong. Jordan Henderson struggled in his first year at Liverpool and his confidence looked low. There were certain training sessions, and some games, where he was just off the pace. But I had also seen that he sometimes trained really well. More importantly, I'd seen bits and bobs in games where I thought that, with a boost in confidence, he could turn the fans around and become a fine player. I decided that he just needed a bit of help and a friendly arm round the shoulder. He's been terrific ever since. Jordan has become Liverpool's captain in my place and I have complete faith in him as a player and as a man.

So when I judge someone early on I don't write them off entirely. A few players have totally surprised me and changed my mind. Javier Mascherano battled at first, and his passing seemed badly awry, but he just needed a settling-in period. At first I was thinking, 'I'm not sure' – but after five or six games he was obviously very good. He's now become an awesome player at Barcelona but it took time for him to show his quality.

Technique and talent still matter most. I knew, for example, that Xabi Alonso was a good player before he arrived from Real Sociedad in 2004, but when we did a passing exercise in the warm-up of his very first session, just seeing Xabi pass a ball over twenty yards, with his effortless touch and technique, convinced me within two minutes that he was going to be a wonderful player for Liverpool and a dream teammate for me.

In contrast, I knew that Alberto, Aspas and Fabio Borini would all struggle to make a lasting impression in English football. Borini is very quick but after two sessions I was pretty sure that he would not make it as a Liverpool striker – certainly not at the level of Fowler, Owen, Torres and Suárez. I was just hoping that, eventually, he might become a Javier Hernández-type player who comes off the bench and nicks goals when you need them most. But Borini was sent on loan to Sunderland. He had his moments but it hasn't worked out for him.

Another big player had left us that preseason: Pepe Reina had gone on loan to Napoli, whom Rafa Benítez had just joined as manager. Simon Mignolet had taken his place in goal. I had a few doubts. I knew Simon had done very well and he had good stats at Sunderland, but it's different when you're a keeper for teams lower down in the league and your goal is being peppered constantly. It's easy then to showcase really good saves on *Match of the Day*. But you get judged on different levels when you're the number 1 at Liverpool. People don't just assess you on your shot-stopping technique. At Liverpool your goal is not going to be under siege that often and so you also get judged on what you're like with your feet, your distribution, and whether or not you can collect crosses.

I knew Mignolet would be a terrific shot-stopper – I would put him up against any other keeper in the Premier League in that respect – and it was also obvious that he was a good guy, as professional as they come, and a keeper who worked hard in training. But I was still not sure how well he would adapt to the Brendan Rodgers system where a goalkeeper needs to use his feet and stay alert after long periods where he's not been called into action. We would find out more, both about our keeper and our team, once the season started.

## Anfield, Saturday, 17 August 2013

The first game of a brand-new season, before the whistle blows and the roar rolls across Anfield, is always sweet with promise. Stoke City at home on a rainy and windy Saturday afternoon in mid-August almost felt like an old-fashioned afternoon of English football – except for the fact that, owing to the demands of television, we were due to kick off at 12.45 instead of the once traditional 3 p.m. At least we were playing before anyone else in the Premier League.

Anfield was in full voice, with 'You'll Never Walk Alone' booming around the ground as we completed our last few warm-up routines. The vast sea of red, with shirts and scarves, banners and flags, unfurled all around me as I gazed again at a moving sight. I could see some huge *Justice for the 96* banners, draped in white with the letters stitched in Liverpool red. My cousin Jon-Paul, one of those killed at Hillsborough, would have been thirty-four. Other flags fluttering in the icy wind simply featured the number *96*. The rest were purely football-driven as we returned to the joy of a game we all loved.

The familiar face of Bill Shankly, as well as my own, stretched across massive flags while other signs were held high. *Make Us Dream* caught my eye again as the Kop's massed choir sang louder and louder. I would have lost that intense feeling, all the deep love and loyalty, if I had left Liverpool for Chelsea eight years earlier. Even if I had swapped Anfield for a ground as famous and grand as the Bernabéu I would never again have experienced the same hair-raising tingle.

I could feel the surging hope and expectation of the Liverpool crowd building inside me once more. 'Here we go,' I thought. 'A new season, a new dream.'

Luis Suárez, of course, was still banned. He sat in the stands, watching us glumly as we limbered up and sent practice passes fizzing along a pitch slick with cold summer rain. But it had been good to hear the huge cheer which greeted Luis in the Anfield car park – and even better to see his goofy smile as he acknowledged the support of the Liverpool fans. In his absence, Brendan had decided to give Aspas his first Premier League start, alongside Sturridge. Raheem Sterling and Alberto were amongst those on the bench.

I walked towards the centre circle. Martin Atkinson, my least favourite referee, was waiting. He had given me enough bookings and red cards to last me my whole career. I can't stand him. I gave half-a-smile to Ryan Shawcross, Stoke's captain, as I shook his hand and wished him luck. I was sure he licked his lips, not to taste the droplets of rain but at Aspas shivering in the cold.

Atkinson spun the coin in the air and it came down heads for us. I said we'd play towards the Anfield Road end in our usual routine. We were saving the Kop for the second half. I turned back to my team. The last words were spoken, the last hand touches were exchanged. All the mess and muddle, and the last-gasp solutions of preseason, were forgotten. I did not even think of Alex and the girls, my parents or my brother Paul. Everything shrank down to the only thing that mattered for ninety minutes and more. We needed to start the new season with a win.

There was a brightness to Liverpool but Stoke, under Mark Hughes, who had replaced Tony Pulis as manager, were typically organized. I floated in a free kick as early as the second minute, a decent ball, but Shawcross rose high to head it away firmly. We looked very mobile, with Sturridge and Coutinho full of dash and verve. They are quality players.

Stoke are a dogged team and they came back at us. We had our first real scare of the season when, in only the ninth minute, Simon Mignolet came out for a cross. Our new keeper flapped nervously and was beaten in the air by Peter Crouch, returning to Anfield in opposition colours, and from the resulting mish-mash Robert Huth thudded a volley against the bar from just ten yards out. We were lucky that the chance fell to a hulking central defender rather than a striker.

A few minutes later, from another of my free kicks, this one hit perfectly, Sturridge buried the ball in the Stoke net with a gorgeous header. Anfield erupted but the assistant's flag went up. Daniel had been fractionally offside; but I was encouraged by the way he had been able to find space so easily in the box.

Kolo Touré was the next to meet one of my dead-ball specials. I took a corner on the right and, seeing our new defender lurking on the edge of the box and ready to charge forward, I whipped the ball in towards the near post. Kolo's header smacked against the underside of the bar. The ball came bouncing down. Touré missed the follow-up and Sturridge smashed it high over the bar from a tight angle.

Sturridge kept causing Stoke problems and he was the right man to finally break the deadlock. Asmir Begović had produced a couple of excellent saves to keep Sturridge out, but in the thirty-seventh minute he was helpless. I played a long crossfield pass to Henderson who found Sturridge. He slipped it to Lucas who moved it onto Aspas. A simple square ball across the edge of the area from Aspas was hit with accuracy and force by Sturridge. It flew through Huth's legs and beat a diving Begović to flash into the bottom right corner of the Stoke net. 1–0.

Daniel raised his arms and stood as still as a statue, cool as you like, as he waited for us to mob him. He had just scored the first goal of the 2013–14 Premier League season; and looked in the mood to make it the first of many.

As half-time approached, Mignolet produced a stunning save, diving to his left to keep out a rising drive from Jon Walters. A few minutes later Lucas cleared off the line. It had been a mixed half but at least we were in front.

We raised the tempo after the break but Stoke were as disciplined as ever. Begović also pulled off a magnificent save to deny Henderson – who then hit the post. Sterling replaced Aspas but Begović remained in the mood. He turned away a free kick from me that had seemed certain to fly into the top right-hand corner.

Stoke scented a breakaway goal, and a point. Anfield felt twitchy. Charlie Adam, our former Liverpool teammate, had come on as a sub for Stoke and he was soon up to his usual trick – trying to score from the halfway line. He would finally nail one, in 2015, but Mignolet kept this attempt out. Stoke came hard at us one last time. Sterling fouled Jerome Cameron and Stoke had a free kick outside our box and down their left flank. Eighty-eight minutes of the game had gone. We pulled everyone back.

The ball curled in and, in the scramble, Daniel Agger raised his right arm as he tried to lift his left foot in an attempt to block the cross. The ball brushed his right hand.

*Penalty.*

We didn't even bother protesting. A Martin Atkinson penalty against me and Liverpool was nothing surprising. But he got it right this time. Agger had handled so blatantly he might as well have punched the ball away. My head slumped. Two points about to be dropped at home, in our first game, at the death. All the hope and promise of the start drained out of me.

I stood on the edge of the area, facing the goal and to the right of the ball. My hands were on my hips in resignation. All eyes were on Mignolet. He had made one great save but he'd been dodgy with his feet all game when it came to distribution. He had also looked lost under that early cross. It had not been a debut brimming with confidence.

In the previous few seasons I'd always had a bit of faith that Pepe Reina might save a pen. I felt less confident with Mignolet because I didn't know him as well.

Jon Walters was all set to take it for Stoke. He's a no-nonsense player, Walters, and I expected him to score. I stood there, watching and waiting as Mignolet bounced on his line holding his arms high in the hope that he might distract Walters.

Atkinson blew his whistle. Walters ran in and struck it hard to Mignolet's right.

Our new keeper dived and pulled off an incredible save, palming the ball away. Simon had only gone and saved it. He was up immediately, on his feet, parrying the rebound from Kenwyne Jones. It was a corner for Stoke rather than a goal. Yes Simon, you beauty.

We all sprinted straight at him. Touré, Henderson and Glen Johnson reached him first. I was next – beating Lucas and Agger and José Enrique in a mad run. I jumped over everyone else and grabbed Simon around the neck while punching the air with my left hand. I was screaming gibberish at him, feeling so happy, but Simon did his keeper thing. He opened his eyes wide, pointed to the corner and started shouting at all of us. He was right. He dragged us back out of ecstasy and we defended the corner. We saw the game out and won 1–0, thanks to that late, late penalty save.

Our season was up and running – half an hour before the rest of the afternoon's fixtures had even kicked off.

'Top of the league!' Brendan Rodgers said with a grin.

Aston Villa away, the following Saturday afternoon, were next. It was another TV fixture and, this time, a 5.30 kick-off. As we boarded the team coach to go to Birmingham it was obvious how everything had changed for me since Carra's departure. We had always sat together; and then he was gone. I was lucky I still had good friends to turn to as our journey began. It was always obvious I would sit next to Chris Morgan, our head physiotherapist and the man who knew more about me and my battered body than anyone in the club, or Paul Small.

Paul is one of our masseurs and a great lad. He had also worked with England which meant I relied on him a lot. Rob Pryce is another physio I trust immensely.

Chris joined us at the start of the 2005–06 season, just after Istanbul and my decision not to leave Liverpool for Chelsea. He was initially the reserve-team physio, doing bits and pieces with the main squad, but Chris was so good at his job that, more and more often, I went to him first whenever I felt a niggle or was worried about a more serious problem.

As the years passed I learnt to trust Chris completely, whether it was during a recovery from injury or him listening to me unburden myself with some of my darker doubts. He helped save my career a couple of times and, at the lowest point, when I thought it really was all over in 2011, Chris and our club doctor, Zaf Iqbal, took me to meet Steve Peters, the psychiatrist who went on to do so much for me during the last three and a half years of my career at Liverpool. Between them, Steve and Chris have helped me, mentally and physically, and I owe a lot to them both.

I remember opening up to Chris. We went to Germany for my first hernia repair. I had surgery on consecutive days, and ever since then Chris has been in theatre to watch my surgeons at work so he can fully understand each procedure. We spent a lot of time together in Germany, between operations and recovery, and our conversations became increasingly frank.

It was the kind of personal chat I normally shied away from in a football setting. But we were so similar in age and background that I began to relax and open up to Chris.

So, on the way to Villa, and every time we were aboard the team coach, it was a given that I would sit next to Chris. There were a lot of young boys on the bus and I generally kept my distance from them. I didn't want to cramp their style because, after all, I was their captain. I was also thirty-three years old while some of them, like Raheem Sterling and Jordan Ibe, were still teenagers and others – Coutinho, for example – had just moved into their twenties. I was an old man to them – and I had done a lot more than any of them. So I made sure that none of them felt intimidated and I always made it clear that I was there to help.

I didn't go out for meals with the younger players or spend time with them away from football. We had the odd joke and laugh but I liked to leave them to themselves. Sometimes they were a bit too quiet when I was around. But I knew that, if I was just a couple of years older, I could have been their dad. It was a scary thought.

I liked what Brendan once said to me before a team-building night out: 'You come and you show your face and you get involved for a while – to show them you're the leader of the group. But you have to give young lads their own space as well and so come out of it pretty early on. Head back home to Alex and the girls.'

It was brilliant advice. I also thought, 'Well, yeah, I'm only five years younger than Brendan.'

Of course, at any occasion involving the whole team I mixed with everyone in the squad, but I could relate much more easily to the older players like Glen Johnson, Brad Jones and Martin Skrtel.

On the bus, I found Chris to be great company and very knowledgeable about the game. He knew me like the back of his hand and understood how to deal with me after a defeat. It took a while but I made it clear that I wanted him to be brutally honest. We really underlined that position after I started seeing Steve Peters. In a way, Steve gave Chris permission to be totally blunt with me.

A thoughtful person, Chris always chose his moment carefully before he told me straight that I had made a mistake or if my standards had slipped even slightly. And, because he never blew smoke up my arse, it meant something if Chris pointed out how well I had played.

Sometimes, when you're in my position, no one wants to tell you honestly how you've done after a match – they're inclined to exaggerate the good bits and gloss over the bad. That's kind, but as an ordinary human being I value having someone I trust, like Chris, to tell me exactly what he thinks.

We'd often text each other our chosen team for the day and, like Brendan, we were happy to keep an unchanged XI for Villa. The manager was looking for consistency and we were on a little roll because, counting the last eight games of the previous season, we had remained unbeaten for nine matches in a row, winning seven of them.

On a beautiful evening, full of the hazy sunlight you get in late August, Sturridge and Mignolet again made huge contributions at opposite ends of the pitch. Midway through the first half, Sturridge hurtled down the left flank before cutting back inside to find me. I played it short to Lucas, who fed Enrique, whose sweeping left-foot pass was stepped over by Coutinho in the D so that Sturridge, again, could take over.

Surrounded by three Villa defenders he showed dazzling footwork as he ghosted past Ron Vlaar and jinked to the right. And then, as the onrushing keeper Brad Guzan tried to close him down, Sturridge dragged the ball wide with his right boot, while still in complete control, before scoring a sublime goal with the outside of his left foot from an acute angle.

Sturridge peeled away, running and shaking his hands in delight, before he turned to find me. We clasped hands above our heads before Touré, Henderson and Coutinho swamped us.

Gabriel Agbonlahor and Christian Benteke, in particular, tested us and we needed Mignolet to be at his shot-stopping best on two anxious occasions. Both attempts were made by Benteke, who was a real handful for Touré and Agger. The first was just before half-time when, with Touré rocking and reeling, Benteke unleashed a shot which Mignolet beat away by diving to his left. Close to the very end, in the last few minutes again, Benteke had an even better chance when set free by Nicklas Helenius's flick of a header. The Belgian hit a half-volley which, diving again to his left, Mignolet turned around the post for a corner. It had been a terrific save which looked even more spectacular as Benteke had been just ten yards away.

Two games, six points. Brendan was upbeat but realistic after the match. Following difficult spells at Chelsea and Manchester City, Sturridge had been transferred to us for £12m eight months earlier. He had scored twelve goals in his sixteen Premier League games for Liverpool. As Brendan said after the game:

If he keeps his fitness, he would be a big threat for any team. Look at him and people would think he might be a Brazilian striker with his physique and his pace and power. England are fortunate to have him because he's a big talent but he knows he needs to be consistent. He needs the games and the goals.

But the difference from when he was at Chelsea and Manchester City is clear. As a young player in amongst superstars, he was fighting for his place in the hierarchy. Here, he's comfortable in terms of where he sits. He's got the England captain Steven Gerrard behind him, advising and guiding him. All his teammates are fighting and running and working and he's very much a part of that. We're all happy for him, and the team, tonight.

# 3. Tangled Celebrations

Manchester United at home, our third league game of the season, was a landmark fixture. Our shared past with United was so tangled, so embittered, it consumed me. I was always desperate to play against them, even if there had been more defeats than victories. It seemed different for Daniel Sturridge. My memories of that game are dominated by the build-up and Daniel feeling he was touch-and-go in terms of his fitness and desire to play. Facing Man U without Luis was tough enough. If we lost Daniel as well, most of our ammunition would be gone.

We stayed at the Hope Street Hotel before the match and had our usual team walk. I positioned myself so that I walked next to Daniel for the whole fifteen minutes. I had to try to persuade him to play. I knew how badly we needed him to get three points against United. Otherwise, we'd have to start with Aspas up front. He'd had a few nice little moments but I was even more sure that the Spaniard lacked the physical power and strength to lead the line for Liverpool in a Premier League game. Our best chance of beating United was pinned to Sturridge leading the line.

Daniel is one of those people you have to boost sometimes with a 'C'mon, you're our main man. We need you – so just go for it.' You never needed to say that to Luis. It was almost as if Luis was indestructible. I don't think he ever missed a game through injury at Liverpool. I had seen Luis walk into Liverpool's treatment room twice; and once was to get a bag of ice before he walked out again. Luis doesn't really do treatment rooms. I remember him playing against Arsenal with a hamstring injury. That's the Suárez mentality. Luis Suárez would run through a brick wall for you.

Some players with unbelievable talent are also born with additional gifts – toughness, resilience, sheer belief. Others have more vulnerability and self-doubt. It's as simple as that.

Luis and Daniel had different mentalities. I knew all about Luis, and I'd since seen that Daniel was someone you had to reassure every now and again. But before the Man United game it was more complicated. He had a genuine niggle and he didn't feel right.

Before the walk I had spoken to Chris Morgan and Glen Driscoll, our head of performance, about Daniel's injury – because I couldn't try to persuade him to play if he was not fit enough. I'd also had enough injury worries of my own where I had needed an expert like Chris or Glen to say, clearly, 'You're OK. You can play. Go with it.'

I asked them: 'What's the situation with Daniel?'

Chris looked at me. 'We think he can play. He has an issue with his thigh but we're sure he'll be fine. We think he just needs an encouraging push.'

Glen agreed, giving me still more confidence.

Daniel had come back from an ankle injury he had picked up with England in the summer. He'd had to undertake an individual preseason fitness regime and then, because we didn't have Luis, he was straight into games.

After Villa we had played Notts County in a midweek Capital One Cup tie. It had not been great. Cruising at 2–0 after twenty-nine minutes, we let the game slip once we moved past the hour mark. County, from League One, fought back and made it 2–2 after eighty-four minutes. We won 4–2 in extra-time and Daniel had played all 120 minutes. We needed him because we were down to ten men in the end. Having used all three subs, we didn't have anyone else to replace Kolo Touré after he went down with a groin tear. Daniel had been forced to battle through; but he still scored two goals.

The new thigh tweak was there, and it was a little sore, but the medical team was convinced it would be safe for him to start against Manchester United. Chris could not be sure how long he would last but he backed me to reassure Daniel that he was medically fit to play. He and the other physios, as well as the manager, had tried to cajole him into playing without any success.

It was yet another of my tasks as captain. But I was probably more like a fan on the walk trying to persuade Daniel – eventually begging him to play. I said if it was no good after ten or fifteen minutes he could come off. I said all the fans, and everyone in the team, would appreciate him giving it a go.

I was trying to boost Daniel, to help him find the confidence in himself to ignore the pain and take a small risk by playing. But I also wanted to win the match. I was desperate to have Daniel on at the start.

'All right,' Daniel said at the end of the walk, 'I'll give it a go . . .'

At last I could turn my attention to United. Even before the season began I thought, 'If United have a bit of an early wobble it's going to be tough for Moyes . . .'

It seemed as if Moyes felt the same. He is an intelligent and strong manager but, once he arrived at Old Trafford, I think he suddenly realized it would be a huge job to replace Alex Ferguson. United won their first game of the season, 4–1 away at Swansea. They then faced Chelsea at home and Liverpool away.

It seemed strange to hear Moyes complaining about a fixture conspiracy. 'Well, the old manager told me those sort of things happened,' Moyes said. 'It's the hardest start for twenty years that Manchester United have had. I hope it's not because Manchester United won the league quite comfortably last year that the fixtures have been made much more difficult. I find it hard to believe that's the way the balls came out of the bag.'

We all knew the Premier League fixtures were generated by computer software and Aston Villa had been given an even harder start than United. Villa had also played their first three games in eight days – while teams like United and Liverpool faced the same amount of league fixtures over fifteen days. In their opening two games Villa played Arsenal – and they won 3–1 away – and Chelsea. They then lost at home to Liverpool. But Paul Lambert wasn't bleating about the fixture list.

I had grown used to the way in which Ferguson and Mourinho had railed against mythical conspiracies supposedly aimed at United and Chelsea. Rafa Benítez had tried the same tactic less successfully when at Liverpool. It seemed to me that Moyes was making a similar mistake.

I prefer to talk honestly to the media. This means that, while avoiding troublemaking quotes, mind-games or trying to put pressure on administrators and officials, I also think there's little point making grand claims. So I responded honestly at a press conference before the United game. I was asked if, after two wins, I felt any closer to winning the league one day.

'I would like to win a Premier League title but at thirty-three I have to be realistic and say there might only be two or three years left,' I replied. 'I'm quite a distance away from winning the league at the moment. I have to take that on the chin, but I'll never give up fighting for it. Getting back into the Champions League might be a more achievable target – but even that is going to be difficult.'

You could argue that both Moyes and I were being defeatist. But I spoke from the heart, and truthfully about our prospects, while I wondered whether Moyes was becoming a little paranoid – a trait I had never seen in him while he did such an admirable job at Everton.

Brendan also sensed the situation and, as a manager, he made more of our old rivals' possible new weakness. It was the first time United would arrive at Anfield without Ferguson at the helm since February 1986. Brendan said he had noticed a change in Man U's mindset since the departure of Fergie and he suggested that they had played far more cautiously under Moyes while settling for a 0–0 draw at home against Chelsea. 'It was drifting towards a nil-nil and there wasn't really a murmur at Old Trafford. When Fergie was there he would be going for the win so the crowd were near enough expecting a goal at the end of the game. Now that seems to have changed a little at United. I can understand the caution – but I would always look to win at home.'

It was a neat dig at Moyes and a way of increasing the pressure on him. I concentrated instead on getting ready for the match. United, even without Ferguson, would be a real test for us.

## Anfield, Sunday, 1 September 2013

We stood in two lines, the eleven players of Liverpool facing the eleven of Manchester United, as the applause echoed around Anfield. We clapped Bill Shankly, celebrating the 100th anniversary of his birth. In our usual red shirts we stood with our backs to the Kop while the United players, in dark blue and black, stared at the mosaic behind us. I had looked at it before we gathered near the centre circle for the minute-long applause.

There is a statue of Shankly outside Anfield. Cast in bronze, his arms stretch out in front of him. Shankly is celebrating another victory, and all he achieved when lifting Liverpool from mediocrity to greatness. The deep lines in the statue of Shankly's smiling face, across his brow and beneath his eyes, speak powerfully of everything he gave to the club. The worry and stress, the love and passion for Liverpool, are carved into his face.

The outline of his statue was captured in the mosaic created by the Kop. Shankly's joyful shape was etched in red cards held by our fans – while 100 was highlighted in the same colour on the other side of the goal. The rest of the Kop was a maze of white. It looked incredible.

I thought of the worry-lines dug into Shankly's face, of his concern for Liverpool, when seeing two homemade banners near the bottom of the stand. The first said:

*SHANKLY 1913–81*
*HE MADE PEOPLE HAPPY*

Another one said, simply:

*Shankly Lives Forever*

Shankly had managed Liverpool for 753 games, in a career lasting fifteen years, from 1959 to 1974. His end at Liverpool was sad and complicated; but his legacy was not only measured in trophies: it was defined by the beliefs and values he instilled into the club. A line of managers ran from Shankly to Bob Paisley to Joe Fagan to Kenny Dalglish. Forged in the Boot Room, and sealed by genius, those four managers took care of Liverpool for more than three decades.

That fact made Alex Ferguson's twenty-six years in charge of United stand out as an extraordinary achievement by one man. Ferguson had made it his mission to bring us down. 'My greatest challenge was knocking Liverpool right off their fucking perch,' he had once said. 'And you can print that.'

It was tattooed into the head of every Liverpool fan. We had never liked each other, as clubs or cities, but the animosity had become deeper. Liverpool had been dominant for so long; and then, finally, United took over under Ferguson. We were the two most successful clubs in the history of English football. And it hurt me that we remained stuck on eighteen league titles while United, who had lagged behind us for decades, devoured one championship after another. They had been on just seven titles, compared to our eighteen, during Fergie's difficult early years.

United went twenty-six years without winning the league. And then in 1996–97, two seasons before my professional debut, their domination began. They sailed past our record of eighteen, much to Ferguson's satisfaction, and had won the twentieth in his final season, just four months earlier. United faced us again as champions and, more than ever, I wanted to beat them.

In Huyton I and every other kid from a Red family had been taught to loathe Manchester United. It was drilled into our brains, hardening our hearts and conditioning our souls as Liverpool fans. Over the years, especially when I was in the same England team alongside great United players like Paul Scholes, David Beckham, Gary Neville, Rio Ferdinand and Wayne Rooney, my feelings became more layered, but they never disappeared.

I still didn't like United, and their shirt is the only one I won't allow in my house. I have a big collection of shirts I've swapped with other players from different clubs – but not one from Manchester United. Yet I respected and admired their best players and my England teammates. We even became friends and I understood what Gary Neville meant when we talked about his infamous quote of hating all Scousers.

Gary had actually said, of his past in Bury and as a boyhood United fan, 'I was brought up in my area to hate Scousers.' He was explaining the conditioning he had experienced – just as I had been raised in Huyton to hate all Mancs. But I respected Ferguson and Roy Keane and Ryan Giggs and so many other of their key characters. I even respected, grudgingly, what they had achieved as a club.

United had their twenty league titles to our eighteen. They had also won eleven FA Cups to our seven. But we had won eight League Cups to their four and three UEFA Cups. Those two competitions didn't compare to the one that really mattered – the premier club competition in world football. Manchester United had won the European Cup three times. But Liverpool had been champions of Europe on five unforgettable occasions.

It was why, soon after Istanbul, people in this city started wearing red T-shirts which carried a clear message: *Hughes to Thompson, Thompson to Souness, Souness to Gerrard.*

Emlyn Hughes had captained Liverpool to successive European Cups in 1977 and 1978. Phil Thompson, in 1981, and Graeme Souness in 1984, also lifted the trophy before it was my turn with the Champions League in 2005. Those five trophies, to United's three, meant we still had European bragging rights over them.

But I yearned for Liverpool's nineteenth league title, and my first, to close the domestic gap on United. I'd had my moments against Man U and I still enjoyed remembering the thirty-five-yarder I had smacked past Fabien Barthez on 31 March 2001 when we won 2–0 at Anfield. I set up Robbie Fowler's second and it completed our first league double in a season over United for twenty-one long years. But moments weren't enough. I wanted more.

I felt the same as Shankly when it came to winning or losing the league. 'If you are first, you are first,' Shankly said. 'If you are second, you are nothing.'

On Bill Shankly's centenary we were fired with belief. It helped having convinced Daniel Sturridge he was fit to play – especially as it was also his twenty-fourth birthday – and we flew at United. We came at them with pace and aggression and, as early as the third minute, we forced a corner.

I ran across to the right, facing the Anfield Road stand, seeing our own fans close to the corner flag and behind that entire side of the goal. The massed horde of United supporters soared up into the highest seats in the distance to my left. It was time for a deep breath as I turned again and stood over the ball. I moved towards it, checked and stopped briefly. I could see Sturridge, one of my targets, was man-marked by two United defenders on the near post. Beyond him, on the edge of the area, alone in space, Daniel Agger waved urgently at me. I raised my left arm.

I stepped up again and took aim with my right foot. The ball rose from the ground in a clean and lovely arc. Agger, unmarked and then barely challenged by Ferdinand, met it perfectly with his head. The ball arrowed towards the net and Sturridge, with his back to goal, helped divert it with a little backwards flick of his own head. David de Gea had been caught out of position and neither Evra nor Tom Cleverley on the far post could react quickly enough to stop the ball flashing past them.

1–0. Sturridge.

The birthday boy hurtled away, his sore thigh and all his pregame doubts obliterated by another goal. Sturridge had showcased his 'ride the wave' dance, where his arms take turns to snake out to either side while he stands there looking cool, after both midweek goals against Notts County. He wanted to do the dance again but Martin Skrtel, in his shaven-skulled way, was having none of it. Skrtel hunted Sturridge down in joy, catching him quickly and wrapping a strong arm around our goalscorer's neck. Sturridge tried to wriggle away but there was no escaping Skrtel. Our big tough bald defender ran down the touchline with Sturridge's head under his arm. Liverpool players on that side of the pitch soon joined them in a delirious huddle.

Ten seconds later I watched Daniel closely as he was finally freed. He lifted both his arms and looked to the heavens in relief. Two fingers waggled skywards in a thank you. His faith had worked. After all his anguish, thinking 'I'm not right, I'm not right, I'm not right', he looked as happy as I had ever seen him.

I glanced across at the bench. Brendan Rodgers and the medical staff were beaming. Our hunch had paid off – and all my pleading during that long fifteen-minute walk with Daniel seemed worth it. He had just scored his eleventh goal in nine games for Liverpool.

United missed Rooney. He had decided, finally, to remain at Old Trafford with the offer of a new contract apparently worth £300,000 a week. But he had cut his head in training a few days earlier, needing ten stitches, and he was out of the Anfield game. Giggs played, a couple of months from his 40th birthday, but he could do little to spark a hesitant Manchester United.

We weren't particularly great either. It was a scrappy game with few chances or memorable moments. Skrtel, who had come back into the side in place of the injured Touré, and Agger were dominant in defence and United became increasingly frustrated. Robin van Persie seemed to nudge his head at Skrtel, who went down, and I was in like a flash just before half-time. Van Persie and I were nose-to-nose, in a serious spot of eyeballing and verbals, before I saw that Skrtel was fine. Big Martin can look after himself.

United were no more threatening in the second half and we saw out the rest of the game pretty comfortably. We had won by the same scoreline for the third match in a row: 1–0

(Sturridge). Daniel did not do much else in the game, but he had got the goal that counted.

The statisticians worked out that we were only the third club in the history of top-flight English football to have won their first three games of a season 1–0, 1–0, 1–0. It had happened twice before, almost one hundred years ago – with Manchester City in 1912–13 and Huddersfield in 1920–21.

The statistic that interested me more was that we were top of the Premier League and the only club with a perfect record of nine points from three games.

It was more surprising to hear David Moyes's reaction. He must have been trying the old Fergie trick of manipulating the headlines by hammering home his biased view of a United performance. It didn't work. Moyes is a very nice man, rather than a fiery dictator, and United had been terrible. The old Everton manager, whom I liked so much, sounded lost and confused. 'I could see why we were champions today,' Moyes claimed. 'I thought we played really well.'

Asked if he was concerned about United's difficulties in the transfer market, Moyes said he was 'more than happy' with his squad. 'After that performance, I wouldn't be worried.'

I headed towards the international break, and two World Cup qualifying games with England, feeling happier and more hopeful than I had for a long time. Manchester United were in trouble; and Liverpool were back where we belonged.

A far more important battle continued. It was still a deeply painful struggle but a year before, on the cold, grey morning of 12 September 2012, there had been a sudden shift of mood. The courageous families of the ninety-six Liverpool fans who had lost their lives during an FA Cup semi-final between Liverpool and Nottingham Forest at Hillsborough on 15 April 1989 had gathered in the city's Anglican cathedral. After twenty-three years of hearing the truth distorted, they were finally given hope as they listened to new evidence.

It was now clear to everyone that, as the families had always argued, there had been an orchestrated campaign to blame our helpless and innocent fans.

The 2012 report finally revealed the truth about that awful day. I could still remember how, in April 2009, Andy Burnham, then the Labour government's Secretary of State for Culture, Media & Sport, had been booed at the twentieth anniversary of the disaster. Burnham came from Liverpool, and he was a football fan, an Evertonian, who cared about us and the tragic events. But nothing had been done for so long that the anger of the families spilled out. He was called a hypocrite when he paid tribute to those who had died – an insult that was accepted by Burnham as a sign of deep anger and hurt. All the issues raised by the Hillsborough Family Support Group had been ignored for two decades.

But, finally, a new inquest was ordered.

Exactly a year on from the landmark day when the findings of the independent panel were heard, still more steps had been taken. It was already guaranteed that the new inquest would begin in Warrington no later than 31 March 2014. And on that Thursday morning, 12 September 2013, Jon Stoddart, the former chief constable of Durham police, said: 'We are exploring all liability, both public and individual. We are looking at unlawful killing – who is responsible for the deaths. Those ninety-six people went to Hillsborough to watch a football match. We want to know what happened, how it happened and why, and who is responsible.'

My cousin, Jon-Paul Gilhooley, had been the youngest of the ninety-six. He was just ten. I was already at the Academy, Liverpool's Centre of Excellence, a couple of months away from my ninth birthday, and we shared the same obsession. We were besotted with Liverpool. It was our club. It was our dream.

We sometimes played football together outside my house on Ironside Road when Jon-Paul joined the huge gang of us in our wild kickabouts. I always remember Jon-Paul and me wearing our red Liverpool kits. We were bound together by football and by Liverpool FC.

My mum and dad, my brother Paul and I watched the news unfold on the television. Our FA Cup semi-final against Forest had been abandoned in the sixth minute. We had listened to the start of the game on the radio but I couldn't understand what had happened. The scary scenes I saw on TV, with people running up and down the pitch, carrying the bodies of Liverpool fans on stretchers, had confused and upset me. I could not sleep that night.

We had no idea that Jon-Paul had been at the game. It was only when Granddad Tony banged on the door at half-eight the next morning that we discovered the loss in our family. Granddad lived in the house opposite and it was obvious that something horrible had happened.

When my parents came into the front room, Granddad Tony could hold it in no longer. 'I've got bad news,' he said. 'Jon-Paul's gone game and he hasn't come home.'

It was almost too much to absorb. Jon-Paul? It couldn't be true.

Granddad told us everything he knew. Jackie, Jon-Paul's mum, had given her son the amazing news. Brian Gilhooley – Jon-Paul's uncle – had managed to get a spare ticket to the game. He asked Jackie if Jon-Paul would like to go to Hillsborough. I imagined how crazed with excitement I might have been had the offer been made to me. A chance to see Liverpool in the FA Cup semi-final? It must have sounded incredible.

It was distressing, at the age of eight, to accept the truth. But it hit the adults around me much harder. They understood. They could imagine Jon-Paul's last few minutes. I could not get my head straight. Jon-Paul had gone to a football match on a spring morning in 1989, to watch mighty Liverpool, and he had never come home. How? Why? *Why?*

At least we were another step closer to justice on that otherwise ordinary September morning in 2013 – a quarter of a century after a catastrophe ripped the heart out of so many families in Liverpool.

My cousin's name is carved into the Hillsborough Memorial near the Shankly Gates at Anfield. Jon-Paul Gilhooley, one of the 96. I thought of him every time I entered Anfield and passed the memorial.

The season rolled on in the early autumn of 2013. During the international break England made more progress in our World Cup qualification group. I scored the opener in our 4–0 defeat of Moldova at Wembley, with Rickie Lambert and Danny Welbeck, who netted twice, getting the other goals. We then went to Kiev and secured a valuable point in a 0–0 draw with Ukraine, our closest rivals in Group H.

As always with England there was a fuss. Sturridge had aggravated his thigh injury in our defeat of Manchester United and missed both England games. He had been named the Premier League player of the month for August and so he was accused of letting England down. The row kicked off because, in an interview with the club website, Daniel had said he needed to focus on Liverpool. He was accused of snubbing his country.

I'm no fan of Twitter but Daniel got it right when, after all the accusations flew in, he tweeted the truth: 'If I do well for my club, I will play for England. If I'm not fit, I can't play. Don't get it twisted. England is the pinnacle.'

After intensive treatment at Melwood he was able to play in our next league game. On Monday, 16 September, we went to the Liberty Stadium to face Swansea City, Brendan's former club. It was a crazy game because Jonjo Shelvey, who had left Liverpool in the summer, was involved in all four goals. Shelvey, a good and honest pro, miskicked, recovered and scored for Swansea after eighty-seven seconds before, almost as if he was saying sorry to his old mates, he tried a back pass with his next touch. It went straight to Sturridge: 1–1 after four minutes.

Shelvey buried his face in his hands just over half an hour later. He mishit a pass to Victor Moses, who had started in place of Aspas, and the on-loan striker from Chelsea fired us ahead. Shelvey started a flowing move and then, using his head, he was on the end of a chipped pass to set up Michu for the equalizer in the sixty-fourth minute. He completed his bizarre set for the night when he was booked for a fierce tackle on Lucas. It ended 2–2 and everyone wanted to interview Jonjo.

Two costly lost points became five when we were beaten 1–0 at Southampton that Saturday. Brendan chose to play four central defenders, bringing Touré in at right-back to replace the injured Glen Johnson, and leaving Enrique on the bench. We were also without Coutinho, who needed shoulder surgery after the Swansea game.

Southampton, under Mauricio Pochettino, were a good side and they featured three players we would sign at the end of the season – Dejan Lovren, Adam Lallana and Rickie Lambert. But we were poor and, even with all our centre halves in defence, we conceded the only goal of the game from a set piece. Lallana took the corner, awarded after confusion between Touré and Skrtel, and Lovren escaped Agger to nod past me as I tried to block the goal at the near post.

Brendan, rightly, was furious:

To first lose possession, and then a goal, with so many defensive players on the pitch was criminal. I would like a much stronger squad, but we have what we have. The only positive from today is that Luis's suspension is over. It will be great to have him back, because technically we were very disappointing. We were flat, right off it. We had one of those days, and it hurts, but I am still optimistic for the rest of the season.


The Luis Suárez script wrote itself yet again. It refused to be downgraded into a less provocative saga and so, inevitably, Luis's first game after his ban ended was against Manchester United at Old Trafford. I guess it could have been worse. It could have been a title decider against Chelsea rather than a Capital One Cup tie. Luis up against Branislav Ivanović, having just completed his ten-game suspension for biting the Chelsea defender, might have seemed even more extreme. But there was a poisoned atmosphere between Suárez and United after a different incident and an earlier ban.

Almost two years before, on 15 October 2011, in a typically tight and snarling league game between Liverpool and Manchester United at Anfield, I went to take a corner in front of the Kop. My attention was focused solely on whipping in a killer delivery that Suárez or Dirk Kuyt might divert into the United net. I had no idea that a squabble had broken out between Suárez and Patrice Evra, United's French international defender.

Luis said later that Evra, who had supposedly been fouling him the whole game, went straight up to him before the corner. Evra asked why he had just been kicked by Suárez. It was the usual stuff you get in a game – except that Suárez chose to call Evra, in Spanish, a *negro*. The exchange continued, the game went on and I knew nothing about it. I didn't even know that, once we got back to the dressing room, Suárez was taken out-side by Damien Comolli, then Liverpool's director of football, who told him that Evra had accused him of racism.

The players began talking about it. But it was only later that evening, when I saw the television footage and the reaction from everyone, that I really understood why it had become such a big deal. Luis and I never spoke about it. I obviously wanted to be there for Luis as his captain and his teammate but I don't think he was comfortable discussing it. He was upset by the whole episode and it was something that got dealt with by other people higher up at the club. The only player who became involved was Dirk Kuyt. He had been standing close to Luis on the pitch and he was aware that trouble had broken out with Evra. Dirk supported Luis when they both appeared before an FA hearing.

I tried to distance myself from the situation. I was convinced that Luis was not a racist, and the support he received from our black teammate Glen Johnson backed that view. But the prob-lem of pitting Suárez's words against Evra's was obvious. Neither player would retract his version. Luis said that there was a difference between Negro in English, where it is such an offensive word, and *negro* (pronounced *neh*-gro) in Spanish. He even said his own wife sometimes called him *negro* because the word meant nothing more than 'black' in Spanish, and that she was calling him 'blackie' because of his pitch-black hair.

I don't think Liverpool or Luis handled the situation par-ticularly well, but Kenny Dalglish, our manager then, was in a very difficult situation. I know many neutral people criticized Kenny for defending Luis too much, and maybe he did. But, as captain, I could understand why Kenny refused to go against Luis. He believed Luis, of course, but there was also the risk of him falling out with our best player, who could then demand a move from the club. Kenny would have been blamed.

Above all else, Kenny will protect his players to the hilt. Maybe such loyalty is sometimes ill advised – but it's one of the reasons I love the man. His love for the club and what he'd be prepared to do for it have always inspired me. For a player to know that he's got that level of backing from his manager is inspirational.

It was another example of the Liverpool way of instinctively defending our own. Some of the players, led by Pepe Reina, decided to wear T-shirts with Luis's face on the front and his number on the back before a midweek match against Wigan on 21 December 2011. I was injured and so I had no idea it was going to happen until I saw the images on television – as the players warmed up in those controversial T-shirts just twenty-four hours after Suárez had been found guilty of racially abusing Evra.

Paul McGrath was one of a few former black footballers who attacked the gesture. 'If I was in Glen Johnson's situation,' McGrath said, 'I'd have thrown the shirt to the floor.' Glen was quick to respond. On Twitter he apparently said, using lots of exclamation marks, 'I will support who I want when I want!!! There are a lot of reasons why I'm standing by Luis Suárez!!!'

Alan Hansen, another Liverpool legend, then made the mistake of talking about 'coloured' players on *Match of the Day*. He apologized but it was far from over.

I can't say for certain exactly what happened between Suárez and Evra. I think only Luis knows whether he was guilty. If he was, as so many decided, then I could not back him. I would never accept any form of racism. But because I had no way of knowing whether it was definitely true or false I had to follow my instinct and believe my teammate.

Luis was banned for eight games. But we all got punished for it because we missed him on the field and it ended up being bad PR for everyone at the club. So we all suffered a little – even if Suárez and Evra were obviously more distressed than anyone.

Then, as if enjoying the tawdry soap opera, the footballing gods intervened. Luis's first match after his racism ban was against Manchester United at Old Trafford on 11 February 2012.

In the dressing room I asked Lucas Leiva, who was close to Luis, if he knew what was going to happen when we faced the United players for the prematch handshake. Lucas assured me there would be no problem. Luis had told him that he was ready to shake Evra's hand.

Instead, we got more controversy as I led my team down the line of United players. A long way behind me, Suárez did not shake hands in the end with Evra. Alex Ferguson called Suárez 'a disgrace' and said he should never be allowed to play for Liverpool again. Nonsense.

Nineteen months down the line, in September 2013, another Suárez ban had ended with another return to Manchester United. The heat was reduced slightly by the fact that Ferguson had retired and Evra was injured. But United were in even more of a mess and had been hammered 4–1 by Manchester City the previous weekend.

Luis was the last of the Liverpool players out of the tunnel. He was booed by the home supporters. But Luis kissed the tattoo on his right wrist, in honour of his family, and our fans roared his name. He offered them a thumbs-up. Luis looked relaxed and he even grinned as he waited for the handshakes. This time there were no missed greetings. Everyone shook hands and at last we could resume as a football team with Luis Suárez at the helm.

Wayne Rooney was also playing again after his injury. A big black protective band was wrapped around his head, covering the gash that had kept him out of the Anfield fixture. The first half was routine stuff but Rooney helped break the deadlock soon after we came back out on the pitch. He took a corner and, with our defence all over the place, found Javier Hernández who poked home a simple deflection. It had been ridiculously easy for United.

For the sixth successive match since the start of the season we failed again to score in the second half. Our 1–0 defeat to Southampton was mirrored at Old Trafford – despite our dominating possession in the last twenty-five minutes. Suárez came closest as, after an inconsistent start, he began to find his rhythm. In the seventieth minute he skinned Jonny Evans and hit a curling shot that just missed. A minute later, and from a long way out, his free kick hit the bar. He also ran his socks off, as I always knew he would. I was sure Luis would get better and better and, if nothing else, the evening slipped away without any controversy.

David Moyes's relief at the final whistle was obvious. He pumped his fist, shook hands with every one of his players and applauded the Stretford End extravagantly. We just trudged off and out of the Capital One Cup. Our targets for the season, already stripped of European competition, had shrunk to the Premier League and the FA Cup. We had no claim to being stretched or diverted. It was time for Liverpool and me, with Suárez, to get cracking.

The first surge started four days later, against Sunderland on 29 September. It ran and ran, despite one defeat and another dodgy display, all the way to Christmas 2013. Our wins were not just routine victories, grinding teams down or sneaking home with another 1–0 as the days became colder and wetter, shorter and darker. They felt different. They felt full of heat and light.

Of course we pressed and ran and pressed again, working our bollocks off, closing down teams at pace, forcing them into errors. We squeezed the life out of them and then frightened them to death with a heavy dose of a potion called Suárez. There were long, dizzying spells of magic from him, and from Sturridge as well, and then Coutinho, another little spellbinder, returned. Sterling, gleaming with promise and power, soon began to start every match and the opposition knew nothing about him. The kid surprised them – just like he had once surprised us with his strength and skill. Henderson brought real energy to the team. Confidence rippled through him in tandem with the team's belief.

I was making goals, setting up assists from open play and dead-ball situations, and scoring a few along the way. Nothing was new to me, but it still felt fresh. There were so many tingling, stunning moments that they began to merge into something more substantial. There was solidity as well as sparkle to our play.

We had our wobbles defensively. Mignolet made a few mistakes, and goals were conceded, but he also kept up his spectacular shot-stopping as well. There were own goals, positional errors in the centre of the defence, but Skrtel was a soldier, tough and hard, and Agger and Johnson and the rest, especially a lovely Liverpool kid in Jon Flanagan, showed we could defend as well as bomb forward when the opposition were on their knees, shredded by the skill, tenacity and speed of Suárez – and the goals both he and Sturridge scored.

Suárez and Sturridge set the tone and everyone tried to match them. Brendan came into his own as a manager. The training sessions were amongst the best I had ever experienced while his man-management was excellent, generous and imaginative. I actually think the standard of training, from Luis's return after being banished during preseason, was the best it had been at Liverpool since the Torres days under Rafa. The intensity, the one-touch passing, was probably even better. I sometimes played in five-a-side games when the opposition wouldn't get a sniff of the ball. We would destroy them. And then little tweaks would be made and the same thing would happen to my team. We would be played off the five-a-side park.

That exceptional standard spread through the whole squad. It was no longer the starting XI and the rest being bit-part players or subs. Brendan managed the squad so cleverly that everyone always thought they had a chance of starting. Before games, and during them, the mood was driven and upbeat. And away from the matches a very healthy atmosphere lifted the club.

Of course, it was painful to be sitting at home on Tuesday and Wednesday evenings, watching Champions League football on television. But, in terms of the Premier League, it was perfect preparation.

The routine at Liverpool is clear. The fourth day before the next game is a strength day – which is all about powering your quads and hamstrings. Then game day minus three will be a resistance day, where the stints are longer and you work on your endurance. Game day minus two focuses on speed, where it's all about sharp reactions and getting yourself ready for the game. The day before the match, you come back into Melwood and do virtually nothing so you're ready to fly in the game. We had an advantage over everyone at the top of the table with that week of preparation unbroken by European games and travel.

And so the cup defeat at Old Trafford mattered less to me than the way we responded in our next league match. Sunderland had just sacked Paolo Di Canio as their fiery manager but I felt sure there would be no new start for them when Suárez turned up at the Stadium of Light in the mood to dazzle. I obviously knew how sharp he had been in training and there was never any worry that, after such a long break, he would need four or five games to settle back into the side.

Luis was quiet and deadly concentrated in training before that game. You could see he was really fired up. I think he had a lot of guilt from having been banned and unable to help the team, and he was determined to make up for it. I would be on my phone straight after training, calling my mates and my dad, saying: 'Suárez is on fire. I told you he was like a man possessed when he first came back to training. But he's taking it to another level now.'

If Luis got a few chances against Sunderland I was certain he would score. It was the same with Sturridge. Keep feeding him and he'll always score for you. I felt real optimism as we headed to the North East.

On a sunny afternoon in Sunderland I took a first-half corner. Touré failed to connect with his header but, at the far post, Sturridge nodded home. It had been more of an opportunistic lunge at the ball, using his shoulder, chest and face as much as his head, but the ball still bounced down into the net.

Deep inside our own half, but with space to move and time to look up, I then hit one of my trademark long cross-field passes. This one landed exactly where I wanted, thirty-five yards away, at Sturridge's feet on the right flank. He ran towards goal, twitching with menace, and then, using the outside of his right boot, flicked it across the face of the goal where Suárez glided in to tuck the ball away: 2–0, Sturridge and Suárez.

As Luis ran away to celebrate he lifted his shirt in honour of his son who had been born two days earlier: *Welcome, Benja. Los Amo!*

I was the first to reach him but I slipped on the verge behind the goal, almost pulling Luis down. I was back up on my feet in seconds so I could embrace him. Apart from the odd howl for us to fuck off, the Sunderland fans watched us in stony silence.

The Liverpool supporters, packed into the away end, were almost beside themselves, singing, *Luis Suárez . . . he can bite who he wants . . . Luis Suárez . . . he can bite who he wants . . .*

We got bitten when Simon Mignolet failed to hold Ki Sung-yueng's hopeful long-range shot. He parried it straight into the path of Emanuele Giaccherini: 2–1, and the Stadium of Light shimmered with sudden hope for the home team.

Two minutes were left when Adam Johnson took a corner for Sunderland. Mignolet made amends. He came out and claimed it comfortably. Simon could tell that the break was on and he urged us forward before throwing it straight to Suárez on the right near the halfway line. Sunderland had only two furiously back-pedalling defenders against a foursome of Suárez, Lucas, Sturridge and Sterling, who were running in a line at the goal. Suárez was in control of the ball, with Lucas haring ahead, hoping for a pass.

Suárez decided to curl it across field to Sturridge. Three Sunderland defenders had made it back into the box but Suárez was waving dramatically at Sturridge. He wanted the ball again, he wanted another goal. Sturridge duly delivered, cutting it back into the area so Suárez could smack it in with his left foot: 3–1. Luis raised his shirt to welcome Benja again, kissing his wrist as he danced away in the sunshine – before turning back to acknowledge his debt to Sturridge.

On the coach home I said quietly to Chris Morgan, 'I think we did well but let's just try and stay in the mix and see what happens.' Neither of us actually thought we had a chance of winning the League. It was more a case of we'd settle for the top four right then if we could. But if we were still in the race with ten games left, who knew how far we might go? I sensed a quiet confidence that we could match any team.

We beat Crystal Palace next, winning 3–1 at Anfield, with goals from Suárez, Sturridge and me. I rammed home a penalty, sending their keeper, Julián Speroni, the wrong way. Unlike Luis and Daniel, I didn't celebrate. I had done my job and, honestly, I expect to score from a penalty every time. Instead of a Suárez shirt-lift and wrist-kiss, or a Sturridge robot-surfer dance, I just wiped the sweat from my nose. No one jumped on me. I think they knew I was too old for any of that stuff after a simple no-nonsense pen. Someone ruffled my hair and that was it. We moved on, top of the league at the end of that warm Saturday afternoon.

Two defining qualification matches awaited England over the next week at Wembley – against Montenegro and Poland. Victory in both would ensure our place at the World Cup in Brazil the following summer. There is always pressure and tension, criticism and uncertainty with England. My attention had already begun to shift to the familiar, testing challenge of playing for and captaining my country.

It was still only the first week of October, and we had just beaten Sunderland and Palace. I would celebrate when it really mattered – once the stress of England was gone and Liverpool started beating our closest rivals. A long road stretched out ahead of me. I could not yet imagine either a fight for the league title or a World Cup in Brazil.

# 4. Qualifications and Positions

I celebrated some goals on Ironside Road as if I had just hit the winner for England in a World Cup final. I was usually Gazza, wearing my England shirt with his name on the back, setting off on a mazy dribble before slotting the ball between the two dustbins which doubled as goalposts. I could also be Gary Lineker, taking a penalty in the very last minute of the final at Wembley and as soon as the ball flashed between the steel bins I would be off on a mad celebratory dash. I was an England hero, an England winner, soaking up the adulation of the whole country as I ran down Ironside Road, yelling with joy and punching the air.

I might have been crazy about Liverpool but Italia '90 also turned me into an England obsessive. It was the World Cup of Paul Gascoigne's brilliance and Lineker's goals, of late nights with my whole family screaming at the TV, of Gazza's tears and semi-final heartache against West Germany. I watched that game at home, having just turned ten, feeling the lump in my throat when Gazza got the yellow card and he started to cry, knowing he would be suspended for the final. As it turned out, Stuart Pearce and Chris Waddle missed their penalties in the deadly shoot-out. England were gunned down. Heartbreak in Huyton, and the entire country.

Out on the street I dreamed instead of ecstatic endings. Little Stevie Gerrard went one step further than his England hero, Gazza, and made it all the way to the World Cup final, where he scored a goal as great as the one I'd just slotted between the Ironside bins. It was a dream as real as the fantasy of winning the league with Liverpool – except it was even bigger.

I played for England often on the streets of Huyton on wet, miserable winter afternoons or sticky summer evenings. It was little wonder that I and my big brother Paul, whom I called Gazza because of his chubby cheeks, idolized Gascoigne. I can't even guess how many times I watched my *Gascoigne's Glory* video as I fuelled the fantasy.

Bryan Robson had been an earlier England favourite. Captain Marvel played in midfield, just like me. When he wore white I forgot all about the fact that Robson was a Manchester United player. I hated United, but I loved Robson. My dad came home one day to find me out in the street, playing football in my England shirt with Robson on the back.

Dad called me inside for a quiet word. What was I thinking? Wearing a Robson shirt – in Huyton? What would the neighbours think? Dad would put up with it behind closed doors, to humour me, and because he also knew how great Robson was for England. But I needed to keep my head screwed on outside. I nodded, changed and went back out into the street in Liverpool red. I still liked imagining I was Robson or, in later years, a Geordie like Gazza or a Lineker from Leicester, even though he'd once been an Evertonian.

England meant an awful lot to me. When a chance seemed to have come up for me to move to the National School of Football at Lilleshall I thought I might be on my way to heaven. Jamie Carragher had gone to Lilleshall two years earlier. Michael Owen was already there, and Jamie Cassidy too, as well as another young Liverpool defender called Tommy Culshaw. I was sure that I belonged at Lilleshall with all the other future England kids. After a trial for under-15 boys, I thought I had played so well that I was convinced I'd get my beautiful invite. I was captain of Liverpool Boys and heading to a dream life as a schoolboy footballer at Lilleshall.

When the letter arrived in the post there were tears. They

told me that I was a great player but all kinds of reasons, beyond football, were taken into account when they made their selection. I had no idea what they were talking about because that's all they said – beyond the brutal fact that I'd been cut and, oh, I shouldn't give up. That did it. I ran upstairs and flung myself down on my bed. I covered my face with a pillow and sobbed.

Dad tried hard to make me feel better. He reminded me how well I had done at the trial. Dad said maybe they thought I just needed to grow a few inches – or get a little more self-confident before they would consider taking me away from home for two years.

I looked at Dad through my tears. Finally, when I could speak, the raw words tumbled out of me. 'I can't carry on,' I said between crying some more. 'That's me finished with football.'

Dad calmed me and, gently, pulled me back. He spoke about Liverpool instead. Liverpool loved me. Liverpool rated me. Coaches like Steve Heighway, Dave Shannon and Hughie McAuley cared about me. They believed in me. It was far from over. As long as I had Liverpool I had hope.

And so I played on. Seven months later the Lilleshall stars who had beaten me to the cut came to Melwood to play against my Liverpool Boys team. They strolled in wearing their National School blazers. I was steaming inside. I would show them and their selectors what they had missed when they turned me away. I could not wait for kick-off.

Michael Owen, Wes Brown and Michael Ball were three of their standout players but I tore into all of them. I played out of my skin. Owen was already a goal machine, and his hat-trick helped the national boys sneak a 4–3 win. We all knew that if Michael had been back in our Liverpool team, or if I had been in the Lilleshall side, we would have produced a rout together. At least the Lilleshall boys all lined up to shake my hand afterwards. I respected them for that and I took each hand with a silent nod. But I ran back to the changing room before the Lilleshall coaches could reach me. I didn't want to hear a fucking word they said – or see any of them. I was bitter.

My England under-15 rejection drove me on for years. I knew why it had hurt so much. I wanted to play for Liverpool and I wanted to play for England. When it seemed as if the second dream had been shattered it took a long time to piece myself together. But I did.

I made my full England debut on 31 May 2000, the day after I turned twenty, against Ukraine at Wembley. It was hard to believe that I was in the same dressing room as Tony Adams and Alan Shearer. I had watched them at Euro '96, when I'd been sixteen and England as hosts had again reached the semi-finals, and again lost on penalties to Germany. That was the delirious summer when the whole country seemed to be singing 'football's coming home', after Baddiel & Skinner and the Liverpool band The Lightning Seeds released 'Three Lions', with 'Jules Rimet still gleaming' after 'thirty years of hurt'. It was the tournament where Gazza scored a wonder goal against Scotland before we actually won a penalty shoot-out in the quarters – and knocked out Spain, who at the time seemed to be even worse big-tournament chokers than England.

Despite being so quiet and shy, I suddenly had Adams screaming in my face, in the old Wembley dressing room: 'Are you fucking ready for this?'

My blood turned cold. My throat was already dry. I managed a Scouse mumble: 'Let's have it.'

The game raced past. I felt amazed to wear the white shirt with my own name on the back. I felt awed to have played against Andriy Shevchenko – and been part of a 2–0 England win under Kevin Keegan, a Liverpool legend.

I won my 100th England cap twelve years later, on 14 November 2012, in Stockholm. We lost 4–2, with Zlatan Ibrahimović

93

scoring all Sweden's goals, including an incredible overhead bicycle kick that flew past Joe Hart from thirty yards out. Before the game, when asked to give my England career a rating out of ten, I suggested 'a six or a seven'. I was being honest rather than downbeat.

Outside of the 1966 World Cup-winning team, which other England players could honestly give themselves an eight or a nine? Maybe I would give some of Bobby Robson's team that reached the Italia '90 semi-final an eight. But there's no one else.

When our hyped-up 'superstars' fall short, and England get knocked out earlier than anyone would hope, the abuse and criticism goes far too much the other way. Players become 'totally useless' and 'completely rubbish'. And that's led to the same old cycle – with the only change in my fourteen years as an international being that the criticism has become more constant. No matter how well you might be playing for England in a good spell, you know it's just round the corner. That's the way you feel when you're an England player. Even when you win against the so-called 'lesser' nations you get criticized unless you beat them 5–0.

It had become obvious to me that one of the problems undermining so many players when they pull on an England shirt is that they are made heroes of far too quickly. The press, and social media these days, are far too keen to claim some kid is great before they've achieved anything of lasting value. It's bad for the players. They start believing that they're giants of the game when in fact they've done very little.

There are also moments, private moments behind the public face of English football, when players are not always handled in the best way. Stuart Pearce taught me that harsh truth in 2012. Pearce had been an important member of the England teams I revered at Italia '90 and at Euro '96. He was a very good full back, a committed player and a passionate Englishman.

Pearce was distraught when, at the end of that unforgettable night in Turin, he missed one of the penalties that cost England a place in the 1990 World Cup final. But it was typical of him that, six years later, he insisted on taking another penalty in a different shoot-out – in the quarter-final of the European Championship against Spain at Wembley. Pearce scored, howled in defiance and England won on penalties – for once.

So I respected Stuart Pearce and, of course, he had become England's under-21 manager and been appointed as an assistant coach of the national team by Fabio Capello. It meant a lot when he called me at the end of England's 2010 World Cup in South Africa. I was at the airport in Johannesburg with most of the squad, of which I was captain, waiting to fly home after the devastating 4–1 defeat we had suffered against Germany in Bloemfontein.

Pearce didn't need to make that call but he was generous. He told me that I was one of the few England players who could leave the World Cup with my head held high – and he praised the way I had conducted myself as captain. He said, 'I know you'll be frustrated and disappointed, like we all are. But your behaviour and your level of training and how you played in the games were all first-rate. You couldn't have done anything different. You were right on it so you should be proud with what you've done.'

And that's why the way he treated me eighteen months later seemed so mind-blowing and upsetting. After Capello resigned in February 2012, and before Roy Hodgson took over, Pearce was appointed caretaker manager for a friendly against the Netherlands at Wembley. I think Pearce imagined he might be in the running for the job, even though his managerial record could not be compared to Roy's vast experience or to that of Harry Redknapp, who was then tipped by the media to become England's next manager.

Liverpool won the League Cup final on the Sunday before the game against Holland. We beat Cardiff, on penalties, and so we arrived later than the rest of the squad at England's training-camp hotel, The Grove, just outside Watford. We went into the England team room – me, Glen Johnson, Andy Carroll and Stuey Downing. Pearce came in and he said, 'Look, lads, I know you had a tough game in the final so you are only going to be playing forty-five minutes against Holland – but congratulations on winning another trophy for Liverpool.'

I thought it was understandable and I had no problems about being told I would only play half a friendly match for England. There had been a lot of talk about who would be captain under Pearce and I thought that might have been his moment to say to me, 'Can I have a word with you outside?' or, 'Could you come to my room for a chat?' It seemed the perfect opportunity to tell me whether I was going to be captain or not. But Pearce didn't say anything.

The following morning I was on a recovery day. Just before the rest of the squad left for training, Pearce pulled me into a toilet at The Grove. He said, 'I just wanted to tell you face to face that I'm going to be picking Scott Parker to be the captain for this game.'

I didn't have much to say because I knew he'd made the wrong decision. Scott Parker is a good player, and he's honest, and I enjoyed playing with him at Euro 2012 later that year when I was captain again under Roy Hodgson. I've got a lot of respect for Scott as a player and a person.

But to pick Scott Parker as England captain ahead of me? Scott was in decent form at the time, playing well, and he is also a leader. But he had very little experience at England level and no experience at all of being an international captain. Kevin Nolan captained him at West Ham – and they had been in the Championship the previous season. I don't know whether it was a dig against Liverpool or something more personal – but my overall perception was that Pearce was doing some muscle-flexing in the toilet mirrors. My guess is that it was a decision designed to focus attention on Stuart Pearce. It was his way of saying, 'This is me. I'm in charge.' He also perhaps thought the London-based media wanted Parker to wear the armband.

He met the media later that day and, discussing his as-yet unrevealed choice of captain, he began a long speech about how he had gone to Afghanistan to give a talk to British troops about the values of leadership. Pearce said:

> On the trip over there I thought: 'Well, how do I approach this? What key element do I believe is fundamental in a leader?' And the one word I could come up with was 'unselfish'. I always want a leader whose teammates know this fella is in it for their greater good, rather than his own. I will attempt to pick a captain who, I believe, has that sort of respect in the other players' eyes. Tony Adams had that, Paul Ince did, Alan Shearer, Terry Butcher, Bryan Robson. For all these guys, the team mattered a hell of a lot before individuals.

The press seemed taken aback a few days later. They had assumed Pearce was talking about me. A few writers even mentioned that Pearce's fellow FA coaches had been surprised he had appointed Parker instead. Of course none of them knew that Pearce actually chose to tell me the news in a toilet.

We had team meetings before the Holland game where Pearce was telling us about his preparations for Euro 2012. He was trying to impress everyone and get a crack at the job. But I think the decision he shared with me in a toilet was one of the reasons he never got the position he craved.

I might have had misgivings about his tactical insights as a coach, but I respected Stuart Pearce until that moment. I just felt he treated me very badly. It was insulting – and it was wrong. I thought it was selfish. It was a political decision to make everyone think he had balls.

Captains do get changed and that's obviously acceptable. But you are owed an explanation. I had taken over as captain when Rio Ferdinand was injured before the 2010 World Cup. In March 2011, Capello decided to make John Terry his captain again. I had no qualms as JT is an obvious leader, a great defender and he has vast experience. But JT had his problems. In February 2012 he was due to stand trial for alleged racial abuse of Anton Ferdinand, Rio's brother. The FA and Capello, who wanted Terry to retain the captaincy, fell out over it. The Italian resigned. Pearce came in as emergency cover but he did not offer one reason in the ten seconds it took him to say he didn't want me as captain.

How would Stuart Pearce have felt if Bobby Robson or Kevin Keegan had pulled him into a toilet at Burnham Beeches, England's old training base, and told him that the expected role of captain was not being given to him – but to someone who had eighty fewer caps than him?

England lost to Holland – and, thankfully, Roy Hodgson was appointed as manager for Euro 2012.

I will always respect Pearce the player – but I have lost a lot of respect for the man after that day in the toilet.

As we reached the crunch period of our World Cup qualifying campaign, with two vital fixtures in October 2013, I hoped I had one last big tournament to play. I had missed the 2002 World Cup through injury and the 2008 European Championship when we failed to qualify. Now, after three European Championships and two World Cups, I had one last tilt at international glory. The 2014 World Cup would be held in Brazil, the greatest stage for every international footballer around the globe, and I was desperate to be there with England.

Roy Hodgson, an intelligent and good man with whom I had forged a close bond, was our manager. I was still England's captain and we had two home games at Wembley, against Montenegro and Poland, to clinch our qualification. Defeat or a draw in either would condemn us to yet another nervy play-off because Ukraine were pushing us hard for the group's only automatic qualifying place for Brazil. The old grinding pressure had returned but I felt good.

England had been here before, again and again. I had also been here before, especially on a wet, awful night at Wembley in November 2007. We'd needed just a point from our final group game against Croatia to seal our place at Euro 2008. Steve McLaren, who had been Sven-Göran Eriksson's assistant for years, had become our manager. I liked Steve and I enjoyed his training sessions and working under him. All the players did. We warmed to him and his coaching methods – but we didn't get the results we needed.

If you don't qualify for a tournament with England then you're in deep trouble. You are going to get slaughtered in the media and by most fans. You and your team are going to be dismissed as total losers who don't care anyway. Of course, the opposite was always true. We cared deeply – so much so that maybe we allowed ourselves to be undone by the pressure.

I still expected us to beat Croatia and qualify. Steve made a couple of big calls which backfired badly. He had dropped David Beckham from the squad when he came in as manager – another example of a new man trying to put down a marker. Steve was wise enough to bring Beckham back into the fold eventually; but he kept our most experienced player on the bench against Croatia. More catastrophically, he also chose to give a young goalkeeper his competitive debut in a qualification decider.

Scott Carson was our keeper at Liverpool. He had just

turned twenty-two and he was still raw. Steve knew Paul Robinson, England's previous number 1, had been through a rough patch but it was a huge gamble to replace him. On a rainy, treacherous night I felt for Carson, and England, when he made a bad mistake in only the eighth minute. Niko Kranjčar had a crack from a very long way out. It should have been a comfortable save. But Carson allowed the greasy ball to slip through his hands. We then went 2–0 down six minutes later and the silence of Wembley, following the Carson howler, turned to jeering anger.

Frank Lampard scored a penalty and we seemed to have been saved when Beckham, who came on early in the second half for Shaun Wright-Phillips, crossed for Peter Crouch to chest down and steer home the equalizer. Croatia were better than us that night and they came again – restoring their lead with thirteen minutes left. We had no answer and, with Steve looking wretched under an umbrella on the touchline, we were washed away by the rain and thunderous booing.

Our performance had been disjointed and disappointing – and the result was shocking. It seemed cruel that most of the derision got heaped on poor old Steve McLaren. He became 'The Wally with the Brolly' and his reputation, which had been built on his excellent coaching at Manchester United and some managerial success with Middlesbrough, was in ruins for a long time.

I thought Steve could have done well as an England manager under different circumstances – but if you don't qualify then a sacking is inevitable. I felt partly responsible for Steve's fate. I was meant to be a big player for England and I hadn't delivered when it really counted. I still cursed the chance I had missed, in Russia, which might have given us the lifeline we needed and made the game against Croatia less nervy.

We endured that horrible night at Wembley and were exposed

again to the harsh truth. At this level of football, the small details can hurt you the most.

It felt important, six years later, to avoid that same fate. The first half against Montenegro was anxious, and goalless, but after the break we played really well. Andros Townsend had a good game and he set up Rooney, and scored one himself, in a 4–1 victory. We were not there yet. We still needed to beat Poland four nights later to secure our World Cup trip to Brazil.

## *Wembley Stadium, Tuesday, 15 October 2013*

This was the kind of night I had dreamed of on Ironside Road. I walked out of the tunnel at Wembley as England captain before a hugely important game. The noise was incredible, with the Polish fans in a crowd of over 85,000 kicking up an almighty din as they set off flares and firecrackers to match the passionate support of our home supporters. Wembley looked stunning under the lights. The pitch gleamed and there were white and red flags and banners everywhere, celebrating England and Poland in waves of emotion and hope.

The tension made it real. I had never felt anxious when playing fantasy football for England in Huyton. But then we never sang the national anthem before a kickabout on Ironside Road. We didn't have a manager like Roy Hodgson willing us on from the dugout, his face creased with the kind of concentration which made it look as if he needed to rip off his tie to allow him to breathe a little more easily. Roy and the lads wanted this badly.

Across Europe we knew that our rivals for the top spot were set for a goal feast. Ukraine were up against San Marino and the only question was how many they would score against a team of mostly amateur players. If we failed to beat Poland then Ukraine would win the group and be bound for Brazil. Wc would be plunged into the lottery of the play-offs.

Poland were a decent side and we had drawn 1–1 against them exactly a year earlier. They also had one of Europe's top strikers and, in the first twenty-five minutes, Robert Lewandowski had a couple of chances. He couldn't score either. The home support was twitchy while the Poles kept on roaring. News filtered around Wembley that Ukraine were already 3–0 up. I was aware that our fans were on the edge of turning from roaring belief into grumbling doubt. Poland had settled into a deep and compact shape and we were frustrated that we couldn't turn our possession into a goal.

Then, four minutes from half-time, it came. Leighton Baines produced a sublime cross into the box. Wayne Rooney buried it with a flashing header. It was one of those moments when I realized that Rooney is really special. Big players come alive in big games. They score at big moments – and that was a huge moment for England.

The game was far from done. We had to get through a whole half and Poland played with real desire. In front of so many of their fans who had found a way into Wembley, they wanted to deny us the win. As the game wore on the 1–0 lead began to look very fragile. I knew that even a draw would feel almost as disastrous as losing to Croatia in 2007. Fifteen minutes were left. James Milner replaced Townsend as we needed more solidity and energy. Frank Lampard then came on for Michael Carrick, giving us even more experience, and another midfielder replaced a striker as Jack Wilshere took the place of Daniel Sturridge. There were less than ten minutes left. Poland were still running and playing.

Sweat rolled down my face as the crowd's unease rolled down from the stands and across the pitch. I forced myself to dredge up one last effort because if we just tried to cling on to our lead we could concede a killer goal. Poland were pushing hard and one of their centre backs hoofed the ball forward again. But Milner intercepted it on the halfway line. He looked up and then lobbed a hopeful little pass in my direction.

Suddenly, I had a sniff of a chance. I was away. The closest Pole was already lagging behind me. I gathered the ball at my feet and my long legs powered across the pitch. I cut back inside, slaloming past a new challenger and the first chasing defender. I was still surrounded by three red shirts. The last man in red and the goalkeeper, Wojciech Szczęsny, closed in fast on me. But I was consumed by the moment. Nothing would stop me.

I stretched out my right foot just as I fell under the rush of my surge. I reached the ball first and dinked it past Szczęsny. The ball arced into the open goal.

I was up on my feet so quickly I could not quite believe it. I started running. And I ran so fast that no one could catch me. My head was up, my mouth was open and I spread my arms wide in celebration. I ran in the direction of the corner flag where I could see the crowd going crazy. People were jumping and screaming as I ran towards them. My arms stretched out wider as if I might fly into the heaving mass of England fans. As I neared them I couldn't stop myself.

I did a long knee-slide, skidding along the wet and glistening pitch, opening my arms once more as if I was ready to hug every single one of them. And then I was up again, grinning and pumping my right fist.

It was a celebration even more abandoned than anything I had done on Ironside Road all those years ago. And this is what makes it even sweeter. The joy was deeper and more intense than I ever imagined it. This was bliss and euphoria packed with meaning. I knew what it meant. We were not only

2–0 up in the eighty-eighth minute. We were over the doubt and worry, for a while at least, and on our way to Brazil.

Rooney and Welbeck finally got me. They jumped on top of me and brought down the corner flag as well. Milner, Wilshere, Lampard and everyone else leaped on top of them. I was buried beneath the pile of white shirts, not even needing to breathe because I was so deliriously happy. They climbed off eventually and I heard the noise while I still lay on my back. I was so happy as bedlam rocked Wembley. What a feeling.

Wayne cuffed me playfully around the face a few times and then lifted me up on to my feet. I turned to the crowd, punched the air and shouted 'Yes!' like a mad man.

I was thirty-three years old and I had just scored the goal that would take us to the World Cup finals. Baines hugged me, as did Phil Jagielka, two Everton players who had played with heart all night. I walked back to the halfway line, on my own again, my head down but my face still lit with happiness. Only football could make me feel this intensely alive. Only football could unleash such joy.

Football is a bear pit. The noise can be deafening. It's not easy to block out the babbling voices and bitter criticism but, after England's qualification, I was looking forward to a quiet and concentrated spell with Liverpool.

On the Saturday after the Poland game I scored another goal – against Newcastle. I drilled the penalty to the right of Tim Krul. It was never in doubt and so I turned away. I didn't smile but as Henderson, Johnson and Suárez ran towards me I spread my arms. A low-key celebration felt right. It was my 100th Premier League goal and we had been 1–0 down.

We had to come from behind again after another defensive mess let in Newcastle. Suárez and Moses then combined down the left and Luis squared it across the face of the goal.

Sturridge rattled in his header. A 2–2 draw. I looked around our dressing room and was encouraged to see that there was disappointment to have dropped a couple of points away from Anfield. We were making progress. We were becoming seriously ambitious.

But I was a little hurt and surprised when the noise from the bear pit broke out again. It was one of the old grizzlies, Alex Ferguson, doing the growling, and so I stopped to listen. Nine years earlier, in 2004, Ferguson had called me 'the most influential player in England, bar none' and suggested that 'anyone would love to have Gerrard in their team'. Even earlier than that, in 2000, when I was only twenty, before we played United, he said: 'Gerrard's physically and technically precocious, a good engine, remarkable energy, reads the game and passes quickly. I would hate to think Liverpool have someone as good as Roy Keane.'

I'd been blown away as I'd read Ferguson's words.

They had even more impact when, against a vicious backdrop that freezing December afternoon in 2000, United fans hammered on our bus outside Old Trafford. They chanted: *Fuck off, scum, we'll fucking kill you, in your Liverpool slum.*

We beat Man U that day, with Danny Murphy scoring from a free kick.

Roy Keane shook my hand afterwards and said, 'Well done.' He didn't need to say it, after a home defeat, and so the praise from Keane and Ferguson meant a lot to me.

Yet, thirteen years later, launching his autobiography on 22 October 2013, Ferguson used his book to insist he was one of the few who had never thought I was 'a top, top player'. He said that I'd 'seldom had a kick' against United and that myself and Frank Lampard had only played so many times for England, ahead of Michael Carrick, because of our 'bravado'.

I wouldn't lose any sleep over his comments but I was slightly taken aback after all his praise even before I'd reached my peak.

My agent, Struan Marshall, had also told me that Man United, under Fergie, had had a decent pop at trying to sign me. Gary Neville would knock at my door during England camps. He'd come in for a chat and let me know how much United would love me to play for them. Gary told me Fergie had sent him.

Now, more than a decade later and out of the game, Ferguson had put me down. Who knows if he really meant it. The United–Liverpool divide won't ever be bridged and we're still rivals in a way. I'm sure I've said a couple of things about United in the past that have annoyed Ferguson.

It became a big deal in the media for a day and text messages clogged up my phone. The only point that actually mattered was that I have real respect for Ferguson. But I wondered how many league titles he thought Paul Scholes or Roy Keane might have lifted if one of them had swapped places with me. I would have done OK in a Manchester United team playing alongside Keane in midfield with David Beckham on the right, Ryan Giggs on the left and Ruud van Nistelrooy up front. I would have managed pretty well in that side.

Anyway, what is Fergie's definition of 'a top, top player'? If he means Zinedine Zidane or Andrés Iniesta or Xavi then, of course, he would be right. I'm not as good as them. But I've played and competed against the majority of leading players and I've always done all right. I've held my own against everyone I've faced. But there have been times when my Liverpool team has been inferior compared to some of Alex Ferguson's sides and the European elite – and that was hard for me to swallow.

As for Michael Carrick, I'm a big fan of him and the way he's played for United. He's done a terrific job. I'm a different type of player from Carrick, a natural holding midfielder. If you look at my statistics and Michael Carrick's they're completely different. So you can't compare Carrick from a goal-scoring point of view to me or Lampard. And you can't really compare me and Lampard to what he can do defensively because of the difference in our midfield roles. Maybe Ferguson was frustrated that Carrick doesn't get enough plaudits, and I think he might be right.

It's all just opinion – just as it was when Zidane was once kind enough to say that I was the best player in the world. I was happy to read it but I also knew it was just one opinion offered by Zidane on one particular day in history. Ferguson chose to make his comments about me on a different day.

I was, however, more concerned about the impact of another set of words from his book. Ferguson made a strange comment after implying Liverpool had paid too much when signing Jordan Henderson from Sunderland for £20m. He didn't like Jordan's 'gait'. Ferguson claimed that Jordan 'runs from his knees with a straight back' and said he was going to suffer from injury later in his career.

Jordan was one of the Liverpool players I cared about most. I'd always had a good feeling that he would become a vital player for the club and the country. I liked him, and I could see a lot of myself in him. He works hard, he's a team player, he wants to win and he comes from a similar background. I remember his mum pulling me to one side when he was having a difficult time – which is normal for a young lad. I could see the concern in her face. She was worried for her boy. He had left Sunderland and when he first came to Liverpool he was a little lost. The move was initially too big for him.

I had a chat with her and said, 'You mustn't worry. I'll do everything I can to help him and, anyway, I know he'll be fine.' I could see what he was doing in training and it impressed me. I already knew him as a person and I was confident it was going to work out for him at Liverpool.

Someone told me recently that Jordan used to have a poster of me on his wall. That's enough to make me feel very old.

But he's a man now and he can look after himself. I can't take any credit for Jordan Henderson turning it round. All I did was reassure his mum. That's one of the best parts of being captain – taking away the worry from other people. I could look at Jordan's mum and say, 'Trust me, he'll be fine.'

It's a responsibility to hold the team together by getting to know their families and listening to their anxieties and doubts. I have now passed on that role to Jordan himself. I will be looking to him and expecting that, as the new club captain, he will do the same behind-the-scenes work needed to keep a happy squad.

When news of the Ferguson book broke, I took Jordan to one side after training. I said, 'Take no notice of it, it's not true. You're playing great and you're going to get better and better. It's just Ferguson having a bit of a rant at Liverpool. We'll accept it and get on with it.'

Jordan nodded and said, 'Yeah,' but I could see in his face that he was hurt. He couldn't understand why Ferguson had singled him out. It was poor from a man of Ferguson's standing.

Jordan went on to have a storming season and so he gave the best possible answer to Ferguson.

I hope that, one day, Sir Alex and I cross paths again. Maybe I could pick his brains, and discover his real opinion of me.

I lost myself in football again. On another sunny Saturday, at the end of that week, we played West Brom at Anfield and tore them to pieces. We won 4–1 and Luis Suárez scored a hat-trick. His first came after a long, mazy run which finished with him nutmegging a defender and firing home. The second was even better. A sensational header, from outside the area, turned an Aly Cissokho cross into one of Liverpool's goals of the season.

I then supplied the delivery, from a free kick, which gave

Luis his third. It was another brilliant header and he ran towards me in delight, his finger jabbing at me as if to say '*You . . . you . . . you . . . !*' It had been my assist but, between us, there was a deeper understanding. I took it to mean that Luis was acknowledging the part I had played in keeping him at Anfield. We jumped into each other's arms like small, excited boys.

Daniel Sturridge hit the bar with a peach of a shot. He then scored the fourth and, on an afternoon of stunning goals, he could have claimed it was the best of the lot. Midway through the West Brom half the ball bounced between Sturridge and me. He brought it under control and I hared ahead of him, hoping for a through pass. But Sturridge had a better idea. He kept running and looked up once, and then twice to check, before coolly chipping the keeper. Boaz Myhill had only stepped a yard away from his line but it was enough for Sturridge to attempt his outrageous dink at speed with an Albion defender jostling him. The ball sailed over Myhill's flying dive and settled neatly in the back of the net. It had been astonishingly skilful. It was a wow moment.

Two magicians were playing up front for Liverpool and it seemed as if they could do anything they liked. Everyone was raving about SAS – Suárez and Sturridge. Brendan Rodgers went out of his way to enjoy himself at the press conference. He said I had produced a commanding performance behind the SAS fireworks and, unable to resist a crack at Fergie, he broke into an even wider smile: 'Steven is a top, top, top, top, top player.'

We played Arsenal next in a top-of-the-table fixture at the Emirates Stadium. There was still some tension between the clubs, over the £40m+1 bid, and we were keen to make a point against Wenger's team. But it was a sobering afternoon. Arsenal outplayed us, winning 2–0 with two fine goals from Santi

Cazorla and Aaron Ramsey. After ten games they were five points clear. Chelsea and Liverpool were second and third, both on twenty points.

Suárez and Sturridge had failed to click against Arsenal. Everyone picked up on the moment when Luis had not passed to Daniel with a chance for a goal. Daniel threw up his hands in exasperation and, even from the outside, it must have seemed plain that he and Luis were not close.

SAS was not a partnership in the mould of John Toshack and Kevin Keegan. Suárez and Sturridge worked instead as two gifted individuals. Brendan often spoke about the fact that they were like soloists vying with each other rather than playing together as a harmonious duo.

They never said much to each other in training but their skill and vision still produced a telepathy on the pitch. It was a dream to play behind them. One would come short, the other would go long and, suddenly, unlike when only Torres was up front, I had two striking options for my next pass. It worked beautifully – though, sadly, not against Arsenal – and each was happy enough if the other scored. I didn't see them having the selfishness of Cristiano Ronaldo, who just has to be the main man.

It never got nasty but there was an edge between them. There probably were some games when Luis was a bit heavy on Daniel. We kept an eye on it but it didn't matter that Sturridge and Suárez would never be mates. If they shared fifty goals a season I wouldn't care if they never said as many words to each other.

Suárez racked up another two on our return to Anfield, in a 4–0 battering of Fulham. I had three assists, there was an own goal and Skrtel got the other with a crunching header from my corner. But we were not the only team flying in Liverpool. Everton, our next opponents, had started brightly too under their own new manager, Roberto Martínez.

In the early summer of 2012 it had seemed as if the new Liverpool manager would be either Rodgers or Martínez. At the time it was exciting but I also felt genuinely sad that Kenny Dalglish hadn't been given longer in his last stint of management at Liverpool. Our league position hadn't been good enough in 2011–12, and Kenny would be the first to admit it, but he delivered two cup finals, which is not easy. He was also my dad's hero and he embodies so much that is special about Liverpool. I wish I had played more than the thirty-odd games I did under Kenny – when I was affected by some serious injuries.

Kenny got a lot of stick because Andy Carroll, Jordan Henderson and Stewart Downing were all dismissed as failures. The media and the fans claimed that Kenny and Damien Comolli, as director of football, had wasted £100m. Carroll and Downing moved on but look at Henderson now. Kenny did a lot of good work – and Suárez was signed by him for just £22.7m.

The owners had kept me updated as they considered Rodgers and Martínez. I also had a couple of conversations with Ian Ayre, the CEO, to find out which way they were leaning. I didn't have a preference because I'd not met either manager then. I also knew they were similar in age and in the type of football they favoured. They had both managed Swansea, and done well, and Martínez had moved on to Wigan and won the FA Cup. I thought either would suit Liverpool but it needed a bold appointment from the owners – and I think they got it right with Brendan. I'm still confident he will have success here but, as we all know, circumstances in football can change very quickly.

Coutinho, from close range, and Suárez with a curling free kick, twice gave us the lead at Goodison Park – only for Everton to equalize each time, first through Kevin Mirallas and then Romelu Lukaku, who made it 3–2 with a powerful header after being allowed too much space. We had heart and fight, though, and in the eighty-ninth minute we scored a dramatic late goal. I took the free kick and Sturridge met it with a perfect flick of his head. 3–3 in a Merseyside classic.

As we moved towards December, second in the table behind Arsenal, and with plenty of assists from me as the goals piled up, I felt strangely unsettled. It was hard to put it into words but I felt a nagging ache of dissatisfaction with myself. I would walk off the pitch after training or a game and be stewing on the inside. No one else seemed to notice it and I was getting good reviews in team meetings and the press. But I could sense the difference. During the previous few matches I knew I had not been firing with the impact of old.

I have always been harsh on myself. That self-criticism and need to improve made me the player I became at my peak. Even in training, deep into my thirties, I'd always try my hardest to be the best player on the pitch. But I could tell I was not quite at my usual level. It had reached the stage where I'd begun to think, 'I need help.'

I've always played football in a certain way, trying things many other players would not even attempt. I want to make a real contribution and produce big moments that help win matches. I could play most games in a comfort zone and keep the ball, taking possession before laying off a simple five- or ten-yard pass. But I'd rather have 80 per cent pass accuracy and set up a goal, than 96 per cent without any significant impact on the game. It's easy to do a steady, safe job. And there have even been times where I've had to do that, when I've had a knock or niggle and I've had to play within myself. But if I'm fit then I'm going to try to play audacious football. The consequence is that there will always be a few errors in my performance.

Even when I've had a game where the press have given me a mark of nine or even an apparently perfect ten there are usually one or two moments when I've tried something and it's gone completely wrong – but that's because I've been searching for a slice of magic.

I don't know how many other players feel able to admit that they need help with their game from time to time. Some might find it difficult to say it out loud but I've always known when to turn to a manager. I found it easy to approach Brendan because not only is he an excellent young manager, he is also a very good man with whom I've never exchanged a single cross word.

I had noticed Brendan's intelligence and tactical flexibility even before he took over at Liverpool. We had played Swansea at Anfield and I'd been impressed with how they passed the ball and how he had set them up. I'd seen that he was trying to get a numerical advantage around our two central midfielders and he'd made it a tough afternoon for me. I remember thinking how rare it was for a side from the middle to lower ranks of the Premier League to turn up at Anfield and show tactical flexibility and imagination while also outplaying us on the day.

So I went to see Brendan in late November 2013. I said, 'I don't feel like I'm firing in the attacking midfield role, I feel a little bit off here.' I felt I was playing at a six or a seven out of ten – but I needed to get an eight or above.

He was shocked at first. Brendan thought I had been playing pretty well. But he listened closely when I said: 'Can you look into my game and my numbers and see how I am doing, physically? Can you also look into my body position and my shape? Could you also talk to the analysis people and the fitness guys? I need some perspective on how I'm feeling inside – because I'm just not happy with my game.'

It was a long list of requests, and a heartfelt plea, and Brendan responded as I knew he would. He reassured me he would give it his full attention and, together, we'd get to the bottom of it. He did exactly that the very next day.

After training, Brendan called me into his office. He had a detailed computer printout of all the positives and negatives of my performances over the past few matches. The first thing he told me was that I was right. He was surprised, but my instinct had been matched by the detailed analysis. More importantly, Brendan absolutely nailed why I had not been firing.

He turned to the video evidence and it was obvious. When we looked at the negative aspects of my play it was plain to see my head movement simply wasn't there. I wasn't moving into position or picking up the angles quickly enough. The tempo of my game had dipped as a result. It was a technical rather than a physical issue because the statistics indicated that I was still producing decent numbers in terms of speed and stamina. This was more about my lack of head movement and my body position and angles of play.

I've never been obsessed with statistical data. I respect the numbers and I use them because I know they're important. But they never tell the whole story. This was a clear example. My stats were solid but my head movement had dipped. That movement is so important because it feels as if you've got to have eyes in the back of your head to play as a midfielder in the Premier League. It's so much more significant now than when I started playing because it's congested in the middle and you have so much less time on the ball. When I watch the best midfield players they've all got excellent head movement. They always check over their shoulders before the ball reaches them, and they all know where it's going next even before it lands at their feet. If you watch midfielders who are constantly getting caught on the ball or are struggling to get their passes away, their head movement is always a factor.

Brendan opened up the discussion. When he had first arrived at Liverpool he had mentioned he could imagine me eventually playing in a much deeper role, almost as a holding midfielder but with the difference that I would still dictate games with my vision and range of passing.

He immediately had my attention. If I played in my traditional role, further forward, it seemed obvious that we were missing a trick. Brendan likes to play at a high tempo and it sometimes felt to me as if we were too slow when I was chosen in the attacking position. We needed a player in that position to get on the ball and move it through the spaces a lot quicker than I had been doing. At the same time I also felt I wasn't spending enough time on the ball. With Sturridge and Suárez up front I was licking my lips at the chance of getting on the ball deeper. I knew their movements were exactly what I needed to spray passes from further back – so that I could release them to do yet more damage.

Brendan and I spoke about Andrea Pirlo, the great Italian midfielder I had faced often, and his enduring ability to shape the outcome of matches. I would never compare myself to Pirlo – because I was a huge fan as well. I had watched and played in many a game which Pirlo had dominated. He epitomized everything I thought best about head movement and body position and angles. I had learnt so much from Pirlo that I was a little flattered to even be mentioned in the same sentence as him.

Pirlo had defined this position for fifteen years. I had played a few games in a similar role but that was the extent of my experience. I had never had a run of games in Pirlo's position – and I knew it was very different from the pure holding role.

I still needed to do a lot more tackling, break up play, win 50–50s and headers before I could start trying to play a little like Pirlo with that depth of vision and subtlety of passing. It could work, with the SAS formation at the head, because there were goals in our team. When I had played as a number 10, the link-up man between the forward and midfield, I'd only had Fernando Torres in front of me. I always felt then that I needed to set up a goal or grab one myself.

Our twist on the Pirlo role was different. My immediate job would be to try to stop attacks and prevent the opposition from scoring. It was almost a reverse role to the number 10. And then once I had the ball and Luis, Daniel and Raheem were running free in front of me I would have space and time to pick out one of them. I would be a creative midfielder, as well as a holding player.

The idea excited me. Brendan and I agreed we would kick it around for a few weeks and discuss it in depth; then, when the time felt right, I would try to play in this deeper position. I was relieved when I came out of the office. Not only had I discovered the missing ingredient in my game but a whole new way of playing now stretched out in front of me. It was a fresh and exciting challenge.

On 1 December we went to Hull. We were missing Daniel Sturridge through injury and so I played in my usual attacking midfield position. After we went behind to a deflected goal, I equalized from a free kick. It was a good strike, picking out a sliver of space in their wall, and I celebrated properly. Victor Moses then missed a good chance but we were all over the place in defence. Kolo Touré was struggling with a back injury and Hull took the lead again. They were playing well but it was a sloppy goal and Kolo went down, clutching his back.

We held our heads in our hands when Hull went 3–1 ahead after more shambolic defence and a Skrtel own goal. It was the first time that Hull had beaten Liverpool in any competition.

At a team meeting Brendan pointed straight at me. He told the squad how I had asked for help. He said I had set an example to everyone. His finger jabbed in my direction: 'He has already won the Champions League. He's played well over 600 games for this football club, and more than a hundred times for England. Steven Gerrard is thirty-three years of age. But he asks me for help to become a better player.'

Brendan let his words sink in and, while I felt uncomfortable, I knew he was building towards his real point. 'At the other end of the scale we have some young players who keep turning up late for training. It's just not good enough. Too many of you are in the comfort zone.'

The manager forced a necessary period of introspection – which matched the mood outside the dressing room. Our fans felt dejected and, fuelled by the press, decided we were in for another season of aimless drifting.

Luis Suárez, of course, believed differently. Against Norwich, on the Tuesday following the Hull disaster, I intercepted their keeper John Ruddy's clearance after fifteen minutes. My header sailed towards Luis. He was just inside the Norwich half, and he allowed the ball to bounce once, twice, before he moved towards it and swung his right foot with exquisite technique. His forty-yard lob soared over Ruddy's head and the Norwich keeper fell to the ground as if he had been shot by a sniper. Suárez was that deadly.

He soon tucked away a Coutinho corner and completed his hat-trick after thirty-five minutes when, with a dart, a shimmy and a little scoop of a pass to himself, followed by a blistering half-volley, he sent Anfield into raptures. Luis looked as if he could not believe it. He covered his smiling face as if he might be blinded by his own brilliance. What could I do, with Suárez in such a mood, but step aside when we were awarded a free kick ten yards outside the Norwich box? He did not disappoint as, with a dipping scorcher, he curled the ball over their five-man wall and into the net. 4–0. Suárez,

Suárez, Suárez, Suárez. It was a joke of a performance, a 10/10 display.

The Kop were in full voice, channelling their inner Depeche Mode, singing about Luis Suárez to the tune of 'Just Can't Get Enough'. Four goals were enough to get them chanting: *Da-da-da-da-da-da / I just can't get enough / I just can't get enough / His name is Luis Suárez / He wears the famous Red / I just can't get enough / I just can't get enough / When he scores a volley / And when he scores a head / I just can't get enough / I just can't get enough / He scores a goal and the Kop goes wild / And I just can't seem to get enough / Suárez / Da-da-da-da-da-da.*

Norwich pulled one back and then Coutinho danced his way through the Norwich half before chipping the ball towards me. I had my back to the goal and so I half turned and used my left foot to hit it, in a restrained bicycle kick, without falling to the ground. It struck the post. Suárez then set up Sterling for our last goal. 5–1.

Suárez's finishing that night had been miraculous. I actually liked his goal on the half-volley better than the long-distance lob, just because the technique and timing summed up his sensational performance.

Three days later the World Cup draw was made. England were in Group D with Italy, Costa Rica and, inevitably, Uruguay and Luis Suárez.

As if we needed a reminder of the threat he would pose to England, and the drive he gave to Liverpool, Luis scored twice more the following afternoon as we beat West Ham 4–1. It was a less happy game for me. I pulled up with a hamstring tear in the fifty-sixth minute and limped off. I would be out for weeks.

On Sunday, 15 December, I was at White Hart Lane – but working as a pundit for Sky Sports, alongside Jamie Carragher. It might have been a game, away from home, where I would start in my new, deeper role. Instead, Lucas took my place in midfield and Suárez replaced me as captain. His rehabilitation from the biting ban was complete.

I watched a majestic performance from Liverpool that winter afternoon. Spurs were totally outplayed. Their manager, André Villas-Boas, was sacked after a 5–0 humiliation – and it was the poorest Tottenham team I could remember. But Liverpool were menacing and ruthless. Suárez scored twice and Henderson, Flanagan (getting his first-ever goal with a fantastic strike) and Sterling sealed the rout. It had been an irresistible display of pace, power and clinical skill.

It was the first time I had watched the team from the outside. I thought, 'Christ – are we really this good?'

Brendan called it 'a watershed moment'. He believed we could have scored more – three shots had hit the woodwork – and that Liverpool had the confidence to sustain a title challenge.

I hitched a lift back to Liverpool with Carra that night. It seemed like old times, me and Carra sitting together on the way back from an away game, except that we were in his car rather than on the team bus. We spoke about Liverpool and football, as always, the whole journey. We both sensed the momentum. The surge had begun. Carra joked that I might not get back in the team.

Sturridge, like me, was injured. But if we could get him fit again, and keep him on the pitch alongside Suárez, we would feel unstoppable. I could hear the excitement in our voices as Carra and I finally dared speak about Liverpool winning the title.

'Maybe this time . . . ,' Carra said.

We fell silent for once, lost in the old Liverpool dream, as we raced through the darkness.

I stared out of the window on a cold winter night. 'Yeah,' I said quietly, allowing myself to admit my new hope at last. 'Maybe we can win it . . .'

# 5. Hard Facts

Liverpool were top of the league on Christmas Day. We had been in the exact same position on 25 December 2008. Brendan Rodgers, in charge in 2013, and Rafa Benítez, our manager five years earlier, offered a fascinating contrast in character, mentality and style.

I often get asked to reflect on past managers and, usually, I smile and have a good feeling for virtually all of them. I have so many happy memories. I've got some bad ones, too, but that's to be expected after seventeen years as a professional footballer. It feels special that, apart from one former manager, I can pick up the phone and speak to all but one of them.

The exception is Rafa. All my other managers are there if I ever need them. I can trust them to discuss anything about my life on or off the field.

Rafa is the opposite to Brendan, who is so warm and welcoming. But it would be wrong to consider them in one-dimensional terms, with Rafa as just the ice-cold tactician and Brendan the very human man-manager. As with every successful manager, and player, they are more complex than they might at first appear.

Brendan came across as a nice man, and a good person, from the start. He also had an immediate understanding of the traditions of the club and showed great respect to everyone connected to Liverpool, from past players to people based at the Academy in Kirkby. But you don't become the manager of a huge club like Liverpool without having a hard, even ruthless

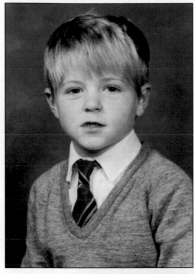

Me aged six.

With Dave
Shannon, former
LFC youth team
coach, in our
matching LFC
jumpers!

Me at twelve years old.

With the youngsters at the Liverpool Academy. I'm in the centre,
below the guy in the green shirt.

Aged sixteen, with the Youth Training Scheme apprentices
at Melwood. I'm on the bottom row, third from the right,
and two to the left is Michael Owen.

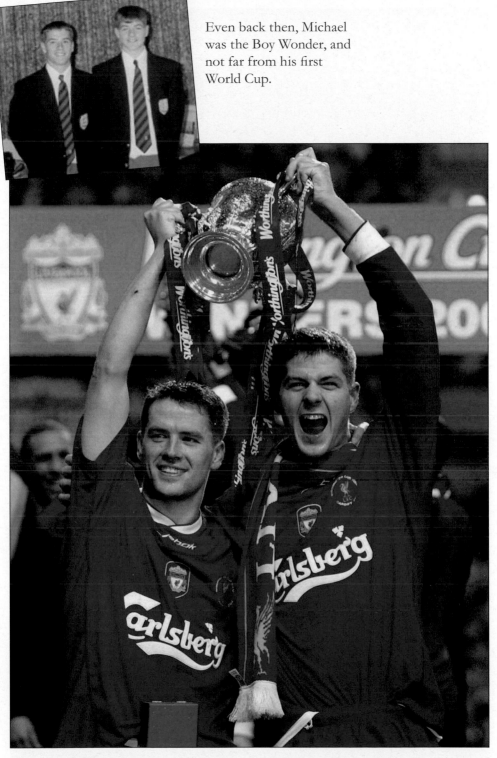

Even back then, Michael was the Boy Wonder, and not far from his first World Cup.

Seven years after being YTS kids mopping floors at Melwood, we were Liverpool teammates lifting the League Cup.

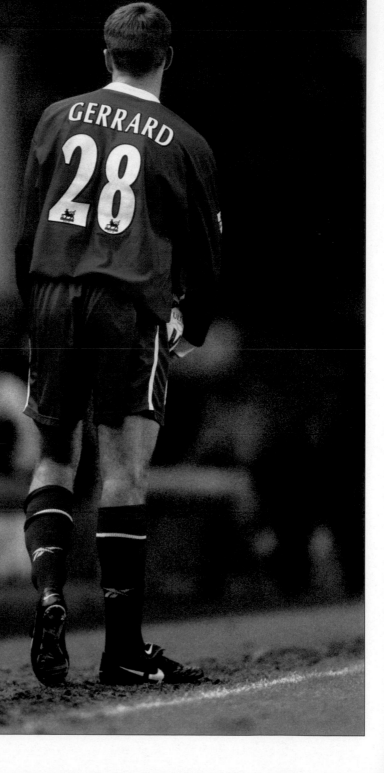

This was my debut match for Liverpool, aged eighteen, as a
late sub against Blackburn.

Getting my first England cap from Kevin Keegan in 2000.

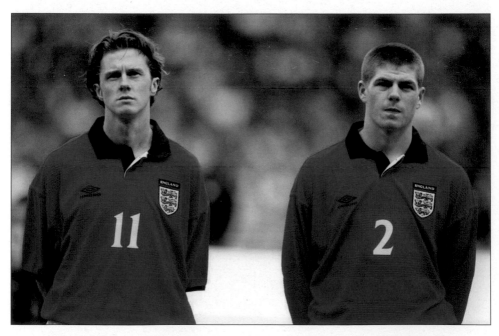

As a kid, I was in awe of Steve McManaman. It was a dream come true
to be a fellow teammate for Liverpool and later for England. This is me
lining up for my debut match, a friendly against Ukraine.

Playing for my country has been one of the
greatest honours of my life.

During a friendly against Hungary at Wembley Stadium in 2010.

*Top left:* At the qualies for the 2014 World Cup.

*Top right:* Celebrating a third goal with David Beckham during a match against Switzerland at the Euros in 2004.

As a former England captain who also made the move to LA, David has always been able to offer me great support and advice.

streak. You need to be prepared to make tough decisions that will cause some hurt.

On his first day at the club, 1 June 2012, Brendan made it clear he would not be retaining Steve Clarke, who had been the club's assistant manager alongside Kenny Dalglish. It might be expected that a new manager would choose his own number two, but the situation was complicated. Steve had helped Brendan in the past when they were both at Chelsea. As an assistant to José Mourinho, Steve had apparently opened the door for Brendan to work at the Chelsea Academy and then with the reserve team – where he was first noticed more widely as a young coach.

I had actually expected Brendan to keep Steve because of the Chelsea connection, but I didn't know anything about their working relationship. This is an example of how weird it can be, being a footballer. One morning you're working with Steve Clarke, the assistant manager, a decent guy who loves to be out training the squad, and that afternoon you get a text from him saying he's on his way down the road.

I had experienced cup finals and league campaigns with Steve and knew him really well – and then all of a sudden he was gone. There's an inevitable sadness when those relationships end so abruptly.

Players have to adapt to change very quickly, but it can be difficult. I remember Gérard Houllier leaving, in May 2004, and I had days at home, thinking, 'Will it be the same to play for anyone else? I don't want him to go.' Gérard had given me my start and, in 2003, he asked me to take over from Sami Hyypiä as captain. Our relationship was so strong it tore me up when he left.

I had to remind myself that I've never gone into a game thinking, 'I'm playing for the manager today.' I always play for my club or my country. So, ultimately, it doesn't really matter who is in charge. I just hope for a strong connection with the manager and mutual respect. That's always the priority.

But so much had changed. Gérard, as my first manager, had been as good as a father to me. All these years later I am almost the same generation as Brendan, my last Liverpool manager.

The role of Liverpool manager carries more weight than most jobs in football. It stems from the success Bill Shankly created, and which Bob Paisley built on to turn the club into a huge institution supported all over the world. Your responsibility when employed by this club, whether as a manager or a player, is to try to add to that history of achievement.

I always felt myself to be a link in that chain of history. At the Liverpool Academy I had been coached by Steve Heighway, who had played for a great team under Shankly. Steve was steeped in the Shankly way, and he was such a part of the Liverpool fabric that the fans sang about him in a famous chant, 'The Fields of Anfield Road'; and so I had a good grip on the changing history of Liverpool through its managers and coaches from Shankly to Heighway, Benítez to Rodgers.

I think that's why I've got the respect of the supporters. From day one I appreciated how hard it was to get into Liverpool's team. I appreciated how difficult it would be to stay there, and to improve. Even when I didn't play well they still saw me try my best. It's exactly the same with a manager. He has to give everything to the job because all of us are here for only a short time compared to the history of the club. You can play for Liverpool, or become manager, but it's only a temporary privilege. The club will be here for ever. It's always going to have top players and top managers. There will be highs and lows along the way but you're only in your position for a certain amount of time. You've got to make the most of it while you're here. Some players don't.

My managers over the years have been diverse personalities, with their own style of working, but they have all passed down the same simple message. They instruct you to be professional and to work hard and be a team player. Those three values are shared by all of them.

On a basic human level I prefer a likeable manager, such as Gérard or Brendan, but in terms of football I really don't mind working with a colder man. An emotionless and distant relationship with the likes of Rafa Benítez and Fabio Capello can sometimes produce more success. It would not be my style if I were to ever become a manager – I'd try to fuse the best of Rafa's tactical thinking with Brendan's skill as a man-manager – but I learnt from Benítez that it's not really important to be close to your players. An edge can sometimes help.

I don't think Rafa liked me as a person. I'm not sure why but that's the feeling I got from him. It probably started even before he spoke to me, when he met my mum. Rafa was appointed as Liverpool's manager in June 2004 – and I was playing for England in the Euros in Portugal that summer. Even though he was being replaced by Rafa, Gérard still loved Liverpool and he remained very close to me. He and my mum flew out to Portugal to watch me play for England against Croatia – and they bumped into Rafa.

Gérard introduced Rafa to my mum. Rafa shook her hand, said hello and then immediately asked her a very blunt question: 'Does Steven like money?'

Apart from a standard 'hello . . . good to meet you' introduction, those were the first words Rafa said to my mum. My relationship with Mum is so close that I heard all about it even before my new Liverpool manager had climbed into a taxi to meet me. I thought, 'What kind of question is that?' but I was so impressed with Rafa's work at Valencia I was still itching to meet him. I even understood that he was probably trying to discover what motivated me.

Our working relationship was ultra-professional but his frostiness drove me to become a better player. I had a hunger to earn a compliment from him – but also a hunger to let him know that he really needed me as a player. I was coming into my prime, I was playing well and I gave him the best years of my career. Maybe he got that streak out of me because of his iciness towards me. Maybe if he had been warm and generous, I might not have had that drive to prove him wrong or to try to get some respect from him.

We were like fire and ice together. Passion surged inside me, while Rafa was the strategic thinker. The distance between us meant that I lost none of my burning intensity – while the icy clarity of Rafa's insights rarely melted.

I used to think he favoured our Spanish-speakers. He was an especially big fan of South American players, which is fine. It caused no problem between us. At press conferences he might call other players by their first name, but I was always 'Gerrard'. It was the same in the dressing room. He would read out the team and use nicknames. But, for me, it would just be 'Gerrard'. I didn't care what he called me. It certainly wouldn't have made me play any better if he'd suddenly started being my mate and calling me 'Stevie'. I just wanted to win the next game and I knew Rafa could, usually, help us achieve another victory.

Rafa was the best tactical coach I worked with at Liverpool and England. When it comes to setting the team up and feeling secure and strong within a structure, he stands out for me. José Mourinho is more than a match for him but Rafa can take a team considered to be the underdogs and still find a way for them to get the win – especially when it's in Europe over two legs.

The only disappointment for me is that Rafa is the one manager I can't lean on now. We no longer have any contact. It's a shame because we probably shared the biggest night of both our careers – and yet there is no bond between us. But in regard to what he does on the training ground and how professional he is as a manager I can only speak highly of Rafa.

If we were to bump into each other at a game or at an airport tomorrow there would be no unpleasantness, but maybe a day will come when we can actually have a deeper and friendlier conversation and reflect on everything we experienced during our time at Liverpool. We have some unforgettable experiences and memories to bind us together.

Istanbul, and Champions League glory, is the obvious highlight. But the 2008–09 season, when we were top of the league at Christmas, remains vivid. It was crammed with stirring comebacks, memorable wins, strange incidents and worry. That season echoed in my head when, five years later, we were again chasing an elusive league title.

We had been on such a roll in December 2013 that, out of the team for a few weeks with my hamstring injury, it seemed right to step back over Christmas, pause, and remember how well we had also been playing five years before – until trouble and strife broke out. The difficulties of late December 2008 and January 2009 were a reminder not to become cocky or complacent. Life, and football, is rarely without problems. I learnt some hard truths during that time. I think Rafa Benítez did as well.

On Sunday, 28 December 2008, we played Newcastle away. Liverpool had beaten Bolton 3–0 on Boxing Day, with two goals for Robbie Keane and one for Albert Riera. But Chelsea had also won and, to retain or even stretch our one-point lead, it was important to maintain our encouraging run. We believed we were in with a great chance of winning the league as we had a very good team. And tactically, under Rafa, we were very smart. I was in form and enjoying playing alongside the likes of Torres, Kuyt, Alonso, Mascherano, Hyypiä, Carra and Reina.

We had also developed a knack of scoring late goals. It started in the first match of the season when, in the eighty-third minute, Torres broke the 0–0 deadlock at Sunderland and grabbed three points. There was such spirit in the side that we didn't get derailed when, frequently, we went a goal or two down. A week after Sunderland, at home to Middlesbrough, we needed Carra to equalize with just four minutes left. His shot took a deflection and gave their keeper no chance. Then, in the ninetieth minute, I struck the winner with a rocket. It crashed in and made the net billow and dance.

I turned away and ran, my arms jabbing to the side as if I was about to take off and fly. I'd recently had surgery on my groin and my preseason had been affected. A winning goal so early in a new campaign gave me just the lift I needed.

The comebacks kept on coming. Down to an early goal from Carlos Tevez, we beat Manchester United 2–1 at Anfield. On 5 October 2008, just five weeks after Manchester City had been taken over by the money-men from Abu Dhabi, we came back from 2–0 down with a couple from Torres and a last-minute winner scored by Kuyt. It was an important victory over the new juggernaut of Premier League football. A week later we were behind again to Wigan and won by the same 3–2 score. Kuyt's winner, this time, was in the eighty-fifth minute.

Then, on 13 December, we were 2–0 down at home to Hull after twenty-two minutes. Ten minutes later it was 2–2. I got both goals. We still dropped two points in a home draw and I knew such results were costly. Manchester United went away that month to play in the FIFA Club World Cup. They were seven points behind us at Christmas – but it was misleading because they had played two fewer games. We could not afford to fritter away anything at Newcastle.

Torres had been on fire the previous season with his thirty-three goals. He then scored the winner in the final of Euro 2008 as Spain beat Germany 1–0 and won their first big tournament. Fernando had spoken to me about how his goal, which broke the long drought for Spain, had inspired him to want to do the same at Liverpool and help bring back the title after a nineteen-year gap. A few weeks before the Newcastle game he had finished just behind Ronaldo and Messi in the vote for FIFA's World Player of the Year.

But his second season with Liverpool had been affected badly by injury. He tore his hamstring in our third league game, against Aston Villa, and had suffered two relapses when trying to return. By the time we reached Christmas he had played so little he had only scored five goals. I had six by then. I was convinced if we could get him back to full fitness we would win the league.

Torres was out for another week and Benítez surprised everyone by dropping Robbie Keane again for the Newcastle game. Robbie had scored three goals in our two previous games.

I had initially been delighted when we signed Robbie because he had done terrifically well at Tottenham alongside Dimitar Berbatov. But he wanted to play as a number 10 at Liverpool. I felt we didn't need him in that position as I was doing so well in the role. He was a good addition to the squad but I worried it could become a problem either for him or me in a battle for the same position. But, more often than not, Rafa played me as a 10. There wasn't room for both Robbie and I in Rafa's team.

I could see why Rafa had his doubts about playing Robbie in front of me. He had none of Torres's pace. Robbie was far better when allowed to drop in behind and pick up intelligent spaces where he could set up and score goals. But it was obvious that his relationship with Rafa would never work. Instead of letting Robbie be the player he had signed, Rafa tried to change him. He had Robbie attempting movements which clearly made him uncomfortable. Robbie would have been a success under most of the managers I played with at Liverpool. But Rafa made it personal. I couldn't understand why Rafa tried to change a top player. Let him play his own game – that's why we signed him.

Ten weeks earlier, after Kevin Keegan had been replaced as manager by Joe Kinnear, a different kind of war had broken out at Newcastle. It was civil war at St James' Park between Newcastle's passionate supporters and Mike Ashley, the club's owner. Ashley had announced he was putting the club up for sale but, on the morning of our game, he changed his mind. The club would not be sold. He promised a new era of success for Newcastle.

I was not in the mood for anything but a big afternoon for Liverpool. After thirty minutes of total domination, Carra, Mascherano and Yossi Benayoun combined down the right and the ball was squared to me across the penalty area. I had plenty of space to drill a shot past Shay Given. It smacked against the inside of a post and ricocheted into the net.

Sami Hyypiä made it two when he headed home my corner. We were 3–1 up when Lucas and I played a one-two before he released me with a lovely pass. After a long run, I chipped a little dink over Given for my second and Liverpool's fourth goal. My hands made a scissor-like movement, as if to say we had cut them dead and the game was over. It was not quite true. Rafa replaced me – the papers said it was so I could be given a standing ovation from the whole ground. I appreciated the gesture from the Newcastle fans but I wondered if it was also a blunt managerial reminder from Rafa to stay hungry. Ryan Babel then won a penalty. It could have been my first Liverpool hat-trick but Alonso scored while I smiled and watched from the bench.

Joe Kinnear, despite the derision being heaped on him, sounded philosophical. 'Liverpool were in a different class. We were threadbare but they played some very attractive football. And Gerrard was magnificent. That's the best individual performance I've seen in a long time.'

There was no need to get carried away with my own display. It was more important that Liverpool had won 5–1 and we were four points clear at the top. We had also played with real dash and style – and absolutely murdered Newcastle. In my post-match interview I downplayed my contribution and pointed instead to a belief that I was probably playing in the best Liverpool team of my career.

To control expectations, I reached for some familiar football clichés. I promised we would 'remain humble, keep our feet on the ground and keep working hard'.

After such a big win, and a very sober Christmas. Rafa had given us a two-day break. I felt ready for a night out – if not on the town, at least in Southport.

I was in a police cell in the early hours of the following morning. It was just the start of a twenty-three-hour stretch in custody. I remember wondering how I had ended up there, when a security guard brought me the morning papers. I looked at my face and name splashed across both the front and the back pages. In the sports pages I was celebrated for my two goals and all-round play against Newcastle the previous afternoon. The front pages were grim. I was plastered across them for being a naughty boy who had been in a scrap in a bar.

The shame burned inside me; but there was hurt too. I had

got caught up in the kind of incident that happens every night in bars in busy cities all over the world. If my name had been Joe Bloggs I would never have been locked up for twenty-three hours. So I was disappointed with the way the police handled my arrest. But I could only blame myself for the mess.

It had started innocently. On the coach home from Newcastle, and buzzing from our stonking win, I texted my best mates. I hardly ever get to have a night out with them and it felt like a rare chance to have some fun. Every one of them was up for a chilled-out celebration. There would be eight of us and we just had to settle on where we would meet.

We knew I couldn't go into the centre of Liverpool. Those days and nights had gone. I was twenty-eight years old, still young, and it seemed a shame that I couldn't go out for a night in the heart of my home town. But as soon as you become well known in Liverpool your life has to change. Even in the daytime it's very difficult to walk through the city centre and be left alone to get on with normal stuff – like going to the shops with Alex or having a coffee. I had not been able to do that for years.

There are Liverpool fans everywhere and I understand why they want to come over and say hello or well done after a win. People are very nice to me most of the time. But I'm not so popular in the blue half of town. Everton supporters can have a right go at me sometimes. Most of them are respectful and decent but a small minority make it difficult for me to go into the city. I still manage it occasionally but I have to duck and dive, and pop in and out very quickly, staying in my car most of the time. Years ago, before I became a first-team regular, I could go to town at nine in the morning and still be there at five in the afternoon. These days I wouldn't have a clue where to go in my own city. This is the life of a player. You have to pick your places carefully.

It's worse at night. At least the vast majority are sober in the day. Drinking can darken the mood and some people become aggressive. It's a bit weird when someone you've never met starts shouting at you. You just have to accept it and, in my position, understand that you have to give up going out in Liverpool. But when you stack up the sacrifices and measure them against the lavish rewards we get it would be wrong to start complaining. We are paid extravagantly, embarrassingly well, and we receive adulation and glory. The abuse and the stick are the flipside, just as not having much of a social life goes with the territory of being a top professional sports star. We still come out of our privileged lives feeling very lucky.

But sometimes, when you're young, you just want to go to a club with your mates. You need a release. That was my mood on the Sunday night of 28 December 2008. And so I made a classic mistake and found myself in the wrong place at the wrong time. Sitting in prison the following morning, I thought: 'Why didn't I just go home and stay in?'

Some nights you can go out and be left alone and you'll be fine. It can help you, as both a player and a person, to relax and let your hair down for a few hours every now and then. But if there's an incident, no matter how small, you are going to regret it badly.

Like most human beings, I'm not a saint. I haven't made too many big mistakes, but I have learnt from all of them. I was only eleven when, with one of my mates, being silly little scallies, I tried to nick some stationery from Woolies. I needed it for school and Mum and Dad had given me the money. But we had other plans: we'd use the cash to buy a Coke and burger instead at McDonald's. Of course, we were hopeless shoplifters, and as I was sticking pens in my pocket and paper inside my coat, the Woolies security guard clocked us straightaway. He made us give him our names and tell him which school we went to and where we lived. I was so scared of my dad finding out that I lied and gave him my aunt's address.

I ran from Woolworths to Auntie Lynn's house. I told her what I had done. I begged her to go and see Dad and explain everything to him first. I wanted him to know how terrible I felt.

It was too late. Woolies had already been on to the school and they had called Dad. He was fuming. I don't think I had ever seen him so angry. What was I doing – robbing in shops? Mum was close by because she wouldn't allow Dad to be too heavy on me, even if I deserved it, but she also wanted me to understand how wrongly I had acted. I knew Dad was right when he warned me that I could lose my place at the Liverpool Academy. If Steve Heighway found out, Dad said, he might decide to kick me out. I was very worried then.

I would have taken the hiding my pal got from his dad. A smack on the bum wouldn't last. But if I ruined everything with Liverpool? It would feel as if my life had ended.

I accepted my punishment: a good earbashing and grounded for three days. It took a while for me to get over my guilt but at least I was never tempted to do anything so stupid again.

I made another mistake as a young pro very early on when, for a brief spell under Gérard Houllier, I was breathalysed and lost my driving licence. I was not much over the limit but Gérard, a bit like my dad, really let rip. And after he calmed down he made his point. 'If your mates want to go to a nightclub, let them. By the time you've finished your career you can buy a club of your own.'

I felt full of regret and, as time passed, I also found it easier and easier to avoid the temptations. It was not difficult to be disciplined because football meant so much to me. I knew that I would become a better player if I stayed in and went to bed early instead of partying with my mates. I also learnt that I could go out a few times a year and enjoy myself. I didn't need to drink a lot. It was enough being out with my closest friends. The novelty was good enough for me.

And so after the Newcastle game I was in a very good mood at the Lounge Inn, an upmarket bar in Southport, when suddenly, out of nowhere, a situation developed. I got into an argument. A scuffle broke out. Over the years people have blown it up into a joke. It was said that I punched the bloke because he was a DJ and he wouldn't play a Phil Collins record.

That's rubbish. The argument wasn't over Phil Collins and the guy wasn't even a DJ. But it amused people to think I'd go over and thump a DJ because he wouldn't play my song. That wasn't the case. The guy was a normal punter and we all got heated over nothing really.

After twenty-three hours in police custody I was charged with assault and affray. The majority of us were charged. It didn't look good, especially when the papers started speculating, with the usual hysteria, that I could face five years in jail if I was found guilty. It was rubbish again and I had real confidence I would be cleared in court. I was prepared to stand up in front of the jury and tell everyone what happened. I was sure that if I spoke truthfully, in front of twelve people who were neutral, they would understand how events had escalated in the bar.

It was very important to me that my form wasn't affected by the incident. And, as it turned out, I think I played even better for the remainder of that season. I just parked it up and put it out of my mind when I was training or playing. The club supported me throughout the whole saga. Rafa was pragmatic and understanding. He didn't play the disciplinarian card with me and, instead, he helped the situation. Rafa employed a guy called Owen Brown as an informal PA. He took me to and from court. I also had a leading QC, John Kelsey-Fry, defending me. With that level of expert help I was confident that my case would be well argued and I would be cleared, so I wasn't too worried about the outcome. And even when there were difficult days, football gave me such a release. I felt free on the pitch, even when the trial dragged on so long.

When at last we were in court the following summer, in July 2009, I was cleared of all charges with the jury unanimously in my favour. This was after both I and the other guy had each given our version of the night's events. In the dock I said I was sorry for what had happened, and admitted that I had punched the other man in self-defence, but I had gone over to reason with him and not to be violent. I explained that I was used to dealing with mither – even at traffic lights.

'What sort of mither?' I was asked.

'Because I am a footballer,' I replied, 'I get supporters coming up to me, Liverpool fans or Everton or Manchester United fans. Sometimes their comments can be derogatory or insulting. So I try to deal with it in the best way I can. I try to talk to them and smooth it over.'

I explained again that I had just gone over to defuse the dispute between us – and to find out why the man seemed to have a problem with me.

After I'd been found not guilty the judge, Justice Henry Globe, told me in court:

The verdict is credible based on the full facts of this case, and you walk away from this court with your reputation intact. You did not start the violence . . . and at all times you insisted that you only ever acted in what you believed was reasonable self-defence to what you understandably, albeit you accept mistakenly, believed was an attempted attack on you. What at first sight to the casual observer may seem to have been a clear-cut case against you of unlawful violence, has been nowhere near as clear-cut upon careful analysis of the evidence.

Even now, I think it's a bit of a scar on my reputation. It still hurts me to talk about it. Even though I was cleared, I didn't come out of court and punch the air. I didn't feel proud or great about myself. I came out feeling embarrassed that I had been involved in the first place. I still regret it, and I regret involving the other guy as well. But it's gone now. It's over, and there are no hard feelings from me. I'm just glad no one was seriously hurt and we could all move on with our lives.

I did not go out at night to anywhere busy for another year. I decided it was better to stay at home. I felt particularly bad for Alex and my parents. I wished I could have kept Alex away from the whole incident but, of course, I had to tell her. I felt so embarrassed when I phoned her from the police station and told her what had happened. She understood and supported me. She also has to be on her guard all the time. Alex likes a night out, and she can go to certain places, but, unfortunately, we live in a time when a minority of people will be looking to cause trouble and dig up scandal.

It has made me realize you've got to be very, very careful in our position. When I first broke into the Liverpool team you had to avoid the press and the cameras if you were on a night out. There would always be one or two snakes with cameras waiting behind bushes or cars to try and catch you off guard. But nowadays everyone who owns a smartphone can be a paparazzo, snapping photographs which are either unflattering or misleading. So there's no longer any enjoyment to be had on a night out. Chances are you'll be on Twitter or Instagram before you get home – and in the press the next morning.

A lot of young players are finding that out to their cost now. I've been there. I've made mistakes. But we're just human beings who happen to be good at football. Why wouldn't we want to go and enjoy ourselves every now and then? In a high-pressure job like ours, a bit of fun can help you on the pitch. I don't smoke, I don't take drugs, I'm anti-everything that is wrong. But one night out still landed me in court. There are fistfights in nightclubs up and down the country every weekend, and they're nearly all forgotten about by the next morning. In 2009 I had to clear my name in the High Court. I'm convinced that happened only because I was a well-known footballer.

My night in a cell had been smeared across the internet and the newspapers on 30 December 2008. It seems incredible now to remember that, just ten days later, on 9 January 2009, Rafa Benítez had a meltdown of his own. Our last league game had been the 5–1 thumping of Newcastle and since then we had played only one other match, beating Preston 2–0 in the third round of the FA Cup. Fernando Torres had made his comeback in that game, scoring as well, and we faced a seemingly routine league fixture that weekend, away to Stoke City.

The big Premier League match of the weekend was at Old Trafford between Manchester United and Chelsea. At least one of our two main rivals for the title was about to drop points. I still don't know what possessed Rafa, but he chose his pre-Stoke press conference to launch his infamous 'Facts' rant against Alex Ferguson.

I went home from Melwood that Friday lunchtime and switched on the TV. I usually do that on media days so I can see what the manager has said. Rafa sat down with his usual half-smile. It looked like it was going to be a normal press conference but then he reached into his pocket for a piece of paper. He spread it out on the table and began to read out one 'fact' after another. Rafa kept saying 'fact . . . fact . . . fact . . .'

and I could not believe what I was hearing. I was grabbing the couch, digging my fingers into the arms, feeling embarrassed for him.

Rafa started by saying that maybe Manchester United 'are nervous because we are at the top of the table'. I immediately looked up and thought, 'Uh-oh, what's happening here?' It seemed so unlike Rafa to start talking in such an emotional way. You could see the anger in him.

'I want to talk about facts,' Rafa said. 'I want to be clear, I do not want to play mind games too early, although they seem to want to start. But I have seen some facts.'

Rafa went off on a ramble about how Manchester United and 'Mr Ferguson' had not been properly punished for various misdemeanours. He listed dates and incidents and concluded that 'Mr Ferguson is the only manager in the league that cannot be punished for these things'.

He then railed against the fixture list and the timing of matches being skewed in United's favour. Rafa was sounding muddled and bitter and paranoid. I wanted to jump behind the couch and cover my ears for Rafa's sake. He was humiliating himself and I had no idea what he was attempting to achieve as his 'Facts' rant went on and on:

> If he wants to talk about fixtures there is another option, that Mr Ferguson organizes the fixtures in his office and sends it to us and everyone will know and cannot complain. That is simple. We know what happens every time we go to Old Trafford. The United staff are always going man-to-man with the referees, especially at half-time when they walk close to the referees and they are talking and talking. All managers need to know this fact. Only Mr Ferguson can talk about the fixtures, can talk about referees and nothing happens. We need to know that I am talking about facts.

Rafa started asking questions out loud:

Are they under pressure? Maybe they were not thinking that we would be at the top of the table in January. But we are at the top of the table and they are nervous. I am not telling the authorities what to do. But I have been here for five years and know how things are going on. I will be watching United's game with Chelsea.

He was still not done. Rafa was on a hopeless roll:

We had a meeting in Manchester with managers and FA about the Respect campaign. And I was very clear, forget the campaign because Mr Ferguson was killing the referees, killing Mr Atkinson, killing Mr Hackett. But he is not punished. How can you talk about the Respect campaign and criticize the referee every single week? You can analyse the facts and come to your own decision and ideas.

It was a disaster. Rafa's 'Facts' speech was compared to Kevin Keegan's outburst when he seemed to fall apart in front of the television cameras in 1996 and said, of United and Ferguson, 'I'll tell you, honestly, I will love it if we beat them. Love it.' Keegan's emotion got the better of him towards the end of that season as Newcastle, having been twelve points ahead at one stage, saw their title challenge falter against United.

I couldn't understand Rafa's thinking in wanting to take on Ferguson, a master of mind games, when we were sitting so calmly on top of the table early into a new year. He got the timing and the tone so wrong. When I met up with England all the Man United players told me Fergie was just laughing at Rafa, saying, 'I've got him. I've got him.'

At press conferences Rafa normally never gave anything away. He'd straight-bat a lot of questions – especially if a big game was on the horizon. It was important to him not to add any pressure to the team. He played into Ferguson's hands. Ferguson loves all that. Why get involved? Sit pretty in the league and deal with a tough game away to Stoke instead of talking about Alex Ferguson and United. Let them get on with their own stuff.

Rafa, for me, made a lot of decisions with himself in mind. He wanted power and control. I didn't like it because fighting with the board, other managers and the press wasn't the Liverpool way. Rafa had fallen out with the owners, Tom Hicks and George Gillett. We were all starting to doubt them, but Rafa talked to the press about problems with his new contract.

Rafa broke the focus of the team. We got asked about it all the time in the media: 'What's all that about? Why's he done that?' We never found out because Rafa didn't say a word to us. I think he felt awkward because he knew it had backfired. That weekend Manchester United hammered Chelsea 3–0. We went to Stoke and drew 0–0. I hit the post near the end of the game and Rafa suggested later that if I'd scored then our subsequent loss of momentum would have never happened.

He was wrong. Something deeper had gone amiss. In January and February we played seven Premier League games and picked up just ten points. In the same period United played eight games and won them all with a haul of twenty-four points. It was a time when we really missed the stabilizing presence of Rafa's former assistant Pako Ayestarán. This was a key factor.

We lost a lot when Rafa fell out with Pako in 2007. We all loved Pako's training and his methods. I always felt so fresh and fired-up when going out to play a match under Pako. He was also a great link to the manager. Rafa was so cold and Pako Ayestarán was the bridge and a buffer for us. He was a fun guy and would explain to a player why he might be starting on the bench or why it would be important to miss a day's training in terms of your fitness. The communication had been perfect under Ayestarán; and when he left it declined. I felt Rafa had changed and I had no confidence in his new staff.

Rafa stopped trusting him and said that Pako was going behind his back. But I still keep in touch with Pako now. He's a good guy and he's managing Maccabi Tel Aviv. They won the first-ever treble in Israeli football in May 2015. So he's done a good job but, for me, he's the perfect number two.

Rafa had brought in Sammy Lee but he actually gave more responsibility to another Spaniard called Pako de Miguel. He was a very small guy who, so far as we could see, was Rafa's yes man. The players had no respect for him and his training was terrible. We tried to keep a lot of Pako Ayestarán's methods but it wasn't the same. The new Pako had nothing about him. No personality. There were other Spanish guys after Ayestarán left. They were nice enough fellows but we would have done better if Pako Ayestarán had stayed.

But Rafa was very stubborn. At the same time he was very good. He brought a lot out of Torres because he used to drive him. It was similar to the situation with me. Rafa demanded more from Fernando. The fact that you did not know where you stood with Rafa made you want to impress him and play for him. I did, anyway. Other players just couldn't stand him.

We still had moments when we looked like title challengers. In the same week that we destroyed Real Madrid 4–0 at Anfield, winning our Champions League last-sixteen tie 5–0 on aggregate, we went to Old Trafford. We were behind after twenty-three minutes when Cristiano Ronaldo tucked away a penalty.

United had some world-class players in Edwin van der Sar, Ferdinand, Nemanja Vidić, Ronaldo, Rooney and Tevez. But they played like a team of individuals. We blew them away after Torres equalized five minutes later. Vidić made a mistake and Torres punished him. Vidić was a very good player but Torres and I terrorized him. He just couldn't handle us and Torres always gave him nightmares. I put us 2–1 up just before half-time, from the penalty spot after Evra brought me down.

As soon as I beat van der Sar I ran down the touchline, in front of the United fans, waving a finger at my teammates to tell them to steer clear. I hadn't planned my celebration – it was off the cuff. First, I kissed my badge, because of the rivalry we had with United, and then I ran straight to a television camera near the corner flag. I planted a great big smacker on the lens, pouting my lips and kissing a hello to the millions watching the game around the world. The game, and the goal, meant that much to me.

Liverpool played really well and Rafa had set us up as if it was a European game. He totally outwitted Ferguson that day and, at his icy tactical best, he created a framework for Torres and for me, with Mascherano, Lucas and Kuyt prompting all the way that afternoon, to destroy United. Rafa was brilliantly calculating, like the coldest of chess grandmasters, while Torres and I played with force and with fire. We felt unbeatable that day, especially as our defence gave us a really solid base from which to counter.

We soaked up the pressure at first and then we just killed them on the counter-attack again and again. Vidić simply could not handle the pace, strength and power of Torres. He was eventually sent off in the seventy-sixth minute for dragging me back. We got two more late on to finish them off. 4–1 at Old Trafford was one of my sweetest victories over United.

There was a little ache, though, because our bad run in January and February meant that United were still four points clear with a game in hand. Our fans were dreaming again a week later because I got my first Premier League hat-trick for

Liverpool. We beat Villa 5–0 at Anfield. There was some title fantasy left but, in the end, too many home draws cost us. We only lost two league games all season but United ended up as champions again and we were second, four points adrift.

Ronaldo was the difference between the sides. I scored twenty-four goals, my best record as a midfielder, and Torres, recovering from injury, got seventeen. Ronaldo got twenty-six goals but he killed off all the weaker teams in the league. We failed to do that. We drew at home against Stoke, Fulham, West Ham and Hull. Those eight dropped points ruined our title hopes, in a season clouded by a court case and a bizarre rant about facts.

I still think that team should have won the league under Rafa Benítez. It was the first of two wonderful opportunities in my career – and we blew it.

The post-Christmas period in 2008 had been fraught off the field. In 2013 it was simply testing on the pitch. We had back-to-back away matches against Manchester City and Chelsea, our two closest challengers. I missed both games as I recovered from my hamstring injury but I travelled with the team on Boxing Day to see us lose, unluckily, 2–1 at Man City. Raheem Sterling had a good goal disallowed when he was wrongly ruled to be offside. Watching from the bench, I felt we played well. We also missed an unbelievable chance with Coutinho when it was still 1–1 – after our Brazilian magician had given us the lead. Álvaro Negredo then scored the winner and it was a shot that Simon Mignolet should have saved. Sterling, set up by Suárez, also somehow missed a late equalizer. We should have taken at least a point from that game.

The match against Chelsea followed a similar pattern. We took the lead, through Skrtel, but still lost 2–1 after another

Mignolet mistake. We also had an opportunity late on as Sakho's header hit the bar. We had done well in both games, without picking up a point, and Mignolet had begun to realize it was a completely different ballgame at Liverpool compared to Sunderland. A lot of players have that reality check where they think, 'Shit, this is a big, big football club.' The pressure gets to them and they make a couple of mistakes on the spin.

I was happy to be back for our next league game, away to Stoke. Sturridge also returned to the squad, initially on the bench, and everyone felt lifted. Brendan and I decided it was time to unveil our new plan with me playing in a much deeper role. Almost six weeks had passed since we had first discussed the positional change and, finally, I could try the switch.

Stoke has always been a very hard ground for Liverpool. Of course it had been our first game after Rafa's 'Facts' fiasco. But, more worryingly, we had never won there in the Premier League. We needed something different to break the pattern. People were very surprised when they saw Lucas playing in an advanced position ahead of me – as I sat in front of the back four. I was finding my feet but I remember doing a lot of tackling as it was such a crazy, free-flowing match. Stoke are usually compact and organized but they had a real go and eight goals were scored.

I found it a lot easier to play more creatively as there were three of us in midfield. I didn't need to bomb forward as Lucas and Henderson were pushing up and Coutinho, Sterling and Suárez were buzzing around up front. We went into a 2–0 lead, through an own goal and Suárez, before Stoke pinned us back after sloppy defending allowed two of our former players, Crouch and Adam, to score. A penalty from me made it 3–2. Sturridge then came on and set up Suárez. They celebrated together like they had never done before.

Walters pulled a goal back for Stoke amid the madness of

the game. Then, near the end, the SAS duo reversed roles and Suárez provided the assist for Sturridge. As Sturridge did his wave-riding dance, which we had not seen for the seven weeks he had been missing, fresh hope rose inside me. We had won 5–3 and, in my deeper role, I could sense something was stirring. Our defence had been all over the place but, going forward, the threat was obvious. We had to be title contenders if we could score five away to Stoke City. I was determined we would not make the same mistakes we had done five years before.

# 6. The Surge

The magic of the FA Cup was bloodied on the day my penis was cut and then stitched shut on an unromantic afternoon in Bournemouth. We were wary of the traditional fourth-round shock as, exactly a year before, we had been knocked out at the same stage of the competition by Oldham Athletic. But the only surprise that sunny Saturday afternoon, on 25 January 2014, was an eye-watering laceration to my private parts. I decided to keep it a secret between me, the medical staff and my very amused teammates. It would have been a touch too gory and scandalous even for the Sunday tabloids.

Bournemouth were still in the lower half of the Championship but, under an impressive young English manager in Eddie Howe, they were on the rise and just eighteen months away from being promoted to the Premier League. They played bright, attractive football and so we went to Dean Court with a strong side. Even though the Merseyside derby was just three days away, Brendan picked Suárez, Sturridge, Henderson, Coutinho, me and an experienced defence. We all wanted to play.

We went ahead in the twenty-sixth minute, when Victor Moses scored, but Bournemouth kept playing well and we had to work hard. Early in the second half, in my new deeper role, I closed down one of their wingers. I tried to block his cross but felt a stinging in my privates. I thought, 'Shit – that doesn't feel right.' I'd slid into the tackle and so I didn't know whether I'd sat on my own studs or if his boot had followed through and caught me. I just knew my dick was stinging like fuck.

After the game I watched the incident again on tape and I saw that his studs had definitely caught me. As he crossed the ball his studs had raked down hard over my wedding tackle. I couldn't look down, obviously, but as the game continued I had a little feel. It made me wince and when I glanced down at my hand I saw the blood. I was trying to follow the game but I was thinking, 'Oh, shit.'

After making sure that the TV cameras were focused on play far away, I took a tiny look. I pulled my shorts a couple of inches away from my waist and managed a sneaky check.

My underpants were bloodied.

I snapped back my shorts, as if quickly shutting the drawer to the crown jewels. My mind was racing, and not just because I could imagine the newspaper headline writers having a field day; I was concerned that something serious had happened.

I discreetly pulled back my underpants as well as my shorts for a longer look.

The gash in my penis looked pretty bad, right across the middle. There was plenty of blood.

I ran over to the touchline, straight to Brendan. I also called over to Chris Morgan and Andy Massey, who had just finished bandaging Martin Skrtel's head. Andy, now the head doctor at Liverpool, was the Academy medic at the time, and this was his first big senior game. Our usual doctor, Zaf Iqbal, had stayed at home because one of his kids was ill.

There was a break in play while one of the Bournemouth players also received attention. It was a busy afternoon for the medical boys. Skrtel had cut his shaven head badly after an accidental collision. The doctor had to put staples in his head so he could continue playing.

I said to Brendan, 'Look, I've got a problem here . . .' I nodded down to my privates.

Brendan looked very puzzled.

'There's a big gash . . . it's bleeding,' I said.

Chris acted quickly. He called a few of the backroom team over and they formed a little huddle so no one else could see what we were doing as I opened up my shorts. Brendan peered down, grimaced and shook his head. Anyone trying to work out what was happening might have wondered if Brendan was refusing to switch to a diamond formation.

I glanced at Chris. He had seen a lot of bad wounds and horrible injuries in his career as head physio.

'Is it all right, Chris?' I asked. 'Can I carry on?'

Chris's face gave nothing away. He said, 'Yeah, you'll be fine . . .'

I took that to mean it wasn't going to fall off. So I played on. The pain wasn't too bad – just the dull ache that follows the sharp hurt of a slicing sensation when your skin first gets cut open. I was more concerned about infection. I'd had a couple of really bad infections in my ankle and groin, back in 2010–11, and I was worried about the grass and the mud. But Chris knew how quickly I pick up infections. I reckoned I must be safe if he allowed me to keep playing. I made it through to the end and we won 2–0, after Suárez set up a Sturridge goal.

Brendan sounded satisfied after the game and he obviously wasn't thinking about me and my injury when he claimed, 'The second half was more comfortable than the first. Bournemouth are a very good side so credit to them. But the character was good from my team. A year ago there were games like this we may have lost. The mentality to up the tempo in the second half was excellent.'

I like to think Brendan was also making a private tribute to my bloodied kecks mentality.

At point I was with Andy Massey. All the lads were falling about laughing, in the way that footballers do when confronted with anything to do with body parts or embarrassing situations. We had won, the atmosphere was good and they thought it was hilarious. I got zero sympathy from any of the lads as I sat there quietly, looking pale and wondering what would happen.

Andy made it clear that it would need to be stitched.

'How many, Doc?' I asked.

'About four, I'd think.'

The lads were absolutely pissing themselves now and you can imagine the jokes about inches and stitches, penis size and my future performances at home with Alex. I might have smiled but I could have throttled the lot of them. A bunch of footballers are the last people you want discussing the state of your sliced penis.

The doc and I went looking for somewhere quiet so he could get his needle out and I could shut my eyes and think of Liverpool, England and the sacrifices of a long life in football. But Bournemouth's medical facilities weren't as extensive as those at Anfield. We had to go into their physio room. It was a busy place and people were streaming in and out. I sat down on a chair, looking sheepish, while a few of their kids came over to shake my hand. They must have thought I was very quiet or shy because I didn't manage much more than a muttered 'All right, mate?'

'I think we'd better get on with it, Stevie,' the doc suggested, but there was no way I was getting my tool out in front of an audience.

Doc Massey spoke to a few people and the room cleared. I took off my shorts and underpants and had one last look. Ouch. I hoped I wasn't saying goodbye to an old friend.

I got a jab first and then, careful not to look at what he was doing, I made small talk with the doc – as you do in such situations, because I could tell he wasn't feeling too comfortable about it either. He'd already had to staple Skrtel's head and now he was repairing my penis. Doc Massey must have wished that he could have stayed at home treating the Academy kids' cuts and bruises.

I didn't talk much, though. I wanted him fully concentrated. He did a good job. I felt no pain as he put in the stitches – four as he had predicted – and I walked back into the dressing room.

There was more of the old banter. Had I stiffened up under the needle? Did the doc know that no feeling was allowed?

I smiled a little more happily this time. The worst was over and the doc assured me I would be absolutely fine – both on and off the field.

After he'd told me the good news, and I had been bandaged up as protection against any possible infection, I asked him the obvious question.

'Can I play against Everton on Tuesday, Doc?'

'Let's see how you get on in the next few days,' he said.

I reckoned I could play with stitches in my dick and still beat Everton. 'Don't worry, Doc,' I said, 'I'm sure I'll be fine.'

I was desperate to play against Everton for more than the usual reasons. Every Merseyside derby generated fear in me. I don't mean just nervousness or that fluttery butterfly feeling we all get in the stomach sometimes; I feared losing to Everton – especially at home. To lose another derby at Anfield would be unbearable. I had lost one before, in 1999, and that defeat had caused me physical, gut-wrenching pain. To make matters worse, I had also been sent off.

Stupidly, I'd booked a table for a meal out that night – expecting that we'd win and I would be celebrating. I couldn't cancel everyone else's plans so I trudged off to Albert Dock and sulked all night. I was just nineteen and a moody kid. In the toilets I bumped into Kevin Campbell, the Everton striker who'd scored the winner. Kevin dropped his kecks and showed me the stud-marks I'd left on his thigh. He was built like a heavyweight boxer and all I could do was say how sorry I was for the tackle and shake his hand.

That defeat had been our last at home in a Merseyside derby, and I knew we couldn't take another at a stage of the season when we were trying to cement our place in the top four. Everton were playing well and, along with Arsenal, Spurs, ourselves and even a struggling Manchester United, they harboured serious hopes of qualifying for the Champions League. Manchester City and Chelsea were already nailed on at the top.

We were approaching the twenty-fifth anniversary of Hillsborough and were also just a month away from the start of the new inquest. It was clear that the tide had finally turned. But I wanted to give the Hillsborough Family Support Group a boost at such a vital point in their long and painful struggle for the truth.

I decided to donate £96,000 to the group before the derby. It seemed right to highlight Everton's contribution over twenty-five years because, more than any other club, they had supported us. I spoke to the press and when I was asked about the donation I said,

> With my own family's connection to Hillsborough it's something I've wanted to do for a while. I think the timing is right to send another message out about how we want justice. Alongside my gesture, I and every other Liverpool fan can only thank Evertonians for their support. I'm not saying that to try to get in any Everton fan's good books because I understand my personal rivalry with them. But it's there for everyone to see. The support they've given us is very touching.

It was easy to speak sincerely of my gratitude to Everton in regard to Hillsborough; their compassion had been sincere. We were united in grief and a desire for justice. Hillsborough, and the families of every single fan we lost, will always matter far more than the next derby. The Everton fans have been terrific with their support, and the club itself has always done whatever it can to help us. Whenever there's a tragedy in the city, or something negative happens, football gets parked up. It's incredible because both sets of fans are so passionate. They basically live for their club – whether they're a red or a blue. For the majority of fans, football is their life. But when a tragedy rips the heart out of our city we come together.

We also felt that unity when Rhys Jones was killed. Rhys was only eleven years old, and a mad-keen Everton fan, a season-ticket holder at Goodison Park with his father and brother. In August 2007, Rhys left training at Fir Tree Football Club, on the Croxteth Park Estate, when he was gunned down, shot in the back in a senseless act of gang violence. He was rushed to Alder Hey Children's Hospital but he died soon afterwards. His parents launched a campaign – In Rhys's Name Get Guns Off Our Streets – which everyone at Everton, Liverpool and across the city supported. It's in those terrible moments you feel the togetherness that unites us. So I wanted to donate the money, and link the tribute to Everton, for the sake of my own family and for every family in the city who had lost someone at Hillsborough.

I was sure a little cut on my dick wasn't going to keep me out – although I was even more determined to keep news of the incident a secret. I could imagine the songs Everton fans would have sung about me had they known what had happened just a few days before the derby.

There was speculation that Ross Barkley, Everton's twenty-year-old midfielder, their local star and my England teammate, might miss the game through injury. But I knew differently. My financial adviser tipped me off accidentally. Barkley was fine. I would be up against him in my new holding role.

Brendan had bigged me up in the build-up, telling the press I could reach the level of Andrea Pirlo and Javier Zanetti in the deeper-lying position and influence games as much as they did. Pirlo seemed to have been around for ever but, playing for Juventus, he was still only thirty-four. Zanetti was forty and still performing for Inter. But most people in the city were more intent on comparing me and Barkley. I was the old man and he was being touted as the future king of Merseyside. It made me extra-motivated.

I had to be right on it because I was aware of Barkley's attributes through playing together at England. I had seen his ability and power. He was the real deal.

I was happy to talk to Barkley when he came to me for advice. Fans in rival halves of this city might find it strange that the Liverpool captain would advise Everton's best young prospect to remain loyal to his club – but that's exactly what I told Ross. I thought he would be better off concentrating on getting better and better for Everton, his hometown club where so many people cared about him. They were pushing hard for Europe so it didn't make sense for him to go elsewhere. Even if I always want Liverpool to finish ahead of Everton it would've been wrong to have given him any other advice.

Apart from my battle against Barkley, I was licking my lips at the prospect of Suárez and Sturridge running riot against Everton's central defenders, Phil Jagielka and Antolín Alcaraz. To me it looked like the biggest mismatch you could see in a Premier League game. Phil is as honest as the day is long, experienced, and my England teammate. He's also a good player but, until he went to Everton, he had been in the Championship. Phil had done really well and, alongside someone like Gary Cahill, I trusted him for England. But, for me, Alcaraz was not a Premier League player. I didn't think he was of Premier League standard at Wigan so it was beyond me why Roberto Martínez should have taken him across to Everton. He had no chance against Suárez and Sturridge.

The Everton game started like a dream for me. I was playing really well and I could feel the power surging through me. I felt great. In the twenty-first minute we forced a corner. I usually take the corners but we had looked at their set pieces before the game. Lukaku tends to mark space in the middle of the box and, like most forwards, he can switch off. I've always believed that if you're defending at a set piece you never rely on a forward. I want my defenders in the most important position. So we thought I could nip in ahead of Lukaku.

Suárez took the corner and Lukaku was nowhere. Alcaraz tried to track me but it was so easy to leave him for dead and bury the header. I ran towards Luis, my arms scissoring to the sides, my mouth open, screaming, but you could only hear an explosion of noise around Anfield. I jumped into Luis's arms and we were pulled into the crowd. When I broke free I saluted with a huge fist pump. 1–0, Gerrard, in the derby.

It got even better. Twelve minutes later Henderson fed Coutinho. He hit a gorgeous through ball which Sturridge ran onto and finished with a composed chip over Tim Howard. Sturridge just nodded again and again as if to tell us that, yeah, of course, it was always a done deal. He did it again before half-time when, following a long pass from Touré, Sturridge produced a wonderful lob. Sturridge didn't ride the wave. He just stood stock-still while everyone jumped on top of him. Skrtel jumped highest, looking like a warrior with his head swathed in a black bandage. No one outside my dressing room knew that I was bandaged in a very different place.

You couldn't keep Luis off the score-sheet. Early in the

second half he intercepted an Everton pass. He was across the halfway line in a flash and he ran and ran, with the ball at his feet, before he put Everton out of their misery with the coolest of finishes. The Kop rocked and chanted: *Da-da-da-da-da-da / I just can't get enough / I just can't get enough / His name is Luis Suárez / He wears the famous Red / I just can't get enough / I just can't get enough . . .*

In the teeming rain, Sterling was brought down by Howard. I wanted Daniel to get his hat-trick so I let him take the penalty. He said thank you but, then, blasted it over the bar. The Kop, wanting a fifth goal, groaned. 4–0 was still very sweet but, as we got back to the dressing room, I had a quiet word with Daniel about his penalty. 'They're not as easy as they look, are they?' I said with the wry smile of a man who had missed a few down the years.

## Anfield, Saturday, 8 February 2014

This was the day it really began. This was the game we discovered how well we could play. This was the day our growing belief took hold.

Arsenal had been playing exceptionally. They were top of the league, two points clear of Chelsea and Manchester City. We were fourth, eight points behind Arsenal. Our place at the head of the table had been dented by those successive defeats between Christmas and New Year. We had also dropped points in draws against Villa, 2–2 at home, and West Brom, 1–1 away. Liverpool still lacked the consistency of champions.

Ten days before we hammered Everton we had been 2–0 down at home against Villa. Sturridge pulled one back in stoppage time at the end of the first half. Then, after fifty-three minutes, I hit one of my crossfield specials. It landed at Suárez's feet and, as he cut in towards goal, he was fouled. I scored from the penalty spot to earn us a point.

After the derby we went to the Hawthorns and Sturridge gave us the lead. West Brom equalized midway through the second half after a Touré howler of a pass across our goal-mouth. We had such control, apart from that horrendous error which left poor Kolo clutching his head in despair. We should have won comfortably. It was time we turned our domination into a consistent run of victories. West Brom became a turning point in our season.

At half-time in that game Brendan had pulled me to one side. He just needed to say one word – 'Perfect' – to confirm what my instinct told me. It felt like I'd had a flawless first forty-five minutes.

Brendan called me into his office a few days after West Brom and he showed me footage of my performances in the deeper role. He seemed very happy as he said, 'Look at the difference, Stevie. This is what we want.' Our analysis of what was going wrong when we first discussed my play in the autumn had been spot on. My head movement was back and I had corrected my body position when receiving the ball. There was more tempo to my play and, apart from creating and scoring, I was also being aggressive and pressing at the right times.

The memory of being outclassed by Arsenal two months earlier was still fresh. I admired Arsène Wenger and his vision of how football should be played and how teams should develop internally – rather than just parachuting in huge stars for hundreds of millions. He believes in improving players himself and he's similar to Pep Guardiola in remaining true to his philosophy of football. Wenger would leave Arsenal before abandoning his core beliefs. I also knew what he meant when he complained how 'financial doping' had unbalanced the Premier League.

Liverpool had usually found it tough to disrupt Arsenal's passing and long periods of possession. You couldn't really take on Arsenal in a contest of pure football. Like most other sides in the Premier League, we had worked out that you had a real chance if you went out of your way to bully them. We couldn't bully the Invincibles – back in the days when Arsenal had big strong men like Sol Campbell, Martin Keown and Gilberto Silva in their squad. Patrick Vieira was another huge presence. Even their most outrageously skilful players, Dennis Bergkamp and Thierry Henry, knew how to look after themselves. They could be very spiky if anyone tried to clatter them.

When we lined up in the tunnel that day at Anfield, with a televised kick-off scheduled for 12.45, I felt even more confident. We weren't just going to bully Arsenal. We would be aggressive and relentless but, even more than that, Brendan had stressed the need for tempo and quality. It was in our hands to be ruthless because we had the quality.

Arsenal were about to begin a crunch period in their season. After playing us, their next eight league games included Manchester United, Stoke away, Spurs away, Chelsea away, Manchester City and then Everton away. In between that brutal run of fixtures they also had to play us in the FA Cup and they were just a week away from facing Bayern Munich in the last sixteen of the Champions League. You either find a special resolve or you crumble in such circumstances. Arsenal were about to crumble.

Per Mertesacker would win a World Cup winner's medal at the end of the season with Germany. I respected Mertesacker but I could see him having fits against Sturridge and Suárez. No central defender likes playing against real pace and to have two strikers running at you, and feeding off each other, is frightening. I knew Daniel and Luis were both feeling good and, since setting goals up for each other against Stoke, their relationship had improved. When a Suárez pass led to Sturridge's tap-in against West Brom, Daniel had broken into a huge smile, pointed straight to Luis and ran to him. The SAS partnership and our whole team were about to give Wenger and Arsenal an absolute nightmare.

We decided to go for Arsenal's throat from the start. We were ready to be breathtaking.

The massacre began after just fifty-three seconds. We had won a free kick down the left side of Arsenal's defence. I stepped up to take it. Skrtel was on the far edge of the pack of red and yellow shirts bunched together in the Arsenal area. I waited until Skrtel began to move. He was in the heart of their box when I struck the ball. It was one of those dead-ball deliveries I got just right. It was dipping and curling in at speed. Olivier Giroud missed it and Mikel Arteta stuck out a leg but the swerving ball flew past him. Skrtel bundled it home with his knee.

Skrtel raised his arm and began to celebrate while, at the same time, looking across instinctively at the referee's assistant to see if he had been ruled offside. The flag stayed down and Skrtel galloped towards the fans at the opposite side of the ground to me. He was going crazy, just like them, and he did a knee-slide which took him into the crowd. Fans were rubbing his bald head, jumping and yelling like crazy. Less than a minute had gone.

Nine minutes later we forced a corner on the same side where I had set up the first goal. I aimed for Skrtel's bald dome and he rose above Laurent Koscielny to steer the ball home with power and precision. That monster header made it 2–0, after ten minutes. Skrtel covered his head with his shirt as he celebrated madly again.

Soon afterwards I intercepted a pass from Özil, who looked shell-shocked, and slipped it to Coutinho who played a long crossfield pass which Suárez volleyed into the path of Sturridge. It should have been our third but Sturridge, trying to lob the rushing Wojciech Szczęsny, sent it wide. Suárez looked frustrated. He knew it would have been a sublime goal.

Suárez then almost scored one of the goals of the season. From another corner, I hit it low and hard to him on the edge of the box. He trapped it, let the ball bounce once while he swivelled and sent a half-volley screaming towards goal. It hit the post and careered straight back at Kolo Touré who could not control the ball. Arsenal, somehow, had escaped again.

They could not stop the storm, though. We were 3–0 up after sixteen minutes. Henderson harried and dispossessed Özil on the halfway line, leaving Arsenal's record signing sprawled on his backside. Driving forward, Henderson ate up the ground, moving deep into Arsenal territory. He slipped the ball to Suárez on the right flank. Suárez played a quick pass into the area where Sterling and Sturridge were lining up. Sterling got there first and steered the ball home. It looked ridiculously simple; but this was football of brutal purity and pace.

Anfield went deeper into dreamland when, after another Özil pass to Wilshere was picked off, Coutinho made his interception count. Just outside the Arsenal half, Coutinho hit a raking pass which Sturridge swept into the net. He spent more time making sure he looked the business Riding the Wave again. Arsenal had been carved open so expertly that Sturridge had a good five seconds to do his arm-waving dance before we swamped him in a sea of red. 4–0. Twenty minutes gone. It had been the most destructive opening to any Premier League game I could remember.

We eased off a little, and didn't score again until the fifty-second minute when Sterling, running onto a fine ball from Touré, tucked home the rebound to make it 5–0 after a desperate Szczęsny had parried his first attempt. The only surprise was that the sixth goal was scored by a devastated Arsenal. Arteta's penalty, after I brought down Alex Oxlade-Chamberlain, made the final score 5–1.

'Maybe it is better I go home and do not say too much,' Wenger muttered afterwards. He and his team looked totally shot. We had blown their hopes for the season to smithereens – even if they were still five points clear of us after twenty-five games. I don't think anyone leaving Anfield that afternoon believed that we would finish anywhere but above Arsenal at the end of the season. Six weeks later they lost 6–0 at Stamford Bridge. They had still not recovered from the mortal wounds we had inflicted on their title dreams in those first twenty minutes.

It had been the worst Arsenal defeat at Anfield in fifty years. In April 1964 Bill Shankly's team had beaten the Gunners 5–0. A month later, Liverpool won the first of three titles under Shankly. Our fans saw it as an omen. I just looked more closely at our current side.

We had the two best strikers in the league in the same team. And we had Sterling, turning into a monster of a player in his small body which was actually so strong and physical. Henderson was growing and maturing. Coutinho was spraying magic all around him. Our defence could be shaky but Skrtel was a leader and capable of doing damage to the opposition at set pieces. And, as captain, I was playing in the holding role and feeling like a million dollars. We were riding one of the big rollers Sturridge liked to imagine he could surf. Our form felt suddenly booming and powerful. I hoped it would last.

There were dips and twists, and we were tested. We travelled to London to play Fulham the following Wednesday and began disastrously. In the eighth minute Touré scored an own goal, falling and then miskicking into our net, which would have been comical if it had not been so distressing for both him and us. A few minutes later Touré accidentally ran straight into the referee, Phil Dowd, flattening him. I didn't think we'd be getting any penalties after that.

I got us going again just before half-time. Aly Cissokho broke up a Fulham attack and the ball fell to me in the centre circle. Playing deep, I had time and space to break forward quickly and then, with the outside of my right foot, send a long pass curling through a gap left by four Fulham defenders. It was a peach, falling right into the path of Sturridge. He slotted it home, off the post, and got back on his surfboard. It had been a world-class finish.

We had to come from behind again and, with eighteen minutes left, Coutinho made it 2–2. A draw was not good enough and we poured forward. In the last minutes, our luck turned. Sturridge was hacked down in the box.

*Penalty!* Phil Dowd had forgiven Kolo Touré.

The nerves were twitching inside me as I walked to the spot. *Don't fuck it up.* I ignored the voice in my head. I placed the ball carefully and turned away. I knew if I missed we would have blown everything we had built up against Arsenal. *Don't fuck it up.*

My hands were on my hips as I waited for the ref's signal. I eventually looked across at Dowd, as if to say, 'C'mon, mate, get on with it . . .'

Dowd blew the whistle. I took a step forward and then moved more quickly. One, two, bang.

I hit it cleanly, to the right of their substitute keeper, David Stockdale. He dived the right way, but he had no chance.

*Goal!* 3–2. I had won it.

I was on my way, running towards the corner flag with that delirium footballers get when we score a last-minute winner and don't quite know how to express our elation and relief. So we run and yell, like little boys lost in joy. But, this time, I suddenly knew what to do. 'It's coming off,' I thought. I reached for my shirt and peeled it over my head. I was wearing a red vest underneath and I must have looked demented with happiness as I kept running, being chased by my teammates, while I twirled the shirt above my head as if I was a cowboy about to use it as a lasso on a cold February night in London.

The Liverpool fans were in that corner of the packed little ground at Craven Cottage. They were bouncing and roaring, roaring and bouncing. As I neared them I leapt high in the air, still waving my shirt as a memento of our crucial victory, before I was swallowed up by my teammates. They were all screaming in my face. I couldn't hear a word. But I knew what they meant. We had done it. We had won. We were now a point behind Man City, three from Arsenal and just four adrift of Chelsea. Twelve games to hunt them down.

In his post-match interview Brendan Rodgers called me 'peerless'. He could have said 'mental' as well.

It had been a see-sawing game, against a team fighting relegation, and we had been nervous. We had made errors and we could have lost. But we wouldn't settle for a draw. We went for the win and we got it. All the passion, and tangled emotion, poured out of me at the end. We had taken another step towards the dream.

On the coach back to Liverpool that night, 'Alive' by Chase & Status boomed out. Chris Morgan and I looked at each other as the 'I feel so alive' mantra echoed again and again as we flew along the motorway, heading away from London and back up to the north. Chris had kicked every ball from the bench. He also looked knackered. But we had felt so intensely alive all night. It was gone midnight when I said to Chris: 'I'm tired too, mate.'

'Little wonder,' Chris said with a smile.

'Yeah,' I said, 'but you know what? I wish it was like this every year. I'd love to be this involved every season.'

If you played for a top-four side, this was how it felt every year. I felt a pang of regret. And it was not regret over my decision to spend my whole career at Liverpool. It was just a wish that I could have been more familiar with the tension and drama of a title race.

I scored another penalty in London that Sunday. But I didn't celebrate. We were 2–0 down in the FA Cup against Arsenal, who were piecing together their shattered season after losing so badly to us and to Bayern in the Champions League. My goal came after an hour but it was the last of the game. We were out of the cup. I was disappointed but, as the weeks unfolded, and we concentrated solely on the league, the benefits were obvious.

One win followed another in an unbroken chain. There were rollercoasters too. After Fulham and Arsenal we were home and cruising against Swansea. 2–0 up, with a lovely pair from Sturridge and Henderson. After twenty minutes we were looking for an Arsenal-style landslide.

Then Shelvey pulled one back for Swansea. A Skrtel own goal dragged them level. I felt the old dread on the inside but I kept playing with freedom and belief. So did the whole team.

An intricate move between Johnson, Flanagan, Henderson and Coutinho delivered the ball to Suárez, whose cross set up Sturridge's headed goal. 3–2. Wilfried Bony then made it 3–3 from the penalty spot after a Skrtel foul. Bloody hell. Why couldn't it be like the 5–1 Arsenal game every week?

Flanagan and I exchanged passes deep in our half. There was room for me to pick out Suárez thirty yards away, with his back to goal. He chested the pass down, swivelled and hit a shot. It was blocked but Henderson, following up, struck it cleanly. Vorm saved it, but like a pinball it fell again to Henderson. Boom! No mistake from the second rebound. We had won 4–3.

It was less complicated away to Southampton: 3–0. Suárez,

Sterling and a penalty from me. A fourth straight win in the league meant we were second, a point behind Chelsea, who had played a game less. Arsenal were third, level on points but with an inferior goal difference. Manchester City were two points further back, but with two games in hand. It was tightening at the top.

The Liverpool fans geared up for the big push. We went to Old Trafford and they unfurled a huge banner – *MAKE US DREAM*. Brendan also knew how to inspire us in his own way. As our winning run gathered pace he started to read out a letter from a different player's family before every game. It was a simple, intimate and very powerful gesture. It made sense that, before we ran out against Man United, the old enemy, he read out loud to the team a letter from my mum to me. Emotion ran through me, making me feel stronger and more determined than ever before.

Our supporters also knew how much it meant to me to beat United and so they sang my name again and again, my song echoing around Old Trafford: *Steve Gerrard, Gerrard / He'll pass the ball forty yards / He's big and he's fucking hard / Steve Gerrard, Gerrard . . .*

As they were singing their hymn to me, in the thirty-fourth minute, Sturridge crossed to Suárez and, in the penalty area, Rafael handled. Penalty to Liverpool.

David de Gea stood very still in the United goal as I faced him. He's a great keeper and there was no fannying about, jumping around or waving his arms in an attempt to put me off. He knew that, with me facing the Stretford End, thousands of United fans would be trying to get inside my head. They didn't have a hope. My head might as well have been encased in ice. I was never going to miss. De Gea dived to his right and I slotted it to the left. 1–0. I made a point of not celebrating, as if to tell all those Red Devils that we were only starting.

Early in the second half, the referee, Mark Clattenburg, gave me another chance from the spot. It was the right decision after Phil Jones clobbered Joe Allen. De Gea guessed right and dived to the left. But he couldn't keep out my spot kick. It flew into the bottom corner: 2–0.

This time I did celebrate, with a knee-slide as well. I even did a reprise of the camera kiss from 2009, when we beat United 4–1. The fans, Liverpool to the core like me, went bananas. Cue my song again.

Echoes of that demolition from five years before broke out again when Vidić was sent off – just as he had been when Torres terrorized him in 2009. It was Sturridge, this time, who turned Vidić inside out before the foul came. Red card, Vidić. A third penalty. A golden chance for me to rack up an Old Trafford hat-trick.

De Gea was sure I'd go right again. He dived right but I went left. I hit the post. I felt sick. De Gea screamed at me but I looked away. *Shit!*

Suárez was denied late on by de Gea, with a great save, but we would still seal a comprehensive victory. In the eighty-fourth minute Sturridge set up Suárez for 3–0. Suárez was ecstatic and he didn't seem to mind that his celebrations ended with his head popping up between Skrtel's legs.

Amid the euphoria, I did step back. I loved beating United and I didn't mind when Wayne Rooney said it was his worst day in a Man U shirt. I'd had my share of thumpings from Manchester United. I knew Wayne would survive. But I felt sympathy for Moyes. He's a good man and I believe he's a good manager. It didn't matter if your name was David Moyes or Pep Guardiola or Louis van Gaal. Anyone taking that job after Alex Ferguson would have been in for a rough ride.

Moyes was also up against a Liverpool side pumping with self-belief. I was not the only local lad. Jon Flanagan is as much a Scouser as I am. Flano was totally onboard during that big ride towards the title. Against United he tackled Rooney, van Persie and Juan Mata before there were even ten minutes on the clock. Flano makes the most of what he's got. He's so strong mentally, and brave. I was devastated for him when, a year later, he was out for most of the season through injury. But in March 2013, Flano was in the form of his life. He was one of the first names on the team sheet because Brendan loved him. He did the job to a T and it was great to see him enjoying it as well. I knew what it meant to him and his family. He's a great lad and just the type of player you need in a successful squad. Flano might not get wider credit for his technique, but he's always there for you. Liverpool fans don't call him the Red Cafu for no reason. In the dressing room he's also known as 'Mini Carra' because he has so many similar attributes.

The games and goals rolled along. We were sloppy at the back and clinical up front when winning by a tennis score in Cardiff – 6–3. But we were behind twice and needed a Suárez hat-trick, two for Skrtel and one for Sturridge to make it a comfortable victory in the end.

Four nights later I enjoyed my goal against Sunderland, a free kick which I curled over the wall and into the top left corner. Sturridge then made it 2–0 early in the second half with a stunning strike. A late Sunderland goal turned the last quarter of an hour into another test of nerve. 'It's about reinforcing the need for calmness,' Brendan said afterwards. 'We were the dominant team but, when it gets to 2–1, it's going to get hairy. But it's important they can think clearly under pressure. The pressure is now on City with the squad they have and the money they've spent – and on Chelsea. The pressure we have is for ourselves, because we are Liverpool and we want to be winners. We are on that path.'

Chelsea were top, with sixty-nine points after thirty-one games. We had one point less after the same amount of matches.

Manchester City were third, on sixty-six points, still with those two games in hand. The odds were in favour of City but their next match was at Arsenal and, like Chelsea, they still had to come to Anfield.

On Saturday, 29 March 2014, the race suddenly tilted in our favour. We were a day away from playing Spurs at Anfield, in Sky's 4 p.m. Sunday afternoon game, and I followed the shock news on television. In a traditional three o'clock Saturday kick-off Chelsea faced Crystal Palace, who were staging a dramatic escape from relegation under Tony Pulis. Chelsea lost 1–0. John Terry's own goal gave us an incredible boost. At the Hope Street Hotel, where we were staying for the night, we watched Manchester City surrender an early lead in the evening game at the Emirates. Arsenal 1, Manchester City 1.

I stared at the league table, blinking to make sure I was reading it right. Chelsea, sixty-nine points after thirty-two games. Liverpool sixty-eight points after thirty-one games. Manchester City sixty-seven points after thirty games.

The truth was plain, but beautiful. If we won our remaining seven matches, no one could stop us becoming league champions. We had won our previous seven: if we could repeat that then the title would belong to us.

Liverpool's amazingly passionate fans absorbed the news and the following day they showed us how they felt. Early that Sunday afternoon the team coach travelling from Hope Street to Anfield slowed to a crawl. I gazed out of the window at the incredible sight we had first seen on the night of the game against Sunderland. The terraced street ahead, and all around us, had turned into an ocean of red. I couldn't see Anfield Road. It was just people and flags, banners and flares. Red plumes of smoke curled up into the air. The same message of hope fluttered again on the biggest banner: *MAKE US DREAM*.

I stood up to get a better view. Most of the players followed.

As the fans saw us peering down at them, the noise grew louder. The songs outside were matched by the thud of hands beating on the bus in encouragement. It felt like we were rocking – but with hope rather than fear. The thumping of the bus, and the songs for Liverpool, for me and Luis as well, echoed all around us as, inch by inch, we crawled the last 500 yards to the ground.

I turned to the players and said seven simple words: 'Look how much it means to them . . .'

There was no need to spell it out. We could not let them down. If we beat Spurs we would be top of the league again. If we then won our next six matches we would be champions.

We played our usual song for that season in the dressing room – 'So Good To Me' by Chris Malinchak. One of the kids turned up the volume. There were just five minutes left before Brendan said a last few words. I glanced around as the lads got ready to step out into the colour and din of Anfield. They looked calm, happy even. We had beaten Spurs 5–0 away, a lifetime ago on a cold December night. I was sure we would win again. I took in a few deep breaths as the song faded away. I nodded to Brendan. There was not much more to say. We were ready.

The game began. Coutinho swept the ball to the right, to Sterling, who fed Johnson on the overlap. Johnson crossed low and hard, aiming for Sturridge. Younès Kaboul got there first but, with his feet tangled, he back-heeled the ball into his own net. 1–0 up after two minutes.

I then broke up a Spurs attack after twenty-five minutes and hit a long clearance which should really have been cut out by Michael Dawson. But the ball squirted away to Suárez. He was away, brushing past Kaboul and, from an acute angle, driving in our second past Hugo Lloris. Flanagan and Coutinho combined with real panache to make it three before Henderson completed the 4–0 rout with a long-range free kick.

We were four points clear at the top of the table, with six games to play. Manchester City had played a couple of matches less and were due at Anfield in exactly two weeks.

West Ham away was the next test. It didn't help that we had problems getting stuck in traffic on the way to Upton Park. The driver had to park and let us off and it felt like we had to walk a long way. Once we arrived, and had started to change, the away dressing room was like a sauna. After the game I made a tongue-in-cheek comment about Sam Allardyce, West Ham's manager. 'Big Sam tried everything,' I said. He didn't like it much, Big Sam, and he had a little bite back at me. It didn't matter. We had already settled everything on the pitch.

Luis Suárez came close with an early free kick and then, in the twentieth minute, his chip left Adrián stranded before hitting the crossbar. Daniel Sturridge missed a good chance and the tension took on another notch of intensity. Then, just before half-time, in the forty-fourth minute, Sakho passed to me, deep in our own half. I could see Suárez lurking and so I hit a long fifty-yard diagonal pass. He controlled the ball and, as he tried to cut back inside the box, it bounced up and brushed the hand of James Tomkins, the West Ham defender. Luis immediately appealed for a penalty and the referee, Anthony Taylor, agreed. He pointed to the spot.

It was one of my biggest penalties. I'd missed and scored penalties in European Championship and World Cup shoot-outs but this one had real, heavy pressure. But I felt brave and confident.

Adrián jumped on his line, waving his arms, but I pretended not to notice. At the whistle, Adrián dived to his right and I struck it sweetly to his left. My smile was full of relief.

We were rocked a minute later, on the stroke of half-time, when West Ham took a corner. Simon Mignolet went up to gather it and he had the ball when Andy Carroll, our former teammate, struck the keeper's head. It was a clear foul and Mignolet lost the ball. It bounced down and was prodded home by Guy Demel. We all protested long and hard, especially Simon, and the referee consulted with his assistant. The goal stood.

In the dressing room we watched the incident again on one of the staff iPads. The referee had made a bad mistake. It was one of those times when you think, 'The luck's not with us today.'

Brendan was strong. He sent us out again, determined to shake off such negativity. Lucas played a lovely little through ball to Flanagan, bursting into the West Ham area. Adrián came charging out and brought down Flano. It was West Ham's turn to object but the ref was right. It was a penalty.

Adrián tried to fox me by pointing to his left. But I went right, as he did, and my penalty had enough pace, power and height to fly into the net.

I ran to our fans behind that side of the goal. They were penned into the away end – full of bliss again.

I was told later that I had overtaken Kenny Dalglish, Dad's hero, in the list of all-time Liverpool goalscorers. It was my 173rd goal and my tenth successful penalty that season. And, since switching to my deeper-lying role against Stoke in January, I had played thirteen Premier League games and scored nine goals. The pressure was intense, but I was playing well.

The team stats on Sunday, 6 April 2014, were more impressive. We had not lost a single Premier League match all year, having played fourteen since New Year's Day. More importantly, this was our ninth straight league win in a row. Nine down, five to go. We were on a roll.

I was an experienced player in my sixteenth season as a professional, but I felt like a rookie in the context of a title charge. I was excited and each morning I drove to training feeling happy that I was moving one step closer to the fantasy that had fuelled me for so long. But, every evening, I also felt drained. I couldn't escape the obsessive talk of the title. We were full of it at Melwood, urging each other on, reminding ourselves how close we were to footballing heaven. Fans were hanging over the walls, shouting out to us, and the street outside Melwood was thick with people waiting to wish us good luck as we drove away.

Usually, I stopped to sign autographs for the kids and to shake a few hands. The encouraging words were repeated over and over. 'Go on, Stevie lad, win it for us . . . you can do it!'

All the way home, whenever I stopped at a traffic light, people would hoot and wave and shout out something about the title. It felt all-consuming. I was desperate to win it because I lived and breathed the club. All my mates are as mad about Liverpool as me. So when I was hanging around with them we spoke about only one thing – the title chase.

Looking back now, I can see I should have tried to switch off more by watching movies or playing with my daughters. Alex and the girls have no interest in football, apart from wanting me to do well and to be happy, and so it seemed as if they were the only ones who were not studying the fixture list for Liverpool, Manchester City and Chelsea – or agonizing over the big games hurtling towards us at Anfield. So I could and should have stepped away from it more and just tried to immerse myself at home in the girls' chatter about gymnastics and dance and school. But I could not stop thinking about football. I drove myself potty.

Even when I tried to relax by watching television, a story about Liverpool and our title chase would come up on the news or my phone would beep with another text wishing me luck. At night, in the dark, trying to sleep, it was also hard. My mind would be swimming with past matches and title deciders before, finally, I drifted away.

The games offered no release. We were so close, in touching distance of becoming champions, that we felt anxious even when playing. Strangely, despite it all, my form remained good. I was playing well and, since the Stoke game in January, I'd had my most consistent spell under Brendan. I might have dreaded everything going wrong in the middle of a game but I didn't allow it to affect me. I played through the tension, and stayed strong and brave.

# 7. Closing In

We made the usual journey from Hope Street to Anfield for another early Sunday afternoon, Sky-arranged fixture. But this wasn't just any game. The streets surrounding the ground were crammed with thousands of fans. Their banners and flags seemed larger than ever and the banging on the sides of our bus even louder than usual. Flares had turned the air a smoky red. The chanting and the singing was deafening as we crawled towards the stadium. Up ahead it looked like the parting of the Red Sea as waves of supporters rolled back to allow the coach to move slowly down a jammed Anfield Road.

I had witnessed incredible scenes after FA Cup final parades and, especially, when we returned from Istanbul to hold up the Champions League trophy to a crowd of around 750,000 in the city centre. But those unforgettable moments had been one-off occasions. They were parties after all the tension and drama had turned to relief and happiness. This was different. Hope and expectation had burst open. We stared in amazement at our fans and their dream.

It felt all the sweeter because, as a club, we had dragged our-selves out of a deep hole. Four, five and even six years earlier those same streets had also been packed with thousands of fans. Their long uprising against our owners, Tom Hicks and George Gillett, which began in 2008, was driven by anger rather than hope. It marked the start of the most difficult years for Liverpool during my career – and a time when football mattered less than the murky deals of the boardroom. Liver-pool's supporters were so affected by Hicks and Gillett that the need for victory over them in the High Court in 2010 seemed to matter more than the league title, which at the time seemed further away than ever.

In contrast to the optimism around Anfield in the spring of 2014, Hicks and Gillett unleashed cynicism, fury and a winter of conflict across Liverpool that it seemed would never end. I could still remember protesting supporters waving huge banners saying *Tom & George: Not Welcome Here* in 2008 and 2009. A year later, as the crisis escalated, the message had hardened into *Tom & George: Not Welcome Anywhere.*

The turnaround from those dark days, when the club was threatened with the prospect of going into administration beneath the weight of debt accumulated under the Americans, seemed incredible. Everyone was talking about league title run-ins rather than legal battles, about Suárez and Sturridge instead of two businessmen. It was what I wanted – passion directed at our football team winning a trophy rather than towards some men in suits who had dominated the headlines at Liverpool for too long.

I've never been interested in the business side of modern football. Ownership, corporate sponsorship and the money that can be made in the game, and squandered or even stolen, has never gripped me. Like most football fans I'd far rather think and talk about my team, or a dramatic game or incredible goal I'd just seen, than about shares and loans, leveraged take-overs and administrators.

Yet money had changed football. Over the years I had been forced to acknowledge that the beautiful game had become just another profit-making industry. Chelsea and Manchester City had been transformed, after years of mediocrity, into powerhouses. My own chances of winning the league with Liverpool had been seriously diminished as a result of those takeovers. I was forced to start caring about who owned which club – because such business matters had a direct impact on Liverpool.

My respect for our previous owners, the Moores family from Merseyside, had always been obvious. In later years I just hoped Liverpool would find new owners who could close the financial divide between ourselves and Chelsea, City and Manchester United. We needed money to buy new players to keep in striking distance of our rivals. But that's as far as my interest in club ownership and takeovers stretched. Could our owners help us become a better football team on the pitch while honouring our traditions?

As club captain, and on those terms, I was happy to talk to Hicks and Gillett in February 2007 with Liverpool's then chief executive Rick Parry. Jamie Carragher, as our longest-serving first-team player and with the best interests of Liverpool at the heart of everything he did, joined us. We met the Americans at the Lowry Hotel in Manchester, a couple of days before England played Spain in a friendly at Old Trafford. Hicks and Gillett were close to completing the purchase of Liverpool for £435m. I had no idea they would need to borrow £185m from RBS to complete the deal.

I was more interested in their apparent plans for the club. They obviously sold themselves very well in the meeting to me and Jamie. Hicks and Gillett said they wanted Liverpool to become a dominant force in Europe, building on our 2005 Champions League success, and they promised money for new players. They planned to build the new stadium the club had discussed for so long. A couple of days later, in public, Gillett confirmed what he had told us – 'The spade has to be in the ground within sixty days.'

They made everything sound exciting and realistic. Jamie and I came out of the meeting feeling really positive and upbeat. But in any job the easiest thing to do is to talk the talk. We're all professionals at talking a big game. The hardest thing is to actually prove you can do it.

At first, they tried. They invested in the team. Five months later, in one of the biggest transfer deals of the summer, Hicks and Gillett approved the purchase of Fernando Torres from Atlético Madrid for £26.5m. The club also sealed multi-million-pound deals for Ryan Babel and Yossi Benayoun.

Torres had that brilliant first season but, by November 2007, Rafa Benítez had already fallen out with the owners over his transfer targets. After the initial honeymoon period Rafa was constantly criticizing Hicks and Gillett to me.

It got messy. A lot of noise poured out of Hicks and Gillett which didn't impress me. Hicks met Jürgen Klinsmann in January 2008 to discuss the possibility of him becoming our manager.

But Rafa stayed, the bickering continued and we went on to challenge for the title in 2008–09. While there was some success on the pitch it obscured what was really happening in the boardroom. It became chaotic because Hicks and Gillett fell out with each other. They had planning permission to build the new stadium but they didn't have the £300m needed for the project. A spade never broke ground. The stadium plan was abandoned and Christian Purslow came in as managing director in the summer of 2009. He was meant to find £100m because it turned out that, under Hicks and Gillett and their loan scheme, at least that much money was needed to pay back the club's creditors.

I know a lot of fans felt Jamie and I should have spoken out against Hicks and Gillett. They probably imagine we have a lot of power when, in reality, we have little. We were also in a very tricky situation. They were the owners of the club and we were just players. Neither of us felt in a position to be criticizing the owners of the club which employed us. It was frustrating because we wanted to speak openly. But we knew if we went public with our personal views it would not help anyone.

I didn't think I had the right, as a player, to become engaged in an argument with anyone above me at Liverpool. The manager was the only one I felt I should speak directly to in my role as captain. He managed the team and we were working together. Anything above that, at boardroom level, was none of my business.

As a fan, and as a player, I always want the owners to be as good as they can be and deliver what they've promised. But I didn't ask for a meeting with Hicks and Gillett. They asked to meet me. And they said to me: 'These are our aims and this is what we plan to do.' I took them at face value and I believed them. And when it all started to unravel it wasn't my place to challenge them in public or to start talking to RBS. I had enough problems in my own job. So I just followed the whole mess from a distance, like any other fan, feeling concerned as it became more and more dysfunctional.

Hicks and Gillett had come into the club as a team and as soon as they started arguing I was worried that the rift would never be fixed. And that's exactly what happened. I understood the fans' anger because they work all week and when they come to Anfield to support their team they want the right people in charge. They were entitled to protest. We all felt angry and let down.

In late 2009 dissent against the owners was in full swing and we were struggling on the pitch. There was a nasty and even venomous edge. Gillett said that his family had received death threats while Hicks's son, Tom Jr, who had been appointed as a Liverpool director, got involved in a cyberspace slanging match with a Liverpool fan who belonged to the Spirit Of Shankly group that was leading the protests. After calling the fan an 'idiot' in an email, Tom Jr sent him another in January

2010: 'Blow me, fuck-face. Go to hell, I'm sick of you.' These were the kind of people who were running our club. Bill Shankly would have been turning in his grave.

A refinancing deal of £237m in loans from RBS meant that a weekly penalty of £2.5m was imposed on Hicks and Gillett's Liverpool holding company. We were told that it would amount to an additional £60m if the club was not sold by 6 October 2010. The financial implications were severe – and there was a very real danger we might go into administration which would also have resulted in the immediate loss of nine Premier League points.

Hicks and Gillett, even though they were still not talking to each other, confirmed in April 2010 that the club was for sale. They wanted to make a killing out of Liverpool, despite their disastrous tenure, and were prepared to wait until somebody paid an outrageous price – which Hicks said needed to be between £600m and a ludicrous £1bn.

RBS stepped in and appointed Martin Broughton, the chairman of British Airways, to see through a more realistic sale. The trouble continued on and off the pitch. We had finished the 2009–10 season in seventh place and Rafa had been sacked and replaced by Roy Hodgson.

The real battle continued to be played out in the boardroom rather than on the football pitch – where Liverpool and Hodgson were still struggling. RBS placed the club's loans in the bank's toxic-assets division. The rest of the Liverpool board, excluding Hicks and Gillett, fielded various offers to buy the club.

On 6 October 2010 they announced that they had agreed to sell Liverpool to New England Sports Ventures of Boston, a company belonging to another American, John W. Henry. Henry also owned the Boston Red Sox and he was clearly a reputable businessman with a proven track record.

Hicks and Gillett tried to block the deal after a High Court ruling on 13 October 2010 that the club could be sold for £300m. An injunction was applied for in a Dallas court to derail what Hicks called 'an epic swindle'. But Hicks and Gillett were finally beaten – and the sale went ahead and was completed by Henry. Fenway Sports Group, as Henry's company became known, were the new owners of Liverpool.

Calm and unity had returned to the club. I felt much more comfortable with the understated and efficient style in which Fenway went about their business. It could hardly have been more different from the noise and chaos we endured under Hicks and Gillett.

I felt relieved that, as we finally reached Anfield on that April afternoon in 2014, we were surrounded by banners and flags urging us on as a team. *MAKE US DREAM* was so much more inspiring than *Hicks & Gillett Out!* The 40,000 Liverpool supporters moving slowly towards the stadium were united in hope. We had escaped a tangled and dirty business. We were lost once more in a simple and thrilling game.

## *Anfield, Sunday, 13 April 2014*

Echoes of our past surrounded us. Fifty years before, at the end of the 1963–64 season, Bill Shankly's first title-winning team featured two players, Roger Hunt and Ian St John, who both scored at least twenty goals in that campaign. We had become the first Liverpool team to match their achievement because, by that stage of the season, Luis Suárez had scored twenty-nine and Daniel Sturridge had reached the twenty-goal mark.

Shankly's team, exactly half a century earlier, had done much else that was identical to us. They had also beaten

Manchester United 1–0 at home, and 3–0 away. On 30 March 1964 they had climbed to the top of the table by beating Tottenham Hotspur – just as we did on that very same date against Spurs. The spirit of Shankly never quite leaves this club.

I led Liverpool out into the commotion and colour of a sun-kissed day at Anfield. Bill Shankly's granite face stared down from a massive red flag as 'You'll Never Walk Alone' rang out with fresh fervour.

Silence soon descended on Anfield. We were just two days away from the twenty-fifth anniversary of Hillsborough. A red-and-yellow mosaic spread out across the Kop in honour of those who had died on 15 April 1989. It was a simple, powerful combination of all the fans we had lost over such a significant span of time: *96 – 25 years.*

Manchester City's players, wearing sky blue as usual, were bowed and respectful, their backs to the mosaic. We faced the Kop and I made a point of looking up at the message, and remembering everything we had been through as a football club, and as a family in Huyton. I was in the middle of our Liverpool line-up. It seemed fitting that I stood between Luis Suárez, the greatest footballer I had ever played with, and Jordan Henderson, who would eventually replace me as club captain when my time came to leave Liverpool. Luis held me around the waist and Jordan gripped my shoulders. I stood tall. I was sad, but much prouder still.

At the whistle, ending a minute's silence, a roar broke out across Anfield. Our line of red separated and I walked forward, turning my mind back to the game. All around me my teammates applauded. Jordan, already sounding a leader, yelled out his encouragement to everyone.

Brendan Rodgers had picked the same starting eleven which had defeated West Ham a week earlier. We were happy that Sergio Agüero, City's title-winning striker, struggling for fitness after injury, was on the bench. They still had a fine side – including Hart, Pablo Zabaleta, Vincent Kompany, Yaya Touré and David Silva. Yaya's brother, Kolo, was on our bench.

It felt as if we were about to play a cup final; and I had not slept well. Before each match we're given little books of analysis to help us prepare. I'd sat on my hotel bed, studying every set piece, both in defence and attack. I overanalysed everything that night and it just felt like a release to finally be out on the pitch.

The familiar old noise of Anfield calmed me. I looked around. We were ready.

Joe Hart took a goal kick which Skrtel cleared with his head. The ball sailed towards Coutinho who flicked it on to Henderson. Jesús Navas tried to close down Henderson but his outstretched foot only managed to divert the ball towards his own goal and the lurking figure of Suárez. His back was jammed against Martín Demichelis, City's pony-tailed central defender, but Suárez spun away. Gaël Clichy clattered towards him, but Suárez bumped him away and broke into space. Suddenly, his wit and strength had carved out an opening.

Three City players ran towards him but Sterling had read Suárez's mind. He darted into the opening. Suárez slipped the ball to him, just inside the City box. Sterling showed brilliant composure and skill. He checked, cut inside Kompany and then, as the defender tried to recover, Sterling went back outside and clipped the ball past Hart. It was a lovely goal. Sterling ran towards Suárez. He was so excited he did not even do his usual celebration where his hand covered his face. 1–0 after six minutes.

Sterling was playing down the middle because we knew that their midfielders were going to press high. Yaya Touré is a great player, and a real threat when he rampages forward, but Brendan had stressed that, on the counter, we could catch him out of position. The plan was for Sterling to take advantage of those sudden gaps and run hard at the heart of their defence.

Touré injured his groin after nineteen minutes, following a long-range pop at goal, and City looked weakened as he limped off to be replaced by Javi García. Sterling was rampant and he set up Sturridge, whose shot flashed past the post.

After twenty-five minutes we had a corner. I allowed Coutinho to take it and, from his perfect delivery, I powered a header towards goal. A diving Hart deflected it over the bar for another corner. I took this next one and aimed for Skrtel at the near post. It was a set piece we had worked on in training that week. My delivery had been on the money for months and I was in the mood for another. I hit it sweetly into the exact area where Skrtel wanted it. My set-piece homework had paid off. Kompany failed to track him and Skrtel climbed free and, with a fast swivel of his neck, the ball flew from his flashing bald head past Hart. It was simple. It was devastating.

Anfield exploded. Skrtel and I met near the corner flag and fell on top of each other, rolling around on the grass like helplessly giggling kids as 40,000 people in the crowd of 44,000 went absolutely crazy. The blue away end didn't move. It barely made a sound as the rest of the ground roared and screamed with happiness. 2–0. It felt like we were closing in on the title, an unstoppable force in red.

We were comfortable. We were cruising.

At the other end of the pitch Mignolet came out and gathered a corner. But it was a sign of intent from City. Slowly, they began to play with more purpose. We still looked settled at the back. Even from another Samir Nasri corner, which Kompany headed towards goal, we stayed strong. Little Raheem Sterling, as powerful as he is small, nodded it off the line. It bounced up and Johnson, who was as brave as a lion, headed it away again and, in the scramble, Mignolet scooped it up in his arms.

There was time for one more City attack. In the last minute of the half, Navas crossed from their right flank. Fernandinho struck a flying half-volley which Mignolet did well to push away at full stretch. We needed to regroup, and just breathe again. City, after being all over the place for half an hour, dazzled by Liverpool's tempo, pressing and some clinical quality, had gained a foothold in the match. I knew it was a long way from being over.

City fought back even more strongly when we came out again. But we played calmly and clearly until they made a big change. The introduction of James Milner, after fifty minutes, meant they were much more direct and purposeful. We were working harder than ever to contain the blue waves – while still causing them problems through Suárez and, especially, Sterling, who was in storming form. Suárez went down too easily, diving, and City appealed frantically for his second yellow card. Mark Clattenburg, the referee, ignored them and we exhaled again. Earlier, he had told me to have a little word with Luis. He was playing close to the edge and I needed to make sure he did not cross the line.

Our problems were mounting. Edin Džeko, out wide on the left, played the ball inside to Fernandinho, who surged across the pitch, moving deep into our territory, before finding Milner, running hard on the right. City were stretching us now. Milner, my England teammate, played a quick one-two with Fernandinho and, close to goal, slid the ball to Silva, who, opening up his body as he fell, used his left foot to arc it past Mignolet. City had pulled a goal back after fifty-two minutes.

Silva shimmered with menace. We back-pedalled and fretted as he fizzed in a dangerous ball which Džeko just missed. This was worrying. We had not even reached the hour mark. For the first thirty minutes it had seemed surprisingly easy. And then it had become a yo-yo game, up and down, round and round. Apart from Silva's skilful probing, Milner had given them a lot more width. City were getting behind us and we were wobbling.

In the sixty-second minute they played an intricate move. Clichy to Nasri, back to Clichy overlapping down the left, and then square to Milner and on to Silva, their magician. Silva back-heeled it to Nasri, who returned it to Silva. The Spaniard tried to jab it across the face of the goal to the waiting Džeko. The ball ballooned off Johnson and into our net.

An own goal: 2–2. I felt my head slump. Mignolet sat on the pitch, arms on knees, shaking his head. A tiny blue section was a noisy hive. The rest of the ground had become a graveyard.

I tried to drive us forward but it didn't feel like we had much left. After our long run of winning games we seemed depleted. I was even more worried now. I knew that this was City's last big test of the season. If they could hold us to a draw, their final fixtures looked relatively easy. We had to get a winner.

Agüero came on. There was more trouble ahead. García found Agüero and the Argentine striker skipped down the left channel. I was just inside our half but I sprinted back as hard as I could. The warning signals were loud and scary. Agüero skinned Skrtel. Our defence fell wide open. Sakho and I were trying desperately to get back in time but it was no use. Agüero saw Silva. He was unmarked and close to goal. Agüero clipped it across and Silva's foot stretched out to poke it home. He missed the ball by millimetres. We had, somehow, avoided conceding another goal. Silva got up and put his head in his hands. He knew he should have buried us.

I was talking loudly again. I was giving us direction and encouragement. We were still in a game we thought we had won, and then thought we had lost. There was still time for Liverpool.

Johnson took a throw-in near their corner flag. Clichy

nodded clear. It bounced towards Kompany. The City captain, one of the best defenders in the Premier League, and one of the first names I had written down when I'd selected my team of the previous season, moved towards the ball. No Liverpool player was near him. Kompany tried to clear it but the ball sliced off his boot towards Coutinho.

Philippe Coutinho hit it cleanly. Boom! The ball flew towards the City net. Hart dived to his left. He had no chance against an incredible strike.

*Goal!* Coutinho, Coutinho, Coutinho. Philippe, you little beauty.

As we chased, caught and embraced Coutinho, Brendan Rodgers raced onto the pitch. He was punching thin air as if on his way to a heavyweight knockout. The City juggernaut was down.

Liverpool 3, Manchester City 2.

Kompany looked devastated. Fate had intervened. A slice by him, and a slice of luck for us.

Twelve minutes were still left. Twelve more minutes of agony. Twelve minutes to the biggest three points of my career.

Victor Moses came on for Coutinho. He ran hard at the City defence. Kompany, this time, held firm. He tackled Moses and the ball spun away into open space. Henderson and Nasri both rushed to win it. There was such momentum in Henderson's run that he knocked Nasri off his feet.

Clattenburg reached for his top pocket, and pulled out a card. It was red. Henderson was off. No one argued with the decision. At that precise moment no one realized just how significant Henderson's red card would prove. He will have learnt a lot from the bitter consequences.

Then, I just knew we needed to cling on. City poured forward again and Demichelis pumped it long, one last time.

It didn't matter. The referee blew his whistle even as the ball flew back into our half. It was over. We had won ten games in a row. We had beaten Manchester City.

The title felt so close now, I wanted to cry. Mignolet, Sakho and Flanagan hugged me. All the emotion tumbled out of me. While they held me I lifted my head skywards. I could not blink back the tears. The relief was overwhelming.

I used my right arm to wipe my eyes. Luis Suárez joined in the celebration. He and the others clutched me.

Anfield watched us. Our fans were not even singing. They were just clapping in joy and almost disbelief. Maybe they were too choked up, like me, to sing. The applause rolled on as City's players trudged towards the tunnel.

I broke free. Again, I brought my arm up to my face, as if I might hide my crying. Skrtel and Johnson reached me next. I was surrounded by a crowd of my teammates. Sterling ran across and jumped on the back of Flano. Joe Allen snuck into the pack. I now wanted my team around me even more. I pulled them together in a tight huddle in the middle of the pitch. I had no idea that a Sky camera was tracking me. I was oblivious to everyone but my Liverpool teammates. They were babbling with excitement.

I needed to talk to them. I needed to tell them that, despite my tears, it was not yet over.

This was the best chance we'd ever had to win the league; the best chance Liverpool had had in twenty-four long years. The players were celebrating. I had been celebrating. But I didn't want us to let it go now. My speech wasn't planned. I just knew I had to get over the message that, look, we've had another scare. We've won a game that could have gone either way. Let's get a grip and get ready to start all over again. I didn't realize how emotional I was until I watched it back much later. I was just desperate to grab hold of the players and make them understand what we needed to do in the week ahead before we next played.

I could feel them closing in tightly around me, their heads down as they listened. My voice was hoarse and ragged, my Scouse accent ringing around the huddle: 'This does not fucking slip now! This does not fucking slip! Listen. Listen. This is gone. We go to Norwich. And we go to do exactly the same. We go again. *Come on!*'

The players gave me a little roar. The huddle parted. I turned to the Kop. I lifted my hands above my head in gratitude. They were singing now with belief and certainty.

*And now you're gonna believe us, now you're gonna believe us, now you're gonna believe us . . . we're gonna win the league . . . we're gonna win the league . . . !*

The old song echoed around Anfield as I walked away, feeling suddenly drained and exhausted. I had just played the longest match of my life.

We were back two days later. It was an even more beautiful afternoon. The sky above Liverpool was a clear and sparkling blue. Sunshine streamed across Anfield during the twenty-fifth anniversary memorial service for the ninety-six victims of Hillsborough. Twenty-four thousand people had filed into the ground, filling the Kop, and also taking their seats in the Main Stand and Paddock, Lower Anfield Road end and Lower Centenary stands.

Ninety-six seats were left empty, a scarf covering each, in memory of every fan we had lost. It still felt raw because the new inquest had begun. There had been six days, so far, of brutal testimony from those who had survived, about those who had died.

Sitting in the Kop, staring down at the pitch, the grass looked very green. My gaze was pulled back towards the centre circle.

The number *96* filled almost the whole circle. The *9* and the *6* had each been made out of hundreds of football scarves, the colours of every team you've ever seen. They lay on the ground but it did not look as if they had just fallen. Each had been draped so carefully that, together with every other scarf, it helped make the outline of the number stand out so vividly.

A little further back there was a circular memento. It stood out in red with the number 96, again, at its heart. Scarves also ringed this tribute which carried the words:

*Never Forgotten*
*96*
*25 Years*

It had also been a sunny spring day at Hillsborough on 15 April 1989 – until the blackness descended. Twenty-five years of dark grief and pain had followed.

In the first years, every Hillsborough anniversary service had felt like a funeral. It felt as though we were burying every one of those ninety-six bodies again. But, as the years passed, the nature and atmosphere of the service altered. The twentieth anniversary changed everything. Anger had spilled out from the Kop that day. The quiet acceptance of a funeral gave way to a demand for justice. Five years on, the mood was different again. There was still sadness, and remembrance, but now there was hope and pride too.

Football can be a greedy and nasty business. It can be crude and cruel. But there are days when the simple beauty and dignity of the game, illustrated by the people who love it, make believers of us all over again.

This was such a day. And even though it was a day when not a single ball was kicked across the Anfield turf it felt even more special. This was a day when football felt pure and good – and a symbol of hope amid the waste and deceit of Hillsborough which had scarred Liverpool for so long. It was a day when all our petty rivalries and burning ambitions were set aside for something far more powerful.

The mood was captured by Everton's manager, Roberto Martínez, a Spaniard, who expressed his empathy and solidarity with Liverpool:

I was only fifteen in April 1989, a football-mad kid from a football-mad family – like many of you here today. And when we heard the news about Hillsborough, as a family we could not comprehend the pain or horror of families receiving the news their loved ones would not be coming home from a football match.

How can you die watching the game you love? That is not right. That is not fair. What happened afterwards was not fair or right either. To have to fight for the good name of those you lost is appalling.

Everton's manager described the work of the Hillsborough Family Support Group as being

truly remarkable. For twenty-five years you have gained the respect of those within and beyond football and the city. I know I don't have to tell you Everton are with you. You know that. We are with you today at Goodison Park, where fans are gathering with the board, staff and players because they want to send their prayers across to you, across Stanley Park.

Applause resounded around Anfield. We clapped hard for Everton, in debt and gratitude, and forgot about our footballing rivalry for the afternoon.

Roberto and Brendan Rodgers had both been born in 1973. They were just seven years older than me. I was conscious how much closer I was in age to Roberto and Brendan than to some of my young teammates. The whole squad sat together on the

Kop, wearing our club ties and blazers. I sat right behind Kenny Dalglish, Brendan's predecessor who had also been Liverpool's manager at Hillsborough, and who had felt the hurt of the families more than anyone else at the club.

Our own manager spoke next. Brendan paid tribute to Roberto and also to some of Liverpool's greatest players as well as to Bill Shankly and Kenny Dalglish:

> I walk in every day past the statue of Bill Shankly and the European Cup at our Melwood training ground. So you don't struggle for inspiration when you are Liverpool manager. But without doubt the single biggest source of inspiration for me is every match day at Anfield, when I arrive at this ground and see the Hillsborough memorial and the ninety-six names. Those who we lost, and those of you who have fought and campaigned tirelessly on their behalf and on behalf of the survivors, you are the true inspiration for us.

At exactly six minutes past three o'clock, the names of those who had died were read out. All across Merseyside, at the same time, church bells tolled ninety-six times. It was hushed inside Anfield, with the silence broken only by the echo of each name. I was conscious of how long it took, and how sad it sounded, to hear all ninety-six names being read in alphabetical order – from Jack Anderson to Graham John Wright.

Andy Burnham, the shadow health secretary, who had been barracked five years earlier, received a standing ovation for the work he had done since in forcing through a new inquest. He said that the anger shown towards him that day, as the Minister of Culture, Media and Sport in 2009, had helped him to

> find the political courage to do something . . . Five years ago things changed, not because of me but because of all of you. Things changed because you made your voices heard and thank

God you did. Your voices carried off this Kop into every living room in the land and into the heart of the establishment. I knew you were right and they were wrong.

Andy Burnham also said he had asked his mother what he should say. She gave him a simple message. He looked straight at me and all the Liverpool players. 'She told me to wish you all the best for the league and to say how fitting it would be if you won it in this of all years.'

Anfield erupted; and chanting broke out. *We're gonna win the league . . . we're gonna win the league . . . !*

He then remembered how his speech in 2009 had been interrupted by a heckler who shouted a stark word – 'Justice' – at him:

That was the moment the dam burst. You were asking the most profound question about our country and how it is run. How can it be that an entire city shouted injustice for twenty years and no one was listening? There is still an uncertain road ahead but the country is with you now. The families will prevail because of all of you. You have made this city stronger and you will make our country fairer. You have given hope to people the world over. What was your call five years ago is my call today: Justice for the 96!

The crowd prepared to sing 'You'll Never Walk Alone' with Gerry Marsden, the man who had taken the Rodgers and Hammerstein song to number one in the early sixties, leading the way.

'Go on, Gerry!' a voice at the back of the Kop shouted.

'All right?' Gerry replied. Anfield rocked with laughter.

'When you walk, through the storm,' Gerry and Anfield began, softly, gently, 'hold your head up high, and don't be afraid of the dark . . .'

It was almost unbearably moving – especially when the singing was mingled with cheering as we reached, 'Walk on, walk on . . . with hope in your heart,' and ninety-six red balloons were cut free in the middle of the pitch. They drifted up into the blue sky while we sang on.

As I followed the flight of one balloon, thinking of Jon-Paul, I remembered the words just spoken by Margaret Aspinall, who had lost her eighteen-year-old son, James, at Hillsborough.

The courageous leader of the Hillsborough Family Support Group turned to Brendan, me and the Liverpool squad. She said, as we chased the league title everyone craved, that we could draw inspiration from the families. 'Stress can be very difficult,' Margaret said, 'but stress can also be good. It gives you fight and I know that's what you are going to do to get this championship.'

A huge roar rang around Anfield. Margaret smiled. 'I just hope I haven't put any more pressure on the players . . .'

We were not alone in facing pressure. All of Liverpool was consumed by the fight for justice and a slice of football delight. As 'You'll Never Walk Alone' faded away, Anfield broke into a long and sustained chant:

*Justice . . . for the 96 . . . Justice . . . for the 96 . . . Justice . . . for the 96!*

There was applause again, long and loud. As the players walked around the stadium we heard, *We love you Liverpool, we do, we love you Liverpool, we do . . .*

Suddenly, almost as if by magic, that fevered chant and the applause broke into another rasping old football song again.

On a sunlit Tuesday afternoon, walking past our fans, full of hope and love, I listened as Anfield sang with one voice:

*And now you're gonna believe us, now you're gonna believe us, now you're gonna believe us . . . we're gonna win the league . . . we're gonna win the league . . . !*

\*

The league table told a pretty story when we went to Norwich. Liverpool, seventy-seven points after thirty-four games. Chelsea, seventy-five points after thirty-five games. Manchester City, seventy-one points after thirty-three games. The two matches that mattered to us since we had beaten City had both gone our way. Manchester City had drawn 2–2 at home against Sunderland on 16 April, dropping another two points. And on 19 April 2014, the day before we played Norwich City, Chelsea had lost, shockingly, 1–0 at home to Sunderland.

I was ready to give the freedom of Liverpool to the whole of Sunderland, and their relegation-haunted manager Gus Poyet. In the space of three days Sunderland had taken five points from our closest rivals. Everything, on the outside, seemed to be falling our way.

We still had problems. Jordan Henderson had been suspended for three games after his red card against Man City. I knew it would hurt us. Jordan was a big cog in the red machine. We would miss his energy and the cohesion he gave to the team. Jordan's importance to us was made obvious by the fact that Brendan asked him to travel down with the team to East Anglia, and to sit on the bench even though he would not be able to kick a ball. His spirit and his leadership would help Brendan and me.

Daniel Sturridge was also out against Norwich, with a strained hamstring, but we still had Luis Suárez. Norwich were Luis's bunny. He had played Norwich in five previous games, and had scored eleven goals against them. I was convinced that Luis would score at Carrow Road again – and even if I was wrong we had other teammates who could take us a step closer to the title.

It was apparent that Philippe Coutinho and Raheem Sterling, who had both scored such crucial goals against City, had become significant players for Liverpool. Coutinho had been brilliant since day one. He came to us as a twenty-year-old from Inter Milan in January 2013 and he had grown month by month. It was sometimes mind-blowing to see what he could do with a ball at his feet in training. Philippe had the quickest feet in the squad and he was the one player I'd be a little bit wary of getting too close to in tight situations during training. Coutinho could make a fool of you. He was that good – and I believed he was on his way to becoming Liverpool's main man and a top player in world football. Watch this space.

Coutinho suited being a gifted number 10. We called them magical players but I think Brendan was the first to refer to him as 'the magician' – and the name just stuck. There was no better word to describe Coutinho on form. He was also a fantastic kid. I loved him to bits, just the way he went about his life and his football. Philippe was very quiet and very happy on Merseyside. And out on the pitch, where it mattered most, he was a dream to play alongside. Coutinho never hid. He always wanted the ball. Of course he'd had some tough games where he had faded but he was still very young. I knew he had a wonderful talent which would shine in the hard games we still faced.

It also helped that, as a fellow South American, Philippe revered Luis. He saw on a daily basis how Luis's hard work and desire to improve made him one of the world's great players. Philippe was inspired – and he was also bolstered by the close-knit friendship of all the Spanish and South American players led by Luis and Lucas Leiva.

Lucas had become one of our longest-serving players. He might have been a Brazilian but he now had Liverpool running through his veins. Lucas was a good friend, a fine player and a rock we could lean on. He would never let us down. Coutinho was bolstered and strengthened by Lucas at every turn.

Raheem Sterling was different in the sense that he came to

the club from London when he was fifteen. He was part of the Liverpool Academy. When he first joined the set-up it was obvious that he had the potential to become a very good player. I just expected it to take longer than it did for him to explode onto the scene with Liverpool and England. Raheem wouldn't say a word at first but he grew with every session and he came out of his shell.

You look at Raheem and you're thinking, 'Kid, you're very small.' But the shock with Raheem was found in the difference between looking at him and thinking, 'Oh yeah, there's a sixteen- or seventeen-year-old frame there' – and then discovering that he's got the strength and power of a man. Even more than an ordinary man. Sterling could always mix it with hard men like Martin Skrtel. No problem. Sterling could carry Skrtel on his back. I've seen him do it in one-on-one situations where he's gone up alone against big strong guys like Mamadou Sakho and Kolo Touré. He'd take on a six-foot-four-inch giant and make it look easy. It was all natural strength because I had never seen him in the gym or pushing weights. He just had it. He was strong and talented.

Raheem was also much tougher mentally than some people might have imagined. I think he was born with that tenacity but, at the Academy, it was enhanced. He was around tough Scouse kids and he quickly learnt the Liverpool mentality and understood what the fans expected. He also had to get used to the demands of playing with the likes of Jamie Carragher and myself. We would be on top of him all the time. Carra and I never really criticized people for making mistakes. But we went in hard on anyone who showed a lack of effort or failed to be ruthless. Raheem had it anyway, that relentless style of playing, but he added an edge.

He would give you everything in training and in matches. Raheem would never ever shirk no matter who you put him up against. He wouldn't let you down – which was very rare for a winger. In my experience wingers can be magnificent or they can be frustrating. They can leave you wanting to pull your hair out. But if Raheem had a bad game it would never be through lack of effort or desire.

So we had the players. But we had the tension and the nerves too. I was guilty of obsessing about winning the league. I probably wanted it too much and so I was worried that, after the high of beating City, some of the team might have been thinking, 'Oh, it's only Norwich next. We'll beat them easily.'

That was the wrong mentality to take into a tricky game, with the home team fighting relegation and you chasing the championship. So I compared the importance of the game against Norwich to a Champions League final in Istanbul. It was my way of hammering home a message that said, 'Look, let's get our heads on straight for Norwich now. If we blow this one, we blow everything.' I wanted the players to start thinking about Norwich immediately after beating City.

Looking back, I can see now that may have been a mistake. Such intensity can sometimes have the reverse effect – especially on the younger players. They can go in a bit edgy, and feel a little scared, whereas you want them going into such a big game feeling confident and as relaxed as possible. I now know I had showed too much emotion in the huddle, and in the build-up to Norwich. But it was hard when I wanted it so badly.

Brendan did a fine job of getting us ready to explode out of the blocks every week – and so he helped channel the tension into something more positive as we walked out at Carrow Road for another Sunday lunchtime kick-off on 20 April. Lucas and Joe Allen were back in the team in place of Henderson and Sturridge. We were soon on our way with another flying start.

Allen, Flanagan and Coutinho exchanged passes before the Brazilian slid the ball inside to Sterling. He was twenty yards out but Sterling didn't hesitate. He let rip and his shot dipped and bent past John Ruddy in the Norwich goal. Sterling ran all the way to the touchline to embrace Brendan – and they were soon surrounded by red shirts jumping up and down. So much for my prematch stress. We were a goal up after four minutes.

Suárez made it 2–0 seven minutes later. Flanagan cantered down the left flank and passed it to Sterling. This time, instead of showing fierce power, Sterling displayed his cool vision. He picked out Suárez in the penalty area. Sterling's pass was so exquisite that Suárez could side-foot the ball into the net. The way in which Luis ran to Raheem, his finger jabbing in delight at his teammate, told us exactly how much he owed to the younger player. Suárez had just scored his thirtieth goal but he looked ready to share it with Sterling.

Our energy soon dipped. Without Henderson to drive us forward, and with me still playing deep, we struggled the rest of that half to impose ourselves. It was as if we had eased down a gear. Both Brendan and I saw the danger signals. I was relieved when, at half-time, he made a tactical change.

We had been playing a diamond formation and Norwich had done the same. After the early goals they matched us. We had five in the diamond, and so did they. Brendan's game is built on outnumbering the opposition. If they play three in midfield we'll more than likely play four. They go to four, we'll go five. So, at half-time, Brendan decided to play Coutinho in the middle of the diamond.

It was a smart move and we looked more controlled. But I felt a little chill when, just like City had done, Norwich made it 2–1 with over half an hour to go. Mignolet came out for a hopeful punt of a cross. He didn't gather it. The ball bounced loose and Hooper rammed it home. I was not sure we would survive another test if, somehow, Norwich clawed back one more and made it 2–2.

It helped having Suárez menace Norwich up front. He came close and then, just after an hour, Sterling conjured up a goal out of nothing. A lazy pass from Bradley Johnson in the Norwich midfield was intercepted by Sterling inside our half. He ran with the ball at speed, Suárez racing ahead as three Norwich defenders tried to work out who was the biggest danger – Sterling or Suárez. They had been spooked by Suárez so many times, not least when he'd scored his scorching hat-trick against them earlier that season. And so they hung back from Sterling. He ran and ran, while they and Suárez waited for the pass. It never came. Sterling swerved past the first defender and swept into the area. His shot took a deflection off the retreating Johnson – giving Ruddy no chance.

Robert Snodgrass made it a horrible last thirteen minutes when his header looped over Mignolet to narrow our lead to a single goal again. Norwich were desperate for a point and they fought hard. They had one last chance when their substitute, Ricky van Wolfswinkel, was allowed a free header. Mignolet, diving low, saved it. We had won, 3–2 for the second game in a row.

Our place in the following season's Champions League had been confirmed. My mind wandered back to the wretched preseason when Luis Suárez had been banned and banished and determined to leave Liverpool and the evening I had felt too miserable even to eat the meal Alex had prepared, because the idea of Champions League qualification seemed impossible without Suárez. If he had left, we would have been doomed to mid-table mediocrity. I was glad we had fought so hard to keep him.

Life, and football, changes so quickly. My preseason dream,

and our objective as a squad, had been fulfilled. We were back amongst the best in Europe. But now that we had done it, nine months on, that achievement was not enough. We had to return to Europe as the champions of England. We had three games left to secure our destiny. The hardest match of all, Chelsea, was next, in just seven days' time.

# 8. The Slip

It was close to midnight and the house was quiet. Alex and the girls were asleep. I was forty hours away from the biggest league game of my career and it felt like my head and my back had both gone. Stretched out on a couch, the lights dimmed and my phone glowing in the murky light, I took another painkiller and checked the time again. It was late.

One of the hazards of being a professional footballer is that, far from feeling like supreme athletes, we often seem a little broken. Our backs ache, our knees hurt, our ankles throb. We break bones, tear muscles, snap ligaments, strain tendons and – well, in my case at least – suffer a lacerated penis. There have been few games, especially since I've been in my thirties, where I've started without having some kind of twinge or concern in the build-up. We get used to playing through pain. But this was far worse.

If we had been facing Oldham Athletic in an FA Cup tie, rather than Chelsea in a title decider, the decision would have been made. I would have been out of the game. For the previous three days I had been suffering from a sore and inflamed back. And then, out of nowhere, the hurt became so acute it felt as if I could not bend over or even move. Hours later I was still pinned to the spot. In agony, I could not even haul myself up and hobble towards bed.

I'd had to take extra care of my back for years. To help manage the stiffness I travelled down regularly to Milton Keynes to see a specialist who used therapeutic injections. I had been so caught up in the title race, and I had been playing well, that I had almost shunted the back issue out of my head for months. But the body is unforgiving. My lower spine pulsed with pain.

I had struggled in training on Wednesday and Thursday, but that was nothing compared with how I had felt earlier that day, during our Friday session, our final piece of intensive work before Chelsea. The medical team had worked on me for hours in the afternoon. Zaf Iqbal, Liverpool's team doctor, had dosed me up with the maximum permissible pain relief and advised me to rest as much as I could at home.

Nothing worked. Ibuprofen was hopeless, Voltarol wasn't strong enough and even Diazepam, which is meant to ease muscle spasms as well as being a tranquillizer, had little impact. The pain deepened.

My head was full of Chelsea, too. It seemed cruel that, having seen off Man City, we had to play Chelsea in our next game at Anfield. I'd had so many bruising encounters with Chelsea over the years. There had been a long run where it seemed as if, almost every year, we were involved in an epic Champions League tie with them. And there had been so many other league and cup matches. We had won a few, and lost a few.

I had come so close to leaving Liverpool for Chelsea in 2005. The reason I stayed in the end was that Liverpool meant so much to me both as a club and as a city. Chelsea and London didn't mean anything. During those distressing days when I felt so torn about whether or not I should stay or go I never once thought to myself, 'I want to play for Chelsea instead of Liverpool.' My head was almost turned because I was thinking, 'I'd love to play for José Mourinho.' I was certain that, under José, I would win all the trophies I craved.

As a manager, Mourinho has everything. He's a great tactician and motivator. He coaches well. He buys well. He fights hard for his squad. He helps his players improve. And Chelsea's impossibly rich owner has always backed him with money and power.

José Mourinho, rather than Chelsea, turned my head. I think he could have got more out of me as a player. I know he would have brought me success. But if I had gone to Stamford Bridge in 2005 who knows what direction my career would have taken. Mourinho left for Inter and Real Madrid, but we all knew he would be back in west London one day.

Between July 2005 and May 2015 Chelsea won the Champions League, two Premier League titles, four FA Cups, the Europa League and two League Cups. That's ten big trophies. In that same period at Liverpool, I have won an FA Cup and a League Cup. Chelsea 10, Liverpool 2: that's why the chase for the league title in 2014 ate me up so much. I wanted that huge championship for Liverpool and, yes, also as a seal of vindication on my certainty, even today, that I made the right decision.

The decision boiled down to a simple choice. Do I want to win trophies with Chelsea – or do I stay loyal to Liverpool? It would have been great to have won so much, and a good experience, particularly under Mourinho, but it would have cost me the love and respect of the Liverpool fans. What mattered more to me? Medals and titles or love and respect?

Chelsea fans are not my people. We've all worked that out over the years. I belong to Liverpool and that's why I decided it would mean so much more if I could win two, three or even four trophies with them. Those victories would last me a lifetime.

Mourinho understood my reasons; but each time he came in for me he was very persuasive. I liked the way he spoke to me and I could see how most of his players were ready to die for him. I remembered him winning the Champions League with

Inter Milan and the devastation of his players when he left. You could see it in their faces. I understood how they felt because they had shared such a big moment in their careers together. I never had that with Rafa Benítez. I would have had it with José Mourinho.

It was clear that, tactically, he could set up his team to win any football match. He could spoil, he could fight, he could do whatever you needed because he was a pure winner. But, more than that, he created a special bond with each squad he managed. You heard it in the way his players spoke about him. You saw it in the way they played for him.

For me, the ideal situation would obviously have been for Mourinho to have managed Liverpool. He was linked with a move to Anfield a couple of times but it never materialized. I know I'm biased, but I think it would have been a perfect match. The Liverpool fans would have loved him, and he would have known exactly how to turn that love into adoration. He would have loved managing at Anfield, too. He always told me about his deep respect for our supporters. José would have had a fantastic time bringing huge success to Liverpool.

Instead, he now stood in the path of Liverpool and me in our quest for an elusive league title. The most difficult manager to beat in the Premier League, and probably Europe, would be in the opposite corner. I knew Mourinho well enough to expect our biggest test of the season. Chelsea's attention might have switched to the Champions League – they were between semi-final legs against Atlético Madrid – but they could still win the league and I was absolutely certain Mourinho would be plotting and scheming to overtake us. He was too proud a man not to want Chelsea to shoot us down at Anfield.

He might have liked and respected Brendan Rodgers, one of his former protégés from their time together at Chelsea, but the master would not enjoy seeing an apprentice effect-ively win the league title against him. It made me nervous, thinking about Mourinho and everything he would have in store for us.

Only the pain in my back could distract me from Mourinho and Chelsea. Late that Friday night it was so bad I felt like climbing the walls of a house which was heavy and silent with sleep. I picked up my phone. It was after midnight. I knew Chris Morgan would understand if a text from me suddenly beeped on his phone.

Hi mate. Sorry. I know it's late. You awake?

Chris pinged me straight back:

Yeah. How are you feeling? How's the back?

I was always going to be straight with Chris:

Head's gone. Worst it's felt. Just taken another ibuprofen and Voltarol. ☹

Chris kept our texts so I can now see that, at the end of each stark message, I added a very sad face. I was resorting to emoti-cons at the dead of night.

Chris had grown used to my sad faces and so he tried to boost me with his texted reply:

When it can go quickly from feeling good to bad, it can also go quickly from feeling bad to good. Don't worry. We'll sort it out tomorrow. Get in a comfy position, relax. Don't keep testing it. Try and get some sleep.

I didn't feel any better. I sent another text:

I've had three hours treatment today, been in the pool, I've rested it, I've had anti-inflams, ibuprofen, diazepam and it's the worst its felt. I'm not confident at all. Night mate. ☹ ☹

It was quarter past midnight and my face was as sad as my text.

Seven hours later, at exactly 7.15 a.m. on the day before the game, Chris texted me again:

**How are you?**

**Not good.** ☹ ☹

We arranged to meet at Melwood at 9 a.m. Chris found me fifteen minutes early. I was eating my breakfast. It was obvious I was in a bad way. I was having to slide my whole body along the long seat before gingerly getting up. He didn't say this to me then but told me later he'd thought: 'Oh no. We're in trouble here.'

In the pool it felt a little bit better. The medical team then did a lot of work on my back and Zaf Iqbal gave me a general anti-inflammatory injection, of Voltarol. They strapped me up so that my back would be supported. Zaf knew that I was determined to play against Chelsea and let me go out for a very light training session.

Zaf had given Brendan the worrying update. He told him we had a real concern – but we needed to see how I coped with training.

Out on the Melwood pitch, I didn't feel right. 'My back felt better than I thought it would,' I said to Chris afterwards. 'But I couldn't play with it.'

We went back to the pool. Zaf and Chris were in a huddle while I was in the water. I moved towards them. I was clinging to the side of the pool.

'Zaf . . . Chris . . . ,' I said. 'Can you get me through this game?'

'Yeah,' Chris said. Zaf was also positive. 'We'll find the best way . . .'

The doc took Chris out for a chat. I stretched in the water, feeling the pain, and waited for their decision. I was still in agony.

They came back into the pool area together. 'OK, Stevie,' said Zaf. 'We can jab the joint.'

I nodded. I was ready for an injection that would take away the pain and allow me to play.

Zaf knelt down at the side of the pool. He explained that it would be a facet injection of cortisone. A facet jab anaesthetizes the joints, reduces inflammation and blocks the pain. The cortisone would free me up and allow me to play.

Chris had pushed for it because he knew I would do anything medically permissible to get out onto the pitch. They'd done something similar with Daniel Agger, and it had worked. It was not a routine decision but, thirty hours before the Chelsea game, it was that or nothing.

'Let's go for it,' I said. I wanted the intervention and I didn't care about the possible consequences. I had to play against Chelsea.

Zaf arranged for a back specialist in St Helens to administer the injection. We walked into the consultancy room a few minutes before 1 p.m. I was anxious to get it done.

The injection brought immediate relief from the pain, as the medical team had predicted, and I could have skipped all the way back to the car. I had sudden confidence that I would be all right.

On Saturday night the Liverpool squad stayed, as usual, at the Hope Street Hotel. My back felt fine, and my head was better too. I still had Chelsea in mind, though, and after some physio and checks which gave me the all-clear to play, I mulled over a number of surreal coincidences. It was weird enough that our league destiny might turn on a match against the manager and the club that had impacted so much on the last nine years of my life. There were other jarring, painful connections between me and Chelsea, between us and them.

The game would feel like a cup final; and the last time I had played Chelsea in a cup final it had ended in disaster. In late February 2005, in the League Cup final held at the Millennium Stadium in Cardiff, we took a beautifully ridiculous early lead when John Arne Riise volleyed in a goal after just forty-five seconds. I was captaining Liverpool for the first time in a cup final and for much of that afternoon it seemed as if I was on course to lift the trophy.

It would have been a relief because, until then, it had been a difficult season. Liverpool were misfiring in the league and I was not willing to sign a new contract until the season ended and we would know if we had made the top four again. There was speculation that Chelsea were preparing a huge bid for me.

We were still winning 1–0, when catastrophe struck in the seventy-ninth minute. I jumped to clear Paulo Ferreira's free kick and attempted to head it away for a corner. Instead, I deflected it into my own net.

ITV's commentary summed up the views of many Liverpool and Chelsea fans in the depths of my personal devastation: 'Stevie Gerrard, many believe, has just scored his first of many goals for Chelsea – and he's scored it as a Liverpool player in a cup final.'

I was crushed by my own goal. The game went into extra time and Chelsea won 3–2.

Mourinho, who had been sent off after he made a point of shushing the Liverpool fans, holding a finger to his lips while he stalked the touchline, consoled our players at the final whistle. We were slumped on the ground. He was very classy in showing us respect – but of course it was blown up and attention focused almost solely on photographs of him comforting me. It was seen as the next stage in Chelsea's wooing of Gerrard.

All I cared about then was that we had lost – and it felt like it was all my fault. I felt I had let everyone down.

It got worse. After my dad had called me, supportive as always, saying, 'Keep your chin up. Forget about it,' a more worrying message arrived while we were being driven back in the team coach to Liverpool. My mate Bavo phoned to tell me that my mum was really upset. He suggested that I give her a couple of hours before I phoned. I texted Mum, telling her to call me whenever it suited her, and I wondered why she had taken the defeat so personally.

When she called me I went cold. Mum told me that, after my own goal, the Liverpool supporters around her and Alex had started abusing me viciously. 'That prick's done it on purpose,' they shouted. 'He wants to play for Chelsea. He wants the money. Him and his fucking missus just want that London money. Gerrard's a fucking traitor.'

I could deal with that but it really hurt when Mum told me that this small group of men in Liverpool shirts and scarves – I wouldn't call them supporters – started chanting that Alex was a slut. She was a slag. She was a piece of shit. They had no idea that they were sitting so close to my wife and to my mum.

We recovered, and we hardened ourselves. Liverpool knocked Chelsea out of the Champions League, in the ghost goal semi-final eight weeks later. But all those tangled memories were a reminder of how games between Liverpool and Chelsea could unleash dark and unsettling emotions.

More bizarrely, the last time we had played Chelsea at Anfield, on 21 April 2013, Luis Suárez had sunk his fangs into Branislav Ivanović. His ten-game ban had followed, with all the subsequent transfer speculation.

Suárez's actions had seemed even worse on a day when, before kick-off, we had honoured the memory of Anne Williams, who had campaigned on behalf of all the Hillsborough families. Anne's son had been one of the victims and her courage and persistence in helping lead the fight against the cover-up was celebrated with a minute's applause. The touching sound of Anfield clapping in unison was also our tribute to the people who had died a week earlier during the bombing of the Boston marathon. Our owners, Fenway, were based in Boston and so emotion swirled around Anfield before the game.

We should have been ecstatic after Luis's ninety-fifth minute equalizer in a pulsating 2–2 draw, or purring over his gorgeous first-time clip across goal that set up Daniel Sturridge for our opening goal. It would have even been acceptable if we had been shaking our heads over his handball – which presented Chelsea with a needless penalty from a Juan Mata corner.

Luis's frustration at that mistake unleashed the demons in him. He went past boiling point when he bit Ivanović. The outrage and long ban which followed were inevitable.

Millions of people had made their mind up and judged him without knowing Luis as a man. It was different in Uruguay. Luis is forgiven an awful lot quicker at home than in other countries. Luis probably can't get his head around the fact that he is judged differently in England than in Spain or Uruguay.

I could only judge him as a friend and as a teammate. I knew he had many faults but I found it difficult to criticize him as a young man, and a star in the spotlight. People make mistakes. We all do. I've certainly made a few, although I've never bitten anyone.

Luis knows that, in the heat of the moment, he can act terribly. His own wife, whom he loves more than anyone in the world, has criticized him for it. But how do you remove it entirely from someone with that fierce winner's mentality – the hunger and warrior spirit. Luis is one of the best players in the world because of that ferocious attitude. It's very rare that a player with Luis's talent doesn't make some big emotional mistakes during his career. I'd seen it with Zidane and his World Cup final head-butt. I'd seen it with Rooney and his red card in the European Championship. I was capable of moments of madness too. They happen in the hot, blurring moment and you regret it for months or even years afterwards.

I just loved having Luis in the same Liverpool side as me. And, despite the strange reunion at Anfield with Ivanović, I was very happy he would be lining up at home in a decisive match against Chelsea.

There was one more twist, too. Fernando Torres was on his way back to Anfield. He would be slaughtered by our fans; but I remembered Fernando fondly. How could I not when we'd played in so many great games together?

Fate has its way with football. If you had dreamed up the script from a Liverpool perspective it would have seemed impossible once Torres left. But it really did turn out that Torres made his Chelsea debut as a £50m player on 6 February 2011 at Stamford Bridge . . . against Liverpool. Our away supporters raged against him all afternoon and Torres was unusually subdued. I wondered if he was haunted by a giant banner at the Liverpool end: He Who Betrays Will Always Walk Alone.

Kenny Dalglish, our canny old manager, who was just acting as the caretaker then, following the sacking of Roy Hodgson, outwitted Mourinho. We won 1–0, the goal coming after a mix-up between Cech and Ivanović allowed Raul Meireles to stab home my cross at the far post. Torres lasted just sixty-six minutes before he was replaced by Salomon Kalou. His Chelsea career never really recovered from that moment and Liverpool's most bitterly passionate supporters regarded it as sweet justice for an act they saw as treachery.

Suárez had only been on the bench that afternoon, having

joined Liverpool twelve days earlier. Three years later, in April 2014, the contrast between Suárez's fortunes and the plight of Torres would be examined all over again at Anfield – even though I suspected that, this time, it would be Fernando who started the game on the bench.

Mourinho had been raging all week. Chelsea were being made to play Liverpool just three days before the second leg of their Champions League semi-final. He had threatened to pick a weakened side in protest. I would have loved it if Chelsea played their reserves against us. But I suspected he'd play one of his strongest teams. I knew Mourinho would bring his A game.

I was worried about how we were planning to play against Chelsea. I've never been able to say this in public before but I was seriously concerned that we thought we could blow Chelsea away. I sensed an overconfidence in Brendan's team talks. He thought we could go out and attack Chelsea – just as we had done against Manchester City and Norwich.

We played into Mourinho's hands. I feared it then, and I know it now. We should have gone into the game with a much more compact formation. We should have made ourselves hard to beat and spoilt the game and been ugly, just like they were. Maybe we could have then got the draw, and even the win we wanted.

As a player I'm more like Mourinho in that I don't mind winning ugly. I've won some of the biggest medals in my career through smash-and-grab tactics. Sometimes we've not been the better team but we've found a way to win. You need that mentality against a serial winner like Mourinho. We could blow away Arsenal and Everton because their defenders couldn't cope with our relentless pressure and tempo. But I felt we needed to approach a game against Chelsea very differently. A 0–0 Rafa-style draw would have worked for us.

I didn't sleep well that night. I was convinced Mourinho would have something up his tactical sleeve to block and hurt us. And we were in for severe trouble if we tried to play the same open and attacking football that had got us to this point. But, at the same time, it was not my place to knock on Brendan's door and discuss tactics with him. He would have been entitled, if I had done so, to tell me to piss off.

The game weighed on my mind. Should I say something to Brendan? He would decide the tactics.

I drove myself mad. My back was quiet, but my head was in turmoil. I kept it all to myself, tossing and turning, and hoping that everything would be fine on the day. On Hope Street, I felt moments of unsettling doubt.

## Anfield, Sunday, 27 April 2014

Mourinho surprised everyone. He picked a strong team but, in one very unexpected decision, he kept Gary Cahill on the bench and replaced him with Tomáš Kalas, a twenty-year-old Czech defender who'd made just two first-team appearances all season, both as an eighty-ninth minute substitute. Kalas had joked on Twitter, just two weeks earlier: 'I am a player for training sessions. If they need a cone, they put me there.'

A training-ground cone of a kid would surely have no chance against Luis Suárez. In the absence of John Terry, Ivanović had been moved across to play alongside Kalas in a makeshift central defence. But my heart didn't soar. I knew Mourinho had his plan in place. He made five other changes from the side that had lost to Sunderland. Ashley Cole, Frank Lampard, John Obi Mikel, André Schürrle and Demba Ba were all back.

We played the same team that had beaten Norwich – with

Daniel Sturridge, still recovering from his hamstring injury, on the bench.

It was another early Sunday-afternoon kick-off, another spring day full of sunshine, another gut-wrenching ninety minutes of tension ahead.

My least favourite referee, good old Martin Atkinson, was in charge. I might have guessed.

Little guesswork was needed to understand Chelsea's strategy under Mourinho. It was obvious after a couple of minutes. At the end of that bitter afternoon Brendan Rodgers for once allowed resentment to get in the way of his class and dignity. He said of Chelsea's defensive mindset:

> There were probably two buses parked today, instead of one. From the first minute they had ten men behind the ball. It was difficult because they virtually played right from the off with a back six. They had a back four, with two wingers back and then the midfield three in front of them. Just putting ten players right on your eighteen-yard box is not difficult to coach. We were the team that tried to win the game in a sporting manner.

It would be a defensive masterclass, as disciplined as it was cynical, but Brendan was infuriated by Chelsea's time-wasting. So was I. As early as the sixth minute Jon Flanagan and I were wrestling for the ball with Mourinho. We wanted a quick throw-in but the old schemer wouldn't allow it. He held the ball behind his back before, as we tried to take it off him, he threw it away. A few more seconds had been eaten up on the clock – and we already felt frustrated. Mourinho, grey and stubble-faced on the touchline, shrugged. He knew what he was doing.

Chelsea had come to spoil our party. Before every goal kick their keeper, Mark Schwarzer, would change sides in the box.

And when he had the ball in his hands he would hold on to it for four or five seconds longer than he needed to. Chelsea then tried to break the game up as much as possible, disrupting our rhythm at every opportunity.

Our first few corners produced nothing. And then, in the eleventh minute, we forced another down our right wing. Suárez took it. I was lurking inside the box, hoping we would find one of our early goals to settle us. Kalas tracked me, sticking close. I got ahead of him and nearly reached the ball but it flashed past and Lucas deflected it towards the Chelsea goal. Cole cleared it off the line with a clumsy swipe. The ball squirted down the goal line towards the corner flag. Sakho gained possession and he looped it back across the area. Suárez met it with a volley which went straight to Sakho. It happened so quickly that Sakho blasted his shot high over the bar.

We would not get another clear chance all half as Chelsea smothered us. Some might call it anti-football but it was deadly effective and terribly hard to play against. We had none of our usual tempo and venom. Even Suárez looked off-colour, his lone opportunity dipping harmlessly over the bar. The blue machine kept choking the life out of us. Kalas was playing like a composed veteran at the back. Ivanović was rock-solid next to him.

Cole came closest for Chelsea in one of their rare attacks, while they also appealed loudly for a penalty when a shot from Mohamed Salah hit Flano's hand. It was never a penalty but Chelsea protested.

Atkinson added on a few minutes of stoppage time as the first half dribbled away. We were also playing for the break. Flanagan found Allen who passed the ball to Coutinho. The Brazilian moved across the halfway line. Every Liverpool player ahead of him was closely marked and so Coutinho turned and played the ball back into our own half to Sakho. Three of us were in a line – Sakho, me and Skrtel. The closest Chelsea players, Ba and Mikel, were some distance away.

It was a nothing moment, an aimless stretch of play at the end of a drab half. Sakho looked across at me. It seemed obvious that he was about to play it safe and square. Ba moved diagonally across the pitch towards me, to close down my options.

Sakho used his left foot to slide his pass in my direction. It was nothing dramatic or risky. Just another routine, run-of-the-mill, bog-standard, predictable cushion of a square pass. I would have received hundreds of thousands of such passes over my twenty-five years in Liverpool colours. It came towards me, sure and steady. I was already moving towards the ball but I looked across to check on Ba. I was still in clear space. There was no danger.

I went to trap the ball but it slid under my right foot. My concentration had been more on Ba than the ball. I turned to correct myself and then it happened.

I slipped. I went down.

I've slipped often in my life. I've slipped downstairs. I've slipped on our kitchen floor. I've slipped on football pitches many, many times, but never as unluckily as this, never in a way which has cost a goal, and three crucial points.

Ba, seeing the ball spill loose, sprinted into the centre circle. He had half a field of open space in front of him.

I was scrambling on my hands and knees but I pushed myself back up onto my feet. I saw the blue blur of Ba flash past me. His right boot knocked the ball away from me.

Ba had momentum now. His long legs powered him forward as I gave chase.

It was not even a race. I was helpless. I knew I couldn't catch him, even though I tried. I ran as fast as I could. But Ba was far ahead. He needed just two more touches of the ball as Simon Mignolet came rushing out to narrow the angle.

All I could say to myself was, 'Bail me out, Simon. Bail me out'.

From just outside the eighteen-yard box Ba coolly slid the ball between Mignolet's legs into an empty net.

I went blank. I kept running on automatic towards the vacant goal, feeling even emptier inside. Ba had turned away to celebrate, almost colliding with Skrtel as he ran.

Inside the goal, I bent down to pick up the ball. My mind was in a daze.

Ba was still alone. It was his turn to be on his hands and knees as he kissed the ground. I walked slowly up the pitch, the ball under my arm. My eyes were closed. I felt like I couldn't go on.

The Chelsea players had reached Ba, burying him in a blue avalanche. I gave the ball away and kept trudging towards the halfway line. I brought a hand to my head in anguish.

Chelsea had scored, after my slip, in time added on for their earlier time-wasting. I felt sick.

The half-time whistle sounded soon afterwards. I could hear the Kop singing one of my songs in solidarity:

*Stevie Gerrard is our captain, Stevie Gerrard is a red; Stevie Gerrard plays for Liverpool, a Scouser born and bred.*

I still felt hollow and burned out.

In the dressing room, I was a wreck. I sat on the wooden bench, in my usual space in the corner, unable to say a word. I caught sight of my reflection in the mirror opposite my seat. I looked ashen and shell-shocked.

The manager came in a couple of minutes later. 'OK, it's happened,' he said. 'We're 1–0 down, but there's still time. We're not playing too well but we need to relax. We need to stay calm. We're trying too hard.'

Brendan was right. I had been straining the whole half to make something happen, so had Luis. Chelsea just kept blunting us. And then I'd slipped.

The dressing room was hushed. 'Look,' Brendan said, imploring the other players, 'if anyone deserves to be bailed out it's him.'

His finger pointed at me. 'Your captain needs you to all pay him back. The amount of times he's pulled this club out of a mess and changed impossible situations and got players out of trouble are the stuff of legend. Now it's time you repay him. You've got forty-five minutes to do it.'

Brendan looked at me. 'Stevie, forget it,' he said. 'It happens. Let's all go out and win this game. We can do it.'

I was still dazed, and I didn't feel confident. It was such a scrappy game, and they were so difficult to break down. I wasn't sure we had the belief to produce any more of the magic that had lit up our season over and over again.

We all tried hard. Sterling steamed towards goal and, just inside the Chelsea area, Kalas blocked him. Sterling went down. I was hoping for a penalty, Anfield was screaming for a penalty. Martin Atkinson shook his head.

The crowd had been quiet early in the second half but they worked to lift us. They built up some noise. It was not the usual Anfield roar but they were trying to drive us on.

I ran in to meet a corner but couldn't connect. The ball slid off Sterling's head to Johnson. His cross was cleared but it fell to Joe Allen inside the D. His shot was well struck but Schwarzer saved it, diving to his left.

Mignolet soon matched him, producing a fine save, also at full stretch to his left, to keep out Schürrle.

I was running forward too much, trying shots from impossible angles, just wanting to make up for the slip. The holding role was not a position suited to heroics. I might have been able to make up for it as a number 10 but I was flailing away now. I was desperate to atone for my error.

Four minutes were left. Another simple pass came my way from Sterling. I collected it easily and passed to Coutinho. We were trying to stay patient and rescue ourselves. Coutinho and Johnson swapped passes before it was played back inside to me. I found Sterling wide on the left. He slid it to Suárez who dinked it back to me. I surged it into the box but my cross sailed over the goal line.

Atkinson got it wrong. He gave us a corner. He owed me one. I took it short, passing it to Sterling, whose dipping effort was punched away by Schwarzer. It rebounded to Suárez who hit his best shot of the afternoon. Schwarzer turned it over for one last corner.

Aspas, on as a sub, took a terrible corner. He passed it straight to Willian. The same Willian I had texted at the start of the season, trying to persuade him to sign for Liverpool, scampered away. Coutinho had to launch himself into a desperate tackle. The ball ping-ponged back and forth before Nemanja Matić intercepted and it fell to Willian again. We were totally exposed. Flanagan was the last red shirt left as Willian and Torres ran at him.

Willian clipped it past Flanagan. Torres was away, Willian close behind him. They ran half the length of the field with not a single player in red near them. It was all over.

Torres took the ball into our area and, as Mignolet dived at his feet, my old teammate slipped the ball to Willian who could walk it into the goal. 2–0.

Mourinho jumped into the air. He then raced down the touchline, beating his chest. He stopped running but kept hammering the Chelsea badge. He was shouting 'Yaaaaaaaa!' all the time.

I looked away. The Kop burst into fiery song: 'Walk on, walk on . . .' I felt that all our hopes had been crushed.

At the end I walked over to Martin Atkinson. I stretched out my hand.

I shook the hands of all the Chelsea players. Anfield was singing my name again. I hung my head low. I didn't deserve it.

Our eleven-match winning streak had come to a shuddering halt, crashing into a big blue bus. We had been unbeaten all year, since our loss on 28 December 2013, sixteen games earlier, against Chelsea at Stamford Bridge. Chelsea had beaten us again, at Anfield, just when we needed the win most.

We were still top, but the destiny of the league title was no longer in our own hands. Manchester City were in control. If they won their remaining three matches they would be champions again. We would be second – and second was nowhere.

I kept walking towards the tunnel. 'You'll Never Walk Alone' rang around Anfield. I just wanted to be swallowed up by the ground. I wanted to disappear down a dark hole.

An hour later I was in the back of the car with tears rolling down my face. Despite my old mate Paul McGratten's encouraging 'there're still a few games to go . . .' I knew Manchester City would not blow it. There would be no comeback this time.

I had wanted to win the league with Liverpool for so long that, now it had gone for ever, I could not help myself. The tears kept rolling.

Eventually, I spoke to Alex. I didn't want the girls to see me in this state. I needed to find somewhere we could be alone, somewhere empty and away from Liverpool.

'Where?' Alex asked.

'I dunno,' I said. 'Speak to Struan.'

I heard Alex talking to Struan Marshall, my agent of many

years. I wiped my eyes and a daze settled over me. The car picked up speed and Liverpool raced past in a blur.

Alex's phone kept ringing. Struan's PA was trying to arrange a flight. Michael Owen knew someone who had a private plane. They would help me out. We just needed to decide where in the world I could go when I was in such a mess.

Suddenly, a name arose in my messed-up head. I had been there once. The only thing I remembered about the place was how empty it had seemed.

'Maybe Monaco?' I shrugged.

Monaco did feel like a ghost town. And I felt like I was in a nightmare for most of the forty-eight hours we were hidden away there. I wasn't suicidal. I knew I had Alex and the girls to keep me going. They were the most important people in my life, alongside my mum and dad. I had my family – but I can imagine that people who are suicidal would feel pretty similar to how I felt then. I was that low; and the worst thing I could have done was face it alone.

I needed Alex next to me. We also asked Gratty to fly over with us. I needed my wife most of all, at my side, and one of my closest mates. That's the type of person I am. I don't know if I could have handled it alone. I just don't know because I had never felt lower.

My phone was switched off. From time to time I would check it. There were many messages. People were thinking of me. Steve Peters, the psychiatrist who had pulled me out of my bleakest spell before this utter nightmare, had texted a few hours after the game, saying I should call him.

I couldn't phone Steve then, because I couldn't speak. I had no words.

I had to take a sleeping pill that night. It was the only way I could stop myself thinking about the slip, and the defeat.

When I woke the next morning I was still locked in a bad dream. But I knew it was real. I knew I had to keep going. I would be numb for days but, eventually, I had to be strong again.

Somehow, I managed to call Steve that afternoon. If anyone could help me I knew it would be him. Steve, sensibly, started by stepping back and putting everything in context. I knew by then that Man City had beaten Crystal Palace 2–0 away in Sunday's late kick-off. They were just three points behind us with a game in hand, and a much better goal difference. But Steve insisted it was not over. He encouraged me just to allow the rest of the season to take its course. We then moved to the heart of my despair.

Steve helped me find some kind of context for the slip. He knew that when I make a mistake on the football pitch, or have a bad game, I've always been honest and open and admitted it. I've done that since day one. So he allowed me to take full responsibility for the slip and accept that it had had a big impact on the game.

But Steve helped me ask a serious question. If the worst happened, in a football sense, and we didn't win the league, would my slip be the only reason for our disappointment? I had to admit the truth. Probably not. We had lost games that I didn't play in. Other players had made mistakes, sometimes more than one. There had also been moments when I had scored late goals, the penalties against Fulham and West Ham were just a few weeks old, and I had won us all three points. Maybe, Steve suggested, Liverpool would not even have been top of the league if I hadn't played so well all season.

It didn't stop me tormenting myself, but Steve did help. He reminded me that, even as footballers, we have a logical human side. But, like everyone else, we also have a chimp in our head who unleashes all our negative emotions. The chimp chatters away, in our lowest moments, and asks, 'But what if you hadn't done that? What if you hadn't slipped? Why couldn't you have been more careful? It's all your fault, isn't it?'

My chimp made me cry in the car; and my chimp made me feel life was hardly worth living.

As Steve told me again, the chimp feeds on negative emotions. I needed to listen to my human self again. I thanked Steve, and said I would speak to him again once I got back home.

In the deadness of Monaco, with darkness falling on that hushed Monday evening, the night after the terrible day before, I allowed myself to reflect more deeply. I didn't just obsess over the slip. My mind opened up and I saw my whole career unfold in front of me.

I remembered the goals against Olympiakos and AC Milan. I remembered the Miracle of Istanbul. I had played my part. But we had also got lucky that night. Milan were a better side than us, but I scored the goal that sparked the comeback from 3–0. I lifted the huge Champions League trophy that night, the greatest moment of my career.

Yes, I had slipped against Chelsea. Yes, I might never win the league. But I had been the king of European football for one night. I always had Istanbul.

Fate, and luck, had sometimes shone down on my skill and hard work. I had scored a screamer of a goal against West Ham, when Liverpool looked dead and buried, in the 2006 FA Cup final. It had been perhaps my finest-ever game for Liverpool. They called it the Steven Gerrard final these days. Who else, apart from Stanley Matthews, gets a final named after him? How lucky was I?

I remembered all the derbies, and my hat-trick two years before against Everton in March 2012. That was the night Luis Suárez and I had felt unstoppable.

How lucky had I been to play alongside Suárez, and Torres, and Alonso, and Rooney? How lucky was I to be going all the way from Ironside Road, in tough old Huyton, to Brazil and that summer's World Cup?

The dark and the light, the elation and the misery, belong together. Yes, I felt terrible; but at least I also knew what glory meant. Most people aren't that lucky. Most people shuttle between more muted experiences their whole lives. Most people aren't as lucky as I've been. I needed to be thankful, and not just tearful.

The past season had been full of despair and joy. I remembered the stand-off between Luis and Liverpool, and my role in resolving it. I remembered the four Suárez goals against Norwich when the Kop had sung, so deliriously, *I just can't get enough.*

I remembered my goal for England against Poland at Wembley, sealing our World Cup place in Brazil.

I remembered the 5–1 win against Arsenal, the 4–0 derby against Everton, the 3–0 thumping of Manchester United.

I remembered all the victorious journeys home from London, feeling knackered but alive with hope. I remembered racing through the dark from Fulham, after taking off my shirt and going crazy because I had scored the winner, and 'I feel so alive' boomed out of the team bus.

I remembered the twenty-fifth anniversary service for all those who had died at Hillsborough. I remembered the moment when Gerry Marsden and the Kop had begun to sing gently, tenderly, 'When you walk, through the storm, hold your head up high, and don't be afraid of the dark . . .'

But I still remembered the slip more than anything. And so, even though I helped get myself back on track, I stayed in my hotel room with Alex most of the time. We went for a walk once, and we sat by the pool for an hour. The second night we went for dinner in an empty restaurant. But I had no appetite. I was still numb.

At least I understood the context of everything. I'm not big-headed. I'm the other way, in fact. I'm probably too harsh and self-critical. But I'm also clever enough to break it down and analyse it and come out with the right answers. In Monaco, as we prepared to go back to Liverpool, I realized a simple fact all over again: I had done my best. That certainty would help me heal. I thought it might take years, but, eventually, with the help of Alex, the girls, my parents, my friends and my family, I knew I would get over my mistake against Chelsea.

Chris Morgan sent one of the first texts I received when I got back to Liverpool on the Tuesday. Chelsea were playing Atlético Madrid the following evening, Wednesday, 30 April, in the Champions League semi-final second leg. Chris had been in touch with me when I was in Monaco, just checking I was OK, and he sent a simple text once Alex and I were back home with the kids:

> Do you want to watch the game tomorrow and have a bag of Haribos?

Chris clearly thought the Haribos might sweeten the bitter taste of watching Chelsea.

> OK. It'll be quite good to watch them get beat. You can come around ours if you want, because I haven't seen my kids much lately.

My friendship with Chris was based on our professional relationship. We saw each other at work, at Melwood and Anfield and while travelling to away games, and we didn't usually visit each other's homes. But these were difficult days and I valued the support of a trusted colleague. Chris arrived early, with the Haribos, which the girls enjoyed. He and I then sat down to watch the game. Torres was up against his boyhood club. Mourinho had picked him to start and, of course, Fernando scored. I was happy for Fernando; but I was supporting Atlético. Chelsea had caused us so much pain I thought we'd enjoy seeing them suffer a little.

Atlético hurt them, again and again. They were stunningly good on the counter-attack. Adrián equalized just before half-time. And then, after an hour, Diego Costa, who would be a Chelsea player a month later, put Atlético 2–1 up. Chelsea had to score two now to survive. We were quite enjoying ourselves; and polished off the few Haribos the girls had left us.

Chris was able to ask me how I was really doing, on the inside. I pulled a face. I was better, but I was still struggling.

'You know what it was?' Chris said of the slip. 'It was just a stud, a bit of grass, a slippery pitch. You can't take the responsibility for that. Ba still had to run from the halfway line. He had to outrun two other players. He had to put it past Mignolet. You were on the halfway line, Stevie. It's not happened in the six-yard box.'

'Yeah, I know,' I said. 'But still . . .'

We brightened again. Arda Turan scored. Chelsea 1, Atlético 3. Bye-bye Chelsea.

I felt better when I went back to Melwood. We were playing Crystal Palace away on the Monday night and Man City had to go to Everton. City had a terrible record at Goodison. Maybe, just maybe, Everton could do us a huge favour.

We were training hard again, and the lads were all great with me. I think they knew I was still in a bit of shock. But I was getting ready to perform well at Crystal Palace. No one spoke to me about Chelsea, or the slip, but I could tell how hard they had all tried in the second half. I knew they had tried extra hard to straighten out the result for my sake, because of

Brendan's words at half-time, and I had been touched. You find out who your mates are in such situations and they were all great with me.

A lot of them really did have extra motivation in wanting to help me win the title, after all my years at the club; but I'd wanted it for them too. We were still in the race together. We were hoping again for a miracle.

City were playing Everton in the early evening kick-off on Saturday. I couldn't bear to watch the game but I was following the score on my phone. After eleven minutes it was 1–0 Everton. Ross Barkley. Hello, could this really happen?

My happiness lasted another eleven minutes. An Agüero goal for City.

A draw would be OK. A draw would be just fine. A draw would mean that the title was back in our hands.

Two minutes before half-time there was another goal alert. I looked down. Džeko. Everton 1, City 2.

Everton needed a win to keep alive their faint hopes of Champions League qualification. But early in the second half Džeko made it 3–1. Lukaku scored another for Everton but City marched on. They were top of the league, ahead of us on goal difference. We each had two games to play. City's were both at home, against Villa and West Ham, two sides with nothing to play for and already thinking of their summer holidays. It felt like our last hope had gone.

We were 3–0 up against Crystal Palace with just eleven minutes left. The old chant of *We're gonna win the league . . . we're gonna win the league . . .* had resurfaced alongside a simpler message from the Liverpool faithful: *Attack, attack, attack!* Our goal difference was fifty-three. City's was fifty-nine. We were still a long way away but we'd given it a real go.

The first goal had come after eighteen minutes. I took a corner and Joe Allen, hardly a giant, headed it home at the far post. Then, early in the second half, I hit a forty-yard crossfield special. It landed at Daniel Sturridge's feet. He controlled it well, cut inside and shot at goal. His strike took a deflection past the Palace keeper for an own goal. Sterling and Suárez combined in the fifty-fifth minute. Suárez scored a lovely goal. He picked up the ball and raced back to the halfway line. We were in the mood for more.

The game gave us three more – all to Palace in a dizzying, sickening nine-minute spell.

A deflected shot started the collapse and then, two minutes later, Skrtel was on the left wing threading a pass into the Palace area. It was cleared away and Palace broke at speed. Skrtel was out of position in central defence and Yannick Bolasie's searing run set up Dwight Gayle. We were unbalanced as a team. Glenn Murray then split us wide open again, and Gayle hammered it past Mignolet. 3–3.

At the final whistle I sank down onto my haunches. Luis Suárez, who was crying helplessly, pulled his white shirt over his face. The television cameras and the photographers crowded round me and Luis, to capture our latest anguish. I pushed them away. I walked over to the Palace players, shook their hands and then went to find Luis. I tried to console him and then Kolo Touré, a substitute that night, stepped in to help.

'I'm here, big man,' Kolo said. He always called me 'big man'. Kolo led Luis off the field. We trudged behind, leaving the joyous Palace fans to their party.

Liverpool had arranged for us to fly back from London on a private plane. The whole squad was muted. Most of the players were on their iPads, listening to music or watching movies. I sat next to Chris and Glen Driscoll. We chatted quietly because we still could not quite get our heads round one of the strangest nights of my career.

'We were murdering them,' I said in disbelief to Chris and Glen. 'I honestly thought we were going to win six–nil.'

I shrugged. It probably still wouldn't have made any difference.

It had been my worst eight days in football. Chelsea, Monaco and Palace. The best dream I'd ever had, winning the league with Liverpool, had just died. I felt horrific.

I looked out of the window. There was nothing to see. The plane did a little lurch as we hit a patch of turbulence. Some of the lads glanced up.

I turned to Chris. 'Mate,' I said, 'all I need now is for this plane to drop out of the sky.'

Chris looked at me.

'If it goes down,' I said, 'I'm not going into the brace position.'

I meant it. I was ready to surrender. If we were going down, well, sod it. I'd had enough.

The plane steadied and everybody picked up their iPads again. I was quiet for the rest of the flight, lost in thought as we flew on into the black night.

# 9. England: The Hope

A small group of scientists travelled to England's World Cup training camp on the Algarve, in Portugal, to help us work on the art of 'Being Comfortable Being Uncomfortable'. There was a logic behind the strange title. It was a programme a team from Loughborough University had devised to help us get used to the extreme heat and humidity we expected in Brazil. Faro was usually hot and sticky but, under the sun in Portugal in May 2014, we were asked to wear three layers of clothing in training. It was one way of getting used to the discomfort of playing our first match of the tournament against Italy in Manaus, deep in the Amazon rainforest.

The plan had a scientific method. Patches were attached to three different parts of our body so that the scientists could monitor our sweat levels and the exact amount of fluids and electrolytes each of us would need to maintain our level of performance. Once that information had been collected they would create specific recovery drinks to suit the needs of each individual player.

England were clearly aiming for a more sophisticated approach than the one I had encountered on my debut fourteen years before, in late May 2000, when Tony Adams had tested my preparation by screaming that unforgettable question into my face: 'Are you fucking ready for this?'

Alan Shearer had been captain that night; I was about to lead England into my third World Cup, and my second as captain. Even without measuring sweat output or electrolyte intake, I knew that playing for England often felt like you were trying to get comfortable inside an uncomfortable situation. I still loved international football, and I had many good memories alongside the disappointing moments, but the media circus and suffocating atmosphere around England before a major tournament was hardly comfortable. It was a testing experience.

I still felt passionate about playing for England; and I still wanted the captain's armband. But I've always felt that the most difficult part of being an England captain is the press conference routine. You're out of your comfort zone and you've got people coming after you. It often feels as if every question has got an angle or they're looking for one wrong word or bad line where they might catch you out. I've survived a few press conferences for England in tricky circumstances. Obviously, the most difficult encounters happen when you've been knocked out of a tournament too early. The questions are at their fiercest and you're at your lowest.

After all my years in the role I had worked out that the best strategy was to speak honestly to the media. Of course, I still needed to be careful. If a teammate was struggling I would never divulge his problem in public. I also avoided criticizing any individual by name. There were even times where I had to say certain words for the sake of the team – so that the manager could have the players in the best frame of mind before a big match.

But 99 per cent of the time I spoke from the heart. I didn't see any point talking to thirty or forty journalists unless I could respond honestly. It was simpler than trying to adopt a media-trained approach where you ended up sounding like a politician bending the truth. You always got caught out, or tangled up in knots, which is why I just tried to talk plainly and sincerely.

If a journalist took an honest statement and spun it, or twisted it, you had to be man enough to accept the fallout. The odd hack did it to me, but there are people who manipulate the truth in every walk of life. In the main, sportswriters' criticism of me as an England player was constructive and fair. And when a few were out of order I took it with a pinch of salt – just as I did when one or two journalists went overboard in their praise of me.

Most of the press guys understood the game and they appreciated that, as a player, sometimes you've got to stonewall. Just before a major tournament or an important game you do need to play some of their questions with a straight bat. But I still think that, more often than not, I was respected by the media who follow England because they knew that, whether the team was doing well or poorly, I'd answer as honestly and as openly as possible. I never hid when it was tough.

It was different in Faro. I actually lied at a Faro press conference on 24 May 2014. It was difficult because it seemed as if the media didn't even want to talk about the World Cup. The first question set the tone. They just wanted to know about my mental state and to hear how I was feeling after the painful month I had endured with Liverpool.

Less than two weeks had passed since the Premier League season ended. We had beaten Newcastle 2–1 at Anfield in our final game, but it had been an awkward and deflating match. I had a new song – and it was sung by the Newcastle fans rather than Liverpool supporters:

*Steve Gerrard, Gerrard / He slipped on his fucking arse / He gave it to Demba Ba / Steve Gerrard, Gerrard . . .*

The Geordies enjoyed singing it, again and again. Let's have it right – they haven't had much else to sing about. I knew it would be a song I'd hear every time I wore a Liverpool shirt in England. It would become a soundtrack for the away supporters of every team we played in the league or any domestic cup competition. I would get used to it.

It was harder to be 1–0 down to Newcastle at half-time, after a Martin Skrtel own goal and a limp display from Liverpool. We needed Manchester City to lose at home to West Ham to resurrect our dead title dream. But City were cruising and 1–0 ahead.

At least we played with much more drive and purpose in the second half. I set up both goals from identical dead-ball situations. I nailed the free kick each time and Agger and Sturridge scored the goals which meant we beat Newcastle and finished runners-up in the league.

Manchester City were champions with eighty-six points. We ended up with eighty-four points and Chelsea were third on eighty-two. Arsenal were fourth, five points behind us.

The press reminded me that if Liverpool had won the slip match against Chelsea we would have lifted the title that meant so much to me. Was I still hurting?

I wasn't in a bad state but the honest answer was, 'Yes, of course.' But the implication of telling the brutal truth was that a story would be generated of how I was still scarred by 'the slip'. I was convinced that once England played a few practice matches and got to Brazil I would be fine. I wouldn't be thinking about Liverpool then. But they asked me about that specific moment. They wanted to hear if I had moved on totally or if I was still stuck in a bad place.

The real truth was somewhere in the middle. I could have said, 'Some days are OK, but some days I still feel shit. I still feel terrible. I've not quite got over the worst disappointment of my life so there are still bad days. How else do you expect me to feel?'

That would have caused a sensation and so, instead, I lied. I said I was in a 'fantastic' frame of mind and focused totally on the World Cup. But I also faced up to the realities of what had happened and tried to turn some deeply negative emotions into a more positive outlook. And there was a lot of truth in the gist of my reaction. I meant it when I said I was thankful to be able to focus on the World Cup. I even managed a small smile.

'Otherwise I would be sitting on a sun lounger thinking back to the last three or four games, going over and over where it's gone wrong and asking myself why and driving myself nuts,' I said. 'I've got to park the slip at the back of my mind and forget about it for the time being because I've got a huge tournament coming up.'

I admitted I had been hurt – but I tried to underline the 'fantastic' positives of the past season to the media:

> I don't like making mistakes, big mistakes, at important times. I've made more than a few throughout my career. As an experienced player you learn to deal with them that little bit better the older you get – but yes, it hurt a lot. Not just the slip, it was more letting the title slip towards the end because we had come so close and had a terrific season. But with experience you look back at the positives as well as the negatives. To finish second in the hardest league in the world and to have the season I've had personally, to watch the likes of Raheem Sterling grow and to see the team do so well, was fantastic.

The honest voice in me still needed to be heard and I conceded:

> I keep saying to myself, 'How and why?' There are no answers because it was a slip. It was so cruel because of the timing, with three games to go. We were top of the league. Of course it's cruel, it's unfair but that's football, that's life. I'm not feeling sorry for myself.

There was no point telling the world then that I had cried in the back of a car on my way home after the Chelsea match. I just said, instead:

For me, Luis Suarez really stands out amongst my generation of footballers.

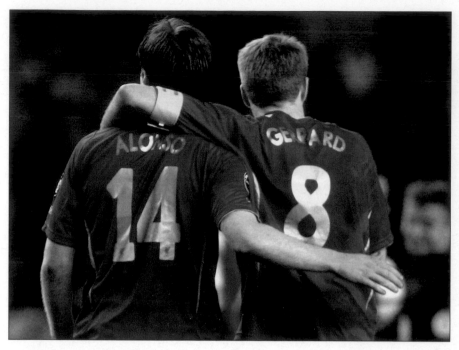

Xabi Alonso would always be in my dream team. He is one of my four favourite football players.

Formerly a Bluenose rival, Wayne Rooney is also a fellow England teammate and a top player.

Fernando Torres is another former Liverpool teammate for whom
I have huge admiration and respect.

Celebrating in a sea of red after clinching the
Champions League title in 2005.

Lifting the FA Cup in 2006 after my best-ever performance for Liverpool.

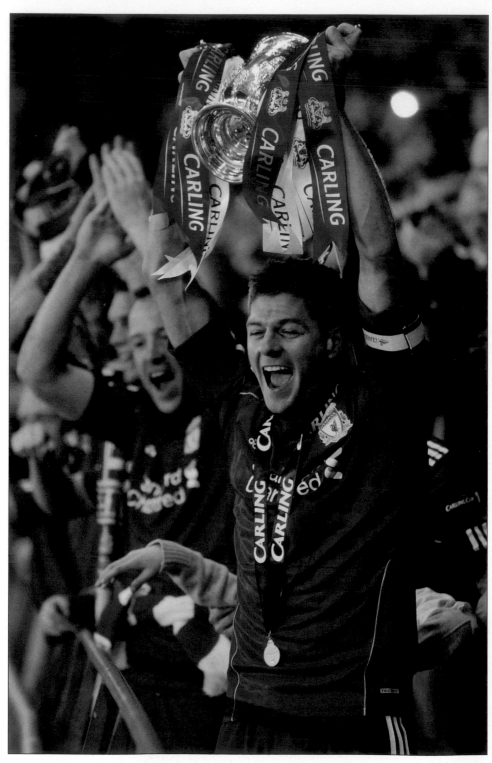

Carling Cup victory at Wembley in 2012.

Celebrating a goal against Everton in 2014.

Kenny Dalglish – a Liverpool legend,
my dad's favourite player, and a great
manager to me in 2011 and 2012.

Celebrating a victory over Everton at the
Premier League match in 2010.

From the highs . . .

. . . to the lows. As we fought for the league title, my slip before that
crucial Chelsea goal devastated me.

I don't want anyone thinking I'm a young, naive, insecure person who goes home and cries in his bedroom. I'm thirty-three years of age with 100-odd caps and 600-odd appearances for Liverpool. I'm big and brave enough to take it on the chin. I take responsibility for the slip and the damage it's done. It wasn't the first mistake I've made. I've made many and I've got over them and I'll prove to everybody in this World Cup that I'm fit, fresh and ready to perform.

It felt important to put on a brave face. I also really did believe we were about to go to the biggest World Cup of our careers. Brazil promised to be a phenomenal stage. It had the wow factor. And so I was excited. I was optimistic. In truth, I was happy and sad at the same time. I think all of us experience those conflicted feelings but, in our media age, in the world of Twitter, it's not easy to express such complicated emotions in snappy soundbites or 140 characters. So, for once, I settled on 'fantastic' instead. I was in a 'fantastic' place.

A white lie, in a black-and-white world, seemed safer than the grey tangle of mixed emotions that shrouded me between the end of the Premier League season and a World Cup in Brazil. I had been through five previous major tournaments with England. I had learnt that it was best to avoid any sensational headlines.

I had vivid memories of my past World Cups and European Championships. I loved the games, even if I never ever enjoyed the camps. I always dreaded the camps. I hated being away from Alex and the girls for that long. But it's worth going through it, the boredom and the daily grind. I knew why it felt so special when we were a couple of days away from the first game of a big tournament. It was then that the hope surged through you. It felt unbelievable, then, to play for England.

*

Four years earlier, in 2010, at the World Cup in South Africa, I was just as excited before our first group game against the USA. I was also England's captain – even if I got the job by default once John Terry hit controversy and Rio Ferdinand was ruled out by injury. Fabio Capello was England's manager but, even though he was almost as cold in his personality as Rafa Benítez, I felt valued by him.

Capello had a weird way of expressing solidarity with his best players. He would never communicate it verbally. Instead he would walk over and give me a shoulder charge. A bump of shoulders was Capello's way of showing you that he appreciated you as a player. I already knew that because he always picked me in his side. But I'm not sure he saw me as a leader – or as powerful a leader as Terry or Ferdinand.

His perception might have been shaped by Franco Baldini, his assistant, who played a key role in many of Capello's decisions as England manager. I got a feeling from Baldini that he thought I lacked a bit of confidence. I think he assumed I was a bit too shy and reserved to be an England captain. He rated me as a player because he went out of his way to tell me on numerous occasions. I was scoring goals most weeks for Liverpool and putting in top performances. They were desperate to see such displays for England but it's a completely different set-up and a different organization. I was striving to meet their hopes but I certainly wasn't as comfortable under their England regime as I was at Liverpool.

I still gave everything and I put in some good performances under Capello and Baldini. But when they made me captain I was affected by knowing that they didn't really see me as a leader. I think they got the John Terry decision right when they made him captain both before and after my first stint in the role. JT's a big leader, and a big personality around the camp. He was in the squad in South Africa but, owing to a personal fallout between him and Wayne Bridge, JT had lost the captaincy. It had a small impact on my confidence as the new leader, knowing that the manager probably wanted JT but had been blocked by the FA. But I didn't think about it too much. I just got on with playing and captaining England in my own style.

Captains lead in different ways. JT does it one way, but I am a much more understated kind of captain, trying to lead by example, and I enjoyed working under Capello. I know a lot of England players didn't like him, but I was prepared to put up with the boredom and the regimental rules of his management because I thought it could bring some success to England.

There was at least a platform for Capello to build his own team. We had reached the quarter-finals of the previous two World Cups. I had been injured in 2002 and missed the tournament, when England lost 2–1 to Brazil in Japan after Michael Owen had scored a fantastic opening goal. In 2006 we lost to Portugal, again at the same stage. I played in that match, in Gelsenkirchen, which will always be remembered for Cristiano Ronaldo's wink after Wayne Rooney, his Manchester United teammate, was sent off after an hour of the 0–0 draw. We lost on penalties. Rooney's dismissal, the Ronaldo wink and the cruel shoot-out enraged everyone at home.

The Portuguese defenders had fouled Rooney, our best player, the whole game. They used cynical tactics to block him and they niggled and riled him in a concerted effort to make him boil over. After sixty-two minutes he and Ricardo Carvalho, who then played for Chelsea, went into a challenge. Rooney stayed on his feet and Carvalho went down as if falling to his death. It was incredible acting. The next few moments were a mess. Rooney stood on Carvalho – he swore it was by accident – and the Portuguese swarmed around the referee begging for him to get sent off. They said it was a stamp.

When the ref reached for a red card I honestly thought one of Portugal's players was about to be dismissed for something he had said. I was shocked when I saw Wayne walking off while Ronaldo winked to his manager, Luiz Felipe Scolari, and the Portugal dugout – as if to say 'job done'.

Wayne talked to me on the bus as we left the ground, all of us in pieces after losing the penalty shoot-out, and he asked me what I thought of Ronaldo's wink. I was so angry that I told Wayne if one of my club teammates had done the same to me I would never talk to him again. Even if it had been Xabi Alonso – and I knew it would never have been Xabi's style – there was no way I would have forgiven him.

He listened closely but Wayne found it in himself to be the better man. He forgave Ronaldo and went out of his way to heal a relationship that had looked ruined that night. It became just another incident in the painful fabric of England tournament defeats.

Penalties were stitched into so many heartbreaking moments and defeats. As a fan I had watched England lose on World Cup penalties in the semi-finals to West Germany in 1990, and in 1998, against Argentina in France, in the quarter-finals, the game when David Beckham was sent off.

As a player I had twice lost to Portugal in quarter-final shoot-outs. In Euro 2004, bad blisters and severe cramp meant I had to hobble off with nine minutes of normal time remaining. I was a spectator again as we went down narrowly on penalties. Two years later, at the World Cup in Germany, I actually missed my penalty against Portugal. I was up third. Frank Lampard missed our first spot kick while Owen Hargreaves tucked away the second. If I scored I'd have put us 2–1 up after three penalties each.

It was a forty-yard walk from the safety of standing in a line with my teammates, arms draped around each other, to the penalty spot. It felt like forty miles. The pressure of the situation, knowing that your whole country depended on you, and that a billion people around the world were watching you, ate away at me.

Penalty-taking was also a new experience for me in 2004. I didn't take many for Liverpool then and I'd never had a chance with England. That lack of experience was very different from the situation eight years later when, being much more used to the pressure, I scored without any problems against Italy in a Euro 2012 shoot-out.

In 2004 I just had my training-ground practice in taking penalties. I had been deadly in training and so I tried to hold on to that certainty as I approached the dreaded moment in a World Cup shoot-out. I managed to calm myself and I was clear in my head that I would hit it to the right. I remembered all my training-ground success. I took a deep breath and got ready to put us ahead.

The referee would not blow his whistle. I looked across at him for four seconds, thinking, 'C'mon ref, any chance?', before he finally gave the signal. Those few seconds were crucial. My mind lurched from fragile certainty to anxiety. I stepped up and took my penalty. As soon as I hit it I knew it was a foot away from my target. It was too close to the keeper, rather than in the corner, and he saved it. I felt hopeless despair as I walked back to my teammates.

Carra was always going to volunteer to take a penalty. He took our fourth spot kick, with the score 2–1 in Portugal's favour. Carra ran up, no bullshit, and hammered it home. My despair turned to joy – and back to despair again. The referee had not blown his whistle. He made Carra retake his penalty, a small death sentence in a sudden-death shoot-out. Ricardo saved Carra's next effort and, inevitably, Ronaldo killed us off when he scored to make it 3–1 with only Ashley Cole left to take one of our designated five penalties. We were out of the World Cup.

Once I recovered from that desolation it seemed obvious to me that you should only pick experienced penalty-takers in a shoot-out. Unless you've been hardened to the pressures of the penalty spot there is a good chance you will come unstuck in such an extreme situation.

Capello also said that he had been surprised by the mental frailty of England. We weren't the only country to suffer from nerves in big tournaments, and during penalties, so I wasn't sure it was just a weakness in English football. It seemed to me that, amongst our European rivals, only Italy and Germany had proved their psychological toughness year after year. I hoped that Capello would translate some of that rigour and mental hardness to England.

He was similar to Benítez in many ways. They both set their teams up in very compact formations. They were organized and they were disciplined. A lot of England players were scared of Capello and they hated his strict rules. I actually didn't mind them because I felt a connection with the man. It was mutual respect. His staff were all Italian and, with the exception of Baldini, their English wasn't great but they also showed that, like their boss, they valued me. They made it clear that, even if I wasn't their ideal captain, I would always have a big role to play for them.

Capello kept his distance but I went onto the training pitch each day believing I would learn something new from him. He had achieved so much in the game and he had an incredible CV. The Italian way is also very professional, very strict. And so if you lacked any kind of professionalism you would not last long under Capello. He certainly didn't miss much. So we gelled because I thrived on the hard work and discipline he instilled into England. The only real downside to Capello was that he would never show any love towards the squad. Mourinho was a master at making the entire squad feel loved. Capello had none of that – but it did him no harm in Italy.

Our time in South Africa during the 2010 World Cup sometimes felt like a real slog. My attitude was that if it was going to help us win football matches then I was prepared to put up with it while hanging around our training camp in the very sparse setting of Rustenburg. It was a challenge. Rustenburg wasn't interesting and there wasn't much to do when we weren't training. But I didn't see any point in complaining. We were in South Africa to play football. The hotel was good enough, the camp's training facilities were good enough. But it became more difficult when the results were disappointing and players started missing their families.

If you're winning football matches the boredom you endure during long tournaments hardly feels relevant. The problems only really emerge if results are not going well and it feels as if the manager is not showing the squad much respect. That gives the players an excuse. They can start blaming boredom or team selection – when, in reality, it all depends on what happens on the pitch and how good you are individually and as a team. England, over the years and especially in 2010, had never been consistent enough.

I very rarely got involved in non-football activities during training camp, and I avoided all the bitching, because I liked getting into a zone and the rhythm of training, resting and preparing for the games. The major tournaments mattered hugely to me and I wanted to make the most of my opportunity to play in them.

And so, as the captain in 2010, I couldn't quite believe it when I heard some of the complaints from the players. They were long and petty and the worst, which sticks out in my memory, was when some of the players came to me to complain that they had to walk fifty yards for a massage. A few of the lads were used to having their massages done in their hotel rooms and one of the players wanted the same routine with England. Some footballers in that 2010 squad had big egos and they behaved like kids from time to time.

Players will complain about everything. I've been guilty of it myself and, as Liverpool players, we have moaned a lot on occasions. It happens. But there was some unbelievable whingeing going on in that Rustenburg camp. I thought it was mind-blowing that some players approached me as captain to make a protest to Capello. I listened to them and I didn't say anything. But, on the inside, I was thinking, 'We've got a really important game in five days and you're worried about walking fifty yards for a *massage*?'

I could have let rip but I was conscious of avoiding any divide amongst the players. So I allowed them their little moan and then I ignored it. I would never go to a manager to talk about such a ridiculous issue. I wouldn't embarrass myself. Of course it blew over and we got on with the games. But it was an insight into some of the different characters you find in an England squad.

We began well enough against the USA in our opening match in Rustenburg. I scored in the fourth minute, when I ran onto Emile Heskey's pass and slid the ball past Tim Howard. It was the perfect World Cup start and we looked comfortable and in control of the game until five minutes before half-time. Clint Dempsey was twenty-five yards out and his shot had no real zip or venom to it. I expected Rob Green to make an easy save. Instead, he had one of those disastrous moments which all keepers fear. He allowed the ball to slip under his body for the softest of goals. It was a shattering moment for Greeny, who is a good keeper, and it took him a very long time to get over the personal devastation.

The game ended in a 1–1 draw. We should have won and all I could do was to try to console Rob, and support him. I told him to put it to the back of his mind and focus on the fact that he was a very good keeper. But I knew he was gone. How can you recover quickly from such an error in a World Cup? You can't – and it absolutely killed him. I felt real sympathy for Rob, even if I had always thought Capello was being brave in selecting him ahead of David James or Joe Hart. Capello got that decision wrong. But, then again, if Greeny had made that routine save he would have kept a clean sheet and it would have seemed the right choice.

Capello then went out of his way to test me as captain. He came to me and said: 'I'm thinking about picking Joe Hart.' It was his way of seeing if I could keep a secret. But I didn't tell a soul and it was just as well because he chose David James instead. Managers do test their captains from time to time and I think that was a case of Capello trying to gauge my discretion and loyalty.

Another problem soon emerged. After we played poorly in a 0–0 draw against Algeria in Cape Town we flew back to Rustenburg. JT, who had played in that match, was put up in front of the media the following afternoon and he spoke his mind. He basically said Capello had picked the wrong team. I had no problems with JT and I've always admired him for being so forthright. He actually came to me later to say that he had not meant to undermine me in any way. I didn't feel undermined and so there were no problems on my part. I just wished I had sat down with JT and asked him who he would have selected in place of the players Capello had chosen.

The only obvious one was Joe Cole. I was playing on the left so if he did mean Cole I don't know whether he felt I should have been playing in the middle ahead of Gareth Barry. It wasn't really an issue for me because I had a job to do and

Capello would always pick the team. JT was going to back his mate and Joe Cole was a Chelsea player. Joe did get his chances in that World Cup when he came off the bench, but he had little impact. But whether that was what JT had in mind or not, I don't think Capello's team selection ruined our World Cup.

JT was probably frustrated – both at our lack of success on the pitch and having lost the captaincy. But personally, face-to-face, JT had always showed me the utmost respect. I was the same towards him because I'm a great admirer of him as a player. There were never any problems between us.

The media, however, began to portray us as a divided squad. Apparently, a few players had met up after the Algeria game at the hotel in Cape Town, and the press depicted it as an attempt at a JT-led Cape Town coup. It was hardly that, although I do think there was an underlying friction between JT and some of the players on one side and Capello and Baldini on the other. The Italian pair had also had their issues with the FA in the build-up to the tournament so there was a lot of niggly tension bubbling beneath the surface.

I don't think Baldini helped the situation because we learnt that he was giving off-the-record briefings to the press. Stuff was leaking out into the media that should have remained private. Players aren't stupid, and we quickly worked out what was happening. I was disappointed that Baldini chose to make those private briefings on behalf of his boss.

Capello didn't have a very good grasp of the language. It caused us some grief. It was fine in tactical briefings because he would use visuals to make you understand clearly what you needed to do. But it was more difficult during games when Capello tried to give new instructions and his English let him down. It was the same in training. Most of the sessions were taken by an older Italian, Italo Galbiati, and his English was poor. So it was problematic, and sessions were slow.

But language barriers, press briefings and moaning players were only on the fringes. The real story for us at the 2010 World Cup was that England were not good enough. We lacked the belief, consistency and quality of Germany and, in the last sixteen, they beat us 4–1.

At 2–1 down, Frank Lampard had a good goal disallowed. It crossed the line but the officials made a mistake. Maybe it would have been a different story if the equalizer had stood. But it's far more likely that we would still have lost because Germany outclassed us for periods of that game. I don't think it was quite as humiliating as people suggest now, or the 4–1 score indicates, but they were better than us, no question.

I'm still not sure if I would call Thomas Müller a truly great player, but he showed that day, as he has done so many times since, that he's a top goalscorer. He got two goals against England but we were more worried about Mesut Özil. You have to credit Müller as one of the best goalscorers in the world. He always seems to score in big tournaments and at key moments, which is one of the hallmarks of a world-class player. I would never dispute that, but whenever I watched Müller, or played against him, I never saw him do anything as brilliant as Messi or Ronaldo.

But in Bloemfontein, in 2010, he did serious damage to England. Müller was not the only one. The Germans' strength has always been to have top players in every position. Even when someone was injured his replacement would be of similar quality. England have rarely been able to make the same claim – which is why our World Cup in South Africa ended in such bleak disappointment.

The atmosphere in the England squad before the 2014 World Cup was so much better than it had been four years earlier. The mood was relaxed and harmonious and our training camp was well drilled and well organized. There seemed so much more unity in the squad, and that was due to one man: Roy Hodgson. I have great respect for Roy. He's a very good person and honesty shines out of him. It also helps that he loves football.

Roy had an excellent CV and great experience. He also had a very mature relationship with the players because he treated us like adults. Roy understands that most footballers don't want to be locked in their rooms when they're not training during a long tournament. If players put the effort in during training, and are professional around the camp, then Roy is happy for them to enjoy themselves and see a little of the real world. And Brazil was enjoyable. I thought it was a lovely place and nowhere near as dangerous as people were trying to make out in the build-up. If you went to the right places it was fine and there was not even a hint of trouble. So at least I got to see a little of a very beautiful country.

We were all set to do well and Roy had made another astute move when he brought Gary Neville into the England coaching set-up. Gary was very important to Roy and to England. He proved himself to be a great sounding board and the perfect link between the players and Roy. We all knew from watching him and listening to him as an analyst on Sky these last few years that he had a deep knowledge of the game. He also proved himself to be tactically astute.

Gary was very proactive in trying to get players involved in 'unit' meetings of defenders, midfielders and attackers. He wanted players to be vocal during these sessions, but there were a lot of young lads in the squad and some of them were scared to speak out, so Frank Lampard and I did most of the talking. I sympathized because I had also been very quiet and even intimidated when I first broke into the England team. I was surrounded by formidable men like Adams and Shearer. It takes time to build your confidence in a national squad. But

Gary was brilliant at getting everyone involved in the analysis of games.

Of course, not everything was perfect and there were some disappointing aspects with training – which reminded me of the difficult time Roy had endured during his brief spell as Liverpool manager. Roy was in charge of the club for only six months. He replaced Rafa Benítez on 1 July 2010 – and he left Liverpool 'by mutual consent' on 8 January 2011.

It was a difficult position for me to be in because I wanted to help Roy – but I had to respect the supporters' wishes as well. I don't think it would have mattered whether Hodgson, Capello, Louis van Gaal or Brendan Rodgers had taken over from Rafa. The fact that the fans were screaming for Kenny Dalglish almost made it mission impossible. Roy also suffered because Fernando Torres downed tools. Torres was already agitating for a move but it got worse under Roy. He obviously wasn't a fan of Roy's methods or training techniques and he had people above him whispering in his ear about moving to Chelsea. So Torres didn't really give much to Hodgson either in training or in matches.

I would walk off the pitch thinking, 'We just didn't have Fernando with us today.' He didn't move. It was hard to know if he was worried about another injury or he had transfer business on his mind – or if he simply didn't like our new manager. It was probably a combination of all three and Roy Hodgson paid the price.

Roy made a couple of bad signings as Liverpool manager. He bought Christian Poulsen from Juventus – supposedly as a replacement for a great player in Javier Mascherano, who was on his way to Barcelona. Poulsen was nowhere near mobile or quick enough to be a central midfielder for Liverpool. He was an experienced player, and a Denmark international, but Poulsen always played it safe. His game might suit other clubs in different European countries. But he was never going to cut it as a Premier League player for Liverpool.

Paul Konchesky was another of Roy's signings who was never going to work out at Anfield. Konchesky was a good lad and I knew him before he joined us from Fulham. He was a tidy player, but he was never going to succeed John Arne Riise. The fans loved Ginger, as we called Riise, and he was very consistent. But he made a big mistake in a Champions League game and he had a tough time after that. Rafa nudged him out and brought in Andrea Dossena as Riise's replacement.

Years later it showed that Rafa had made a bigger mistake than Roy in the transfer market. Dossena was nowhere near good enough to play for Liverpool. He was a decent guy and he had a professional attitude but he would have struggled to get in my reserve team. Konchesky was better but the harsh truth was that he was not good enough to play left back for Liverpool. The fans saved most of their derision for Poulsen. They booed and barracked him and his confidence was quickly shot. So Roy made his share of mistakes.

I tried my best to persuade some good players to join us, without any luck, because I wanted to help Roy as much as I could. But everything was stacked against him. Roy was only a few months into the job when we had the massive court case against Hicks and Gillett. Fenway took over as owners and I think they quickly understood that the majority of fans had wanted Kenny before Roy was appointed. So Roy was right up against it and as soon as we had a few inconsistent results the pressure started to escalate. Throw in the fact that your star striker has basically given up while he waits for a move, and you're in deep trouble.

Roy tried really hard because Liverpool was his dream job. I think he would have succeeded if the club had been more stable. But he was on a hiding to nothing. It even reached the point where Roy tried to tailor his training sessions around Fernando. I remember we did team shaping for a couple of days on the spin. That's basically when the team plays against no opposition. You pass it about to get your rhythm and style of play in synch – and to give Torres confidence in front of goal. At the time Roy didn't know that Torres had downed tools. He just thought Torres was lacking a little belief and sharpness. But it wouldn't have mattered what kind of sessions Roy put on. Torres had little faith in Hodgson and he was just desperate to get away.

I tried to spark some performances out of the team so we could buy Roy a little more time. But when a manager is under pressure at Liverpool and the fans turn against him then there is no way back. The fans are very powerful at the club and if they want someone else in, especially if it's a Liverpool legend like Kenny Dalglish, then you're a goner.

I still rated and respected Roy and I was happy, after he had a decent spell at West Brom, when he was appointed England manager. Roy succeeded Capello on 1 May 2012 and, despite having such little time to prepare, he did a fine job for England at that summer's Euros. We finished top of our group after drawing with France and beating Sweden and Ukraine.

The same old fate awaited because we lost to Italy in the quarter-finals on penalties. But I had my best ever tournament as an England player. Roy got more out of me than any other England manager had done before. So I was hopeful we could have a decent World Cup in Brazil. I was under no illusions about us winning the tournament – I knew we were not good enough – but I expected us to get out of the group, even though it was a tough one with Italy, Uruguay and Costa Rica.

When the draw was made, the FA Chairman, Greg Dyke, was caught on television making a throat-slitting gesture. Roy smiled but he understood it was going to be very difficult. Italy, our toughest test, were our first opponents as well, and I was slightly disappointed with the level of our training, which I didn't think was intense, sharp or aggressive enough on a daily basis. Some of the sessions were far too slow. Maybe it was down to the heat or some tiredness after a long season and a lot of travelling. But there was no place for excuses at a World Cup.

I went back to my hotel room a couple of times before the Italy game and I wasn't very happy. It didn't look good when the standard of training was so slow and predictable. I'm not sure who was at fault for that because I think sometimes it's up to the players to create the tempo and the speed and the aggression. At first it's almost always quick and intense. But then the starting XI begins to become obvious and some of the players who are going to be left out feel sorry for themselves. The whole group is soon affected. I think that happened on certain days in Brazil.

Gary and I spoke about it and there were times when he was disappointed with certain sessions himself. There were also some very good training sessions in between but it was another sign that England needed more consistency at the highest level – in training as much as playing.

The day before England played Italy in Manaus I felt really good. I felt powerful and fit. I obviously knew that we were in for an awkward game because Italy are always going to be a challenging team in a World Cup match – but I knew that Roy wanted us to play much more aggressively and at a faster tempo than we had done during the 0–0 draw in Euro 2012. He had made a bold selection, picking bright young attacking players in Daniel Sturridge and Raheem Sterling. It was going to be a 50–50 game but we were ready.

In the European Championship, during our quarter-final in Kiev against Italy, I thought that we had showed Andrea Pirlo too much respect. He was obviously a great player – and everyone raved about his performance and the fact that Italy had dominated possession. In the build-up to Manaus we became sick of hearing that, two years before, Italy had control of the ball for 75 per cent of that match in Kiev. Pirlo, we were told, had played more passes on his own than I and England's three other midfielders combined. But I looked at it differently.

Pirlo had not really done anything magical in that game. He dinked his penalty, which was magical, but in 120 minutes of play he didn't really hurt us. Pirlo had a lot of the ball and sprayed some lovely passes around but he didn't actually do any huge damage. Daniele De Rossi hit the post from quite far out but, in general, we were always in that game in Kiev. Italy looked technically superior, but if we'd held our nerve and won on penalties – only Wayne Rooney and I scored in the 4–2 shoot-out – we would have made the semi-finals of Euro 2012. Small details are so vital at this level. You are a shoot-out away from being a hero.

Italy had stagnated since then and I felt that we had real dynamism and pace in our team. We were also capable of playing a fluid system and keeping better control of the ball. I knew Gary was impressed with the style and tempo of Liverpool's play and Roy had watched a lot of us as we made our title surge, when I had been the single pivot. Ray Lewington, one of the other England coaches, spoke to me beforehand, and a couple of times in Brazil, about my playing in the single pivot role. I had got used to the position and I would have been happy if we'd gone down that route.

But a few days before Italy the tactics changed. Roy decided that we would play with two sitting midfielders, with Jordan Henderson joining me in a holding role. I thought it was a waste of Jordan's best attributes because his game is based on energy and bursting forward. He's happy to go box to box. In choosing to play him in a sitting role I felt we would be forcing him to be much more subdued. I would have liked us to have taken the shackles off Jordan and let him power forward while I held the formation together as the lone pivot.

I think Roy was concerned about the temperature that Saturday evening and the sapping humidity of the Amazon. FIFA had ruled that there would be 'cooling breaks' – three-minute stoppages to allow the players to drink the fluids their bodies needed – only if the heat exceeded 32°C. We were expecting to play close to the edge.

'When things don't go right, the easy way out for footballers is to look for an excuse,' I said at my final press conference. Memories of South Africa were still clear in my head and I wanted to send out a strong message.

> You look at other people and point fingers and blame others and say: 'Well, that wasn't right, this wasn't right.' But, for me, the FA have left the players with no excuses in every tournament I've been in. They try their best and this time they have put everything in place. They have done everything they possibly can for the players to perform.
>
> When the whistle goes against Italy, you are on your own. You are with your team and you have to have belief. I think we are in a good place. The squad is very talented, with a good blend of players who have vast experience at this level, and have had great careers, and young exciting talents. This is the perfect opener for us. The confidence and belief we would get if we do get the right result could be massive.

I spoke honestly as I made my final point before our World Cup finally began:

> I will be proud leading this group of players out against Italy. I believe in my teammates, but I will be even prouder if we

come home from this tournament with our heads held high knowing we have gone out on to the pitch and given everything we have got for the public back home. And, looking at the lads and being around them, I get the impression they are ready to give everything they have got. It's here now. All the distances and the miles we have covered, the heat preparation, we have done all that. There are no excuses now. It is time to walk the walk.

# 10. England: The End

*Arena da Amazônia, Manaus, Saturday, 14 June 2014*

I had started playing football on a cold and hard stretch of cement on Ironside Road and I had ended up in the steamy and tangled Amazon rainforest. Manaus was a city that could be reached only by plane or by boat. Only football could have brought me here. Only football could have given me such a bridge across the world. On a fevered Saturday evening in Brazil I was happy to be this deep in the jungle.

I had been lucky enough to play in all the great European football cities, whether it was Barcelona or Madrid, Milan or Turin, Dortmund or Munich, but the accompanying trip around the world, from Huyton to Istanbul, Gelsenkirchen to Bloemfontein, Kiev to Manaus seemed even more surreal. I felt lucky all over again as I changed into my England kit in our dressing room at the Arena da Amazônia.

It was hot and humid, but not unbearably so. The weather men had got it right, predicting a temperature of 30 °C with humidity of 58 per cent just before the 6 p.m. kick-off. Sweat rolled down the faces of my teammates but I liked to think it was more from our warm-up routine than any excessive nerves. I wanted them to feel excited rather than anxious.

The World Cup had exploded into life the previous night when the Netherlands had ripped Spain to shreds in Salvador. It was a 5–1 thrashing studded with memorable goals – and it had been a shock to see the defending world champions, with great footballers like Xavi, Iniesta and Alonso, annihilated. The Dutch had outstanding players too, and Robin van Persie and Arjen Robben had each scored twice, but it was an encouraging sign. Maybe the predictable old order could be demolished in Brazil.

We had been slated for our performance against Italy in Kiev in 2012. The media decided that Pirlo was the artistic master and we were the toothless, clumsy fools. But Italy had still not been able to beat us in open play that night and we had a much pacier team in Manaus. After the season we'd just had I think there were few quibbles from England's fans that our starting XI included five Liverpool players – Glen, Jordan, Raheem, Daniel and me.

Roy and Gary's game plan was for us to play positively and attack Italy from the outset. We opted for a 4-2-3-1 system with Sterling running hard down the middle, just behind Sturridge. Sterling, with his sudden bursts of pace and deceptive strength, was given licence to play with freedom in an attempt to stretch the Italians. He would also need to occupy Pirlo. Rooney would play on the left. It was typical of Wayne that he agreed, without complaint, to sacrifice himself and do a worker's job down the left while Raheem played in the number 10 role they both favoured. I had played with Wayne for a long time and he understood the importance of being flexible and accepting a position which would help the team. He often did the same at Manchester United.

My only concern was that Wayne was much sharper tactically than Raheem – which was to be expected when you compared their very different levels of experience. I worried a little about Sterling's ability to read the game against Pirlo and Daniele De Rossi. But I knew Sterling would be fearless going forward and it was a bold strategy from Roy. I was sure no one would accuse us of lacking courage or attacking intent by the end of the night.

Playing Henderson in a more advanced role would also have been possible if we had less doubt about our defence. Glen Johnson, Gary Cahill, Phil Jagielka and Leighton Baines were good players, and I got on with all of them, but it was obvious to me that England's best defender, our only truly world-class defender in the wake of John Terry's international retirement, had not even been selected for the squad which travelled to Brazil.

The exclusion of Ashley Cole seemed a real error of judgement to me. He and I were not especially close, but I was convinced he should have been in Brazil and he should have started against Italy in Manaus. In every tournament I'd played with Ashley he had probably been England's best player.

Cole was thirty-three, the same age as me, and he had played outstandingly in five major tournaments. He had 107 caps when, in May 2014, Roy decided to leave him out and take Leighton and eighteen-year-old Luke Shaw to Brazil as our left backs. Leighton was a close neighbour of mine in Formby. He was intelligent and likeable and a top Premier League defender with Everton. But there was a difference between him and Cole – and I'd always known it in the years they had vied for the same position with England. Ashley Cole was world class and, like John Terry, he was the kind of defender England needed at the World Cup. And for me, Shaw wasn't ready.

If Cole and Terry had walked out onto the pitch in Manaus I was pretty sure the Italians would have been more worried about how they might get around our defence. It was one thing to excel in the league, as Baines had done consistently for so long, but it was something else altogether to play in a World Cup against the best attackers on the planet.

Roy thought Baines would offer us more going forward than

an ageing Cole, and his strategy placed less emphasis on defence and controlling possession than on attacking Italy at speed. It was brave and exciting, but I was wary of the Italians' guile and experience. Only three members of our team – Rooney, Johnson and me – had even started a World Cup match. Three of the Italian starting XI – Andrea Barzagli, De Rossi and Pirlo – had received World Cup winners' medals after the 2006 final against France.

They were very strong in midfield – with Pirlo, De Rossi, Marco Verratti and Claudio Marchisio all having distinct qualities. It was harder to gauge how Italy would be at opposite ends of the pitch. Buffon, one of the world's great goalkeepers and a key member of that 2006 World Cup-winning team, had been forced to start on the bench after injuring his ankle early that morning. He had been replaced by the Paris Saint-Germain keeper Salvatore Sirigu. Italy would be weaker without the calm and commanding presence of Buffon – while who knew how the chaotic but gifted Mario Balotelli might influence the game up front?

Italy's manager, Cesare Prandelli, was a sly old fox. Earlier that week he had made a joke. Prandelli said he'd had a dream in which his team won the World Cup after playing seven different formations in seven different games. I think it was his way of reminding us that Italy, who had won the World Cup four times, were tactically more sophisticated than England.

That contrast, between our mostly young and pacey team and Italy's more seasoned, fluid tacticians, underpinned the endless appeal of the World Cup. I knew that the game would be watched around the globe but my thoughts were mostly of our fans at home. The pubs in England would be heaving, just before 11 p.m. on a Saturday night, with the game beaming back from the rainforest on huge screens while everyone screamed and roared us on. I sensed there was much more realism in 2014 as most people realized that we did not have the players to win the World Cup – unlike all those dashed hopes the country had harboured since our lone victory in 1966.

The players knew what it meant for us to play well, to get out of the group stages and then go as far as we could in the World Cup while the whole country went crazy on hot summer nights back in England. I did not need to say much in the dressing room. Roy Hodgson was also not a big grandstanding talker just before a game. He allowed me to say the final few words as the team gathered around me. I had a very simple message.

'Let's not have any regrets when we walk off that field at the end of tonight,' I said to the players. I reminded them of the need to give everything of themselves, to play hard, to stay smart and disciplined – and to enjoy it. But most of all, thinking of my past disappointments with England, I said the words again just before we left the dressing room: 'No regrets.'

Pirlo and I stood with our teams behind us in the tunnel. He looked like a bearded old warrior. Pirlo was also coming to the end but, God, what a player. He was one of the mighty giants of European football. Everyone said he couldn't run, but he still had searing vision and a beautiful range of passing. We were old adversaries, and I admired him greatly. It was weird to think I had spent the second half of the past season playing in a Pirlo-type role for Liverpool. It was only a variation on Pirlo, though, because we remained very different players.

He seemed typically Italian, while all the attributes (and flaws) of English football ran through me. I poured my heart out in a game, and I would run and tackle more than Pirlo. He played in a more subtle way but, well, I'd proved over the years I could also read a game and hit a lovely long pass too. I looked forward to one more epic battle against the maestro.

Over the years, fate had been both cruel and kind to the pair of us. We had played against each other in two Champions

League finals, in 2005 and 2007. The victories were split one apiece. After Pirlo suffered the indignity of Istanbul he said he had almost wanted to stop playing football. The hurt of surrendering a 3–0 lead with Milan had scarred him as deeply as the slip against Chelsea had wounded me. Two years later, Pirlo and Milan had gained their revenge over me and Liverpool in the final in Athens. I could hardly bear to think about that game, which we lost 2–1. Pippo Inzaghi scored the first of his two goals that night when a Pirlo free kick took an unexpected deflection off him and flew into the net. Inzaghi knew nothing about the goal and he embraced Pirlo in gratitude. The night would belong to Milan, Inzaghi and Pirlo.

Even such huge games at the peak of European football suddenly seemed dwarfed by the magnitude of a World Cup in Brazil. We both knew that this would be our very last World Cup. I had turned thirty-four a couple of weeks before, on 30 May. Pirlo had celebrated his thirty-fifth birthday eleven days earlier. This was our last tilt at international glory.

We seemed to wait in the tunnel for an age. It felt very hot and Joe Hart, standing behind me, used the towel around his neck to wipe the sweat from his face. I now knew why they had used a special material for the seats in the stadium to avoid them buckling in the heat. I tried to look cool and stared straight ahead; but it wasn't easy. I glanced across the tunnel. Pirlo and I exchanged a knowing look. I reached out and offered my hand. He took it with a wry little smile and a nod. I nodded back, with deep respect.

The Italians were so cool they could wear white tracksuit tops over their blue shirts as if they were waiting for a kick-about on a cool autumn evening in Milan. We were already stripped down to our playing kit of white shirts, white shorts, white socks – and we were still sweating more heavily in the jungle heat.

Joe wiped his brow again, flexed his neck and kept chewing gum in my ear. I could tell he was itching to reach the solitude of his goal. The four match officials, dressed in red, stood in front of us, blocking our path. We could hear the songs of the English supporters and the clamour of the Italian fans.

Eventually, we were given the signal. It was time. The Dutch referee, Björn Kuipers, who had taken charge of the Champions League final between the two Madrid teams exactly three weeks before, led us out into the arena, pausing briefly to scoop up the match ball from a plinth that had been placed just outside the tunnel. Suddenly, as the roaring din hit us, it felt very real. I hoped my young teammates would not shrink in those heart-skipping moments.

As we waited for the national anthems I turned to look down the line of my team. They seemed OK and, at the far end, Sturridge squirted water all over his face.

The music started. I mouthed the words to 'God Save the Queen', but I just wanted to start playing. At least I could breathe again when the Italian anthem boomed out. The cameras would be mostly on Pirlo. Their anthem sounded like a jaunty and jolly military march. Pirlo would be the warrior at the head of their army.

Italy's players belted out the words. They were off-key, but they were up for a battle. Italy always welded passion onto technique. It explained why they were so hard to beat. I heard their players cry out and clap once the anthem ended.

It was handshake time. We stood stock-still while the Italians walked down our white line. Pirlo put up his hand to grasp mine. I took it with another smile and a nod to a rival. The other players for the Azzurri followed. I heard the slap of our hands against each other, one after another, each a thunderclap above the bellowing arena as Italy's and England's fans began chanting.

Pirlo and I soon exchanged a far more formal handshake in

the centre circle. We also swapped pennants as mementos. The ref spun the coin. I won the toss and we shook hands with the officials. The sky above us was a bruised purple. It was very hot in the arena.

I barked out a few more encouraging words to my young team, clapping again and urging them on.

Balotelli and Marchisio stood over the ball in the centre circle, waiting for the whistle. At last it came. Our World Cup could begin. Balotelli tapped the ball to Marchisio who slid it back to Pirlo. He turned and clipped it across to Gabriel Paletta, my old teammate – even though Paletta, as one of Rafa Benítez's more disastrous signings, had played only a few games for Liverpool before he was transferred to Boca Juniors. It was Paletta's first competitive match since changing his nationality from Argentinian to Italian. The ball was knocked forward, in a hopeful punt, towards Balotelli. Cahill intervened and cleared it.

After three minutes Pirlo received the ball and Sterling, unsure whether to close down him or De Rossi, backed off. It was easy for Pirlo to sweep a pass out to the right. Antonio Candreva was given so much space that he could calmly feed Matteo Darmian. It was only Darmian's second cap for Italy but the full back drove hard down the right and whipped in a cross. Jagielka hoofed it clear but an ominous pattern had been established. Prompted by Pirlo, Candreva and Darmian had found an easy way around Leighton Baines.

Our young players were brave. Sturridge picked up a clearance from Cahill in the fourth minute and he found Sterling just inside Italy's half. Sterling decided to run, as if he was playing for Liverpool against Hull rather than for England against Italy in the World Cup. He still had a teenager's bravado and the blue shirts retreated. Sterling had a dip from twenty-five yards. The ball flew towards goal and a roar echoed around the

England end. It looked to some of our fans as if Sterling had scored. He had just found the side netting but it was an impressive first attempt. Italy suddenly knew that Sterling and England were not afraid.

Jordan Henderson forced Sirigu to dive low to his left to keep out his driven shot a couple of minutes later. We looked threatening even though Italy dominated possession. Our biggest problem was down the left as the overlapping Italian rookie, Darmian, now at Manchester United, kept getting at Baines with the help of Candreva. It was two against one.

Hart made a smart save from Candreva but after twenty-one minutes the Liverpool axis took charge. Henderson won the ball and slipped it inside. I drove forward, releasing Sterling, who zipped the ball across the face of the goal. Danny Welbeck just missed a toe-poke of a chance to put us a goal up. It was encouraging; and a couple of minutes later the roles were reversed. Welbeck set up Sturridge and only desperate Italian defending kept us out.

Darmian kept pushing back Rooney and taunting Baines. After thirty-two minutes he flicked it across to Balotelli, whose header was weak. It had been a big chance for Italy. The heat and humidity pressed down on us – but there was a breathless pace to much of the play.

Italy forced a corner, again down our troubled left flank. Candreva took it quickly, playing the ball short to Verratti who hit a diagonal pass in the direction of Pirlo. Sturridge tracked the Italian, who shaped to shoot. But then, with a little touch of his old mastery, Pirlo sold Sturridge an outrageous dummy. He stepped over the ball and allowed it to roll towards Marchisio. None of us were anywhere near him and so Marchisio could trap the ball at leisure and then roll his studs over the top of it. He rifled his shot into the bottom right corner of the goal. Hart had little chance against such power and accuracy. 1–0 down, after thirty-five minutes.

Marchisio ran towards their bench, gesturing to his team-mates to follow him. I watched him go, feeling empty in my gut. The Italians were soon jumping on top of each other in a heap on the touchlines, their blue shirts ringed with dark sweat. They were lost in bliss.

We were quiet. All our effort and perspiration, and we were behind.

I walked around the team, especially the younger players, and encouraged them again. We were playing well in patches – but we could do better. We couldn't shrink now. We had to go again. C'mon, they're not that special. We can get a goal back before half-time.

Italy began to knock it around, stringing twelve, thirteen, fourteen passes together. But the ball was cleared in our half and it broke to Sterling. He was in the centre circle. Sterling ran at pace, moving deep into Italian territory. He played it wide to Rooney, on the left. Rooney showed the class of a great player. He powered down the left and then unleashed an absolute gem of a cross. It flashed past a struggling defender and found Sturridge near the far post. It was easy for Sturridge to steer it home with a half-volley.

1–1, after a beautiful goal, full of the pace, movement, vision and quality I knew we had at our best. Sturridge knew it too and he was on his surfboard, showing the Italians and the Brazilians the old sight we had become so familiar with on the Mersey. Riding the wave, his arms waggling to either side, Sturridge was ecstatic to have caught a big one along the Amazon.

Amid the mad celebrations on the touchline, England's physio, Gary Lewin, went down like he had been shot. He soon had to be stretchered away with a dislocated ankle. Only football could unleash such craziness.

I knew we needed calm. There were only seven minutes of

the half left. I just wanted us to get back to the dressing room so we could sort out the tactical problems, especially down our left side. Hendo agreed. He spoke urgently to Rooney while I talked to Baines. We needed to close down the increasing threat of Darmian and Candreva.

Play resumed and we managed to keep the ball for a minute, passing it crisply to one another, but Italy were soon looking for another goal. The blue shirts rolled towards us but we pressed hard. Darmian got away down our left again, and his shot just flew over the bar. Bigger scares unfolded in the second minute of injury time. My pass was intercepted and Italy broke quickly. Pirlo, on the edge of our box, slid a through ball to Balotelli. Hart came rushing out but he was caught between Balotelli and the goal. The Italian attempted a little dink of a chip over Hart's head – and Jagielka did well to get back and clear it off the line. Italy regained possession and, after some quick interpassing, Candreva hit the post.

We needed the break. We needed a breather. We got it. 1–1 at half-time.

Back in the dressing room we also needed to untangle a tactical mess. Sterling had played very well offensively, but Italy were clever. When they broke from the back I thought Sterling had some rabbit-in-the-headlights moments. He was unsure whether to track Pirlo or De Rossi. I felt we were crying out for two number 10s – Rooney and Sterling pressing their holding midfielders – or a diamond. I thought Gary and Roy got it spot on. They moved the hard-working Welbeck to the left and Rooney was brought inside to a more natural role for him alongside Sterling. But we needed to make sure our full backs played with more certainty. They sometimes looked scared to press because they felt exposed against Darmian and Candreva.

We started aggressively in the second half and I found it frustrating. It was not my place to argue against the manager as he urged us forward in a bid to maintain the momentum of the first forty-five minutes. My instinct was different. This was not a Premier League match. It was our opening World Cup group game. A mindset of 'We must beat Italy' didn't make much sense to me. It smacked of inexperience in our team.

Why didn't we just shut up shop and go for the draw? It seemed similar to the game at Anfield when we tried too hard against Chelsea, went a goal down after a mistake and then panicked a little. We had done well against Italy and struck back immediately. But I felt we were a little gung-ho in the second half instead of showing patience and concentration. Out on the field I was trying to get the message across that a 1–1 draw would be a decent result. I am certain now that if we had managed to take a point from Italy then we would have got out of the group.

But we poured forward, the England fans roaring us on, and when Italy regained possession we defended poorly. Five minutes into the second half, just when we should have been at our most cautious and disciplined, we were sloppy. Baines could not get close enough to Candreva. The Italian danced away and then cut back inside. He had so much freedom and, as he looked up, he saw that Cahill had allowed Balotelli to drift smartly away from him. It was a fine cross from Candreva, under no pressure, and Balotelli had so much space at the far post to score with a downward header. From just a few yards he could hardly miss. It had been a simple, almost routine training-ground goal for Italy.

We tried hard the rest of that half to equalize and Sterling, Rooney, Welbeck and Ross Barkley, on as a substitute, all had their moments. But Italy were used to holding on to a lead and, deep into injury time, they came closest to another goal. Pirlo rattled the crossbar from a free kick thirty yards out. The game was up. England 1, Italy 2.

A 1–1 draw would have been a very good result, so Balotelli's winner felt like a hammer blow. We were drained and disappointed, after playing so well in sustained spells. At times we had outplayed Italy but we had been too keen to try for the win. We were back under terrible pressure in the World Cup – again.

A couple of days later, at our team hotel in Rio de Janeiro, Roy and Gary asked me to talk to the squad. We were in a desperate situation. One more defeat and our World Cup would be over. The failure to leave Manaus with a point seemed more frustrating than ever but I knew I had to lift the squad and explain the dangers that awaited us on Thursday in São Paulo against Uruguay – and Luis Suárez.

Playing in the World Cup for England always felt like a dramatic saga and so it seemed inevitable that the do-or-die stakes would involve Suárez.

The stakes had been raised for Uruguay too. They had lost their opening match, 3–1 to Costa Rica. Suárez had been on the bench, having not yet fully recovered from keyhole surgery to his knee. There was public speculation about Suárez's availability against England. I knew there was no doubt. Suárez was burning to play against us.

Gary Neville kept asking if I had spoken to Suárez since we'd been in Brazil. I explained that we had swapped texts but I'd never once asked him if he was fit and available to play against England. There was no need. I already knew one of the Liverpool physios had been out to check on Luis. I got the message that he was ahead of schedule. Out of respect for Luis I didn't ask for confirmation that he would start against us. It was easy enough to read between the lines. Of course Luis would face us.

Luis had some serious points to prove. He had ended the

Premier League season with a clutch of awards. Voted the play-ers' player of the year, and the football writers' player of the year, Luis might have thought he had rehabilitated his name in England. But he felt a bitterness and hatred towards the English media. He still felt he had been badly treated. Luis also harboured resentment towards the FA because of the way they had dealt with him during the Evra scandal. And then, a day after we lost to Italy, Roy said he didn't believe Luis could be regarded as a world-class player. I obviously disagreed.

I didn't say anything to Roy but I did think 'Uh-oh' when I heard about it. Having a dig at Luis Suárez in the build-up to such a massive game was not Roy's brightest idea. He's a very intelligent, cultured and well-read man, but Roy didn't know Suárez like I did. On the surface his comments were measured. Roy initially praised Suárez, saying, 'He has got the potential. He is a wonderful footballer.' But he then suggested: 'You can be a great player in your league but for the world to recognize you are one of the all-time greats you have got to do it at the World Cup. If you are really going to put him up there with Maradona, Pelé, Beckenbauer and Cruyff, and Pirlo, this is the stage you have got to do it on.'

It was a reasonable observation – but it was the wrong thing to say. I knew Luis would regard it as provocative and disre-spectful. I knew he would use it as additional motivation to make our game in São Paulo his defining answer to all those who had criticized and doubted him in England.

At first, before we turned to Suárez I wanted to convey a wider message to the squad. I kept it brief. Looking around me, I said if we didn't get it right against Uruguay on Thursday, then each and every one of us faced a terrible summer. It would be a long and frustrating month where, away from each other, we'd mull over everything that had gone wrong again and again. I explained how I had suffered in the past – and how much all England players suffer when you leave a tournament earlier than expected. We could go anywhere we liked on holiday but there would be no hiding place.

I was not out to scare anyone. But we had a lot of young lads in the squad and it was important that they understood the importance of the game against Uruguay. We needed everyone to be focused and right on it, both individually and collectively. If we played as I knew we could, we would wake up on Friday morning with three points and feeling on top of the world.

I turned to the topic of Suárez next. I did stress that, while he might be a dream to play alongside, he could be very sneaky to face. We could not leave him alone for a moment. We had to make sure that a couple of us had our eyes trained on him throughout the whole game. 'Be ready for him,' I said, 'because he's lethal if you give him just a little space.'

I stood up and walked across to the tactics board because it was time to be as clear as I was serious. I wrote down all Suárez's strengths and his very few weaknesses. I reiterated what we all knew – that he could be wound up and made to explode – but I felt it was more important to stick to the techniques of trying to blunt him. I said to the whole squad: 'When the ball is coming towards him you've got to keep him facing his own goal. More than anything he wants to turn and face you. He wants to run at you and into you. He'll try and run through you because he wants ricochets, he wants contact. So don't get too tight to him.'

Everyone nodded. I also said to forget about his injury. He was not a normal player. He did not need a game or two to find his rhythm. I expected him to be explosive from the start. I had one more line to add. 'Also, never ever think that it's fine and you've got him sorted. You can never relax against him. Suárez will come at you again and again.'

## *Arena de São Paulo, São Paulo, Thursday, 19 June 2014*

It was a cool and drizzly afternoon in São Paulo. All the heat of the rainforest was long gone. We could have been back at Anfield – which had been the venue the last time England had played Uruguay. That friendly had been held in 2006, back in the days I loved when, with the new Wembley still being built, England used to play fixtures all over the country, many of them in the north. We had won 2–1 and only Wayne Rooney and I survived from that England team.

Eight years later Wayne had been brought back in the middle to play as our number 10 while Sterling would start on the left. Our side was otherwise unchanged from the team which had lost narrowly to Italy. Uruguay, meanwhile, were galvanized by the unsurprising return of Luis Suárez. He was the last player I wanted to be facing – but I took heart from the fact that, apart from Luis, and Edinson Cavani, Uruguay looked little more than a workmanlike team.

For the first thirty minutes we were comfortable. We weren't playing sparkling football but we were keeping Suárez and Cavani in check. Suárez was not looking quite as sharp as he usually did and I felt confident. Of course he had some cheek about him and he shocked Joe Hart when he tried to score straight from a corner. Hart had to beat the corner shot away with both hands. But we came much closer to scoring first. I took a free kick from wide on the left. I found Rooney rising high but his header smacked against the crossbar from a few yards out.

Then, in the thirty-ninth minute, a little slice of luck opened up a dark box of magic. I felt desolate that the luck went against me and the dark magic was unleashed by, firstly, Cavani and then, mostly, Suárez. Nicolás Lodeiro and I contested a loose ball near the halfway line and it ricocheted off me. It spun away into our half and Cavani was soon running hard down our right channel. I could see Suárez gliding into the box. Jagielka was trying to track him but as Cavani shaped to cross the ball, Suárez pulled away. He was suddenly, terrifyingly clear. Suárez was already climbing and twisting in the air as the ball curled in from his left. Hart could sense the danger but, before he could do anything more, Suárez had cushioned a header of looping power and precision over him. It had been an unbelievably good goal.

I had celebrated every one of Suárez's thirty-one goals for Liverpool during his peerless season. This time I could only watch as, screaming with joy, he ran to the sidelines. He was embraced by his teammates but he was more intent on finding Uruguay's physio so that he could show his gratitude. Suárez had regained the fitness he needed to punish his old enemy, and friends like me and his Liverpool teammates.

There was still hope. We were at least as good as Uruguay and we dominated possession. I still believed we could win the game. At half-time I said that we were playing a bit too deep, and showing them a little too much respect. We needed to watch Suárez more closely than ever but we had little else to fear. One of our problems was that we were trying to get the ball to Rooney when he was forty yards from goal. We needed to have Wayne on the ball near the box, where he could really hurt them.

Uruguay had a couple of chances early in the second half but we survived. There was little of the zip and high tempo we had displayed against Italy, in much more draining conditions. No one in a white shirt, apart from Rooney, looked ready to take a grip of the game. But we kept trying and, finally, with fifteen minutes left, we had the breakthrough. Sturridge found Johnson overlapping down the right. Running at speed, and showing great control, Johnson cut inside a defender and clipped a ball hard across the face of the goal. It was a deadly delivery and Rooney, five yards from goal, steered it past their keeper with his left foot. We were jubilant. Rooney's first-ever World Cup goal – 1–1.

It felt like time to settle for a point. We were comfortable and a draw against Uruguay and victory in our last game against Costa Rica would almost certainly see us qualify. The bulk of possession was with us, 62 per cent, and we just needed to be careful when Uruguay broke and counter-attacked. Just as against Italy, when the score was also 1–1, I wanted us to be cannier and cagier. But England's gung-ho gene would not be denied. The team wanted the win. We started to chase the game.

We had so many players piling forward, trying to score and become heroes, that we began to feel outnumbered on every transition. We were all over the place whenever attack had to switch to sudden defence. Suárez was lurking. I wanted us to be patient, to build and prod, and move with solidity. Maybe we would create only one chance in the last ten minutes but that could be all we needed. Instead, it seemed as if we wanted to whip up another new chance every time we had the ball.

In the eighty-fifth minute Uruguay's keeper, Fernando Muslera, gathered the ball safely. He then launched a long kick over the halfway line. I began to back-pedal towards it, in my own half. I waited for the call of 'Mine' from one of the centre halves behind me. It seemed a routine clearance for an alert central defender moving forward as he faced the ball. There was silence behind me and as Cavani rose for the flick-on I jumped with him. But it's hard when you're back-pedalling to get enough height on your leap. The ball skidded off the top of my head. I had misjudged the flight.

Jagielka and Cahill were out of position. The ball bounced

past them, at speed. Suárez had seen how it would all unfold. He had turned and raced towards our goal even as the ball skimmed my head. Suárez was away once more with his frightening speed and brutal menace.

This was nothing like Demba Ba hurtling towards our goal after I slipped. I still had hope then that Simon Mignolet might bail me out – or Ba might miss. But with Suárez I knew there could be only one outcome. I had played alongside him for two and a half years. I knew what Suárez did to such chances. He devoured them, and he would devour us, along with our World Cup dream.

Suárez allowed the ball to bounce and bounce before he took a touch and then, fleetingly, another. Suárez smashed it past Hart for his second killer goal. Uruguay 2, England 1, five minutes from time.

The old emptiness took hold of me at the final whistle. Luis came to find me. He had been substituted after his goal and he wore a sky-blue training top. Luis knew there was nothing he could say. He had won; I had lost. But we were friends. He rested his hand on my head. I looked down and, for a few more seconds, his hand remained in place. And then, with a nod and a last handshake, Luis Suárez was gone.

I was dejected. I felt bad that it was my head the ball had skimmed off and into the path of Suárez. Once we had changed and made our way in silence to the team coach I reached for my phone. I texted Jamie Carragher to ask him about the header. It was my task to deal with any clearances in front of me. But I didn't feel that I should be back-pedalling to win a ball sailing over my head near the halfway line. Roy Hodgson had said the defence should have called out and dealt with it. But I wanted Jamie's opinion – as both an honest critic and a former central defender himself.

Carra also felt it had been a defender's ball – and once I had gone for it then the centre backs should have been prepared for the worst. But it was a collective fault. I hadn't dealt with the header as I should have done – and it was a crime for us to have given Suárez so much space. We all deserved to have fingers pointed at us. It hurts but if you can't accept being blamed then don't become a professional footballer, don't try and play for Liverpool or England.

I also needed to accept the harsh truth. None of us had played well enough. We did not deserve anything better. We had to take our punishment.

It seemed a very long time since the October night, eight months before, when I'd scored the goal against Poland that sealed our qualification for the World Cup. Ever since then, while under no illusions about England's limitations, the minimum requirement once we reached Brazil was to get out of the group. But we had failed miserably. We were out of the World Cup sooner than any other England team of the past.

Before our final, meaningless game against Costa Rica, there was an England press conference. I suppose I could have ducked out of it, I could have refused to do it or made some excuse, but it felt important to face the media. On 22 June 2014, I think I shocked some of the writers who had covered my England career over so many years.

I felt like shit. I looked like shit. There were black circles under my eyes. I had hardly slept the last three nights. I hadn't shaved for four days. My stubble was hard and spiky.

I walked into the media centre in Rio's Urca district. There were journalists everywhere. I recognized most of the old faces. I knew many of them by name. I even trusted a few of them. I did not say hello to anyone. I did not even nod to those I knew best. I just sat down on a chair behind a desk. Roy Hodgson was next to me.

I stared into space, waiting. I already knew the first few questions. I had heard them before. I had sat at the head of a press conference in South Africa in July 2014 after we had lost 4–1 to Germany. This was worse. This was far worse. We were out of the tournament and we still had a game to play. This hurt even more deeply. This was a penalty-shoot-out level of despair. It felt that raw.

And, yes, I was also badly wounded because of deeper, personal reasons. I knew I would never play in a major football tournament ever again. It was over. Six tournaments; six different scenarios of heartbreak.

Someone took the plunge and asked the inevitable question. How did I feel?

I thought it was a legitimate question for an England captain to answer after two straight defeats had ended our tournament. And so I answered honestly. I was 'hurting bad'. Some of the writers looked down. I didn't want any sympathy, but they were only human too. They felt compassion. I kept talking. I felt 'broken'. The anguish spilled out of me.

But this would not have been an England press conference without some controversy. My pain was not controversial. It was too real to be doubted. There were other voices, however; other issues. I knew this was not about me. I still flinched, this time with anger, when I was asked to comment on Harry Redknapp's apparent claim that the modern Premier League footballer didn't really care about England. Harry had been in the running for the England job before Roy was appointed. He said that some of his players at Spurs thought there was 'too much aggro' playing for England.

I couldn't believe it when I first heard it. I still didn't believe it. 'Name them,' I said bluntly. 'We need names.'

There was silence. 'Come on, name them,' I repeated. 'Is it Aaron Lennon? Kyle Walker? Andros Townsend?'

I couldn't believe any Spurs player had tried to get out of an England call-up. Some of the names and faces reeled through my head. Jermain Defoe? Never. Jermain had felt destroyed that he had missed out on the World Cup in Brazil. Peter Crouch? Ledley King? Scott Parker? Michael Dawson? Tom Huddlestone? I didn't believe any of them would have avoided playing for England. There were others but I did not want to think that even one Spurs player could have let down England.

Roy was just as riled as me. 'It's certainly not Jermain Defoe,' he said. I knew how hard Roy had found it to break the news to Jermain that he had not been picked for Brazil. Struan, who represents both of us, had also told me that Jermain was devastated.

'If it's the case, it's disgusting,' I said. 'They didn't want to play for England? Who? Who does he [Harry] mean? I don't know who he means.'

Roy could hear the edge in my voice. 'I agree with Steven,' he said. 'In the two years I've been here, I've seen a greater interest in playing for England, so Harry's comments come as a bit of a surprise. If you make comments like that, you have to name the players. I could name *a* player with an educated guess, but "players"? It's unfair to ask people to look back historically like that.'

Everyone could see how much I cared. I cared so much it tore me to pieces. The World Cup had left me with feelings, I said, of 'frustration, pain. The season for Liverpool ended badly for me. I was coming out of that, trying to put it to bed, trying to get some positivity back. This is exactly what I didn't want to happen, the exact way. The last couple of days have been grim. It hurts. It's killing me not to have any positives to speak about.'

I looked up. There was no need to hammer home any message about the commitment and damaged hopes of England's players. I just needed to speak the truth one more time. 'No one in this group wants to go home,' I said. 'No one.'

We all knew we were on our way home after our final group game against Costa Rica ended in a drab goalless draw in Belo Horizonte on Tuesday, 24 June 2014. We finished bottom of Group D. Costa Rica were top, ahead of Uruguay and Italy. England had finished six points behind a tiny island with a population that was virtually the same as the number of people crammed into south London. Costa Rica surprised everyone and they had done extremely well.

We tried to win that last game, for the sake of our pride, but we were not good enough to get three points against Costa Rica. It told us exactly where we belonged.

A few weeks later, on holiday in Spain, I watched Germany, the eventual winners, destroy Brazil 7–1 in the semi-finals. The hosts, the world's greatest football nation, had been humiliated. Even in the group games I could see the Germans were streets ahead of England. I don't think they would have beaten us 7–1 if we had played them in Brazil – but it would have been a defeat as bad as the 4–1 we'd shipped against them in South Africa. We had also faced them in a friendly at Wembley in November 2013 and, even without many of their best team, Germany had outplayed us.

In Brazil the problems of England's national football team were clear. It was obvious that the media needs to be more balanced. I think players need to be more balanced. At the moment you get hysteria because we have the most exciting and the most competitive league in the world. Clearly, it's not the best league in the world from a technical perspective, but young players shine in the Premier League and they become media superstars overnight. Such manufactured fame does no favours to anyone outside the kid's agent and his sponsors.

I remember liking something Roy Keane said on television. It struck a chord with me. He said it's very difficult to become a superstar or a legend. Those kind of claims can be made only after you have won some important tournaments on the European and world stage and performed consistently over a very long time. I don't think we need more than two hands to count the real superstars and the genuine legends of modern football.

So there needs to be reality and balance in the media towards England – but, as importantly, that same perspective needs to be instilled into our current crop of international players. When England do reach the World Cup or the European Championship the competition is tough. You suddenly realize there are very good players from every corner of the world. There are excellent teams and intelligent managers because, obviously, this is the highest level of football.

I've experienced both extremes during my England career, so I accept it. I can take the abuse because I also remember how much unearned adulation we received for so long. And, of course, I fell for some of it too. I might wish I had totally ignored being told how great we all were in the press. But I think it's true to say that I only ever felt that when, deep down inside, I thought we were good enough to reach the last four in a major tournament.

The 'golden generation', as some people liked to describe the era of Owen and Beckham, Scholes and Ferdinand, Lampard and me, and Rooney too, got plenty of stick in the end. But looking back, a couple of quarter-final performances from that crop of players wasn't too bad. It wasn't great. But it wasn't as disastrous as some people now claim. With a bit of luck in penalty shoot-outs that team would have reached the last four of a major tournament and that would have been no small achievement.

We didn't make it in the end. And so only the players in three

England teams can claim more than a modest six or seven out of ten over the course of their international careers. Maybe the Euro '96 team. Probably the Italia '90 squad. And, of course, way above all of us, as the only really genuine England legends, the 1966 World Cup-winning squad remain the shining example.

West Germany were the losing finalists at Wembley that year. It was the pinnacle for England, but just one final in a very long list for the Germans. Someone told me the other day that, since 1954, Germany have won four World Cups, been a losing finalist four times and reached the last four a total of twelve times.

England specialize in hype and criticism, and constant soul-searching, while allowing countless mistakes and bad decisions to add to the confusion and disappointment. It seems as if the Germans put all their energy and intelligence into finding solutions and planning clearly.

They also produce very good players; and their media don't hype them up and tell them that they're superstars before they have done anything of note. A German player becomes a superstar only once he has a World Cup or European Championship winner's medal. Our players are often told they're superstars even before their first England call-up.

A manager like José Mourinho would not have allowed our players to get ahead of themselves. And it made me stop and think when I read José's comments just before the World Cup started, as he remembered how close he had come to signing a contract to become England's manager. José said he was ready to commit himself to the job – saying he was 'this close' as he gestured to the small space between a pen and a piece of paper – when his wife stepped in and persuaded him not to sign the deal. His wife said he would not be happy without the daily contact of working with a club squad and so he decided to turn down England.

It would have been a fascinating combination. Apart from keeping our heads in check, José would also have given the squad the protection it needed from outside influences. And he would have played the media a treat. He would have taken a lot of pressure off the players as far as our media commitments were concerned. That's all part of what José does so well.

José Mourinho in tandem with the best England team I played for, between 2004 and 2006, would have been the most compelling of all combinations. During those years we played 4-4-2 under Sven-Göran Eriksson. Sven was a very good manager, but I think José was more tactically astute and sharper with the media. There were times when 4-4-2 could be quite positive and used against a lot of national sides. But, for me, it's been very outdated for a long time. Yes it can work if you have two centre forwards who are relentless in the way they work for the team. You also need two great athletes in central midfield who can cover a lot of ground. But over the last decade and more the best teams have always managed to get a numerical advantage in the middle of the pitch. A rigid 4-4-2 will be absolutely killed by the right team. Imagine playing 4-4-2 against Spain? You would be in for the longest ninety minutes of your life.

José, unlike Sven, would never play 4-4-2. He showed, even when he was with Porto, he would never be so naive. And so if José Mourinho had managed England in 2004 and 2006 I'm convinced we could have reached at least one major final. I think Rafa Benítez could also have steered us to a final in the Euros or the World Cup. But the only problem with Rafa is that a lot of the players would not have enjoyed playing for him – and over a long tournament there would be pressures and tensions. That's why José Mourinho stands out as the manager I wish England had appointed during my time as a player. Imagine what he could have got out of a group that included

Beckham, Scholes, Owen, Terry, Neville, Rooney, Campbell, Ferdinand, Lampard, Cole, Gerrard and a few others. It was the stuff of football fantasy for me.

Back in the real world, I didn't feel humiliated in Brazil. I just felt bitterly disappointed. We'd played three games and hadn't won one. We'd scored just two goals. We'd conceded four. The irony was that, in the first two games, we were probably too positive. I think we got caught. Roy got some criticism at Euro 2012, where we were a bit too defensive and negative. He felt as if he was left with no option but to go for the jugular. But that also damaged us because I'm not sure it's Roy's way. For a long, long time he had always been an organized manager with two banks of four in a standard 4-4-2. Modern football is very different now and you have to be much more sophisticated tactically.

But Roy, essentially, is a dogged manager. He's very organized, very compact and he is similar to Benítez in preferring to play midfielders who graft for you in wide areas – rather than attacking dribblers and wingers. I think the criticism we received in 2012, losing on penalties to Italy, was unfair. It made us more positive in Brazil but we came unstuck.

We had a squad of honest lads who did their best. We never got the breaks we needed and some big moments in games went against us. In the end, we were just not good enough to have progressed further. I think, collectively, all of us involved in English football during that campaign have to take responsibility for the let-down we suffered in Brazil.

We all sometimes fall into the trap of believing that we're better than we are, and we start to dream. There's no harm in dreaming as long as you temper your dreams with realism.

At least there's always another fixture to be played, always another qualifying group, another tournament to aim for. One day, maybe, we'll get it right.

I didn't know that my last-ever appearance for England

would be against Costa Rica. I hadn't made the decision then to retire from international football. Roy Hodgson is a good manager and considerate towards the whole squad. So I understood the reasons when he suggested that I and a few others who had played against Italy and Uruguay should start the Costa Rica game on the bench.

Soon after we'd arrived in Brazil it had been fairly clear who would be in the starting XI for the first two games. A little bit of fight and intensity went out of training – and Roy tried to get that back before Costa Rica by being respectful to the squad players and giving them some World Cup experience.

I accepted it as the right decision. The rest of the squad had come a long way. They deserved a run out. I also knew I'd be coming on in the second half.

At the end of the game, I walked over to the England fans. It was one of the most touching moments of my international career. They gave me a wonderful reception. It meant all the more because I knew many of them would have been there on that unforgettable night in Munich, in September 2001, when I'd scored a goal and we'd pulverized Germany 5–1. They had just sat through a humdrum goalless draw, at the end of a terribly disappointing World Cup, which had cost each of them a lot of money. But they rose to their feet to cheer and applaud me.

I was moved by their unwavering support. But it hurt, too, because a lonely thought echoed in my head. 'Imagine the reaction we'd get from these fans if we ever won a big tournament . . .'

I held my hands above my head, applauding our supporters, thanking them for being so generous, and the thought echoed again. 'Imagine what it might have been like . . .'

On the team bus an hour later, I looked out of the window and said my own private little goodbye to Brazil and the World

Cup. At least I would soon see Alex and the girls. My phone buzzed. Another sympathetic text? The WhatsApp icon shone on my phone. I opened the message. There were just a few words accompanying two images. I had been sent a photograph of Giorgio Chiellini's shoulder. The Italian defender, who had played against us in Manaus, was touching his bare and bruised skin. His shoulder had been bitten. The second photograph showed Luis Suárez clutching his teeth.

I just could not believe that Suárez had done it again. But in my heart I knew. He had bitten Chiellini. I felt gutted for Luis, and sick for Chiellini. It was unforgivable – and I knew Luis would soon have to admit the undeniable truth for the third time in his career.

What a season – for Luis Suárez and for me. We had shared the pain of his isolation at Melwood when he had been banished from training and banned for biting Ivanović. I had convinced him to stay. Together, we had almost won the league for Liverpool. We went to the World Cup. Suárez punished England for all the past slights and humiliations he thought he had suffered. Uruguay also beat Italy. They were into the last sixteen of the World Cup. But, in the end, Luis Suárez was about to suffer the same fate as England and me. He was about to be kicked out of the World Cup. We were all going home early.

I stared at the images in despair. Oh, Luis. Not again . . . not again.

# 11. The Merry-Go-Round

My work as Liverpool captain hardly ever stopped. Even during the World Cup I took a little break from fretting over England to try to magic up some transfer business. Brendan Rodgers was keen on the idea of persuading Alexis Sánchez to join Liverpool from Barcelona. He knew there was a strong chance Luis Suárez would be making the journey in the opposite direction. Sánchez was, obviously, a terrific footballer and his intense energy, desire, speed and work rate made him the exact sort of star player who could slot into the type of team we were trying to build at Liverpool. He impressed again for Chile in Brazil and Brendan and I agreed I would do my usual off-season hustling.

I was up against it because we knew Arsène Wenger was also in the hunt for Sánchez. Wenger was in Brazil and Sánchez was top of his shopping list. We had gone to war against Arsenal the previous summer over Suárez – and won that fierce battle. Wenger's regal managerial reputation and suave charm tended to dazzle most players he met in person. But I was hoping I could ride the wave of our fantastic 2013–14 league season and persuade Sánchez that Liverpool were still a better bet than Arsenal. I knew that if we could land Sánchez it would help hugely to soften the blow of losing Suárez.

Luis had his agreement that he would give Liverpool one final huge season and then no one would stand in his way if Barcelona came in for him. I had secretly been hoping that the thrilling title chase of the past season might help change his mind, especially as we were now playing Champions

League football again. But any hope of clinging on to Suárez disappeared the moment I opened up my phone in Belo Horizonte and saw the Chiellini bite. It was obvious Luis would be banned again for a long time. And I knew that he would never come back to play in England, where he had his harshest critics.

I tried hard with Sánchez because I really did believe we had a chance of getting him. I stepped back onto the texting merry-go-round and followed the usual routine when approaching a player. Sánchez was great in the way he responded; his English was good and we had some detailed text exchanges. I could tell he had real respect for Liverpool and he said he would love to play in the same team as me. I said I definitely planned on playing for another couple of seasons but, just when I thought we might be getting somewhere, Sánchez pointed out, politely but honestly, that he appreciated my career was coming towards the end and he felt he needed to be careful before signing a contract with Liverpool.

Essentially, he wasn't really certain of Liverpool's future and had a lot more confidence in Arsenal. I appreciated the fact he was open and candid about his reasons for choosing Arsenal, as being in London was another attraction for him and his girlfriend.

A few weeks later, on 10 July 2014, Arsenal confirmed that they had signed Sánchez for £35m. I was not surprised that Wenger's persuasive powers had clinched the deal. The Chilean would become one of the signings of the season – and well over a year later I still wondered how Liverpool's 2014–15 campaign might have turned out if Sánchez had chosen us instead of Arsenal.

My other texting target of that World Cup summer was ridiculously optimistic. Brendan asked me to take a crack at trying to talk Toni Kroos into signing for Liverpool. He just smiled when I said we'd be pissing into the wind with this one. We both admired Kroos immensely as a player. I knew Real Madrid were gearing up to make Bayern Munich an offer and so I felt a bit awkward when I texted Kroos at first. The German midfielder was on his way to winning the World Cup with his country and Real were the champions of Europe. But God loves a trier, and so I gave it a whirl.

Some of the best footballers in the world can also be the most respectful. Kroos was super-respectful and he didn't make me feel like I was a total idiot. But, of course, he would soon sign for Real Madrid. We had a nice little exchange of texts and I said well done and good luck.

'We were always on to a loser with that one,' I reminded Brendan.

The mood back at Melwood in July 2014 was different from the paranoia of a year earlier. We had resigned ourselves to losing Luis but we were clearly aware of the need to sign a striking partner for Daniel Sturridge. Brendan was working hard to fill that hole while I was deep into my other team-building role. Apart from texting possible future players it was also my task to boost my teammates. I always believed that we needed someone in the squad to take on the mantle of the main man.

From the outside some fans might have assumed that I saw myself as the kingpin at Liverpool – because I was the captain and our longest-serving player by miles. But I never thought of myself in that way. I was always on the hunt for a goalscoring star who could be our key player. It was in keeping with the Anfield tradition to anoint our best striker as Liverpool's figurehead. I saw a gleaming chain stretch from Kevin Keegan and Kenny Dalglish to Robbie Fowler and Michael Owen to Fernando Torres and Luis Suárez. Those were our heroes – and, in training, I loved pitting myself against the likes of Torres and Suárez to improve as a player.

I had more responsibility and influence than other players – but I always went out of my way to tell someone he was the most important person in the team. It was my job, when we signed a new star player or when a new season began, to motivate him. I would be in their ear daily, Fernando's, and then Luis's: 'You're the main man. It's all about you today. None of these teams want to play against you.' I'd be pumping them up every single day, making them feel great. When they were down, I'd pick them up. When they looked like they had a cob on I'd sort them out and make them feel special again.

Of course, I understood the importance of team unity and I would also try and make sure that everyone felt they were equally important to me. But, on my own with the top player, I'd make it clear. To be successful and to compete at the highest level we needed a world-class striker – and he would be my favourite.

As soon as I accepted Suárez was as good as gone my plan was to pump up Daniel Sturridge, and I spent the summer of 2014 telling him how good he was and how much we needed him. I had no idea then that Daniel's season would be affected so unluckily by injuries – but during the build-up to a new campaign I invested a lot of hope in him. His twenty-one league goals the previous season meant that he had the potential to become even better and keep us in the top four. A deadly striker goes a long way to ensuring Champions League qualification – and two of them, as Suárez and Sturridge had proved, can drive you to the brink of the title.

In early July we were out on the A-team pitch, having just finished a preseason training session at Melwood. Brendan called me over for a chat. He said, 'I'm trying desperately to get a forward in and I really want Loïc Rémy. What do you think?'

I was a fan of Rémy's and definitely thought he was good

enough for Liverpool. He had ability and pace and would be a great asset alongside Sturridge. Arsenal and Chelsea were also interested so we needed to move decisively. Rémy was under contract to QPR and, while they had spent the previous season gaining promotion to the Premier League, he had enjoyed a successful loan spell at Newcastle. There was a release clause in his contract: if any Champions League club offered at least £8.5m for him, Rémy could leave QPR.

Brendan was confident we could get him and, for once, I met our transfer target in person rather than having to text him. Rémy and I met in Switzerland during preseason. There was no need for a sales pitch; Rémy was really looking forward to playing for Liverpool. Why couldn't all transfer targets be so easy?

Of course a straightforward deal soon went wrong. Our doctors picked up a problem during Rémy's medical. The deal was off. Rémy was angry and he felt Liverpool were wrong. He ended up signing for Chelsea instead. I just knew we were in trouble without another striker to take the load off Sturridge.

On the opening day of the season Raheem Sterling and Sturridge scored in a 2–1 win at home against Southampton, a club we had plundered. We had signed three of their players that summer – Rickie Lambert, Adam Lallana and Dejan Lovren. The big surprise for me was the £20m we paid for Lovren. Southampton didn't want to sell him so they held out for a lot of money. A £20m defender, for me, is the calibre of John Terry or Jamie Carragher. I didn't know enough about Lovren to gauge whether he warranted such a huge outlay.

His first training session, however, made an unbelievable impression on me. I thought, 'Yeah, that's why we've paid £20m.' He was putting his body in the way of shots. He was heading the ball away every time. His communication in

English was good. Lovren looked a rock that day. I still think that he is good enough to play for Liverpool at centre half for a long time. But he went on to struggle with his confidence in his first season at Anfield as fierce media criticism affected him.

It can have a big impact on some players when, after two or three bad games, they get destroyed in the papers, on *Match of the Day* or on Sky by Carragher and Neville. Players do read their reviews. They hear the pundits and take notice of them. Some footballers just bounce back, which is how I've always tried to react – by trying to go out and prove the 'experts' wrong. But other players go into their shell and the criticism affects them for quite a long time. There were a couple of times when I had to put my arm round Lovren. I needed to boost him.

Even after the tough opening season he went through, I still think that he has the character to settle down and do well for Liverpool. He's a good defender. But we'll need three or four years to judge whether he was worth £20m. It helps that Lovren is a lovely feller who wants to succeed. He works hard and he's professional. Those attributes are vital.

The same can be said of Lambert. He immediately proved himself to be a true professional who worked incredibly hard every day. It meant a huge amount to Rickie to be signed by Liverpool because he had been born in nearby Kirkby. The club had let him go when he was fifteen – after he had spent five years at the Academy. I could imagine how crushing that must have been because I still remembered my pride at being an Academy player when I was a teenager. But Rickie didn't give up. He had to fight to make it as a professional footballer and before he and Southampton were promoted into the Premier League he had played for Blackpool, Macclesfield, Stockport, Rochdale and Bristol Rovers. I had great respect for the way he had turned himself into an England international after that long battle through the lower ranks of English football. So it must have seemed like a dream summer for Rickie when, in June 2014, he signed for Liverpool and went to Brazil with England's World Cup squad.

I liked the fact that he loved Liverpool. That passion and professionalism meant his attitude never wavered even when it quickly became obvious that he would only be a squad player at Anfield. He would come off the bench a lot, and remain behind Sturridge and whomever else Brendan might be able to sign before the transfer window closed at the end of August 2014.

Brendan eventually came to me at Melwood in mid-August. We had a chat on the training pitch. He said, 'You know we've missed out on a couple. I'm basically left with no option but to have a bit of a gamble.'

Brendan paused before he spoke again: 'The gamble is Mario Balotelli.'

My instant reaction was, 'Uh-oh.' I'd never met Balotelli but I'd heard all the stories about the indoor fireworks and José Mourinho describing him as an 'unmanageable' player. I could see that, in the right mood, he was a quality footballer but the rest of his career seemed like a spectacular waste of talent. That was my opinion of Balotelli. But I also had to admit that, when he played for Italy, he seemed able to switch on his gift like he was snapping on a bright light.

When he scored the winner against England in Manaus, a month earlier, he showed all the movement which made him so difficult to mark at his best. I spoke about this more positive impression to Brendan. There was no point harping on about Balotelli's negative public image.

'Well, if you get the gamble right, and you feel able to manage him,' I said to Brendan, 'maybe it can work. When I've played against him for England a couple of times he's been very, very good.' I also told Brendan that, up close to him on the pitch, you could see that he was a big, powerful guy.

Balotelli had the potential to be a world-class striker, as well as the touch, the power and the finishing. I mentioned his mentality but Brendan had the confidence he could be the manager Balotelli needed.

I understood the gamble. We didn't have another top striker alongside Sturridge. Lambert would be a decent back-up but we needed someone with a special talent. Balotelli had it and I believed that if Brendan could work a miracle and sort out his head we could have one of the best £16m signings in the world. We are still waiting.

Brendan still sensed my underlying reservations because he spoke a little more about why he thought it could be worth the risk. Brendan implied that Balotelli didn't have anywhere else to go – and it seemed as if Liverpool would be Balotelli's last chance to shine at a major club.

He would be offered a strict contract. Any bad behaviour would be punished. Brendan said he would meet Balotelli at Melwood while we investigated the only other option for us – Samuel Eto'o.

He might have had a big ego but Eto'o had won the Champions League with Barcelona and Inter. There was a winner's mentality inside Eto'o, which is why Mourinho, who had managed him at Inter, brought him to Chelsea. But Eto'o, at thirty-three, was winding down and there were worries about his fitness and injury record. It was decided that while Brendan sat down with Balotelli our fitness coach, Jordan Milsom, would spend time with Eto'o in Paris. He'd run some tests and then Brendan would make the call.

A few days later I got the nod from Brendan. He was going to take the big gamble. We were going to sign Balotelli. I heard the same 'uh-oh' at the back of my head. I had mixed feelings.

I reminded myself that I had always allowed every new

player to come into the club with a clean slate. Balotelli's reputation tested that resolve but I tried my best to be open-minded when he arrived for his first day of training on 26 August – a day after we had played our second match of the season and lost 3–1 at Manchester City, one of Balotelli's former clubs.

He made an immediate impression. We were doing work on our defensive set pieces and Balotelli said to Brendan: 'I don't mark on corners. I can't.' I nearly fell into the goalpost. I was thinking, 'What are you? Six foot three, and one of the strongest men I've ever seen on a football pitch? And you can't mark on a corner?'

Brendan was very firm. He said to Balotelli: 'Well, you can now – and if you can't then you're going to learn.' That was the first conflict between Brendan and Balotelli, on day one, but the manager stood up to Mario really well. From that point, Balotelli started marking on corners. And he even went on to stop a few important goals over the coming months.

Balotelli made his Liverpool debut on 31 August 2014, away to Tottenham, and he did well. We won 3–0, with goals from Sterling, me and Alberto Moreno. Tottenham's new manager, Mauricio Pochettino, had taken over a poor team. He was a good manager but he needed time to get them playing with some kind of rhythm. We played well that day – almost to the level when we had beaten Spurs 5–0 and 4–0 the previous season. Balotelli wasn't outstanding but he worked hard for the team and he had two or three chances to score. He even looked like a team player.

It would not last. Daniel Sturridge was injured ten days later, while training with England. He would be out for many weeks. Suddenly the Mario gamble was in jeopardy – because I knew that Balotelli would simply not put in the work we needed from a lone striker. Everything became more tangled, and more difficult.

*

The day after we beat Tottenham, Luis Suárez was back at Melwood. I wished I could have said he was back to play for Liverpool again. But Luis had come to say goodbye. He had also brought me a present. It was a Barcelona shirt with the number 9 on the back and Suárez written above it. Luis still couldn't wear his new shirt for real because, after his World Cup bite, and the third of his career, he had been banned even more heavily. Apart from missing nine matches for Uruguay he was banned from all 'football-related' activity for four months and fined £66,000. He had not helped himself by, initially, protesting that the bite had been unintentional.

'In no way did it happen how you have described, as a bite or intent to bite,' his lawyer had written on behalf of Suárez when a FIFA disciplinary committee found him guilty of biting Giorgio Chiellini. 'After the impact I lost my balance, making my body unstable and I fell on top of my opponent. At that moment I hit my face against the player, leaving a small bruise on my cheek and a strong pain in my teeth.'

It was a crazy defence and FIFA had rightly insisted that the bite was 'deliberate, intentional and without provocation' – and delivered their punishment. On 30 June, Luis finally apologized in a public statement:

> After several days of being home with my family, I have had the opportunity to regain my calm and reflect on the reality of what occurred during the Italy–Uruguay match on 24 June 2014. The truth is that my colleague Giorgio Chiellini suffered the physical result of a bite in the collision he suffered with me. For this I deeply regret what occurred. I apologize to Giorgio Chiellini and the entire football family. I vow to the public that there will never again be another incident like this.

I knew Luis was still hurting from the fallout, and the fact that he alone had caused it. I concentrated instead on the happier story, for him, of his £75m move to Barcelona. I knew the history of his attachment to Barcelona and what it meant to him and his wife to finally be on their way to Catalonia. Eleven years earlier, when he was just sixteen, Luis visited Barcelona for the first time in order to see his girlfriend, Sofi. She and her family had just emigrated from Uruguay to Spain. They lived in Castelldefels, a short way up the coast from Barcelona.

Luis was heartbroken at losing his girlfriend, and he swore to Sofi and to himself that, through football, he would find his way back to Europe and, eventually, Barcelona. Before he said goodbye to her and flew back to Montevideo, sixteen-year-old Luis and Sofi slipped inside Camp Nou so he could take a photograph of the empty stadium. She was afraid they would be caught. But Luis got his photograph – and now he had turned his dream into reality.

He and Sofi, now his wife, and their two children, Delfina and Benjamín, would rent a house in Castelldefels. It completed a love story, and a football fantasy. Despite my sadness at losing him as a teammate, I could only be happy for Luis. I had no doubt he would be a great success at Barcelona, playing alongside Messi and Neymar.

We sat for a while in the same part of Melwood where, almost exactly a year before, I had persuaded Luis to reject Arsenal and stay for another season at Liverpool. We both still hurt a little over the fact that our amazing last campaign together had not ended in the title we craved. But we had our memories; and our friendship.

It was also striking that, before he left Melwood for ever that day, Luis spoke to me about Philippe Coutinho. 'Make sure you look after him,' Luis said of Philippe, 'he's a good kid.' That told me how much Suárez rated Coutinho as a player. I knew they were close, because all the South Americans and Spaniards loved Luis. But it struck a chord with me when Luis singled out Philippe as our most special young talent. It echoed my own view.

Philippe is wonderfully gifted and I expect him to become Liverpool's leading player. Many Liverpool fans already regard him as our main man. He has just signed a new deal and he and his wife — who are a lovely couple — seem settled here. But I also know that the Spanish giants, Barcelona and Real Madrid, will come looking for Philippe in a few more seasons, just like they did with Luis. And that's when it will get tricky for Liverpool because the lure to go to one of those two clubs is so strong for any South American or Spanish player. Until that happens, Liverpool should really treasure Philippe.

I was already keeping an eye out for him. But ever since Luis spoke to me on his last day in Liverpool I've taken even more care. If I had been out for a while, through injury or suspension, I would always make sure that I texted Philippe before or after a game. I knew we needed to keep hold of him as long as possible.

I don't often use social media but, when I do, I'll post a photo on Instagram. On 1 September 2014 the Melwood snap featured Luis and me — and the Barça shirt he had just given me. We were both smiling as we held the shirt between us. 'He's back bearing gifts,' I wrote on Instagram. 'Emotional saying goodbye to the main man this morning. Best wishes to a phenomenal player.'

Luis went on Twitter later that day to send a last tweet from Liverpool, a photograph of him with me, Glen Johnson and Jon Flanagan:

Today I could say goodbye to some friends, it was exciting to remember the good moments that we lived together. Thank you for all the joy you gave me!!!!! Great picture with @Glen_johnson, @ jon_flan93 and Steven Gerrard!!!!

My own future with Liverpool seemed to have been strengthened by my retirement from international football. The news was announced on 21 July but the decision had actually been made while I was still in Brazil. Out of respect to Roy Hodgson I agreed to think it over for a few more weeks.

Brendan Rodgers played a key role. I'd had a brief chat with him before the World Cup to say that I might be about to play my last games for England. I said we would see how the tournament went and we agreed to discuss it with an open mind when the time was right.

Brendan kept in touch by text and also by calling to wish me good luck before the group games began. We then spoke again between the Uruguay and Costa Rica matches because I needed to find out our preseason training plans. I also thought it was the perfect chance to bring up the topic of my future with England.

Roy was very keen for me to stay on. He had made that plain when we spoke after the Uruguay defeat. Roy said he wanted me in any capacity that suited me – whether that was remaining as captain or just as a player. We had spoken very informally, as we were both still in pain after the two World Cup defeats, but Roy implied that we could even pick and choose the England games I played. He said he would be comfortable if I didn't even attend certain squad get-togethers for low-key friendlies or even routine qualification matches. If he didn't feel he needed me to start then I could use that as recovery time back in Liverpool.

I didn't think such an arrangement would be fair to the other players. If England won a game 5–0, without me, it would look odd if I came straight back in for the next match. But I had such a strong relationship with Roy that I agreed to think about it.

Steve Peters had been with England in Brazil and he stressed how much Roy wanted me to stay on. Gary Neville also had a chat with me. He said, 'Look, take your time. This squad needs you because we've got a lot of young players. Go home and think about it.'

I was thirty-four years old and, because of my relationship with Liverpool and the supporters, my priority was to gauge Brendan's reaction. He said, 'I understand how big a position you're in for England. You're captain. You don't give that up easily.'

But everything changed the moment Brendan started talking about managing my games. He said, 'It's fine by me if you do want to stay on with England. I can certainly tailor your games.'

I took a troubled backward step in my head. I was not looking to limit my Liverpool career.

Brendan spoke about his plan to bring in at least five new signings. We needed a bigger squad, especially because we were in the Champions League, and he was willing to rotate me. He made it clear that if it was a big game then I remained a first choice – but he could ration my Liverpool appearances a little if I wanted to continue my England career.

It was the most important phone call of the whole season for me. As soon as I heard Brendan saying he could tailor my appearances, my decision was made. I said: 'I don't want my Liverpool games managed – so I'll retire 100 per cent from England.'

Brendan was happy from a Liverpool perspective. But he suggested that I talk to Roy and think it over after chatting to a few more people. It was then that Roy asked me not to make any hasty announcement. He was going away for a break, and I was doing the same with Alex and the kids. So we agreed that, once I got back to England, I would give myself three or four weeks to make a final decision.

I spoke to Jamie Redknapp, Gary McAllister, Jamie Carragher, Didi Hamann and David Beckham – all the usual
former teammates I turn to when I need some advice about
football. I had another chat with Brendan and I spoke to Struan
Marshall, my agent, and to my dad. I also discussed it with a
few of my closest friends, outside of the game. I was already
90 per cent there in my head – because I had basically decided
I would retire from England during that first chat with Brendan
about managing my games.

Only one person disagreed with my instinctive reaction.
David Beckham was very firm. He said: 'Don't retire. Don't
walk away from England. If you do, you might regret it.'

I knew David had really missed it when Steve McLaren left
him out of the squad after the 2006 World Cup. He fought his
way back into the team and ended up playing 115 games for
England, one cap more than me.

But once I had spoken to Becks in detail, he listened closely.
I told him I was paranoid about becoming a squad player and
he softened his stance. He said he understood and respected
my decision.

Roy was also very understanding and our relationship is still
strong. We stay in close touch and I was very happy when the
FA agreed that he should remain as England manager. I firmly
believe Roy is the best man to be in charge of England. The
fact that England were unbeaten for the whole of the 2014–15
season, even if the opposition was not always the strongest,
supported that belief.

Once my decision had been confirmed, and made public, I
was confident everything would be fine. My existing deal with
Liverpool was due to expire in June 2015 but Brendan had told
me that he had asked the owners to sort out my contract and
give me the year-long extension we had discussed. I was relaxed
and looking forward to building on the success we'd had the

season before and, without any England games, I expected to feel fresher and play well for Liverpool. Everything seemed very clear and very positive.

The business of football makes a habit of becoming complicated. It became a little troubling on the field when, after our 3–0 defeat of Spurs in London, we lost two successive games – 1–0 at home to Aston Villa and 3–1 away to West Ham. I was heavily man-marked in both games and I found it difficult in my now-established deep-lying midfield role. I think Premier League managers had devised a new way of stopping me after I had done so well the previous season. So they started sticking a man really close to me. It was as if they had decided I could destroy them if I was given time and space.

Gabby Agbonlahor was the first player who was really sent out to do a specific job on me. When we played Villa he was on top of me the whole game – apart from when he actually scored the only goal in the eighth minute – and he gave me few options. I could only play it short because Agbonlahor was so committed to stifling me. He didn't even bother looking at the ball. He just watched me the whole time, and stuck to me like the stickiest glue. It worked for them and they won the game.

Sam Allardyce repeated Paul Lambert's strategy the following week. Stewart Downing was all over me, and it worked again. You have to credit both managers for getting their tactics right. The press made a big deal of it and, I think, they forgot that there were nine other Liverpool outfield players who were not man-marked. It's the way the media works in England. But I was frustrated by the way I was being blocked from playing my normal game because, during the previous season, so many of our attacks had started from the holding position.

It was also difficult because even when I broke free from my man-marking shadow we were so much less mobile up front without Suárez and the injured Sturridge. Balotelli wasn't giving me many options on his own. At least against Spurs, the combination of Balotelli and Sturridge, with Sterling at number 10, had given me plenty of choices with my passing and we'd won 3–0.

I was also not as sharp and as quick as usual, which often happens in the first few months after a World Cup. There was an additional hangover from having lost the best player in the league, and one of the best players in the world, to Barça.

I went to see Brendan to discuss concerns about my form. It was not as deep a conversation as we'd had before, when we had settled on the decision for me to switch position, but it was another plea for help. Brendan was very balanced in his response. He said, 'Stop being too hard on yourself. Anyone playing in your position for us right now would find it hard because our options up front are so much more limited.'

He also pointed out that I should take it as a compliment that teams regarded me as such a threat that they sacrificed one of their players in an attempt to smother me. We agreed that we would do various drills in training in order to work out ways I could find space for myself again.

Our next game was against Everton at home. Brendan decided we should change formation to a 4-2-3-1. By playing two holding midfielders Brendan said, 'If they're man-marking you then you can push up higher because we'll have the other man sitting to give us that security at the back.'

It worked a treat playing with two holders in me and Jordan Henderson. Steven Naismith was at number 10 that day for Everton and he tried to follow me early in the game. But he kept turning round and arguing with his midfield, complaining that he was pressing alone. Their central midfield looked uncomfortable and once he had to go and press Hendo, I could make an angle and get on the ball and start playing more naturally again.

We were easily the better side. Balotelli and Lallana both went close and we should have been awarded a penalty midway through the first half. 'It was practically a save,' Brendan complained later of the moment when Gareth Barry's arm got in the way of a stinging drive from Sterling. 'Short of grabbing the ball with both arms it could hardly have been more obvious.'

Martin Atkinson, as mentioned before, was always our least favourite referee and it seemed a typical decision from him towards Liverpool. He also booked me, as usual, but he did award us a free kick in the sixty-third minute. I curled my strike around the Everton wall and it flew into the top corner. I ran and celebrated like I had not done for months. In this city, from our own fans and Everton fans, there is sometimes a tendency to write off a player – to say, after a couple of difficult games, 'He's finished, he's done . . .'

I was reacting to that knee-jerk opinion as well as to the media, who had hammered me for my performance during the West Ham game. I was Liverpool's strongest performer against Everton and we were winning deservedly when, out of nowhere, in the 90th minute they scored a wonder goal. Lovren cleared the ball and, from twenty-five yards out, Phil Jagielka swung a boot at it. It simply flew into the net – a sensational goal from anyone, let alone a central defender.

So I'd been just seconds away from having scored the winner in the derby. The focus would have been on my return to form and Liverpool getting back to winning ways after we had lost three of our first five games. Instead, attention switched to Jagielka's 'incredible strike', as his manager Roberto Martínez rightly described the goal. 'It might just have been the best strike I've ever seen.'

I had silenced some of the doubters, if not all of them, as we turned our attention back to the Champions League. On the last day of September we travelled to Basel – a city where I had once been doubted and criticized fiercely by my own manager.

It was mid-November 2002, the day before we flew to Basel to play a decisive Champions League group game, and I had been summoned to the manager's office at Melwood. Gérard Houllier was not alone. He looked angry and he was flanked by his assistant coaches, Phil Thompson and Sammy Lee, as well as Joe Corrigan, the goalkeeping coach, and the head scout Alex Miller. I was twenty-two years old and it looked like I was about to be lynched by a five-man mob.

Gérard had gone out of his way to nurture me during the three and a half years I had been playing for the first team. But all the kindness seemed to have drained out of him. Gérard set about me from his very first question.

'What's eating you, Steven?' he asked.

I just looked down. A few weeks before, on 26 October, just as my slump of form deepened, Gérard had subbed me against Tottenham at Anfield. I felt humiliated seeing my number being held up in front of the Kop by the fourth official. On the inside I knew that I was acting like a spoilt brat. But I was still just a kid and my head was in a terrible mess.

I stormed off the pitch, walking straight past Houllier, and headed down the tunnel into the loneliness of an empty dressing room. The boss sent in Doc Waller to bring me back out.

'No chance,' I snapped.

Doc Waller could see the fury in my face and he left me to stew alone. Gérard was not impressed. He fined me and dropped me to the bench for the next game against West Ham. I got back into the side the following week, against Middlesbrough, but I was subbed again.

And so the Melwood inquest began. Questions were fired from all angles by the five middle-aged men facing me. What's the matter with you? Has it all gone to your head? Have you got a problem? Is it your family? Do you want to talk?

I might have been able to talk if Gérard and I had been alone. But the scrutiny and hostility just made me clam up even more tightly. They came down harder on me. My attitude was terrible. I was not training hard enough. I looked too big for my boots.

It seemed a bit much that, apart from the manager and his assistant staff, I was being torn to shreds by the chief scout and the goalkeeping coach. I still remembered how I and the other YTS lads used to howl every morning while, on ball-pumping duty, the stinky fog of Joe Corrigan's morning bowel-movements settled over us. The power of a Corrigan shite seemed endlessly funny. And now Big Joe was pitching in – along with Miller, Lee, Thompson and Houllier. They were all on my case.

Eventually, when there was a break in their fuming, I spoke up. 'Have you lot finished?'

Before anyone could answer I walked out the manager's office. I didn't care if Houllier dropped me for the game against Basel. It felt as if my whole world was falling apart.

I didn't talk to anyone until we got to Basel and we were in our hotel rooms. I was sharing, as usual in those days, with Danny Murphy. We were very close and I trusted him completely. I told Danny what had happened at Melwood but, far more importantly, why I was so distressed.

My mum and dad were in the midst of separating. I was in pieces. Once I started earning decent money I had bought us a nice house in Whiston. My parents moved in with me. I wanted my brother Paul to join us because we were such a close family, but Paul didn't want to leave Ironside Road. It was still home to him. So we agreed that Paul could stay in the family house and Mum and Dad would live with me in Whiston.

It was meant to be perfect. I was playing well for Liverpool and life was great. Mum and Dad were with me and they had plenty of time to enjoy themselves. There were no more financial pressures and all the boring day-to-day headaches were meant to disappear. But I would come home to the new house and hear the arguing. Mum and Dad always tried not to argue when I was around as they didn't want to upset me. But by the autumn of 2002 it was clear they were splitting up for good. They had fallen out of love and both wanted to go their separate ways.

I can understand it now, and everything has worked out, but at the time I was devastated. My game suffered and my mood plummeted. I felt helpless.

Danny pulled me through the nightmare of that Basel trip. He was the best person I could have spoken to because he understood. His own parents had been through the same turmoil. At the end of our conversation Danny said: 'Don't worry. You'll get through this. Just try and forget what's happening for a while and go out and play football.'

I was surprised to have been picked by Gérard for the game against Basel. Having lost both home and away to Valencia, managed then by Rafa Benítez, and drawn 1–1 against Basel at Anfield, we had to win our final match in Switzerland to qualify from the group. Basel were in a determined mood and their squad had just spent time at a camp in the Black Forest to prepare specifically for this Champions League decider. I was nowhere near ready and I didn't play well. We were 3–0 down at half-time.

As soon as we walked into the dressing room, Gérard shouted: 'Steven – shower.'

It is one of the worst humiliations in football – being hooked at half-time. It got even worse when I heard that I was being replaced by Salif Diao.

'Keep your chin up,' Joe Corrigan said as I headed for the showers.

'Fuck off, you,' I replied.

My embarrassment was sealed when, without me, Liverpool came back to force a 3–3 draw. I was pleased Danny got one of the goals. But we were still out of the Champions League and at the post-match press conference Houllier had a real go at me. He basically called me a Big-Time Charlie. 'Once a player starts to believe everything that is written about him and thinks, "I am King of the World", there is difficulty and danger,' Houllier said.

I might have had a stroppy attitude – but I hardly looked as if I was swanning around like the King of the World. I was hurt by Houllier's comments. He went on to say that 'Gerrard's having a terrible time. I have stuck by him but he just wasn't good enough against Basel. We missed the good Steven Gerrard, the Steven Gerrard that we like.'

The bad Steven Gerrard was outraged. The story was all over the papers, so when Gérard called I barely spoke to him. He claimed that the press had blown up his quotes. But Paul Joyce of the *Daily Express* told me that Houllier had been quoted accurately by all the papers. Joycey is the journalist I trust most and I knew that Houllier was simply covering his tracks. Even the England manager, Sven-Göran Eriksson, was interviewed about the uproar and he admitted to being surprised that I had been criticized so publicly by my own manager. The usual Liverpool way was to keep such bust-ups in-house at Melwood.

My dad had seen the papers. 'What's going on, Steven?' he asked.

I shrugged and stayed silent. Dad said we all knew why I

wasn't playing well. 'It's because of what's happening in the house between me and your mother. Gérard knows that – doesn't he?'

It hurt too much to talk. 'You have told him, haven't you?' Dad asked.

'No,' I said quietly. 'Why would I?'

Dad couldn't believe it. He insisted that I talk to the manager. When I said I didn't want to, Dad asked for his number. I shook my head.

'Right,' Dad said, as he headed for the door. 'I'm going down the training ground to speak to the manager.'

I tried to stop him but Dad was fuming. It was a long and painful wait. Eventually, about an hour later, my mobile rang. It was Gérard. He sounded different, much softer and kinder. Gérard said my dad had explained everything to him and Phil Thompson. Would I come in to see him – for a meeting between just the two of us?

At Melwood I heard what my dad had said: 'It's my fault and Julie's fault – not Steven's. He's off his game because of us.'

It can't have been easy for Dad, talking about the break-up of his relationship, but neither he nor my mum could bear the thought of me being affected by their problems. They resolved to sit down and sort out everything calmly. I was sad that the marriage was over but I remained as close as ever to both of them. Gérard was also very supportive. We shook hands and I felt relieved.

When I returned home to Whiston I thanked Dad. 'I know it's been tough for you,' he said. 'I haven't seen you smile for ages, Steven. And you're not the happiest of people anyway . . .'

I laughed then; and my mood lightened. I could breathe again. I could smile again. I could start playing football again.

A couple of weeks later, as my form returned, Gérard referred to me again in a press conference. 'We have missed him, but the good Steven Gerrard is finally back.'

Nearly a dozen years later, on 1 October 2014, we were back at St Jakob-Park in Basel. I felt much older, and wiser even, than I had been as that anguished twenty-two-year-old. My family life was settled again – and Mum and Dad were thrilled to see me happily married to Alex and to be grandparents to our three girls, Lilly Ella, Lexie and Lourdes.

We were also under slightly less pressure going into the game against Basel this time round. We were in a decent-enough Champions League group. Real Madrid, as the holders, were the runaway favourites and Basel had made a habit of beating English teams like Manchester United and Chelsea. But we believed we were better than Basel while the fourth team in Group B were the Bulgarian club Ludogorets Razgrad. Not many people had heard of Ludogorets but we'd struggled at home against them in the first match two weeks earlier. We won 2–1 only after I scored a penalty in the third minute of injury time. But if we could get a good result against Basel we would take a huge step towards qualifying for the knockout stages.

I still had not heard anything about a new contract. In late September Brendan asked me if the owners had been in contact with my agent. I shook my head but I was relaxed. I trusted Brendan implicitly and he said he was sure that Fenway or Ian Ayre, Liverpool's managing director, would be in touch with Struan Marshall any day to sort it out.

Before the Basel game I was asked about the new contract in a press conference. Had I received it yet? I had to be honest and say no.

When Brendan held his press conference he was glowing when asked about me:

This is a genuine superstar and this country hasn't produced many of them. He still strikes a ball better than almost anyone – both with his passing and his shooting. He is a joy to work with every single day, both as a football player and a human being.

With him in our team he's been a real catalyst for everything the team has done in the last eighteen months. Some of the criticism he's had shows the level he has been playing at consistently. The fact that teams are now man-marking him shows you the influence of his game.

Asked specifically about my contract, Brendan said:

It's something we are looking at as a club, and with Steven and how he feels. He is still in a real good physical condition. He's thirty-four, he trains every day, he never needs a day's rest. He wants to work. He will play and prepare himself right the way through to the very end. When that is, we will see.

Brendan was also asked about my substitution against Basel twelve years earlier:

I've spoken to Steven about that night and I know he had an experience that really helped him. He obviously had a fantastic relationship with Gérard Houllier but he was a young player who learnt from very early on that you need to perform and prepare.

Unfortunately, we didn't get either our preparation or performance right against Basel in 2014 either. I think Brendan got suckered by the media, who had turned it into a match-up between him and Paulo Sousa. They had both managed Swansea, with Rodgers taking over from Sousa in the summer of 2010. There was a lot of press chat before the game about which manager's team might play the prettier football. Brendan was very confident in his prematch presentation of the Swiss side and the clear implication was that they weren't a good team. We were overconfident.

If we'd had Suárez and Sturridge up front, with Sterling behind them, we would have dismantled Basel and most teams in Europe. But we only had Sterling of those three – and Balotelli was playing up front again on his own. We had been better against Everton but if I'd been in charge I would have said, 'We have to do this differently tonight.'

Instead, we were far too open and Basel beat us 1–0. I was disappointed because we should have come away with a point. It doesn't matter who you are playing – an away draw in the Champions League is a good result. There is little sense playing expansive, lovely football if you're going to lose the game.

At half-time Brendan slaughtered us. He said I was the only one in the whole team who was managing to pass the ball from A to B. We were better in the second half, but we still didn't have anyone capable up front to grab us a point.

I was interviewed on Sky after the game and I questioned the performance of my teammates. 'They wanted it more,' I said of Basel, 'which is very disappointing. We didn't deserve anything. We were too soft all over the pitch and conceding again from a set piece isn't good enough.'

Some people were surprised I was so blunt. What did they expect? Should I come out and say we played great – when we didn't? Nine times out of ten, my style is to put my arm round the players and encourage them. But we were crap against Basel. If anyone wanted me to defend them after such a performance then I would have preferred not to have been captain.

I also made a point in the press conference which was a message to Brendan. He picked up on it and he made the same point at our next team meeting: 'When you go away in the Champions League you can't be soft. You can't be open. You can't play the same every single game.'

I have huge respect for Brendan as a coach, and as a man, but I had experienced many more years of Champions League football than him. I know it's a ruthless competition and I think we all learnt a harsh lesson that night in Basel.

But even if we had been switched on tactically, and been much more compact, we still would have struggled. Balotelli started the game and he was hopeless. After his promising debut against Tottenham he had lapsed in training and the subsequent games. His demeanour was very poor. I made up my mind pretty quickly after that about Balotelli.

There was no friction between us. We got on fine. I still tried to help him and I kept looking for chances to praise him. But I could see Mourinho had been right when he said Balotelli is unmanageable. He is very talented, with the potential to be world class, but he'll never get there because of his mentality and the people around him. Balotelli's always late, he always wants attention, he says the wrong things on social media. For me, he doesn't work hard enough on a daily basis. You're always fighting a losing battle with Balotelli. He does too many things wrong.

The pattern of the rest of the season was settled that night for Balotelli in Basel. I became frustrated being his teammate – because I knew that, if his mind was right, he had so much more to give. If you said to me now, pick any striker in the Premier League with the best physique, power and touch then I know who I would choose. If you could somehow change his mentality then I would consider Mario Balotelli every time. Even after the contrasting seasons they had I would pick Balotelli before Harry Kane on pure ability. If you could set aside a player's mentality I would probably choose Balotelli before any current Premier League striker because he's got all the tools to be the best. Unfortunately, ability means little without the right mentality.

As we headed out of Basel that night, back in October 2014, I looked across at Balotelli and Rickie Lambert. It had been another game in which Lambert had started on the bench and just come on for the last ten minutes. But Rickie had tried hard again and he had not moaned about his situation. He was thoroughly professional as always.

I would play Lambert all day before Balotelli – just because of his mentality and desire to work hard for his teammates. Managers are always influenced by what they see in training and so maybe that's why Mario didn't play much.

If you could transplant Rickie Lambert's mentality into Mario Balotelli's body you would have a world-class player.

# 12. Contracts, Decisions and the Night of the 8-Iron

Another month disappeared and still I waited. I was no longer sure whether Liverpool would offer me a new contract. The text messages flew in from the local football correspondents. 'What's happening?' they asked me. 'Have the owners been in touch?' 'Will you be here next season?' They made up a loop of three interlinked queries and the answer to both the first and the last question was a simple 'I don't know.' The middle question could be answered with a straight 'no'.

My agent had yet to be contacted by the club's owners or by Ian Ayre. Struan had only spoken to Brendan Rodgers who told him what he had told me in numerous chats in his office over the past few months. Brendan wanted to keep me. It just needed Fenway or Ian Ayre to pick up the phone and talk to Struan to sort out a deal that suited me at this stage in my career.

I had known some of the writers for a long time and I sensed their surprise. I was in my twenty-seventh year at the club, stretching back to my first signing a form in spidery handwriting to join the Liverpool Centre of Excellence at the age of eight. I was approaching my 700th game for Liverpool's first team and I had been the club captain since 2003. It was not as if I was just a kid looking for a new deal. My age was an obvious factor and I was realistic enough to know that I was approaching the end of my career. I was willing to discuss a new contract on that basis – especially as Brendan was emphatic that he wanted me at Liverpool.

Yet month after month, August into September into

309

October into November, there was only silence from the club I had cherished since I was a very small boy. That love, from me towards Liverpool, stayed constant. I was not unsettled by the lack of communication. Brendan reassured me that his own conviction had not changed. He still saw me as central to his plans both this season and in 2015–16. I could only assume that the men in charge of the club's finances were stalling and avoiding early negotiations with Struan – or that they thought there was no rush. Maybe they thought it was a foregone conclusion that I would stay.

In late October I was asked by one of my two main sponsors, Lucozade, to agree to an interview with the *Daily Telegraph* and the *Daily Mail*. I had been with Adidas and Lucozade for years and I preferred to focus on working for them rather than collecting a whole range of different sponsors. The latter strategy might have been more lucrative but I liked being loyal and limiting my commercial work in order to concentrate on football. I was relaxed because the interview would be carried out by Chris Bascombe and Ian Ladyman. I had known Chris for years, since he'd been on the *Liverpool Echo*. I was also comfortable talking to Ian.

The interview was published on 30 October 2014 and I told the writers: 'I won't be retiring this summer. I will play beyond this season. We will have to wait and see if that's at Liverpool or somewhere else. That's Liverpool's decision.'

In terms of quoted material we left it at that and spoke instead about Liverpool's stuttering start to the season, losing Suárez and my vague hope that Mario Balotelli might still become a success at Anfield. I was at my diplomatic best in regard to Balotelli. There was no point saying in public I had already begun to lose faith in Mario. In regard to the contract, I could have made more of it but I still harboured serious hopes that the club would soon talk to Struan and we could settle on a deal acceptable to both parties. But I was happy to send out a plain message that I would keep playing football – whatever Liverpool decided.

We went to Newcastle on 1 November and lost 1–0 in another fitful display. But attention after the game focused on my lack of a contract. Brendan was quizzed about it and he was as clear as he could be in the circumstances:

> It's quite straightforward. I had a meeting with Steven's repre-
> sentative explaining the situation. I very much want him to be
> a part of what we are doing here. He's been a brilliant captain
> for me. I relayed that to the ownership. I'm sure everyone will
> go away with that and hopefully his representative will organ-
> ize a deal. Steven is very much part of what I'm doing here.
> He's a unique player; a unique talent.

We waited another week and then, finally, Struan got a message from Ian Ayre. The club wanted to offer me a new deal. Could they talk?

Struan arranged a meeting with Ian. It was a big day for me. I had high hopes for my final contract from Liverpool; but I just wanted to get it settled so I could get back to thinking only about football.

Struan called me after the meeting, much earlier than expected, and I said to him, 'How did it go? How long were you in there?'

Struan said, 'Fifteen to twenty minutes.'

'Really? Fifteen minutes?'

Struan knew why I was surprised. It seemed like a very short meeting to decide the conclusion to my Liverpool career. Struan explained the situation. Liverpool had offered me a deal. But it was pretty much a case of 'this is the offer'. There was no point in Ian and Struan talking for longer after such a clear message.

I was at home, listening to Struan on my mobile. I thought, 'OK, I've waited this long to find out what they want to do and this is the offer? It's time to think carefully.'

Perhaps it was not meant for Liverpool and me to move into a twenty-eighth year together. It seemed as if I wanted them more than they wanted me. I was a bit unsure at that point. But I was also much calmer than I had been in 2005. Back then Ian's counterpart, Rick Parry, had made me wait for a new contract even though we had just won the Champions League final. It had felt then as if my young blood was boiling. I was much more thoughtful at thirty-four. But I was also taken aback. I thought Struan and Ian would talk for an hour or so and we would move forward positively.

In a fifteen-minute nutshell, Liverpool offered me a new deal. It was for a one-year extension with a 40 per cent pay decrease. The bonuses were very good but they contradicted everything that Brendan had said to me. Brendan had told me, in a different nutshell, 'Look, you're not going to start as many games. We're going to manage your games and your minutes to make sure you're fresh for the games that really matter.' But the club were offering me bonuses for clean sheets, games that I'd start in, goals, assists and whether we finished in the top four. They were all part of the package. I was confused. My game time was going to become less and less but they were offering me a contract with performance-related incentives? I had no quibbles with the money being offered. If they had offered me that very same deal in the summer I would have been happy to sign it. But I had just walked away from England to commit myself to Liverpool.

A substantial decrease in my pay was only to be expected. At thirty-four, I was not the player who had lifted the Champions League trophy ten years earlier. I also understood that I would have to play less – but I still valued myself as a top player and an important part of the team. I was still the captain and I was disappointed to be offered a performance-incentive contract after all my years at the club. I thought they would have known that, apart from pride in my own performances and an enduring love for Liverpool, I didn't need any incentive to try my heart out.

In a perfect scenario, Liverpool could have offered me a one-year deal which included the chance to make a transition to the first-team staff. Such a deal would have been more appealing than a year as a squad player. A year with Brendan and his staff would have been an invaluable experience – which players like Ryan Giggs, Phil Neville and Gary Monk had enjoyed at other clubs.

I believed I could read between the lines of their offer. To me there was a stark message from Liverpool: whether we're right or wrong, it feels like it's time. Enjoy your last six months with us and then start afresh somewhere else.

Since our poor Champions League performance in Basel we had lost twice to Real Madrid – 3–0 at Anfield and 1–0 in the Bernabéu. We were set up correctly at home against Madrid. I played as one of two holding midfielders and we were more compact and we did try for the tactical cage around their main players. When Ronaldo had the ball we quickly got two or three around him. But the problem playing Madrid was that they had five or six world-class players. You might stifle one, but then the other five would have more freedom.

There was a gulf in class and Real were in their best form. They had the swagger and confidence of champions. We played well in patches and caused them a few problems – but we didn't have a single forward who could put away the chances.

Balotelli was in trouble again. He swapped shirts with Pepe as we walked off at half-time. The manager was understandably unimpressed. Mario was replaced at the break.

The return match in Madrid made me nostalgic for March 2009. We had beaten Madrid 5–0 on aggregate in the knockout stages – winning 1–0 away and 4–0 at Anfield. The home demolition was one of my sweetest nights of European football and it prompted Zinedine Zidane to make his generous claim about me: 'He's the best in the world. Forget about Messi, forget about Ronaldo. It's Gerrard.'

I got two goals at Anfield and Fernando Torres and Andrea Dossena scored as well. We had a good team, with Mascherano and Alonso playing behind me and Torres, but Real had a great side that night: Iker Casillas, Sergio Ramos, Fabio Cannavaro, Pepe, Gabriel Heinze, Arjen Robben, Lassana Diarra, Fernando Gago, Wesley Sneijder, Raúl and Gonzalo Higuaín. Rafael van der Vaart, Guti and Marcelo came off the bench.

They sauntered into Anfield thinking they were going to turn us over. One of the Madrid papers ran a front page with a photograph of Liverpool's ground. Above it was the headline 'So this is the famous Anfield?' And there was another below it which said 'So what?'

The atmosphere was incredible and we blew them away. They could not handle our tempo, pace and intensity of play. Torres was sensational that night, and it was probably one of the best performances I've ever seen from him. Pressing from the front, aggressive, fast, powerful and lethal, Torres gave Sergio Ramos and Pepe a terrible evening. You could see the game meant so much to him, against his old team's bitter rivals, and they just could not control Torres. He opened up so much space for me to shine. Real Madrid left Anfield in total shock that night.

Five years and four months later it was my turn to be shocked. On 4 November 2014, in Madrid, Brendan fielded a deliberately weakened side. We were due to play Chelsea at Anfield on the weekend and he decided that Balotelli, Sterling,

Coutinho, Henderson and I would start on the bench against Real. He supposedly wanted us fresh for Chelsea while he was banking on wins against Ludogorets and Basel in the final group games to take us through to the last sixteen.

That was the night, tucked away in the depths of a dugout at the Bernabéu, when my disappointment ran so deep I almost made up my mind it was time for a change. If Brendan's managing of my games meant that I would have to miss playing against Real, in Madrid, it seemed as if I had seen the end. How could I go on playing for Liverpool another year if these were the kind of empty nights that awaited me?

I came on in the second half, with Coutinho and Sterling, and while it was only a 1–0 defeat it did feel like Brendan had surrendered even before kick-off. My career would never be the same again.

The following Saturday, Chelsea were back at Anfield. I think almost everyone who follows English football knows how close I came to leaving Liverpool for Stamford Bridge in July 2005. The saga has been well documented. I have written about it before and its skeleton can be unearthed by a quick search on the internet. But only I can reach deep within myself to dredge up all the conflicting emotions I still remember so vividly. They almost tore me apart on 5 July 2005 – before, late that same night, I committed myself all over again to Liverpool.

That summer day and night nine years before represented the hardest twenty-four hours of my life.

It had begun more than a year earlier. Even when I was playing for England in Euro 2004, at a tournament where Wayne Rooney was on fire and we looked to be in with a serious chance of going all the way to the final, my future was being questioned. My England teammates were asking me if I was on my way to Chelsea. Liverpool had just finished the Premier League season thirty points behind Arsenal and I had serious doubts we would be able to qualify for the Champions League at the end of the following campaign.

In the 2004–05 season I made it clear to Liverpool that I would discuss a new contract only once I knew whether we would be in a position to sustain a Champions League challenge. Some people might say I was being selfish then but I was in my prime as a footballer, roaring into my mid-twenties, and I needed some guarantees I would be at a club which could close the thirty-point gap between us and the league leaders. I wanted to stay at Liverpool – but I also wanted to play at the highest level.

It turned out to be another disappointing Premier League season, and we finished outside the top four, but we had a better time in Europe. We made it all the way to the final in Istanbul, and the club knew that I was ready to commit myself to a new contract. I was expecting Liverpool to sign me up, especially as they had already spoken to Igor Bišćan and Didi Hamann about their new contracts. Looking back now, it seems as if they could have issued a contract offer in the week building up to Istanbul. Would even earlier not have been the perfect time to give your young captain a lift before the biggest game of his life? Sign him up and keep him secure.

But I heard nothing from the club in regard to my contract either before the final or after we had won that amazing game. When I was interviewed soon after I had lifted the monster trophy up into the Turkish sky I made it clear that I expected to stay at Liverpool.

'I'm sure the manager and Rick Parry will want to sit down really soon and a decision will be made,' I said before I gave into jubilation. 'But how can I leave after a night like this?'

I wanted to stay. But I heard nothing all through June and the first few days of July. It gave Chelsea, and especially José Mourinho, a chance to really get into my head. I'm still not sure, all these years later, why there was no approach from Liverpool to me. I've heard that Rick Parry was away on holiday – and Rafa Benítez was on his break as well.

An element in their thinking encouraged a little complacency: 'He's just won the European Cup, why would he want to go anywhere else?'

I had two years left on my contract. Compare this with early 2015 when Raheem Sterling was in the same position and Liverpool set about trying to sign a new deal with him. And Sterling had not just won the Champions League.

There was neglect in my situation in 2005. I don't know who was to blame – but should they have offered me a contract after the Champions League final? Yes. I think so. I still feel they should have come to me in the very next week and said, 'Let's sort this out.' It would have killed off all the speculation and saved everyone a lot of heartache.

It didn't help that my relationship with Rafa was so distant. I became a little paranoid. I kept asking myself, 'Does Rafa really want to keep me? Or does he want to get as much money as he can for me and build a new team around players he really likes?'

I was also confused because I wasn't asking for anything out of the ordinary in terms of football's inflated economy. I was asking for the going rate paid to a top midfielder in Europe. Chelsea offered more money, but that didn't matter. We won the Champions League on 25 May. When I had still not received a formal offer from Liverpool five weeks later, on 1 July, I told Struan to start moving and find out what was happening.

He called Rick Parry and told him that, in the absence of a new contract, I was prepared to leave, albeit reluctantly.

'I need a few more days,' Rick said.

The latest delay gave confidence to Chelsea. They made a

formal bid for me of £32m. Liverpool rejected it and Rick said the offer was on its way to Struan. My head was so messed up I began to wonder if they were now just producing a contract as a way of showing the fans that they'd tried to keep me while they flogged me to Chelsea. I decided to find out. On 5 July I told Struan to issue a verbal transfer request.

Rick went public with the news and the rest of that day passed in a distressing hum. There were rolling media reports and I stared at the television footage in disbelief. I watched fans burning a Liverpool shirt with my name on the back. For the sake of the cameras they poured petrol on my old number 17 shirt, with GERRARD branded into the material, and set it alight outside Melwood.

Six weeks before, on one of the most famous and joyous nights in our history, I had started the comeback which ended in Liverpool glory. We were welcomed home by ecstatic fans. We felt adored because we had pulled off the Miracle of Istanbul. It seemed disturbing to then watch my name go up in flames outside Melwood. At least the culprit got £40 from the press for his stunt.

I was still sensible enough to know that only a few fans had reacted in such a way. But the intense scrutiny, the consuming nature of being the lead story on the national news that day, upset me. I didn't want that kind of attention. I didn't want the abuse. I actually just wanted to play football, ideally for Liverpool, and to try and win a few more trophies. It was that simple – and yet everything had become so dark and tangled. I didn't feel wanted. I didn't feel they had acted as quickly as they should have done.

I felt my head would burst and I was popping paracetamol like they were Smarties. I was on the verge of hyperventilating with the stress of it all.

Alex was great. She made it clear that she would back me

whatever decision I took – whether I went to London or stayed in Liverpool. She and Lilly Ella, our only daughter then, would be with me wherever I ended up. I worried about my wife and little girl, wondering how they would adapt to a new life in London, while the same old doubts about my football career raced around my pulsing head.

I knew I had to talk to my dad. We arranged for me and my brother Paul to meet up at Dad's that night.

It all came tumbling out. I asked Dad, 'What do you think? What shall I do?'

Dad was calm and, before he said much, he had me talk through my own feelings. I told Dad and Paul that I didn't think the club had shown me the love I needed. I didn't feel that they had acted as quickly as they should have done. Chelsea were serious about me and the Mourinho factor dominated much of my thinking. Mourinho had turned my head. I wanted to play football for him. But as soon as I made everything sound so clear I got lost – and I started talking about Liverpool all over again. I spoke so much more about Liverpool than Chelsea.

I was so close to leaving Liverpool for ever but that hour with my dad and Paul changed everything. Unlike those players surrounded by people who just see the money piling up, I had family who loved me. The questions they asked concerned my welfare, not my bank balance: 'What's best for you? What do you want? What will mean more if this happens or that happens? Can you handle the Kop turning against you? Can you accept the fact that you'll never play for Liverpool again?' These were the kind of questions, none of them to do with money, that we picked apart inside the four walls of my dad's front room. We all knew I would make millions more if I went to Chelsea. But the money was irrelevant. Dad boiled it down to my driving force – the hope that I would succeed and win trophies as a footballer.

Would it mean more to me to win two or three trophies with Liverpool than double or even triple that number with Chelsea?

The question hung in the air. While I turned it over in my head, Paul spoke up. I think he was desperate for me to stay a Liverpool player – but he was my brother before anything else. He said, 'Whatever you decide to do, I'm with you . . .' There was no pressure from Paul, just support. But he has said many times, since that night, 'I'm so happy you stayed.'

My dad said: 'If you look me in the eye and tell me you want this Chelsea move 100 per cent, then I'll be with you all the way. But I don't think you do.'

I didn't look Dad in the eye. I was far from convinced about Chelsea. I was thinking only of Liverpool.

Dad sensed it. 'Don't walk away,' he eventually said, with powerful simplicity. 'Don't leave the club that you love.'

At eleven o'clock that night, after the most draining day of my life, I called Struan Marshall. 'Tell Liverpool I want to stay.'

Rick Parry might have been the most surprised man in Liverpool when his mobile rang a few minutes later.

I signed my new contract on Friday, 8 July 2005, after I had told Rick to remove the escape clause – which had previously specified that I would be allowed to move to another club if Liverpool were not performing on the pitch. I never wanted to think about leaving Liverpool ever again.

The internal debate was far less tortured in the winter of 2014. It had been different in the summer of 2005, when there were flames both outside Anfield and inside my head. At the age of thirty-four I could adopt a measured approach as I weighed up my options and decided whether I would stay for another year at Liverpool, with all the doubt and uncertainty that would entail about my playing future, or seek out a potential new career in America. It helped that I had ruled out many of the complications.

Unlike in 2005, when I'd faced the upsetting prospect of returning to Anfield to play against Liverpool in the blue of Chelsea, I was now adamant that I would never sign for any club that might play a competitive match against Liverpool. That ruled out every club in England and Europe. America was my only realistic alternative to remaining for another year with Liverpool. I felt strangely relaxed as I decided, for once, to put my family first and consider a future that might be good for all of us – rather than just my football career.

When Struan told me about Liverpool's offer in November 2014 I could easily have sent him back to insist on negotiating improved terms. But the pain of being on the bench against Real Madrid mattered more. The financial side of any deal didn't really interest me – and so Struan never discussed anything more with Ian. I just spoke to Brendan. I said, 'Look, we've had the offer and it's not about money. It's more me needing time to think what's best for my future.' Brendan understood and, as always, there was a very good exchange between us. He said I could take as long as I needed to make up my mind.

Soon after the reduced contract offer had been made by Liverpool, the club asked me to appear in an advert for Nivea. It was clear that I was still important to Liverpool off the field. But I turned it down.

In the end Jordan Henderson stepped in and when I saw the ad on television I was mightily relieved. Doing those kind of ads just isn't me. I've had tons of offers to advertise products bare chested and I've always said no. Maybe that's why, unlike most leading players, I've never asked for an image rights deal with Liverpool.

Struan has checked with me a few times. 'Should we get an image rights clause in the contract?' – and I've always said 'No.'

I've heard other players around the dressing room talking about image rights and how much it will earn them. Personally, I think it's disgusting for a player to ask for image rights from his club. My belief is that when you sign a contract with your club then you sign your image rights over to them. They pay you well, anyway, and you're working for them. Maybe it's different if you are Messi or Ronaldo.

But the Nivea advert was one request from the club I could turn down. I have fulfilled so many commercial obligations for Liverpool over the years because it's part of my responsibility as captain. I had reached a stage of my life where I wasn't prepared to do any more. I'm too old for all that now, anyway, but I could give you a long list of stuff I've turned down over the years that would have brought big financial rewards. My career has been about football: neither vast amounts of money nor a celebrity image really interests me.

Of course I've got three kids to worry about, but I became financially secure in my early twenties. I know how lucky I've been that I've not had to make any decision concerning football or my future on a financial basis for the last dozen years or more.

So I had no problem when it became apparent that if I decided to play Major League Soccer in America with LA Galaxy, it would be for less money than I would have received if I had stayed at Liverpool. And it's also why, at the same time, I turned down that €13.5 million net deal to play in Qatar for two years. That sort of money would obviously have been more than I'd ever earned, but Qatar wasn't the right place for me and my family.

America was much more appealing. MLS would allow me both to continue playing the game at a decent level for a few more years and to spend some proper time with Alex and the girls – away from the pressure-cooker of life in Liverpool.

Professionally, I could not have accepted becoming a squad player. I remembered watching Frank Lampard – a great player, and a close contemporary of mine – sitting on the bench for Manchester City week after week after he left Chelsea. I don't think I could have followed the same route. I always want to be playing.

I felt that even more acutely on 29 November 2014, on the sixteenth anniversary of my Liverpool first-team debut, when Brendan had me start a match at home against Stoke on the bench. We were between our final Champions League group games, and I could see the sense in being rested, but I didn't like it much.

Many people just see the wealth and glamour of a life in football. They don't perhaps understand that it's also difficult playing for a club like Liverpool. It's testing on the pitch – and far more challenging off it. In my home city you meet Liverpool and Everton fans wherever you go and it becomes impossible to lead a normal life.

I can only be myself, the person I really like, when I'm not on edge or having to be careful all the time. That happens only when I'm either at home or at Melwood. It's the same for most footballers at the top level. People sometimes forget that, if you take away our wages and fame, we are just normal human beings who like doing what everyone else likes doing. We're not that special. And that's why I've always felt it's important to stay grounded. I want people to respect me as a person and as a player rather than as someone who is just lucky enough to earn millions. It's more important for me to be as normal as possible.

But even something as simple as taking the girls for a swim at the local pool or picking them up from their dance classes or gym lessons is often not possible. I can't be an ordinary dad because I'm swamped by football fans, either cheering me or abusing me, wherever I go. That's wearing, even when things are going well and people just want to pat you on the back or shake your hand, but I certainly don't want to put up with all the abuse when I'm with my girls.

When you're an international, the same thing happens all over the country. Even in London I get stopped every couple of minutes for a picture or someone comes over to the table when you're having a meal with your family. After seventeen years in my surreal and pressured world of professional football, I'm desperate for some stress-free anonymity.

Especially over the past year or so, I sometimes take my concerns home with me. Alex understands because it's my job and she knows that I love it, but I began to feel in late 2014 that it was time I put her and the kids first for a change. In America, I could do that.

When we started talking to people in MLS it became clear that it was likely to be a choice between LA or New York. Two or three other clubs were also interested but I was always pulled more towards the idea of LA. The hustle and bustle of New York is not really my scene. I prefer the more laid-back lifestyle of California.

I spoke to Robbie Keane and David Beckham and they raved about Los Angeles and LA Galaxy. Becks sent me so many texts about LA. He knew Alex and the girls would love it out there. He also said, 'The football can be challenging, with the travelling, the heat and the humidity. But the level is improving all the time. You'll love your teammates, you'll love the club. It's a good set-up, good facilities but the key will be you'll absolutely love it with your family.' He ended by saying: 'I miss it every day.'

Thierry Henry also gave me some advice: he was still playing in New York but he said, 'If you get the chance, go to the MLS. LA Galaxy are a very good organization.

As winter in England began to bite I felt more certain. It would soon be time for a change.

In early December 2014, as the end closed in on my Champions League nights, I became more reflective at home. The great victories and the harsh defeats unfolded in a blaze of colour and a maze of memories. I also amused myself by remembering the most bizarre and hilarious European encounter of all – when we played Barcelona at the Nou Camp on 21 February 2007.

The real shenanigans had taken place on the Algarve where, a week earlier, we had gone to prepare for the game at a special warm-weather training camp. It was meant to be a team-bonding exercise because we were the clear underdogs. We went into the game thinking we needed camaraderie and togetherness to survive against a slick Barcelona team in front of a fevered crowd of 88,000. So the idea was that we would train hard and prepare well but Rafa Benítez had also agreed we could have one free night to enjoy a couple of beers together as a team. He expected us to be back at Vale do Lobo around 11 p.m.

I know that part of Portugal so well that the breakdown was probably my fault. After years of playing golf on the Algarve I knew that the place for a good time, and a little bit of karaoke, was Monty's. I called the owner and made a booking. I then took everyone down there and we were having a brilliant night – until the karaoke got a bit out of hand. It's all a little hazy now but I remember Craig Bellamy pressuring John Arne Riise to go up on stage and belt out a song. Bellamy was winding up Ginge mercilessly. He had not forgotten that Ginge had missed the Christmas party a few months before, where, as a new player, he was meant to sing a song. Bellamy kept saying 'It's your go, Ginge, it's your go! You can't get out of it this time, you ginger bastard.'

Riise is a bit like me. He's not a karaoke singer. He turned on
Bellamy and said, 'No, you fucking get up. You're making such
a fucking noise, being on my case, you get up and have a go.'
Bellers didn't like it. He's a bit of a hothead and he and Ginge
were soon nose-to-nose. It got a bit too heavy – all that 'I'll
fucking kill you, you ginger twat!' while Ginge really did look
ready to murder Bellamy.

We calmed them down eventually, and Ginge went back to
the hotel with the hump. He was sharing with Daniel Agger.
Daniel didn't want to leave Monty's because he was still having
a good time and so Ginge said he would leave the latch off their
door so Agger could get in without waking him up.

The rest of us stayed on at Monty's. People went over the top
on the booze. I remember Jerzy Dudek being in a terrible state.
Normally Jerzy's the nicest fellow on the planet; but after a
night on the drink he came out of Monty's wanting to fight the
security guys and the police. He wanted to take on the world. I
think that's when most of us realized, a little blearily, it was
time to call it a night.

I got back to my room and I'd only been there a few minutes
when I heard the boss outside my door. Rafa banged hard,
sounding pretty pissed off. I answered the door, trying to look
like I'd been in bed a few hours.

'What's going on?' Rafa said. He was colder than ever.

To maintain my just-woken-up scam I threw in a few blag
yawns and rubbed my eyes. 'I dunno, boss,' I said, trying not to
breathe alcohol fumes all over Rafa.

'Riise and Bellamy are fighting,' Rafa said icily. 'Where is
everyone else?'

'Leave it to me, boss,' I said. 'I'll go see what's happening.'

There was a party in one of the lads' bedrooms. It was
carnage and Steve Finnan looked like he had either seen a ghost
or witnessed a murder. I soon worked out that it was closer to

murder. Finn had got back to his room and found Bellamy in a raging mood. Bellers said, 'Right, I'm going to get him.' The Welsh wizard took an 8-iron, his favourite club, out of his golf bag. Finnan was very worried then because Bellamy looked half-crazy. He went off to Ginge and Agger's room, carrying his 8-iron. Finn chased after him but Bellers was quick.

Of course the latch had been left off the door and so Bellamy went straight in and started walloping Riise with the 8-iron. Ginge, who was in his boxer shorts in bed, went into protection mode, covering himself up. Finnan arrived and managed to stop Bellamy doing any more damage.

It was like a morgue at breakfast the next morning. We heard that the club had received a police complaint about Jerzy's behaviour and Rafa was not happy. Everyone was very hungover and Ginge's legs were covered in bruises. It didn't look good and it was already all over the internet. The papers back home went to town. The club was furious as it was disastrous PR – a player attacking his own teammate with a golf club just before a big Champions League game was not the kind of behaviour that went down well with anyone, from owners to sponsors. I think some of our fans might have enjoyed it because it was a crazy story. But it was serious too.

Bellers and Ginge were completely different characters and I always expected there might be fireworks between them. They both fancy themselves. I'd seen teammates go head-to-head before, and there had been a couple of handbag moments and some nasty banter flying around, but never anything that dangerous.

If I had been in Ginge's shoes I don't think I would have stood for it. It was totally out of order – especially over something as stupid as an argument in a karaoke bar like good old Monty's. Rafa handled it with a surprisingly light touch. He wasn't pleased but he got the players to shake hands and he

moved us on quickly. In a weird way it was almost as if the incident helped the team – by taking everyone's mind off how
intimidating it was going to be at the Camp Nou.

The media were all over it and the party line was that Bellamy would not be allowed to play. But the TV, radio and
newspaper boys didn't know Rafa like I did, and it was no surprise to me when he told us the team. Riise was playing, bruised
legs and all, and so was Bellamy. Rafa's strategic brain took
charge. He cut out all the emotion of Monty's and the night of
the 8-iron.

Rafa likes to play deep and compact when away to big teams
like Barcelona. And so you need speed on the counter-attack.
Bellamy had electric pace. It made sense that Rafa played him.
And he knew we needed Riise at full back and on the counter,
too, against the reigning champions.

Even when Deco scored early, to put Barça 1–0 up after just
fourteen minutes, our spirit stayed strong. As Bellamy would
insist, we were still in the swing. A few minutes before half-time
Xabi Alonso's free kick found Finnan, who, having recovered
from being the main witness to the 8-iron attack, whipped in a
beauty of a cross. Bellamy drifted away from his slack Barcelona marker and powered in a header towards goal. Victor
Valdes tried to scoop it out but the ball had crossed the line.
Dirk Kuyt followed up and knocked it in again – but it was a
Bellamy goal.

Our ecstasy turned to hilarity when we saw the Bellamy
celebration. He made space for himself and swung an invisible
8-iron. I was pissing myself at the sight of Bellamy's craziness.
But I felt for Ginge. I knew he was still very upset as he
really took the golf club assault to heart. I would have felt the
same.

Ronaldinho and a long-haired Lionel Messi came close but
so did we on numerous occasions. Valdes kept out my free kick

and Kuyt should have scored. But there was no stopping us on the follow-up when Bellamy, of course, showed lovely vision to find, naturally, Riise. Ginge hit a right-foot screamer, rather than his usual left-foot thunderbolt, into the Barcelona goal. His celebration, and ours, was riotous. Ginge did not reach for his imaginary 8-iron. He slid along the glistening green turf and screamed.

We beat Barcelona 2–1 that night. Riise was very diplomatic. 'It was destiny for both of us to score, I think,' he said. 'Both Bellamy and myself have had a difficult run-up but we've put it behind us when it mattered. His celebration didn't bother me. Look, he's had a difficult time as well and I could see it meant a lot to him. I'm happy for him, as is the whole team.'

Bellers just grinned. Rather than feeling the hand of destiny, he was 'gob-smacked'.

Liverpool went all the way to the Champions League final that year. We lost to AC Milan in Athens – and maybe missed a trick by not returning to the Algarve and Monty's for a team-bonding session before the final. I'm not sure if Ginge ever really forgave Bellamy but, between them, they gave us one of our greatest Champions League memories as not many teams win at the Camp Nou.

Ten years is a long time in ordinary life. In football it feels even longer. Ten years is an age. It's almost an era, a whole generation of players and games. So much had happened to Liverpool and me over the past ten years. We had won and lost two Champions League finals. We had been in the High Court and a title race. We had been through three sets of owners. We'd had four different managers – but just one captain.

I had become club captain in 2003 and led my country as well. I had got married and become a father to three girls. I had passed the 690-game mark for Liverpool and won over a hundred caps for England. I had also decided it would soon be time to swap Liverpool for Los Angeles.

There had been times of tumult and delight, worry and glory, uncertainty and utter conviction. Most of all, it had been an unforgettable ten years between Liverpool playing at home against Olympiakos on 8 December 2004 and the visit of Basel to Anfield on 9 December 2014. Both games were desperate Champions League group deciders. In 2004 we needed to beat Olympiakos by two clear goals to qualify for the knockout stages. Ten years later it was simpler. Victory over Basel, even by a single goal, would be enough to help us qualify for the last sixteen of the Champions League after a scrappy round of group games.

I felt the weight of years when it was pointed out that one of our key players, Raheem Sterling, had turned ten on the day of our memorable encounter with Olympiakos. He would turn twenty the day before we played Basel.

Liverpool had signed seventy-five players, over those ten years, at a cost of £520m. I had seen a staggering number of footballers walk into Melwood between 2004 and 2014. I watched every single one of their first training sessions with close attention, wondering whether we'd bought a star or another dud, a king or a prat, a Xabi Alonso or an El Hadji Diouf, a Luis Suárez or a Mario Balotelli.

It was clear Alonso was royalty after our first training session together, and Rafa Benítez, who had been so clever to buy him in the first place, was equally stupid to sell him to Real Madrid five years later. The loss of a great player hurt even more than the arrival of five bad new signings. When Rafa arrived at the club as our new manager before the start of the 2004–05 season, his first four buys were all Spanish: Josemi from Málaga, Antonio Núñez from Real Madrid, Xabi Alonso from Real Sociedad and Luis García from Barcelona. It helped sweep in a small Spanish revolution which transformed the club and ended in our becoming champions of Europe at the end of Rafa's first season.

Alonso already had a Liverpool connection even before he arrived at the club. At Sociedad he had been coached by John Toshack, one of the great Liverpool strikers and an astute manager. Toshack paid a lot of attention to Alonso, who became captain at Sociedad at a young age, and so the links were already in place. Alonso was a revelation at Liverpool from 2004 to 2009 and, by some distance, the best central midfielder I ever played alongside.

It was a disastrous decision to sell Alonso, and especially for just £30m – which looks a snip now when you reflect on all he has achieved subsequently, both at Real Madrid and Bayern Munich and with Spain, winning the Euros and the World Cup. I blame Rafa entirely for the loss of Alonso.

Rafa phoned to ask if I would help him sign Gareth Barry, my England teammate. He actually wanted Gareth to replace Xabi. Gareth was a very good player but Xabi was world class. It was crazy; but Rafa got it into his head that Alonso was not for him. He wanted Alonso out, and Barry in as his replacement. Alonso went back to Spain, and it saddened me.

Xabi Alonso could still be playing for Liverpool, six or even seven years later, so why should he have left at the age of twenty-seven – when he still had almost three years left on his contract? Mascherano wanted to go, and he refused to play on until he got his move. Torres came to me to ask for help to leave, and he downed tools until he went to Chelsea. Xabi Alonso never once said to me he wanted a move.

I think more about the special players we lost – Alonso, Torres and Suárez – than the terrible signings with which we got lumbered. I don't really want to waste time thinking about El

Hadji Diouf but it's worth highlighting his wasted seasons at Liverpool as an example of how it can all go wrong. Gérard Houllier, a very good manager and a usually wise judge of character, signed Diouf in the summer of 2002. Gérard bought Diouf for £10m from Lens – solely on the recommendation of his former assistant, Patrice Bergues, who had coached Diouf there.

In the 2002 World Cup Diouf played very well for Senegal and they reached the quarter-finals. I understood why Gérard rushed through the signing, but he did not really know Diouf as a person. He was one of three new signings which were meant to turn Liverpool into Premier League champions. We had finished as runners-up to Manchester United the season before and a combination of Diouf, Salif Diao and Bruno Cheyrou was supposed to drive us to the title. It was probably the biggest waste of £18m in Liverpool's history. We finished the season in fifth place and Diouf had sealed his place at the top of the list of Liverpool signings I liked least.

It seemed to me that Diouf had no real interest in football and that he cared nothing about Liverpool. For example, the way he spat a huge globule of gunky phlegm at a Celtic fan in a UEFA Cup match at Parkhead in March 2003 summed up his contemptuous and spiteful demeanour.

A few people have since asked me if I saw any comparison between Diouf and Mario Balotelli – and I've always said no. I've got respect for Balotelli; I've got none for Diouf. Balotelli can be endearing sometimes – and that's never a trait that you would associate with Diouf. The only positive aspect of the otherwise ugly signing of Diouf is that he worked hard on the pitch. He always wanted the ball, and he never hid. But after a while I decided Diouf simply wasn't your usual foot-baller. It seemed to me as if football got in the way of his social life.

At least Balotelli can still make me smile sometimes, I have a small hope that, one day, his career might work out and he can prove his potential on a regular basis.

Balotelli had cost £16m of the £120m we had spent building a team to play Basel in our last Champions League group game in December 2014, but on the day he was not even in the squad as he was struggling with a mild groin complaint and a more complicated dent in his mentality. I tried to concentrate on Basel – but everyone kept reminding me of my 'wonder goal' against Olympiakos.

It was the curse of growing old as a footballer. There was always another anniversary, and another echo of the past, to remind you of a faded time. There was always another game, whether it had ended in victory or defeat, to offer up an omen for today. Sometimes the anniversaries and matches, the nights and the goals, blurred like the ghosts of my past.

Some, however, will always stand out like beacons in my head. Olympiakos is one, Basel is another, though the reasons couldn't be more different.

# 13. Wonder Goals and Injury Blues

*Anfield, Wednesday, 8 December 2004*

The Kop, aflame with colour under the dazzling floodlights, looked incredible at night. I led Liverpool out of the tunnel and turned to gaze at the soaring sight. It was a vast ocean of red, streaked with white and yellow, and the booming noise seemed louder than a wild storm at sea. The small mascot holding my hand shivered with excitement as we stepped out onto the famous old pitch. It was just as I remembered it the first time Dad took me to Anfield.

That had also been on a Wednesday night, 26 November 1986. Liverpool vs Coventry in the Littlewoods Cup. I was nearly six and a half, probably a little younger than the mascot holding my hand as we walked out alongside the Olympiakos players for our final Champions League group game.

The burning images and emotions of that night in 1986 had not faded in my mind. Most of all I couldn't believe Dad had allowed me to go to the game with him – *on a school night!*

We sat low down in the old Kemlyn Road stand. On that Wednesday night in November '86 I'd also stared at the Kop. I was blown away by excitement.

It was the first time I saw the sea of red. I also felt giddy with happiness. The noise was so loud I was tempted to use my hands to cover my ears. But I didn't. It was amazing. I loved the singing and the chanting.

I remembered it all. But, mostly, I remembered how beautifully green the Anfield pitch looked beneath the bright lights.

Liverpool beat Coventry 3–1. Jan Molby scored all three goals. Every goal was a penalty. *Three penalties?* I remembered thinking: 'This can't be real. I must be dreaming.'

Eighteen years on it felt very real. The grass was just as green. It glistened as I looked across the perfect playing surface. We could do with a penalty tonight. Three would be impossible, the stuff of Jan Molby and boyhood dreams, but one goal, even a penalty, might be enough to get the win against Olympiakos.

The day after the Molby penalty-feast, on the Thursday afternoon following a sleepy day at school, I turned Ironside Road into Anfield. I imagined the hard concrete was Anfield's green grass. I pretended the tight rows of terraced houses were the Kop and the Main Stand and the Kemlyn Road end. And I turned into Jan Molby. I scored at least three hat-tricks, slotting each penalty between the steel dustbins that made our goals. I loved playing the match all over again in Huyton with me at the heart of it all.

On that different, much more serious winter night in December 2004, my gaze was drawn back, as always, to the Kop. A Spanish influence now added even more flavour to the Liverpool support. Behind the goal at the Kop end, a banner had been made to look like the Spanish national flag. A huge wash of yellow was trimmed by two red borders. The red Liver bird was in the middle of the big yellow band, surrounded by four red stars representing our four European Cup victories. Along the borders the words *Rafa's Red Men* had been stencilled in gold.

Facing the goal, and down at the bottom, to the right, my eye picked up a new sign that had begun to do the rounds at Anfield on European nights:

Paisley Won It 3 Times
Fagan Made It 4
Rafa Leads The Reds
Another ¿Por Favor?

Who said you couldn't get an education through football? My Spanish was getting better with every new game and every new Kopite banner.

My maths was already pretty good and the numbers made simple reading. After five games for all four teams, Olympiakos were top of the group with ten points. Monaco were second with nine while we had seven points. Deportivo de La Coruña were already out of the race after they had drawn just two games – but one of those had been at Anfield. That goalless draw against the bottom club meant we had to beat Olympiakos. The goal difference tally was plain. We either had to win 1–0 or, if Olympiakos scored, by two clear goals.

I was still only twenty-four and, even as captain, I had not quite yet worked out how to temper my honesty on the eve of a massive match. At a press conference on the Tuesday I spoke emotionally about the consequences of not qualifying for the Champions League knockout stage and being relegated to European football's second-tier tournament if we finished third in the group. 'It would be a disaster for the club, and for me personally, to be in the UEFA Cup on Thursday,' I said. 'For myself, it has been frustrating playing in the UEFA Cup for the last few years. I've already won it and it plays second fiddle to the Champions League. As a player and as a club, I don't settle for second best. The Champions League is where I want to be.'

It was one way, inadvertently, to ratchet up the pressure on my own team – with me sounding as if I thought I was just as big as the club. I didn't actually think that, not even at my most youthfully arrogant, but I could not curb the sound of my own ambition. Everyone knew that the rumours of me leaving Liverpool for Chelsea had begun the previous summer and I was not willing to discuss a new contract until I had some idea of the club's Champions League potential for the following season. In case anyone missed the clarity of the situation, I hammered it home again. 'I don't want to wake up on the morning after the match and be out of the Champions League. If we don't qualify for next season, I'll have to consider my future.'

The narrative of the tie was driven by my quotes. It might not have been the smartest prematch press conference I've ever given – but it was red-raw with the truth. I couldn't get rid of the thought that I might never play again for Liverpool in the Champions League if we didn't overcome Olympiakos.

At that same presser I also tried to sound confident and matter-of-fact:

Some people say that having to win one–nil or by two clear goals will be difficult. But if you told me before the group started we'd be playing Olympiakos at home needing a one–nil win to qualify then I'd have signed up for that. I'm not worried about them scoring. If they do, we'll need to score three; but that's OK, we'll try.

Of course we would try; but I was also terrified of conceding an early goal. In private, when it was just me and Carra in a corner of the dressing room, I said, 'We cannot give away a goal. If we slip up once, we'll have a mountain to climb.'

Carra agreed.

I was anxious. I didn't want our Champions League dream to end.

We were lucky to have Sami Hyypiä and Jamie Carragher at the heart of our defence that season. They were the equal of any central defensive partnership in Europe. I had known about Carra for years, but Sami showed me how special and thoughtful he could be when, in 2003, Gérard Houllier appointed me captain at just twenty-three. It meant that Sami had to relinquish the armband. When I went to see him, feeling sheepish at being his new skipper, Sami went out of his way to stress that he would be there to help me every step of the way.

Sami and I almost combined early on against Olympiakos. I took a corner, down our left flank, and found Sami at the near post. His header flashed just past the goal.

We had to defend as well. A dipping free kick from the Greeks fizzed in and I had to head it behind for a corner. It was going to be a testing night even though Anfield roared its support with wave after wave of song. We came closest to scoring in the first twenty minutes when Xabi Alonso's dead-ball delivery was struck so perfectly that I just needed to stick out the back of my boot to send the ball flying towards goal. My arms shot up in a ritual celebration before I saw the yellow-and-purple ball smack against the post. We had come so close to getting the early goal we needed.

After twenty-six minutes the black-shirted Greeks were awarded a free kick just outside our D. We had six in the wall and three other players close by as our keeper, Chris Kirkland, shouted at us to get tighter. Rivaldo lined up to take the shot. The great Brazilian had done little for twenty-five minutes – unlike three years before when, playing for Barcelona, he'd terrorized me and Liverpool. We couldn't get close to him in 2001 when Barça won 3–1 at Anfield. He was three years older as an Olympiakos player but, still, we looked helpless as with two steps and a left foot he clipped it over the wall. 1–0, Olympiakos.

Kirkland raged at us. But I gave him a bollocking for allowing a free kick to sail into the middle of the goal. He had been out of position. It was Kirky's fault. I still got a booking for booting the ball away in frustration. I would be out of the next game – and it felt as if we were already out of the competition. We needed three goals to rescue ourselves now.

Rafa was strikingly calm during the break. He just got out the white board, made a few tactical tweaks and said some simple words which were easily understood: 'Djimi [Traoré] off. Florent [Sinama Pongolle] on. Three at the back. Be brave. No mistakes. Let's have a go. We have forty-five minutes to stay in Europe. Go and show me how much you want to stay in Europe. Go and show the fans.'

Two minutes into the second half we felt inspired. Rafa's change had worked. Harry Kewell drove down the left wing and squared it across the goalmouth. Sinama Pongolle nudged it home, running into the goal to pick up the ball and race back to the halfway line. Rafa didn't celebrate. He just made a point of studying his watch. We had forty-three minutes to score two more goals. It sounded easy but it was devilishly difficult.

Kewell and Milan Baroš combined with me and when the ball arced back in my direction I hit it on the flying half-volley. It zipped under the squirming body of the Greek keeper and into the goal – but the whistle had already sounded. My equalizer was disallowed because Baroš had fouled Gabriel Schürrer. I held my despairing head in my hands.

I was thinking, again and again, 'Is it going to be our night? Is it going to be our night?'

Both teams had chances but after eighty minutes it was still 1–1. We needed two more goals in the last ten minutes. We forced a free kick a minute later. Xabi Alonso took it and Kewell went down. We appealed for the penalty but it was ignored as the ball bounced to Sinama Pongolle. He crossed and Núñez's header was palmed away by Nikopolidis – but straight into the path of Neil Mellor. Another of Rafa's inspired subs, Mellor smashed it home. He had been on the pitch for less than three minutes. 2–1 to Liverpool.

Anfield rocked and roared. We did a strange series of

celebrations. We ran towards each other to yelp and touch hands so quickly they looked scalding hot. It was our way of saving time by racing back into our half so we could restart play.

Rafa didn't celebrate. On the touchline he just peered at his watch again, as if his icy brain was coldly calculating the number of seconds we had left to unleash more mayhem across Anfield.

All I knew was we had nine minutes to score the goal that would save our Champions League season.

Stress and tension ran through us as we waited for Olympiakos to kick off again. They tried to waste a few more seconds. Carra and I were trying desperately to rally the team above the noise of Anfield, telling everyone to stay calm. Victory was still possible.

Five more minutes dribbled away. Kewell and I exchanged passes and I drove in a cross. It was a deadly looking ball. Mellor went down and we all appealed again. No penalty.

Four minutes shone on the clock. Four minutes to save ourselves.

Carra was on the attack. He had the ball at his feet. Carra was off on a dribble. That showed how desperate we'd become. We were ready to try anything, but even I couldn't believe my eyes when Carra then did a Cruyff turn, dragging the ball back and spinning through 180 degrees to cut back inside on the edge of their area.

I was in the middle of the pitch, thirty yards from their goal. I put my hands up high in the hope that Carra might see me in acres of space.

Carra, instead, chipped a clever little ball to Mellor. As Mellor rose in the air I moved towards him.

'*Set it, set it!*' I screamed.

Mellor heard me. He saw me. Mellor nodded the ball in my

direction with a firm but expertly cushioned header. It bounced once and then, in a lazy arc, looped down towards me. It was about to bounce again when, running at speed, I hit it on the half-volley. Opening up my body to get the right angle and my full weight behind the shot, I hit it perfectly from twenty-five yards.

It was a screamer. It was an absolute wonder of a strike that would change my life for ever.

The yellow-and-purple Champions League ball flew like an arrow, like a stonking great missile, into the right-hand corner of the Kop-end goal. Boom.

I ran towards the Kop, pumping my fists in joy, my arms moving in frantic tandem with my legs as I sped towards our supporters. They were going crazy. I gave the air an almighty slug before I pointed madly, using both arms, at a fan who looked like he was about to explode with joy.

He stretched out his hand and I kept running towards it. I thought, 'I'm going in . . .'

I hurtled towards the crowd, my teammates chasing me hard. Liverpool fans, who had spilled out of their seats to run towards me, rolled down the Kop in waves.

'Yeah, I'm with you,' I thought as the faces flooded towards me. 'I'm one of you. I'm fucking coming in . . .'

The crowd just sucked me in. I was soon lost in the middle of that roaring red sea of joy.

The six-and-a-half-year-old boy who had been blown away by a Jan Molby hat-trick of penalties, in a Littlewoods Cup Wednesday-night thriller, would not have believed what would happen to him eighteen years later.

I've had to watch the Olympiakos goal again and again, over and over, year after year, at awards evenings and anniversary dinners. The sequence is so vivid. Carra's cross comes in from out wide. Mellor is there and I knew the only thing he could try and do was set it. If Mellor ever had his back to goal he would always set it anyway. He was quite limited in terms of technical skill but a great poacher and finisher. The only question I had in my head, all those years ago, was could Mellor execute it right? He did, and as the ball bounced towards me I knew that, if I got my body angle right and connected cleanly, I could score. It was still a difficult ball to hit but I caught it like a dream. As soon as it left my foot I knew it was going in because of the contact I'd made. It was as sweet as one of those golf shots where you nail it and you don't even feel it. It was a big, big goal for me and the club.

The Sky commentary is now seared in my brain. 'Here's Carragher,' Martin Tyler says on screen, 'trying to stay cool ... Mellor ... lovely cushioned header ... but *Gerrrr-raaaaaarrrrrdddd!*'

Midway through Tyler screaming my name, Andy Gray's shriek erupts. It follows the blistering trajectory of my strike. '*Ohhhhhhhh-hhhh! You beautyyyyy! What a hit, son! WHAT ... A ... HIT!*'

Gray, a former Evertonian, a Bluenose, was lost in the howling bliss of an unforgettable goal.

I hit it sweetly, devastatingly, perfectly. It was a good enough goal to have unleashed cries of admiration if I had scored it at an ordinary training session on a freezing Wednesday morning at Melwood. But the real wonder of the goal was wrapped around its timing on a fevered Wednesday night, with four minutes left of an agonizing Champions League decider. It flew through the cold December night and into my future life – to be played over and over again as the moment which set us on the path to becoming the champions of Europe that very season.

Watching it now, I can see my conviction and desire. I screamed at Mellor to set it in the hope I would have one more chance in the game. I just needed Mellor to lay it off, nodding it down in my path, and I would try to bury it.

On the screen, when it gets replayed, after the Gray scream has finally faded away, Tyler says, 'Well, you'd take a tap-in in these circumstances. But what you have seen is a Champions League strike as good as anything the competition has produced in this and many a season.'

The goal comes again, in another loop. Gray takes over and then decides to step back. 'You don't need me to explain it,' he says. 'Just watch this. Let the pictures tell you everything. This is special. Have a look, boys.'

It often makes me smile at this point because Rafa is still not celebrating. He is walking around in a circle on the touchline, on his own, looking a little dazed. A beaming orange-jacketed steward rushes to embrace him. Rafa stands stiffly, like a small Spanish boy being hugged by a distant white-haired relative he's never met before. Eventually, as the ecstatic steward clings to the manager, Rafa pats the man a couple of times. It was the Rafa equivalent of me going crazy, flying into the Kop to be swallowed up by my crying, screaming, whooping people.

The pictures on screen cut away from an unsmiling Rafa to me. In the centre circle, I'm gritting my teeth, pumping my fist into my palm, reminding everyone to concentrate, to not let an even later goal slip. I look so young, and so determined.

'He didn't want to wake up tomorrow in the UEFA Cup,' Martin Tyler explains. 'He was saying that yesterday. And with one swing of his gifted right foot, Steven Gerrard says, "Champions League knockout stage, here we come."'

## Anfield, Tuesday, 9 December 2014

I stayed true, and loyal, and ten years and a day after the Olympiakos goal, I was about to lead Liverpool against Basel in another European group showdown at Anfield.

Real Madrid had fifteen points, having won all five of their games. Basel had six points, and Liverpool and Ludogorets both had four points. We had the better goal difference and the Bulgarians had to play their final game in Madrid. Second place in the group would be a straight fight between Basel and ourselves. It was much less complicated than the Olympiakos saga. We just needed to win the game. The score didn't matter. A win would get us into the knockout stages, and mark a small step of progress during a difficult season.

It seemed as if everything rested on our new players matching the indestructible will which had fuelled our very different side against Olympiakos, of which I was the only survivor. I was the last man standing – and so there was a deep focus on me and the anniversary of my goal, not least by Brendan Rodgers:

> This competition has a great history for Liverpool and that game against Olympiakos is part of that history. This game against Basel is an opportunity for these players to qualify and to write themselves into the same folklore. We cannot be reliant solely on Steven. It has to be about a team performance against Basel. We need others to be a catalyst for the team. That is the nature of Steven's game. There are very few world-class players around so when you are a world-class talent the responsibility falls on you, but this is about the collective. We need the whole team functioning at the top level to get a result.

Anfield has a spirit unlike any other football ground I've experienced. There is a power and force to the Liverpool crowd that can sometimes make you believe they're capable of sucking the ball into the opposition net. The noise against Olympiakos during the last twenty minutes was the most intense I'd heard – until a few months later when it was even louder against Chelsea in the second-leg of our semi-final win over Mourinho's team.

There is also an intelligence to the Anfield crowd. They understand football and I think that's why, against Basel, the crowd was strangely subdued. It was as if, after a drenching downpour, they knew we didn't have the same fire and fury, the skill and precision, to kill off the Swiss team, whose fans in their small section of the ground were much more boisterous than ours.

We were ragged and insipid in the first half and Basel played calmly and coolly. They also showed great skill. In the twenty-fifth minute, after some intricate play just outside our box, Fabian Frei hit a scorcher of a shot past Simon Mignolet. We were 1–0 down and in need of two goals.

*Attack, attack, attack . . . !* the crowd chanted with sudden fury as we chugged along. I knew we needed to light some kind of fire inside us at half-time.

Brendan changed the team at the break. Enrique replaced Moreno and Lazar Marković came on for Lambert. Fifteen minutes later Marković and Behrang Safari both chased a ball. Safari had been Basel's best player. He also turned out to be their best actor. As Marković swung his arm back, to win the chase as he ran, his fingers brushed Safari's nose. The Basel man went down as if he had been smacked in the face by a crunching uppercut. The referee reached for his red card. Marković was off and we were down to ten men.

We were not about to give up. I urged and cajoled and tackled and ran as the rain rolled down my face. One thunderously hard challenge from me won the ball back against Taulant Xhaka. I ran on and their keeper, Tomáš Vaclík, had to dive bravely at my feet. The crowd was lifted; and the noise and belief returned.

We could still do it. I felt the old conviction surging through

345

me. In the eighty-first minute I stepped up to take a free kick on Basel's right. I hit it with venom and dip. It cleared the wall and flew into the top corner. The keeper had no chance.

1–1. I set off on my run, pumping my arms to the side, believing it could happen all over again.

Ten years before we had needed two goals in the last nine minutes against Olympiakos. Now we only needed one.

All the subdued murmuring of the crowd had gone. The roaring red sea was back.

I had just scored my forty-first goal in 130 Champions League games. I was hungry for number forty-two.

Sterling menaced the Swiss, twisting and turning this way and that, and the ball ricocheted towards Jordan Henderson. Anfield was seething and believing as Hendo chested it down and then caught it with a treat of a half-volley. The ball flew towards goal but their keeper, diving at full-stretch, turned it away.

The last few minutes went too quickly. We strained and tried but then, crushingly, we heard the final whistle. I sank down onto my haunches. My hair was soaked with sweat and rain. I wiped my face and stayed down. It was over. I would never play another game of Champions League football.

It was time to tell the world. I had already informed the club that I would be leaving for America at the end of June 2015. I could have kept it quiet but it wouldn't have been fair to the manager. Uncertainty about my future had begun to dominate the agenda. Brendan was asked about it constantly.

I had said to Struan, 'I want Brendan to be the first person to know that I'm going to move on and then the club can decide how to deal with the news?'

So I went to see Brendan and told him the news. I didn't mention that I had begun to accept my leaving was inevitable on that dismal night on the bench in Madrid. Instead, I said: 'Let me tell you right now, man to man, face-to-face, nothing will change. I'm going to train hard every single day and I'm available to try and contribute from now until the end of the season. I'll give you everything I've got.' It was, as always with Brendan, a conversation full of mutual respect.

Tom Werner, the club chairman, called me from Boston. I got on well with Tom and John Henry and, as owners of the club, they had treated me decently. I could tell by Tom's voice that he was bitterly disappointed and surprised I had decided to leave. But he was very respectful. He asked me why and I explained my reasons and stressed that a couple of years in America would be good for me and my family. We had a good chat for twenty minutes and I'm going to stay in touch with him and John. Whenever they've been in Liverpool they've always asked to meet me for a coffee so they could keep me in the loop with their plans. I think Liverpool are in good hands with Fenway.

Before I went public, Struan's phone started to ring. Other clubs were hearing hints that I might be leaving Liverpool. The first offer to talk came in from the Turkish club Beşiktaş, and their then manager Slaven Bilić. Monaco were next. They came in strong. Paris Saint-Germain were also very keen. David Moyes called Struan a couple of times, to see whether I would be interested in playing for him at Real Sociedad.

A few English clubs called, but I wouldn't play against Liverpool. There was interest from Tottenham and their manager, Mauricio Pochettino, asked to be kept in the loop. It was good to hear Pochettino still rated me. I was sure I could play in the Premier League for another year but there would not have been much of a buzz doing the same thing all over again with Tottenham. Struan knew I didn't want to play against Liverpool.

I was slightly interested in PSG and Monaco – and staying

347

in Europe crossed my mind. But how could I come back to Anfield if there was a European game? So I made it clear to Struan. I said, 'No chance. I don't want to stay in Europe. It's time for something different.'

Qatar came in big and there were a couple more offers from the Far East. But we'd had the initial conversations with the MLS people and I felt sure LA Galaxy would be the best move for me.

All it needed was for me to speak to the press and the fans. A statement, released on 2 January 2015, confirmed that I would be leaving Liverpool for America at the end of the season. I was touched and moved by the plaudits and tributes which rolled in almost immediately.

I had also done an interview with Claire Rourke of Liverpool FC TV after we'd drawn with Leicester City on New Year's Day. We were 2–0 up at half-time after I scored both penalties. But Leicester grabbed two quick goals soon after the break. I just wanted to get the interview done. It would be screened on the club's TV channel a few days later.

Even before they started filming I felt a little choked up. I had to remind Claire that we'd only do the interview on the condition it didn't get too emotional.

Claire was good but the interview was still raw. 'I always knew it was going to end one day and it would be an emotional decision,' I said. 'Now it's real, it's a strange feeling. I think about me and the club as one. It was a tough decision but the reality is I'm thirty-five in the summer. Hopefully I will return one day.'

I suddenly realized I had just started to say a very long goodbye to the club I had loved all my life. I wasn't quite sure if I could survive five more months of such deep emotion. It already felt brutal and tough to talk about leaving – and the year had just begun.

'I'm not twenty-four,' I said, trying to sound practical again. 'I wish I was twenty-four. I wish I'd met Brendan when I was twenty-four because I think I'd be sitting here talking about a lot of titles we'd won together. But the reality is that Brendan came into this club when I was thirty-two years of age.'

Claire had planned to read out some tributes from the manager and my teammates. I had to shake my head and say, 'It would break me.' But Claire did read a few moving words from Margaret Aspinall of the Hillsborough Family Support Group. I couldn't talk. I really was speechless.

I could feel myself welling up and nearly choked, but I got a grip after I took a deep breath:

> There'll be plenty of time for tears and sentiment at the end of the season. The aim now is to finish the season strong from a personal point of view – and to also achieve something for the team and try to cheer the fans up. They've had a difficult six months like the rest of us . . . but I'd like nothing better than to leave with a trophy and with us in top form. We'll try and go for a trophy and forget about Steven Gerrard for a bit.

On Monday, 5 January 2015, we had a proper game of English football. A third round FA Cup tie between AFC Wimbledon and Liverpool, held at their little ground at Kingsmeadow, in Norbiton, evoked memories of the 1988 final at Wembley. It was the year when, much to my horror as an eight-year-old, Wimbledon's Crazy Gang beat Liverpool 1–0. In the twenty-seven years since then, matching the span of my time at Liverpool, Wimbledon had been taken over, bought out and moved to Milton Keynes – where they were renamed and 'rebranded' as MK Dons.

I understood and identified with the anger and solidarity of the old-school Wimbledon fans who refused to accept their changed identity. They started all over again as AFC

Wimbledon. They had moved up through the tiers of non-league football slowly and steadily. They were now a football league club again – and played in the equivalent of the old English fourth division.

It was an uplifting story and AFC Wimbledon even featured a cult hero in their sixteen-stone striker Adebayo Akinfenwa. 'The Beast' was also known as 'The Strongest Man in English Football'. He was a Liverpool fan and I was, apparently, his favourite player. That still didn't stop the big man, who had a surprisingly light touch, from scoring an equalizer after thirty-six minutes. I had given us the lead when, after clipping it across to Javier Manquillo, I raced into the box and muscled my way between two strapping League Two centre halves to score with a stooping header. It was one way of showing everyone I was as committed as ever.

In the second half, with us needing a winner, I curled a free kick over the wall and into the top corner. Neal Ardley, AFC Wimbledon's manager, said he had shown his keeper James Shea countless videos of me scoring such free kicks. They were kind enough to smile after the game.

'That's Steven Gerrard,' Shea said. 'That's what he does.'

Ardley, a former member of the Crazy Gang, was even more generous: 'We got outdone by a world-class player in the end.'

I was happy to swap shirts with The Beast. We wished each other good luck and, on the long journey back to Liverpool, I allowed myself to dream. The 2015 FA Cup final would be held at Wembley on 30 May, the day I turned thirty-five. I had my perfect, fairy-tale ending in mind.

As if galvanized by a new fantasy, Liverpool hit form. We won four out of our next five league games, while drawing the derby 0–0 at Goodison. We beat Sunderland and Villa away, and West Ham and Tottenham at home. It felt as if we were on the march again. I scored against Spurs, a penalty in the fifty-third minute. But a quarter of an hour later I was forced to limp off with a hamstring injury.

It didn't feel good and later that night the medical team confirmed the grim news. I would be out for three weeks – at least. The physios and doctors knew how much every game, and every minute in a Liverpool shirt, mattered to me as the end loomed. But we had been through so much, after so many surreal and career-threatening injuries, that they didn't need to say anything. I knew how lucky I had been in the past.

Chris Morgan might tell you that he has worked on the periphery of my career. Physiotherapists tend to play down their roles in a footballer's life because their great decisions are never noticed while their bad choices, when they send a footballer back out onto the field too soon, can haunt them and the player for years. It's a business where they get little gratitude – apart from that shown towards them by the footballers, like me, who owe them so much.

There have been two occasions where Chris helped save my career, and my sanity, when all seemed threatened or lost. In 2011 it felt like my groin and my mind were ruined for ever, blown to smithereens by pain and despair. Chris came to my rescue.

I'd had groin problems my whole career, adductor muscle pain and numerous surgeries on my hernia. My groin, and the gracilis [a small muscle in the inner thigh] release I'd needed, had cost me my place in the 2002 World Cup. It was a chronic issue and I'd already had a revision of a previous hernia procedure to reinforce the lower abdominal wall. But in March 2011 I had suffered a groin avulsion. It's an injury that's as nasty as it sounds because, basically, the whole of your groin muscle comes off the bone.

It happened after I did a Cruyff turn at Melwood. I managed

to walk off the pitch and get to the treatment room. As soon as I hobbled in, the medical team knew I was in trouble. 'What happened?' Chris said, worry lining his voice.

I shook my head. 'My groin's just exploded.'

It was a dramatic word, but 'exploded' had a measure of accuracy. They soon worked out that I had pulled the adductor longus tendon off at the bone. The avulsion had occurred where my adductor muscle attaches onto my pubic symphysis area.

Your adductor muscle primarily helps when you swing your leg across your body. It is possible for such an injury to heal itself because it can form a new attachment lower down. Some footballers actually play with a half-attached adductor and they get assigned a secondary cleft – a little gap which helps them manage their movements. But as soon as I heard from the surgeon that, if we followed that non-interventionist approach, I could lose power when making a trademark cross-field pass, I was adamant. I wanted surgery. If all went well, the surgeon assured me, the adductor muscle would feel as good as new.

I was happy to take his advice and he also reassured me that Frank Lampard had come back from the same injury. I would be out for twelve weeks but I would make a complete recovery. It ended my season but Chris said he would come out to Portugal with me in the summer. I would be ready to play again long before the start of the 2011–12 season.

It was vital to have a strong core around the groin and adductor area because, in a typical Premier League game, I would run eight miles and a mile of that distance would be covered at high speed. There was always plenty of twisting and turning of the groin and the adductor. Some players believed that massage was the key to everything but our medical team had a strong belief that active rehabilitation, strengthening and hard work were essential in ensuring that the surgery was successful.

I nodded. After the surgery I would be ready to put in as much hard work as we needed.

The operation seemed routine and it left me with a neat four-inch scar. It was another to add to the collection. But we soon hit a problem. I kept suffering from discomfort and, sometimes, pain in and around my pelvis. Chris, the Liverpool doctors Zaf Iqbal and Peter Brukner and the surgeon Ernest Schilders all examined me – and gave the all-clear. It was still early days. I just needed to relax and allow the adductor to heal.

We thought some sun would sort me out. I was longing to get to Portugal and feel back to normal again. Alex, the girls and I went out for our summer break – and Chris took a working holiday with us. We would go to the gym in the morning and evenings to work hard and he would leave me to enjoy my holiday with the family the rest of the time.

It was frustrating. We kept needing to pull back in terms of our targets for the first of July – the day I hoped to start preseason training. Anything as simple as a high knee-step or a lunge would hurt too much. They were the basic exercises we needed to strengthen the adductor.

We devised a new plan that we would pick up the pace at Melwood. I would, surely, be fully rested and recovered by then.

The plan went awry. On my first day back at Melwood, after we'd done some lengthy but gentle warm-up routines, we decided I would go for a little jog. I knew I couldn't kick a ball but, surely, I could manage a ten-minute jog around the training fields. I had made some progress in the pool and on the alter-g, a weight-bearing treadmill which enables you to jog without placing any stress on your body.

I was looking forward to it, the simple mindless pleasure of being outside and moving one foot in front of the other at a steady pace. I had not run for a very long time.

My feet began to move. One, two, three . . . and by the time I had taken my ninth and tenth step I had to stop. My face was a mask of pain.

I could not run another step. It was excruciating; and it was frightening.

What was going on? I was a professional footballer and I couldn't even run ten paces. My operation had been twelve weeks earlier. I was meant to be fit and flying by now.

It was obvious that the medics were also concerned. Part of their job was to study the clinical side and then pinpoint the reasons a player might be feeling pain. Such explanations always helped ease the stress and the worry. But they were not sure what to tell me. All the tests the doctors had since run showed that the surgery had been successful. Yet I still felt completely crippled.

They had explained years earlier that I picked up more injuries than many players because I was hyper-mobile. That meant I had real flexibility around my joints. It was great in the sense that flexibility helped my football. The downside was I was also more susceptible to injury. But my latest injury had apparently been resolved by surgery.

Chris and the doctors studied a new set of scans. They went through each of them in detail with me. They showed me that, when I tore off the adductor, I had also stripped away the ligament underneath the pubic symphysis. That explained why my movement was hampered and it perhaps indicated some instability. It was suggested that the gapping in my pelvic area was causing the pain. There was not much we could do about it except wait for the ligament to heal properly.

A week later, feeling a little better, we had a meeting with all the medics and it was decided I'd avoid running for a while. I'd switch to cycling.

Melwood felt very empty, with the first-team squad away on a preseason tour, but Darren Burgess, the club's head fitness coach, soon called me. He asked me to do a twenty-four-minute bike ride. 'Do this one for a physical hit,' Darren said, 'and let me know how you get on.'

The plan was to build on that first real test on the bike. Jordan Milsom, a good friend of mine and a top fitness coach, would be there to monitor me and the readings. I climbed on the bike and I began to pedal.

Wow, it was so painful. After two or three minutes, with sweat already beading my brow, and my face stretched into the wrinkly grimace of a very old man, it felt like I was having to ride all the way from Liverpool to the Trafford Centre in Manchester while sitting on a saddle of nails. That's how agonizing it felt.

After five minutes I gave up. I had to stop. I surrendered.

I left a message on Darren's voicemail. 'You cannot put me through that again,' I said. 'Something's not right. It feels serious.'

I was getting lower and lower. 'It's not feeling good,' I told Jordan and Chris. 'It's excruciating.'

'Where exactly are you feeling the pain?' Jordan asked.

'Sort of behind the balls,' I said.

They looked worried.

'Yeah,' I said, 'it feels like someone is trying to knife me behind the balls.'

We didn't laugh. I was beginning to wonder if I would ever be able to kick a ball again. It had been almost four months since my fateful Cruyff turn. At this stage I was meant to be ready for a full-scale game. But my body had given up.

The pain was sporadic. I could go for hours feeling fine and then it would suddenly knife me when I was doing something as simple as getting in or out of my car.

'It sounds like the pain is being caused when you open up the pelvis,' Chris suggested.

'Could be,' I said. 'There's something going on between my privates and the middle. There's something underneath my pelvis. It feels like my pelvis is opening. It's like a great big gapping.'

Zaf Iqbal and Chris took me back to the surgeon, Ernest Schilders, who had done the operation at the Yorkshire Clinic near Bradford. Schilders was a fine surgeon, from Belgium, whom the club had relied on for years as our hip and groin specialist. I trusted him and I was even more worried when he could not identify any reason for the stabbing pain. We told him about the aborted jog, and the abandoned bike ride. Schilders looked bemused. He again said that he was completely confident the surgery had been successful. Schilders thought we needed a fresh pair of eyes. He suggested I see a pelvic specialist down in London.

It was sounding more and more serious. I couldn't jog. I couldn't ride a bike. I couldn't kick a ball. And there was no chance I could jump up in the air and head it. I wasn't able to do much at all.

Zaf, Chris and I travelled down by train to London. I had plenty of time to talk to them. They tried to keep my spirits up but we all knew that there was a real danger I might not improve. We had to face the possibility that, over fourteen years as a first-team player, so much damage had been done around the joint that the whole pelvis had been made unstable. Without a supporting structure I was finished as a hyper-mobile player, and probably as any sort of player. As soon as I tried even the most basic movements my whole pelvis felt like it was shearing.

Zaf and Chris encouraged me. Maybe the pelvic surgeon would come up with a simple solution. Perhaps it would be possible to pin the pelvis?

I shuddered when it was explained that it would be similar to putting a bolt through the joint.

Terrific. I didn't feel good as we met our latest specialist, the pelvic guy, and I waited to hear if he was about to tell me it really was all over. He was very thorough and, after a long examination, he went back to the scan taken that morning.

'Look here,' he said, pointing to a shadowy smudge. 'You've got all of this white fluid here. I don't know how much fluid you should have after this procedure because it's not one that I do. But you need to find out what's going on with this fluid. You'd better go back to Schilders.'

We were going round in circles. But, on the train journey back to Liverpool, Doc Iqbal explained that a build-up of fluid usually indicated an infection. It was confusing as he had already carried out a full battery of blood tests for infection. The clearest sign of an infection is a high white blood-cell count and mine had remained normal throughout the long haul. Maybe Schilders would have a brainwave.

An appointment back in Bradford was arranged with Schilders for later that week. Zaf and Chris asked me to rest up as much as possible at home.

The body works in miraculous ways and maybe it decided that my poor old heart and brain had ached enough. It began to do something very strange. The next day, at home, my wound opened a little. It seeped out white, yellowy, gunky pus.

A clean, perfectly stitched scar opened up – less like a flower than a nasty weed with white and yellow buds on the top. What the fuck was going on now? I found a cotton wool pad and dabbed it clean. More gunk began to ooze out.

I was so scared of what I saw I took a photo of my wound. I

was having a serious panic. I sent the image to Chris with a message:

What the fuck is this?

Chris texted back:

This is v good. Will call in 2 mins. This means it really is an infection.

I messaged him –

That's good?!?

– after sending another photographic update.

Chris called me. I told him that I'd just had to use another pad to clear the next hit of pus.

'It's great news, Stevie,' Chris enthused. I must have grunted dubiously because he quickly explained that my pain had almost certainly been caused by the pus pushing the joint apart. It also caused the sensation of instability in my pelvis. We had been worried that something had become seriously unhinged in the pelvic area. But, instead, the build-up of fluid had caused immense pressure on the joint and essentially forced it apart. No wonder it had felt unstable.

Chris got me back to Bradford quickly to see Schilders and have a repeat MRI scan. It was clear as day, they said, after they had examined the scan. They could see the build-up of pus jammed right between the joint and my pubic symphysis. The apparently normal post-op fluid was probably a raging infection which, bizarrely, hadn't been picked up by any of the tests.

I began to understand. No wonder it had felt as if I was being stabbed in the bollocks.

While we waited for them to run a test on the pus, to confirm it was the infection they all suspected, Chris took me for a coffee in Shipley, on the edge of Bradford. He was fired up.

'We need this to be an infection,' he told me. 'If this is an infection you'll be fine. You'll be sorted.'

I was suddenly desperate. I wanted to be infected. I was praying silently for an infection.

An hour later the results were in and there was absolute confirmation. I was infected. I felt like punching the air. What a result!

Schilders smiled. He understood. He was also relieved. There had been a 1 in 10,000 chance of picking up an infection during surgery. I got the one – and it explained everything. But it was all right. I would go into the Spire, a hospital in Liverpool, and spend a week recovering. They would pump me full of antibiotics and kill off the infection.

There was a chance I would be playing again in late September 2011, early October at the latest. I could not stop smiling as I headed off to hospital for a week.

I had no idea then I would soon feel far lower than I'd ever done before. Yet another mysterious injury, and a deep depression, loomed over me. The worst was on its way.

At first there was only good news. In hospital my pain diminished rapidly. The pus had been drained away and I felt a noticeable improvement in my movement every day. My recovery had begun.

Within a week of getting home I was back at Melwood. I was able to jog freely a few days later. I could ride a bike without pain. I could soon run. I could jump. I could kick a ball. It was a beautiful feeling.

I was still nervous. I had been out for six months and had lost confidence in my body. I wasn't sure if my groin and pelvis would stand up to the rigours of training. But within a few days I felt like my old self again. I felt normal, at last.

I made my comeback on 21 September 2011. We played

Brighton in the League Cup and it was my first game of football in six months. After such a long lay-off I started on the bench but, 1–0 up after seventy-five minutes, Kenny Dalglish sent me on as a sub. I replaced Luis Suárez. I would have loved to have played alongside Luis again but it was enough just to get out on the pitch at the Amex Stadium.

After six minutes I stretched out my leg and blocked a shot. The ball ran loose and I was away. I pushed forward and then found Craig Bellamy, who set off on a mazy, scampering run. Bellamy set up Dirk Kuyt for our second goal. Brighton pulled one back in the very last minute but we had won and were through to the fourth round of a cup we would go on to win the following February.

I gave my shirt to Craig Noone, a good friend of mine who had played well for Brighton that night.

There were even bigger smiles as my comeback continued with two more wins against Wolves and Everton away. I was feeling close to my best again as we prepared to play Manchester United at Old Trafford on 15 October.

In training the day before the game, we were working on some set-piece moves when Daniel Agger's boot caught me. His studs grazed my ankle. It was nothing really, just a little 'ouch' moment. After training I went to the treatment room. They cleaned it up, gave me a bit of compression to stop any swelling, and we all chit-chatted about United and how much I wanted to beat them.

It was not the greatest game, and it would eventually be remembered only as the spiky contest during which Suárez was accused of racially abusing Evra. But before that story broke, I opened the scoring with a free kick in the sixty-eighth minute. I went the whole hog, running, kissing the badge and launching into a long knee-slide of joy.

'To experience all that emotion again was fantastic,' I said in

The Liverpool fans are amazing – loyal through and through.

I'll never forget the singing and the banners and the noise of the crowd at Anfield when I made my emotional farewell.

After my final match at Anfield,
all the Liverpool players
wore No. 8 shirts.

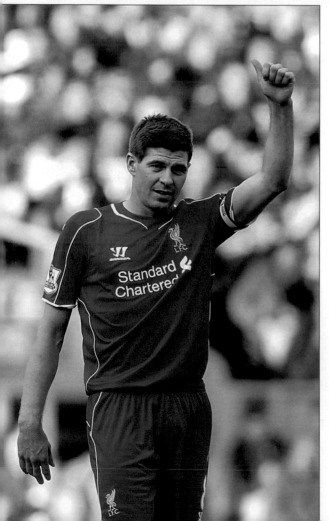

I've always been a one-club player
and leaving Liverpool and these
fans was the toughest decision
I've ever had to make.

The disastrous final match against Stoke wasn't the send-off I had hoped for.

It may not have done much for our fortunes but I was pleased that
I managed that one final goal for Liverpool.

Being introduced to fans at LA Galaxy.

Warming up ahead of my debut.

My debut match for the team.

Receiving the PFA Player
of the Year Award in
2006.

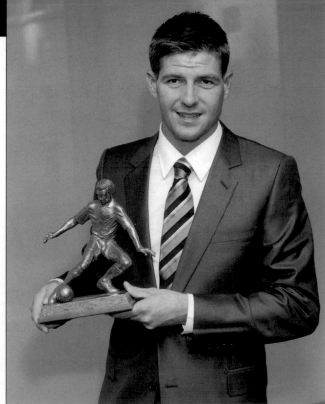

FWA Footballer of
the Year in 2009.

With my lovely wife Alex outside Buckingham Palace.

*Below:* Meeting Her Majesty the Queen when I collected my MBE was more nerve-wracking than any cup final match.

My family, Alex and our girls, are such a rock in my life.

Lilly and Lexie wearing red before a game in 2009.

Twenty-seven years after joining the Liverpool Academy aged eight, I'm leaving with a career full of memories, heartbreak and triumphs. Now I'm looking forward to the next chapter in LA, with my girls by my side.

the post-match interview. 'I couldn't even say it was a great free kick. I was trying to put it over the wall but it went round the side. It's nice to have a bit of luck at long last.'

United equalized in the last ten minutes and soon the world of football was consumed by the Suárez–Evra saga.

My own new set of problems were just about to begin. It started with an ache in my ankle. It felt different from a sprain. There was just a dull throb. I mentioned it to the physios but there was no obvious problem when they bent it back and forth and from side to side.

Fate intervened. Chris saw me walking to the treatment room. He was strolling behind me and, without saying anything, took a sharp intake of breath. Chris saw a swelling in the back of my ankle. The swollen flesh was hanging over my flip-flop.

Chris told me later that he was disturbed. He thought, 'That isn't right.' Chris was used to seeing swollen joints and this was different. The swelling looked soggy. Chris kept this quiet from me at the time but he went straight to see Zaf Iqbal. They both feared another infection.

Chris iced the ankle but he said nothing to me about their infection worries. He just listened to me babbling on about making sure that I could play at West Brom that weekend.

Chris told me his concerns had begun to deepen. He normally liked working on ankles because they are such pliable joints. Chris would dig his thumbs into an ankle and move the contours naturally. But there was no such movement in my soggy ankle. Zaf was even more worried that the infection might have penetrated the joint. Although he didn't say so until later, he knew they needed to establish whether the pus was both in and outside the joint. If it was only on the outside they could drain it away. But if pus had penetrated the joint it would be extremely destructive. Pus is not ordinary fluid. It softens the cartilage in the joint. If I tried to play a game of football with pus in the joint it could shear the cartilage right off my ankle.

Chris said that Zaf just wanted to do a quick check on the ankle. Zaf walked in and pulled out a great big needle. They looked very serious. The needle slid in and yellow pus filled the syringe. Zaf disappeared so that he could study the results. Not wanting to worry me, they kept their darkest fears to themselves. I went back on the club's Game Ready compressing machine in an attempt to reduce the swelling before West Brom. I had no idea of the lurking trouble.

On the Friday evening, the night before the West Brom game, we had dinner at our hotel near Birmingham. Zaf sat next to me. I noticed he was checking his phone more than usual. I now know why. He was waiting for an email containing the results of my test. He was quiet as he read the message on his screen. The test confirmed the worst. The graze caused by Daniel Agger's boot had healed but, beneath the skin, an infection had already moved into the joint.

Zaf started by telling me I was out of the game. I would not be playing against West Brom. Zaf was suddenly very blunt. 'We're going straight to the hospital,' he said. 'We need to get this infection out of you – fast.'

I was worried then. Another infection, another operation, another stint in hospital: an ominous pattern was starting to emerge.

We met Chris in Liverpool and then Zaf returned to Birmingham as he needed to be on duty with the team. Chris took charge. He had booked me into the Spire again and had arranged surgery. The earliest it could be done was late the following afternoon.

Chris explained the severity of my injury. If I had played against West Brom with an infected joint, it would almost certainly have been the last game of my career.

I looked at Chris in disbelief. He was not joking. He stressed how lucky I had been.

'Lucky?' I said, having cursed my misfortune over the last eight injury-ridden months.

Chris pointed out that it was just luck that he had been walking behind me, and I had been wearing flip-flops, when he saw the bulge of flesh. I had been so determined to play I would not have complained to anyone. And if the fluid had not been drained or tested no one would have guessed that I was about to step onto the field to play a Premier League match with an infected ankle joint. I really had been very, very lucky.

Chris Walker, the aptly named foot-and-ankle surgeon at the Spire, soon made it plain. He told us that if I'd tried to play against West Brom the continual stop-start movements would have resulted in a definite shearing of the ankle. The pus would have then peeled the cartilage away like a grater shaving slivers off a chunk of cheese.

As it was such a career-threatening injury they needed to evacuate all the pus and infection under anaesthetic. I would then have to keep my foot in a non-weightbearing boot for the next six weeks in order to help the softened cartilage repair itself. I had no choice. I had to go under.

Liverpool's match against West Brom kicked off at 5.30 p.m. on Saturday, 29 October 2011. I was already unconscious then and lying on the operating table. Chris, as usual, was with me in theatre so that he could observe the procedure. He looked up at the clock on the theatre wall just as the surgeon's scalpel sliced open my flesh. It was 5.31 p.m.

'Watch this,' Walker said to Chris as he stepped back. Yellow fluid gushed out of my ankle, spilling onto the hospital floor.

The poison poured out of the joint and the surrounding ankle tissue. Around eight minutes after they began surgery they could start to clean up the wound. At that exact time, 5.39,

Liverpool were awarded a penalty. If Chris and Zaf had not acted so quickly I would have tried to take that penalty with my infected foot. I was, again, very fortunate. Charlie Adam was also happy. He took the penalty in my place and scored. Liverpool went on to win 2–0, just as I began to stir and open my eyes from the anaesthetic.

I drifted in and out of my drugged sleep all night. In the morning, early on a cold and drizzly October Sunday, it felt as if the poison had moved into my head. I felt terrible.

The gloom deepened as the days passed. I might have been in a weightless boot but it felt as if a deadly load was pinning me down. I felt so desolate I thought I would never be able to lift myself again. I began to imagine the end. I was thirty-one years old and I already felt like a washed-up has-been. The groin and the first infection, followed by the ankle and another infection, had been too much for me.

Finally, I told Chris how bad it felt inside my head. 'I'm down, really down,' I said.

I'd sunk so low that I didn't know how to break free and be myself again. I was in the grip of depression.

I had no motivtion to get out of bed. I felt there was no light at the end of the tunnel. I had no idea when, or even if, I might ever play again. It was obvious that a life without football for me would be devastating.

Chris listened closely and he nodded when I said two more lines. 'I think I need to see someone. I think I need help . . . I am feeling low every day.'

# 14. The Chimp, the Stamp and the Letter

I met Steve Peters for the first time on an icy day in the winter of 2011. He lived up in the hills a long way past Oldham and Stockport. Chris Morgan and Zaf Iqbal took me because I was on crutches. I had also needed some convincing to make the journey. I felt even more depressed at the thought I actually needed to see a psychiatrist. Despite what I'd said to Chris after my surgery, it didn't seem the right fit for me.

Over the years there had been times when I'd felt moody. Some days I could be grouchy or just a bit miserable. Like most people, I had my off days, but I'd never been so down before. Everyone had ups and downs in life, good days and bad days, and I was no different. The surest sign of my balanced approach to life was that I almost always knew the reason for a sudden dip in my mood. It usually seemed football-related and I felt low, for a brief while, because of a game we had lost, a mistake I had made or because one of my teammates wanted to leave us. I could rationalize everything and get back on an even path. But after the groin, the ankle and the twin infections, everything was knotted and twisted.

I still understood the real reason for my feeling so low. I was worried that I would never get my fitness back to play football at the level I'd maintained for so many years. That was the reason I'd told Chris I needed help. But I was sceptical when he mentioned a psychiatrist. The idea of me in therapy sounded pretty weird.

Chris had heard about Steve Peters from one of the

Liverpool doctors, Peter Brukner, who had been blown away by an amazing presentation he had given at a conference. Peter has since become the doctor for the Australia cricket team and he was already with them when the batsman Phillip Hughes died tragically after being struck by a ball. He was a key figure in helping the Hughes family during that terrible time.

When he was still at Liverpool we all respected Dr Brukner's opinion. He had raved about Steve Peters, who was best known for his work then with cyclists like Chris Hoy and Victoria Pendleton. I still wasn't sure but, at the same time, I was so low that I needed help. 'You know what?' I eventually said to Chris, 'I'll try it. I feel so shit I'll try anything.'

On a freezing and icy afternoon the roads were treacherous. It took us an hour and a half to get to Steve's house. By the time I had dragged myself out of the car, hoisted myself up on my crutches and started to shuffle down the path to his house I was terrified I was going to slip on my arse. It would be the next thing to go wrong and I'd tear a few ligaments or break a bone. That was my state of mind as we approached Steve's front door.

We made it in and I managed to sit down without slipping off my crutches and breaking my neck. It was a start, at least. Steve was very easy to talk to and I opened up without too much prompting. After I had told him a little about the injuries, and the past eight months, I admitted that there was some good news. The rest of my life away from football – Alex, the kids, my whole family, my friends – was fine. They were always my support network and I valued and loved them. The only problem was that no one could really offer me much support or comfort when it seemed as if my career, my life in football, might be taken away from me too early.

Steve was very good at that first meeting. He probably said words to me that other people were wary of ever saying. He was harsh but fair. Steve also asked me some tough and searing questions: 'Well,' he said, 'if you never kick a ball again, so what?'

I looked at him in shock. Steve didn't shrug when he said those same two words again: 'So what?'

Steve then pushed on to give me my answer. 'You've got three beautiful little girls who sound happy and healthy. So you're a dad. You're also married, to a lovely wife, who supports you every step of the way. You're a lucky man to have such a fantastic family. You've also had an unbelievable career. You've played for Liverpool for thirteen years. You've won the biggest trophy in club football. You've played so many times for your country. You live in a very nice house. You're financially secure for the rest of your life. What are you worried about?'

I didn't say anything but I nodded.

'So what's the worry?' Steve asked again.

'That my career might be over,' I said in a quiet voice.

Steve spoke even more firmly then. He told me how he knew of some young sportsmen and women who had been forced to retire after six months, before they'd had a chance to achieve anything. They had no medals to show for a lifelong commitment to their sport. They had no money. How lucky was I compared to them?

Steve opened it up to say that people were in trouble in all walks of life. Some men gambled everything and ruined their lives. Others drank their lives away. How did their broken lives compare to mine? My life was fantastic.

He was right, of course, and I listened closely. This was when I first found out about the 'chimp'. Steve told me how many of us allowed our chimp, the illogical side of our brain, to run ourselves down. The chimp forced us to try and look for the worst outcome and shut out all hope and common sense. My chimp had taken charge of my life and he was running riot. The chimp was causing havoc. Every morning I woke up he said to me: 'You're not going to play again. You're done, it's over.'

When I was young and single, and football was the be all and end all, I really would have believed there was no point to life if I couldn't play the game. I would have been wrong but it might have been more understandable because of my youth and naivety. But I was no longer a naive teenager. I was thirty-one years old, a husband and a dad of three. Football was no longer the most important part of my life. My family came first – even if I was still besotted with the game and desperate to succeed. Football came second now – and so I knew I could survive without it. I might even still be happy.

Steve had more to say. 'You will play football again,' he said emphatically. 'I've spoken to your doctors and they've got no doubt. You will be fine. You'll get over this and you'll play as well as you've ever done. But you need to take control of your mind again because the chimp is absolutely hijacking you and it's running your life.'

I decided I'd get my fucking chimp in a headlock and I'd fucking muzzle him. But I thought it best not to swear in front of Steve. I just smiled instead. And it was a real smile, a proper smile, one of those smiles that had disappeared from my life for months.

We agreed that Steve and I would meet regularly from then on, just to keep the old chimp in check, and to make sure I was in charge of my head again.

I got back up on my crutches and shook Steve by the hand as I thanked him. I used my arms to hoist myself up and out of his house and I didn't even worry about slipping on the icy path.

*

More than three years later, in March 2015, I was still seeing Steve Peters on a relatively regular basis. He had bolstered and steadied me ever since that first meeting at his house. Steve was especially strong when, after I clawed my way back to fitness, I started playing again. I led Liverpool to victory in the Carling Cup final in February 2012 at Wembley. We beat Cardiff City 3–2 on penalties, after my cousin Anthony Gerrard missed their final spot kick, and I lifted another trophy, my first under Kenny Dalglish, above my head.

·I was not entirely happy because, like Anthony, I also missed my penalty, when Tom Heaton pulled off a brilliant save in the shoot-out. Steve Peters spoke firmly to me. 'You're too harsh on yourself,' he said, echoing a mantra he'd quoted at me over and over again. 'Even when you're not giving a ten-out-of-ten performance you're still one of the best on the pitch.' Those were the kind of things Steve would say as he filled me with renewed confidence. He also suggested that I needed someone – someone who was neither a family member nor one of my close friends outside football – to be honest with me. I needed someone I could vent my anger and frustration to and someone who would tell me bluntly how I had done. Chris was the obvious person. He was bright and clever and without any bullshit. Chris was given permission by Steve to be brutally frank with me – and to also make sure that I kept my perspective at all times.

Chris was there for me when, after my hamstring injury against Spurs on 10 February 2015, I missed Liverpool's next seven games. The team had done well without me and were again pushing for the top four and a Champions League place. Liverpool had lost only one of those seven matches, when we were knocked out of the Europa League by Beşiktaş in Turkey.

Our next game was away to Swansea, on Monday, 16 March,

and I was fit to play. Brendan insisted, rightly, that he would not allow sentiment to sway his selection when he decided whether I would start the match or be on the bench at the Liberty Stadium. At the same time he was generous in his praise:

> This guy is one of the greatest players in the history of the Premier League and arguably the greatest player of this club. Stevie always puts the team first. Whether he is playing or not playing I have huge respect and admiration for him as a player and a person.
>
> But I am not one that makes emotional decisions on whether I like someone or not. For me it is about finding the right balance in the team so that we win. Stevie still has big qualities that we will need between now and the end of the season. But what you have seen over my time here is that I rely on the team. I will always pick the best team I feel to win a game.

Liverpool were on a strong run of form and two weeks earlier, on 1 March, we had beaten Manchester City 2–1 at Anfield. Joe Allen played well in my position and Jordan Henderson and Philippe Coutinho scored the goals. I had heard the opinion of some Liverpool fans. They decided that I was past it and not good enough to get back in the team. Liverpool no longer needed me. They were entitled to their opinion but, logically, using the Steve Peters technique of stepping back and looking at the situation without excessive emotion, I was able to set aside those views. Not every fan knew a huge amount about football. Sometimes their opinions were expressed loudest – 'We don't need fucking Gerrard any more' – after three or four pints.

I knew what I still had to offer. I also knew that a Premier League campaign lasted for thirty-eight games. It was about more than just beating Manchester City at home. The lesson from the season before, when we followed the exact same winning score against City, 2–1, by losing our next home match to Chelsea, had been tattooed across the memory of our failed title challenge.

I was also pragmatic. I understood the logic in not changing a winning team. I realized that I might need a little time to get back the rhythm and tempo of my play after missing seven games. And so I was absolutely fine when Brendan took me to one side and explained why I would start on the bench against Swansea.

It's always difficult watching a game from the dugout when you're fit enough to play. I'd done it a few times already that season, from Stoke City at home to Real Madrid away, and it didn't get any easier. Someone asked me after the Swansea game if I ever hoped my team would do badly without me – so I would be picked for the next match. The immediate truth was that, being a Liverpool fan as well as a player, I would never sit on a bench and think, 'I hope we don't win today.' I still want the three points first as a supporter.

But my feelings were complicated at the Liberty Stadium. Apart from wanting to come on against Swansea I was desperate to start Sunday's home game against Manchester United. Since I had made my announcement confirming my departure at the end of the season, it was hard to avoid being asked how I felt about a series of 'last times'. How did I feel about playing in my last Merseyside derby? How did I feel about playing my last Carling Cup tie – when we lost narrowly in the semi-finals to Chelsea? How did I feel about facing Man U for the last time? All I knew for sure was that I did not want to be watching my last game against United as a substitute.

So, for once, against Swansea, I was hoping Liverpool might start without absolute composure and certainty. I wanted play to fall in such a way that the need for a very experienced thirty-four-year-old captain, operating in a deep-lying midfield role, became glaringly apparent. I sat on the sidelines, on a cold Monday night in Swansea, consumed by those private thoughts.

In a way, I got what I wanted. We didn't concede a goal in the first half but we were outplayed by Swansea. They outnumbered us in midfield and, under their manager Garry Monk, played fluent, attacking football. We were much more jittery and fevered. It seemed pretty obvious from the bench. Liverpool needed to calm down and string some passes together, not try to bomb forward at every opportunity in an effort to score as soon as we got the ball.

The confidence a young team had picked up on its recent winning run was misplaced. It looked to me as if the kids imagined they could play every game in the same way. They tried to have an immediate crack at Swansea – and ended up forcing the play. We needed to win back the ball first, and then retain it. We needed to stay patient and then, when the openings inevitably came, attack Swansea with a much more structured tempo. We needed confidence that, eventually, the goal would come. I thought the game was tailor-made for me to step in and help Liverpool take control.

I was also still enough of a fan to wince whenever Swansea looked like they were about to take a deserved lead. Simon Mignolet was in fine form and he did well keeping out dangerous shots from Bafétimbi Gomis and Gylfi Sigurdsson. Skrtel made a couple of last-ditch headed clearances and Lallana deflected a fierce drive from Jonjo Shelvey. We all trudged into the dressing room at half-time, knowing how lucky Liverpool were to still be in the game at o–o.

Brendan was fuming. He slaughtered the team and pointed straight at me. 'One of the hardest decisions I've had to make is to not put him straight back in the team. One of the best players in the fucking world and I've kept him out because you've been playing well. You've been on a winning run. So I left out Steven Gerrard. I gave you all a chance. I stayed loyal to the team.'

There was silence in the room as Brendan looked at the players. And then he said, bluntly, almost bitterly, 'How fucking wrong was I?'

A few of the kids looked down as Brendan continued. 'So you get my trust and yet here we go again . . .'

The atmosphere was strained. 'Does he have to go and put his cape back on and save us yet again?' Brendan asked, pointing at me as if I was Superman. 'You know what? I am going to have to tell him to put his cape on in ten minutes and turn this game around for us – again.'

I felt a little embarrassed when Brendan said those words. I wanted to come back on as soon as possible, but I didn't feel much like a superhero. I just wanted to play well, win the game and nail down my place against United.

Brendan allowed his words to die away and then he switched into a much more strategic way of thinking. He was, once more, impressive in the way he read the match. Our formation simply didn't work against their diamond. We had been playing the box formation with two holders and two number 10s. They played the diamond and absolutely destroyed the box. We always looked overrun in midfield and so Brendan, smartly, switched us to a matching diamond. We went man for man with the idea that, when I came on after fifteen or twenty minutes, Henderson would have more space to push forward. I would keep Swansea occupied and the game would open up. But we also needed much greater physicality, intensity and tempo to win the one-on-one challenges – and that would start with us pressing Swansea much higher up in their half.

'I'm just asking you to be men,' Brendan said before he sent the team back out. He nodded to me. I should be ready to come on.

The signal came after sixty-four minutes. The number 18 lit up the fourth official's board. Moreno was off. The board gleamed with my number 8. I touched hands with Moreno and ran onto the field. Jordan Henderson sprinted across to me. He hadn't been asked to do it, but he handed me the captain's armband.

There was no cape around my shoulders but, within four minutes, we had the goal we needed. It came about through a huge chunk of luck rather than the power of a comic-book hero.

Daniel Sturridge flicked the ball into the path of a rampaging Hendo, suddenly able to pour forward, and the race was on. A Swansea defender, Jordi Amat, was closer to the ball and he made a sliding tackle to win the challenge. Amat's clearance struck Henderson's leg. Hendo knew nothing about it but the ball ricocheted off his shin and arced over the surprised head of the Swansea keeper Łukasz Fabiański – who was stranded. The lucky break had fallen our way.

We were composed and gritty for the rest of the match. The 1–0 victory meant that, after twenty-nine games, we were in fifth place, just two points behind Manchester United and three adrift of Arsenal. Manchester City had lost the previous weekend, surprisingly, to Burnley, and they were now only four points ahead of us. We all had nine games to play and Brendan spoke about chasing second spot again – as we all knew Chelsea were marching relentlessly to another title:

> It was a wonderful demonstration of the character and resilience in the team, especially after our first half. We just weren't anywhere near it but we knew we were going to be better in the second half. We also changed the structure – I thought

second half we really dominated the game. Everyone talks about fourth, but it's the same every year for me. We do our best to finish as high as possible. And I think that Manchester City's result gives us an opportunity to finish second. We've just got to take our mentality and the run and the confidence we have at the moment into every game.

On the long journey back from Swansea, travelling through the cold black night and reaching Liverpool only after two in the morning, I had plenty of time to think.

The game against United had assumed even more of a personal edge than usual. There were always two teams I wanted to beat more than any other – Everton and Manchester United. That had never changed but the emotions of the last four months were still swirling around me. The difficult personal decision to leave Liverpool, and the rawness around making it public, had been followed by injury and then the bench against Swansea. I wanted to make up for lost time and for the time I'd never get back after my final season ended. One last game against United offered the chance of one last win over the team we had hated most on Ironside Road.

Everton were the Bluenoses, and we always wanted to beat our local rivals, but they were Scousers in the end. When I stormed into tackles on Ironside Road, grazing my knees but winning back the ball, I often imagined I was robbing a United or Everton player and driving on to score the winner against them at Anfield.

At least I felt much more hopeful that Brendan would pick me for his starting XI on Sunday.

I had received a clear-cut message from him earlier in the season. At a point when I had not decided my future, Brendan called me into his office and we had a really good conversation. He said, 'Even though I'm managing your games it's important for you to understand that I'm trying to help you stay fresh. I can't bc flogging you every game because I won't get the best out of you. Sometimes, I'll give you a break and you'll come back fresh and you'll do well.'

His words made a lot of sense and I agreed with him. Brendan then said, just as I was getting up to leave, 'Look, I also want you to know one more thing. If we've got a very important game, a crucial game in the league or a cup final, then it's obvious. You're my number one pick. I put you in, and you're my captain. What you've given me since I've walked through this door, made my mind up a long time ago. If we've got a big game, you're in . . .'

We were out of the Champions League and the title was long gone. But we were closing in on fourth place, and Manchester United, our fiercest rivals for decades. A home game against United felt like the biggest game of the season. So I felt confident I would be selected.

I was tired, though, as our journey home from Wales dragged on into the early hours, and the odd stray thought nagged at me. Liverpool had been unbeaten for the last thirteen league games – and our last defeat had been 3–0 to United at Old Trafford back in December. After that loss Brendan had switched to a 3-4-3 formation which, as if by magic, just clicked.

We had racked up our fifth straight league win, and had kept clean sheets for the previous six away games. The stats were impressive, as was the points haul of thirty-three from the last thirty-nine. What if Brendan decided to keep the pattern of the team-run – and held me back in reserve.

I had a small talk to myself. Keep the chimp in check. Stay logical. Everything Brendan had said to me earlier in the season and in the dressing room against Swansea made it clear. Of course I would start for Liverpool against United.

*

I trained really well on the Wednesday and felt sharper and hungrier than anyone in the squad. That was always my aim at Melwood; but the long absence and the anticipation of a vital game against United intensified my appetite. I felt fit and ready, and we still had four days to prepare.

It seemed as if Brendan and I were thinking alike. On Wednesday night, at home with Alex and the girls, I received a text from the manager:

> You've trained so well the last couple of days, can we have a chat?
> Can you come to my office in the morning before training?

I was already in bed but I replied instantly:

> Yeah no problem, thanks.

I might have sounded casual in my text but I was much more excited in my bed. I read Brendan's text again.

'I'm going to be back in the team here,' I thought. 'He's thinking Man United, at home, massive game. He needs me for this one.'

I lay in the dark for the next hour, thinking about every-thing, while Alex slept peacefully next to me. United had played really well the past weekend against Tottenham and, finally, they were starting to gel under Louis van Gaal. They were going to be a real test for us. I wondered who Brendan might leave out to make way for me, and what kind of formation he would choose. He might opt to shuffle our line-up but keep Joe Allen and Jordan Henderson because they had both done well in recent weeks. I assumed he might stick to the diamond we had used in the second half against Swansea. I couldn't wait to get into Melwood in the morning – and to Anfield and the game on Sunday. Eventually, I drifted off to sleep.

When I woke in the morning I felt fired up. Once Brendan and I had met I knew it was important for me to train even harder than ever – just to prove how right he would be to trust me. I felt happier going into training than I had done in months.

Brendan was in his office when I arrived. He started smiling as soon as I walked in and stretched out my hand to say good morning. Brendan was still smiling as he leant back in his chair and said, 'How are you feeling?'

'Yeah, I'm fine, good,' I said. 'No problems.'

There was a little pause then Brendan said, 'Look, I'm desperate to get you back into the eleven. But the team has done so well I'm going to go with the same lads that started the other night.'

A sudden lump formed in my throat. I looked at Brendan and, in that mad moment, I had a split-second decision to make. Do I have a go at him?

I went the other way. I went the right way. I decided to stay professional. 'No problem, fine,' I said.

'OK?' Brendan said.

'OK,' I nodded. 'I respect your decision.'

We left it at that. I walked out and got ready for training.

My mind was swimming. I couldn't believe it. It felt to me, then, like a classic case of muscle-flexing. My relationship with Brendan was too good for him to need to make a point to me. But I wondered if this was his way of showing the press that he was strong enough to make a difficult decision. There had been a lot of talk about me in the media when I'd been injured and the team had been doing well. Would I walk straight back into a winning team at the age of thirty-four? This seemed a chance for Brendan to show his authority and send out a clear message that this was his team.

I was certain it was the wrong decision. I had understood the selection against Swansea because I was just coming back then. But I should have been in the best XI to beat United. Even at my age, and in my last months at Liverpool, the team were better with me in my place, and as captain.

I can respect Brendan's decision now, even if I obviously still believe it was the wrong one, because he wanted to show loyalty to everyone who had done well for him. But it hurt me, especially because of our previous conversations and the fact that his Wednesday night text, which had been full of praise, had misled me. I'm sure he didn't mean to give me the wrong impression but his text confirmed in my mind that I would be selected.

Players are players the world over. If you're not in the starting XI the manager is a so-and-so. The world is against you and you go home feeling sorry for yourself. We're all the same in the end. We're like spoilt kids. We feel the same as men as we did as eight-year-old boys. We want to be picked for the first team.

I've learnt, with experience, that sometimes you have to look at yourself and say, 'Why aren't I in the team? What am I doing wrong? Do I have to analyse my game and improve on a specific aspect?' I like to believe that I'm further ahead than a lot of players in being able to take that perspective. Many footballers sulk or go into their shells, and I don't. But I wasn't on the bench very often. It was still the shock of the new. I handled it professionally around the training ground and in the dressing room but, on the inside, I felt wounded. I felt frustrated and angry.

Steve Peters saw me on the morning of the game and he's since told me that he really regrets not spending longer with me. He says now that the warning signs were stark. I had spoken about the need to clear my head of all negative emotions and try to be as professional for the team as possible. But Steve says that the last thing I said to him that morning haunts him. As I turned to leave I said that I felt like a caged animal.

Steve wishes now that he had made me stay with him and calmed me down – because caged animals don't last very long on a football field.

379

## *Anfield, Sunday, 22 March 2015*

It was a sun-kissed afternoon at Anfield but I could see from my cage in the dugout that Manchester United were much the better side. They were passing the ball with slick confidence. But it's easy for a team like United, which is full of good players, when the opposition don't put in a decent tackle. For some strange reason, Liverpool did the opposite of what we were meant to do. We backed off and allowed United to dominate.

The first goal came after fourteen minutes. Marouane Fellaini slipped it to Ander Herrera who, with Liverpool slow to press, had time and space to move forward. He then looked up and hit a pass, full of vision and incision, which split us open like a peach. Juan Mata ran onto it and, as Mignolet tried to narrow the angle, the Spaniard fired it across the keeper and, with a deflection off the right post, into the corner of the net. It had been such a simple goal.

We were so mediocre that it did not take long for Brendan to send me down the touchline for a warm-up. Adam Lallana had been clattered by Phil Jones after twenty-two minutes. He looked like he was just winded but Brendan was sending out a plain message to all his players on the pitch. Each one of them was dispensable if they kept playing so poorly.

I ran towards the United fans, stretching my legs as they opened their throats. They pelted me with abuse – and their favourite song echoed around the away end:

*Steve Gerrard, Gerrard / He slipped on his fucking arse / He gave it to Demba Ba / Steve Gerrard, Gerrard . . .*

After a while, when they got bored, they swapped it for another chestnut:

*You nearly won the league, / you nearly won the league . . . and now you better believe it / now you better believe it / you nearly won the league.*

The anger in the caged animal grew and grew. I should have forced myself to take a few deep breaths. But I was boiling with intent to make a point that I should have been in the starting XI. I also wanted to answer the critics who had been circling around me the previous few weeks.

Lallana continued but it was obvious after thirty minutes that I would be on at half-time. Van Gaal had worked out Brendan's box formation and United were swaggering. Anfield was very quiet.

I warmed up again, as Brendan had told me I was coming on for Lallana. It was another opportunity for me to concentrate on bringing some purpose back to the team. Instead, I felt angry and determined to make a shuddering impact.

We had stood off United in the first half and made very few tackles. It went against everything built into my DNA. I had once said that 'tackling is a big part of the game which usually sorts the men from the boys'. Tackling and collisions mattered against Manchester United. From Huyton to Melwood to Anfield, for more than twenty-six years, I had always felt compelled to show fire towards United. They were the enemy. You never rolled over against United. If they got one over you, you fought back. You went in harder, with just a little more crunch, just to let them know it really was personal. They did the same to us.

Everything about the game on that sunny Sunday afternoon had become painfully personal.

Brendan was mortified by Liverpool's performance. It must have been in his mind that the press would make a big deal of van Gaal winning the tactical battle in the first half – because it was an admission and a statement to call for me at half-time.

I ran onto the field with the team for the second half. It was a warm afternoon and the sky was a very pale blue. The Kop erupted in a welcoming roar as they caught sight of me. Jordan

Henderson came over and we wrapped our arms around each other and said a few encouraging words. I was primed for the start. While we waited I looked around Anfield, my ancient battleground, and did a last few warm-ups, rotating my torso from the hips, tugging at my shorts, impatient for the game to get underway.

Martin Atkinson blew for the start of the second half. Coutinho rolled the ball to Sturridge, who turned and slid it to me at the base of the centre circle. I played a neat and controlled one-two with Allen. Herrera moved towards me, snapping busily at my heels, and I had to cut back to break free from him. Allen and I exchanged passes again. The ball was back with me and, already immersed in the game, I looked up. I hit a long diagonal pass and found Emre Can on the right, thirty-five yards away. Applause rippled around Anfield.

Can brought my pass down with his chest. United were still pressing hard and Can had little option but to come inside and feed it back to me. I scooped the ball past Herrera to Allen who prodded it back. His return pass to me was slightly short and it spun towards Mata.

I was determined not to let Mata get the ball. I went in hard, with a fair but slamming tackle. I cleaned out Mata, who went flying, and I won the ball. The crowd bellowed its approval.

I was involved again, immediately, as Sakho played it once more to me.

Herrera was hurtling towards me to shut down space. I was too quick for him. I completed a simple pass as Herrera came flying in with his sliding tackle.

His right leg stretched out invitingly on the Anfield turf. I couldn't stop myself. Without even giving myself time to think I brought my left foot stamping down on Herrera. I felt my studs sink into his flesh just above the ankle. It had to have hurt him.

Herrera clutched his ankle and writhed around on the ground. I raised my arm above my head and then gestured angrily. I was trying to deflect attention away from me because the whistle had already made a shrill blast.

The assistant referee had an unimpeded view. His flag shot up seconds after the stamp. He must have spoken into the referee's earpiece because Atkinson was walking fast towards me.

I knew I was in trouble. But I'm still a footballer and so I pointed at myself, almost in self-defence, as if to say: 'What? *Me?*'

'Yes, *you*,' Atkinson's walk said. I didn't like the look of his walk. I didn't like the look of his face.

Fellaini and Rooney were close by. Wayne looked at me. He knew I was gone. He had been in the same position as me in a World Cup game against Portugal. He spoke to Atkinson as the ref reached for his top pocket.

I knew it was going to be a red and so I kept carping about Herrera. I might as well have a moan because I knew I had to go.

I wasn't ready to leave meekly, not with the wrath sinking so slowly into despair.

Martin Skrtel ran across to protest. I appreciated him trying to defend me but, with his shaved head and tattoos, Skrtel did not look much like a silver-tongued barrister. He had no chance. And I, of course, had no chance with Atkinson. The referee got it right but I still felt sick as he jabbed his finger at me and then made a show of pointing to the tunnel.

I waved angrily at Atkinson and swore under my breath. And then, as if to say, 'OK, I know, I know . . .' I turned away and walked towards the touchline. I kept muttering to myself and shaking my messed-up head.

'What have you just done?' I asked my chimp. 'Are you fucking stupid?'

Behind me, Herrera was back up on his feet, arguing with Atkinson over the yellow card he had been shown for his late challenge on me.

The Manchester United fans didn't care. They revelled in my misfortune.

It had taken me just thirty-eight seconds to get myself sent off against Manchester United. Thirty-eight seconds in which I had been at the heart of every small cameo of action and ferocious display of rage. It had been, in the end, thirty-eight seconds defined by anger and a kind of madness.

Liverpool, down to ten men, lost 2–1, following a sublime second goal for Mata, a consolation for Sturridge and a penalty save by Mignolet from Rooney. After the match, I faced the cameras. I was, at least, honest: 'I need to accept it, the decision was right. I've let my teammates and the manager down today. And even more importantly I've let all of the supporters down. So I take full responsibility for my actions.'

I was asked to explain why I had boiled over: 'I don't know. Probably, just the reaction to the initial tackle. I don't think I should say too much more on it. I just came to apologize to everyone in the dressing room, all the supporters, all the players because I also take full responsibility for today's result.'

That night, at home, feeling ashamed and embarrassed all over again, I spoke to Alex. I told her how angry I had been since Thursday morning – but how disappointed in myself I now felt. I was thirty-four years old. Surely at that age, especially as a professional, I ought to be capable of controlling myself during a game of football?

I had kept my anger well hidden – from Brendan, from my teammates and even from Steve Peters. Steve had thought I was doing OK until I compared myself to that caged animal.

Alex, of course, knew how I had been feeling. She lives with me. She knows me. She loves me. And so that night, while we sat up late and talked, she made an admission herself.

'I just knew something like that was going to happen today,' she said.

I looked up in surprise.

'Just by watching you these past three days,' Alex said. 'You've not been yourself. I could tell it was eating you up.'

Alex tries hard not to interfere in my career. She doesn't follow the game much and she never tells me what I should or shouldn't do as a footballer. Instead, she just trusts me to do the right thing and, most of the time, there are no issues. I try to be fair and decent, but I have my bleak moments. I succumb to emotion. I give in to frustration and anger.

I was sent off eight times in my seventeen-year career as a Liverpool player. It works out as under one dismissal every two seasons – or once every eighty-eight games. It's not the worst disciplinary record in the world – but I'm also aware of how far removed it is from the career of a player like Gary Lineker, who did not pick up even a single booking in all his years playing for club and country. But he was a poacher rather than a tackler.

It seems significant that half of my dismissals have come against two clubs. You can guess them.

Manchester United and Everton; twice against each.

When my emotions are at their highest, and the outcome of the match against fierce local rivals matters most, I'm always closest to the red zone – and the red card.

I've had to accept that I'm a player both inspired and tormented by emotion. My most significant goals for Liverpool – against Olympiakos and AC Milan in the same victorious Champions League season – were scored amid deep emotion. At the same time the lowest moments, the defeat against Chelsea and the stamp against Manchester United, were also fuelled by the extreme emotions I experienced during the build-up to both matches.

Many of the thoughts that had consumed me in Monaco almost a year earlier, when I was grieving the Chelsea slip, returned. The same truth applied. The conflicted emotions of football, of just being alive, of being gifted yet flawed, of being lucky and fated, of Istanbul and Hillsborough, were wrapped around each other.

I was banned, correctly, for three games. I would miss two league matches, against Arsenal and Newcastle, and an FA Cup quarter-final replay against Blackburn Rovers. The idea of playing my final match for Liverpool at Wembley on my thirty-fifth birthday, in the FA Cup final, shone still more brightly in the murk. It was turning out to be a messy end but I felt sure there would be one last twist. And nothing would be sweeter than playing a massive game, a cup final, on my very last day in a Liverpool shirt.

And so, after a few days, I was calm and almost philosophical in the wake of the stamp. I would let fate take its course. There was nothing else I could do, back on the sidelines again, but wait for the last few weeks of the season, of my football career in England, to unfold in front of me.

I already knew the fixture list by heart and so I didn't need to check. My ban meant that I had only two home games left as a Liverpool player – against Queens Park Rangers and Crystal Palace. But at least, exactly a week after the Man United disaster, I had another chance to play at Anfield.

On 29 March a Gerrard XI faced a Carragher XI in a charity match at Anfield – with the proceeds being donated to the Liverpool FC Foundation and Alder Hey hospital. We aimed to raise as close to a million pounds as we could manage. It felt a relief to be able to do some good after all the bad news.

The idea of the game emerged when the Liverpool Foundation approached me. They said, 'Do you want to put on a game and half of the money can go to your foundation and the other half to the club's foundation?'

I turned them down initially. It was just over eighteen months since the charity match for my foundation when we played Olympiakos before the start of the 2013–14 season. I said, 'No. It will look like a second testimonial and I don't want to do that to the fans. They gave me the best testimonial I could have wished for – and I don't want to be asking people to put their hands in their pockets again.'

They soon came back to me and said, 'Look, can we do it in a different way where we raise money for the Liverpool Foundation – which is mostly community projects to help disadvantaged children. You can then pick a hospital for the other 40–50 per cent of the money.'

It sounded a much better idea and so I said, 'OK. But why don't we spread the other 50 per cent between all the local charities – while making sure that the bulk of it goes to Alder Hey?'

The Liverpool Foundation liked the suggestion and it made me happy. Alder Hey is the main hospital in the area and every supporter needs it. We all need it in Liverpool.

I also said that I didn't want my name leading the way. 'Instead of making it my game, why don't we make it the city's game?' But I was happy to be used behind the scenes – so that the players would be invited on my behalf.

The initial aim had been to involve Everton and their non-international players, with Roberto Martínez acting as the other manager for the day. But Everton wanted half the gate for their foundation and Liverpool wouldn't allow that to happen. So none of Everton's players were involved, unfortunately, but we still had a perfect day, with a perfect turnout.

I was touched by the response from so many great footballers, both former teammates and old rivals, when we asked them to turn up and play for nothing. My squad was full of my old favourites – Luis Suárez, Fernando Torres, Xabi Alonso, John Terry, Thierry Henry, John Arne Riise, Glen Johnson and my cousin Anthony Gerrard. Carra's squad wasn't too shabby either – including Pepe Reina, Didier Drogba, Gaël Clichy, Craig Bellamy, Lucas, Mario Balotelli and Craig Noone.

It was fantastic to see everyone together and all the memories flooded back – of Luis and Fernando, of Ginge and Bellamy's 8-iron madness, of battles with Chelsea and JT and Didier. Most of the players were friends of mine, and had a special bond with Liverpool, but the likes of JT, Didier, Thierry and Gaël could easily have said, 'Sorry, I'm busy. I've got something else on today.' But they all turned out and Carra's team went 2–0 up after goals from Balotelli and Drogba. I pulled one back with a penalty before half-time.

We had to respect all the clubs who employed the players and so some of the day's stars, like Luis and Fernando, only played the second half. But I had my fantasy football moments. I was back alongside Xabi again, the best centre midfielder I've ever played with, and up front we had Luis and Fernando together. They had a ball.

I loved it. Brendan was managing my team and Roy Evans was in charge of Carra's XI – but the sight of Luis and Fernando in front of me made me a little giddy. I ignored instructions, again, and started playing as a number 10. How could I resist when I was behind Suárez and Torres?

Anfield was in the mood, too, and the old songs resounded around a packed ground. *Stevie Gerrard is our captain, Stevie Gerrard is a red; Stevie Gerrard plays for Liverpool, a Scouser born and bred.*

It made me nostalgic to hear Luis's song again, to the old Depeche Mode tune of 'Just Can't Get Enough'. As soon as

Luis left the bench the roaring chant began: *His name is Luis Suárez / He wears the famous Red / I just can't get enough / I just can't get enough . . .*

We were awarded a penalty in the sixty-seventh minute. I offered it to Luis. I thought it would be great for him to score again in front of the Kop. Luis said: 'No, you take it.' I know Luis wanted me to get my second goal – but I also think he would have hated the thought of missing one too.

I stepped up and scored. Anfield was happy – and I was surprised and moved when the Kop began to boom out its appreciation of Fernando again. After all the bitterness and rancour of his move to Chelsea, and the loathing that would be heaped on him whenever he came back to Anfield, it was emotional to hear our fans singing in his honour again: *His armband proved he was a Red / Torres, Torres / You'll Never Walk Alone it read / Torres, Torres / We bought the lad from sunny Spain, he gets the ball and scores again / Fernando Torres is Liverpool's number 9!*

There was even more zest and sparkle from Fernando when he heard his old song. I think he probably enjoyed the game more than anyone. He said to me afterwards, 'I'm so happy I got a second chance here. Before it was always in the back of my mind – being booed at Anfield. But I'm at peace now. I can move on . . .'

There had been so many glimmers of movement and class between Suárez and Torres I started dreaming a little. How would it have been to play as a 10 behind those two – with Alonso and Mascherano in midfield, Carra at the back, and José Mourinho in the dugout as Liverpool manager? How many league titles might we have won then? It was the stuff of fantasy.

In the real world, Suárez and Mascherano, of Barcelona, would soon face Alonso and Bayern Munich in a Champions League semi-final. I was gearing up for my own fantasy – of getting over my ban and playing two more games at Wembley in the FA Cup semi and the final.

It had been such a happy day, and it was made complete when John Terry handed me an envelope.

'It's for you,' JT said, 'from José . . .'

'Really?'

'Yeah,' JT said, 'I wonder what he's put in that?'

I turned over the envelope and laughed. The back had been sealed with Sellotape and signed by Mourinho. 'Well, mate,' I said to JT, 'he's obviously signed it because he doesn't want you to know.'

JT also laughed and I appreciated again the classy effort he had made in coming up to Anfield for the day. We shook hands and I went to find a quiet place to open the envelope.

It was a handwritten letter, on Chelsea notepaper, from José Mourinho to me:

*Dear Steve,*

*I know this isn't yet over but first of all I want to congratulate you for the fantastic career at your heart club. Secondly, I want to let you know my feeling of how sorry I am, for never seeing your work. 3rd, enjoy the day with your friends and family and your stadium, your fans, your memories. 4th, the most important thing, 'Be happy every day of your life with the smile of your kids!'*

*Respect*
*José Mourinho*

The words were not inspired by any plan to woo me away from Liverpool. Those days were gone. This was just a kind message from one man to another.

The letter meant so much I knew it would soon be framed. I would keep it for ever.

# 15. Dreaming

As we moved into April the end suddenly felt too close. I was banned until the middle of the month so I had just weeks left to call myself a Liverpool player. I felt a tug of sadness, but consoled myself with the thought that there was sure to be another twist or turn. A smooth ending seemed unlikely but I knew that, as always with me, there would be drama and emotion.

Liverpool were already locked in a different kind of drama with Raheem Sterling. In terms of football, it was obvious that Sterling and I came from different generations. I spanned diverse eras of Liverpool history, reaching almost three decades, as an Academy junior, a YTS kid and then as a professional. I was one of the last links to the Liverpool legacy which stretched back from me to Kenny Dalglish to Steve Heighway to Bill Shankly. Raheem Sterling and Bill Shankly stand at opposite ends of my Liverpool story. They could not be more different.

The first whispers around Sterling had begun to rustle back in December. I'd had a quiet word because I knew that the papers, and his agent, Aidy Ward, would be more involved in talking about a possible transfer than a kid who was just about to kiss his teenage years goodbye. I liked Raheem and so I advised him to keep his head down and concentrate on playing the kind of sparkling football of which we all knew he was capable.

On 1 April, Raheem agreed to a long and, in my view, ill-advised television interview with the BBC, presumably with the agreement of his agent. In the interview, Raheem protested, 'I don't want to be perceived as a money-grabbing twenty-year-old,' while at the same time being clear that he wasn't going to make a decision about Liverpool, who had offered him a new contract apparently worth £100,000 a week, until the end of the season.

The interview backfired badly on Raheem. He lost the support of those Liverpool fans who felt that he was debating whether a football club as famous as theirs, which had won five European Cups and developed him as a player since he joined their Academy at fifteen, was good enough for him. There was widespread public ridicule of Raheem, which would soon worsen.

I didn't come down hard on Raheem. I had also once been at the heart of a storm about my own future, fuelled by doubts over whether Liverpool would remain Champions League contenders. But there was a difference between me and Raheem. When a few Liverpool supporters burned my shirt in July 2005 I was twenty-five. I had just captained Liverpool to victory in the Champions League. I had also won the treble – the League Cup, the FA Cup and the UEFA Cup in 2001. Raheem hadn't won anything yet.

He had played just eighty games for Liverpool then. The previous season, behind Luis Suárez and a fit Daniel Sturridge, he had burst to prominence. He had also played really well for just under an hour, before fading, against Italy in a World Cup match. Raheem clearly had the potential to become a special player, but in April 2015 he didn't appear to be anything more than a good, and very promising, young Premier League footballer. He clearly needed to learn much more, both tactically and technically, while working on his final ball and trying to add goals to his tally. As a deep-lying holding midfielder I had scored more goals that season than Raheem. If he really wanted to classify himself as a forward he needed to be approaching the twenty-goal mark most seasons.

If I had been staying on as Liverpool's captain I would have been all over Raheem. But I was sensitive to the changes. I would soon be gone and so I limited myself to a few private chats. I basically said to Raheem, 'You must do what you and your people want to do but, personally, I think Liverpool are a great club for you. You're going to start, you're going to play. You can grow. You can learn. In a couple of years you'll be an even better player. If you want to move then, it's your decision. But, if I were you, I would be going nowhere.'

I thought he should get at least 200 games under his belt with Liverpool before he even started talking about moving. Judging from my own career, those first 200 games are when you learn the most and gain your bedrock of experience. Some players move too early and they're never the same again. I had seen it with Franny Jeffers when he went from Everton to Arsenal too early. You could say that Jack Rodwell made a similar mistake in leaving Everton for Manchester City. Raheem could be one of the exceptions but I'm always a bit paranoid about a young kid moving on too early to a club where he can be quickly cut adrift. We will have to see how Raheem rises to the challenge, as gaining a regular starting place at City could be tough.

I also believed the argument about him needing to play for a Champions League club simply clouded the issue when he was just twenty. If Liverpool don't make it back into the top four in the next two years he can still play in the tournament for eight years after that. There were years when I hadn't been involved in the Champions League and it didn't do me any harm. I still went on to win it. It looked to me as if his representatives were using the Champions League as an excuse to agitate for a transfer. Maybe I will be proved wrong and Raheem will enjoy instant, and endless, success domestically and in Europe. I will be fascinated to see how he does at City.

There is so much money swilling around in football now, because of the television deals, and it seems to be getting worse. I think we'll see players moving an awful lot more than they used to because agents will always be looking to push for the next move. They feel, 'This is my chance to get a really big deal – and if I don't push it through I'm scared it might not come round again.'

My own agent, Struan Marshall, has allowed me to stay true to my philosophy – which is to focus on football. It's something my mum and dad handed down to me, the idea that you should just 'be the best you can be and everything else will take care of itself'. You avoid becoming greedy. You concentrate on becoming a good footballer rather than a 'personality' or a 'brand'.

I knew that, with Manchester City lurking, Raheem Sterling was already good enough to get into Manuel Pellegrini's team. If you asked me who I would pick between Sterling or Samir Nasri the answer is obvious: Sterling. But I believed that if he kept his head down, and concentrated on football for the next five years, we would be comparing Sterling to far better players than Nasri in 2020.

All the signs pointed to Raheem leaving Liverpool when he carried out that disastrous BBC interview – where he also claimed to be 'flattered' by potential interest from Arsenal, who just happened to be our next opponents. He was quieter than usual in the build-up that week but I knew he had the mental strength to withstand the scrutiny. On the field, he's never been one to blend into the background.

Alex and I had sold our house to Brendan and were renting another while we prepared for our move to America. In one of those strange twists of fate, it turned out that Raheem used to live in the house we were renting. Sometimes I would be so preoccupied after training that I'd drive on autopilot from Mel-wood to my old house before suddenly realizing that the manager lived there now.

A week before Raheem was splashed all over the media I had already decided to follow him in the televised match at the Emirates and then write a report as part of my course work towards obtaining my UEFA 'B' licence as a coach. So, banned from playing and in Raheem's old house, I got out a pad and a pen and switched on the TV to watch him play in that Easter Saturday-lunchtime fixture. I was ready to do my homework on Razza.

It was fascinating to analyse Raheem against Arsenal because he was under immense pressure. That allowed me to assess his mentality. In terms of tactics, he played through the middle, which he regards as his favourite position, and I thought he coped well. Arsenal won easily, 4–1, but Raheem was Liver-pool's best player. It was a reminder of his quality and resilience. I gave him a small tick in my assessment that day.

I was still training but, in my free time, I immersed myself in work leading towards my coaching licence. It was an eye-opener in the sense of how different it was from playing. I was so used to making a quick point while playing in the middle of a training session – and I now had to learn how to step back and find the language to explain something much deeper to a broad group of players. It was thought-provoking and I could understand why many top footballers are just not cut out for coaching.

I actually liked it – even if I don't see myself ever becoming a coach who puts up the cones, takes sessions, sets up posses-sions, shooting practice and all the routine day-to-day drills. If I did decide to work at a club in the future it would be as an assistant manager or, ideally, the manager. But coaching is interesting – even if some of the 'B' licence packs can seem tedious at times. When I'm trawling through stuff on nutrition and psychology there are moments when I think: 'Oh God, I don't want to be a dietician.' Or, 'I don't want to be Steve Peters.' I'm already doing it. I'm eating good food every single day. I'm analysing my mental state. But I appreciate I have to prove to the examiners that I have a solid grounding in all these areas and can deal with players' situations on a daily basis.

I have since completed and passed my 'B' licence and will now take a break while I concentrate on playing football with LA Galaxy – and then crack on with my UEFA 'A' coaching licence once I'm back in England for good. The idea of becoming a manager one day is intriguing but I still really don't know if it's the road I will follow.

Once my playing career is over in America I want to explore various aspects of management. I would love to spend some time with a few top managers. How could you not learn a lot if you had a chance to sit down and talk in detail about management to Mourinho, Wenger, Hodgson and Rodgers? I would love to pick their very astute brains. The same goes for Pep Guardiola. I'd love spending a week watching Pep work as a manager. Of course, we once played against each other, and Xabi Alonso has said he could help set it up. And I'd love to spend time back at Liverpool, shadowing Brendan, soaking up as much as I can about the challenge of management to see whether I like it and if I am cut out for it.

I want to see what a manager really does, how he handles meetings and what gets said behind the scenes. I think the experience I've gained over the last seventeen years would help me – as would all the knowledge I've gained from my past managers. But any success I've had as a player won't automatically make me a good manager or coach.

If I had smart people around me, and the right coaching team behind me, I like to think I could succeed as a manager.

But there are no guarantees – which is why it is so interesting. I sometimes allow my mind to wander and think, 'Wouldn't it be amazing to manage Liverpool one day?' Of course; but right now I can't know if I'd be good enough or if I would even be asked to do the job or any other work with the first team in the future. First and foremost I'd have to feel confident that I could be a successful manager. I would never take the job on the back of my name – or just because some fans would like me to step in on the basis they'd once supported me as a player.

I know that being manager of Liverpool Football Club is a huge job. It needs the right man with the right credentials and know-how. So for me, at the moment, it can't be anything more than a 'maybe'. All I can really say is that it is a lovely dream – but I simply have no idea if it will ever happen or if it's even realistic to talk about it.

It's still quite fun to fantasize a little. If, totally hypothetically, I was going to become Liverpool manager one day I know who I'd love to have as my assistant: Xabi Alonso or Jamie Carragher. They are very intelligent, have a deep knowledge of football and are special men. The players would respect them, the fans would like them and I think we would work really well together.

I've never mentioned it to either Xabi or Jamie, so I think they'll be surprised if they read about it. Xabi might go on to be a great manager himself – and so I feel a bit embarrassed admitting that a managerial fantasy would be him working alongside me.

If I did become a manager, and it could be at a different club or maybe at under-21 level, it would be important to have picked up knowledge and experience. So maybe I would start as a number two or a number three. Or I may just take a different path away from management.

I've already begun doing some work in the media, as an occasional pundit for BT Sport, and that will give me an opportunity to step back from the playing side of the game and take a more analytical role. I would not want to do too much television work as I'm not suited to the weekly grind of going from one routine league match to another. But doing a little for BT will allow me to watch players closely and talk to managers while perhaps shadowing some of the top men, if they were willing.

It was fascinating for me to do a little coaching of the under-16s at Liverpool. The Academy at Liverpool falls under the remit of the manager. So over the last ten years we've had an Academy run in three contrasting ways because we've had three very different managers – Dalglish, Benítez and Rodgers. Brendan's pretty good because, even though the reserves and the under-21s train separately from the first team, he invites them and some of the Academy kids over to Melwood. But, if the kid is based at Kirkby most of the time, he'll still be in his shell when he arrives for the occasional session at our main training base.

I believe the club itself should run the Academy with one unified strategy. This would help consistency to emerge while the kids themselves could feed off the inspiration of training at the same venue as all the first-team stars they'd love to emulate.

While I was coaching the under-16s a couple of boys really caught my eye. Trent Arnold has a terrific chance of making it as a top professional. He's quite leggy but he's got a lovely frame and seems to have all the attributes you need. Having just turned sixteen, he's still not strong enough at the moment, but that will come. He has the right attitude and comes from West Derby, home to Melwood. So Trent is another Scouser and apparently, just as I tried to be John Barnes and Steve McMahon, he grew up pretending to be me while playing in the Merseyside parks. He can play as a number 6, a holding midfielder, but he's versatile and I've seen him fill various positions. I know England are all over him.

Herbie Kane also stood out. We signed him from Bristol City a couple of years ago and he plays in central midfield. He's got a little bit of ruthlessness about his play, which you need in this position, and he's a big presence for England at under-16 level. Trent also has that mean streak, in the best possible way, and he and Herbie look capable of developing the physicality they will need to match their technique in the Premier League one day.

They both knew I rated them because I'd pull them aside for one-to-one sessions – and I always asked the main under-16 coach Pepijn Lijnders if I could have the two of them in my group. They offered what I needed for my coaching assessments and I also knew if I asked them to do something they would deliver at a slightly higher level to the others.

There were other talented kids and it was good to compare them. After a few sessions you could work out which ones had a big ego or an attitude which meant they were more interested in the new boots they'd just been given than in hardening themselves as young pros.

A lot of players can make it on talent alone and they'll earn a good living, but the footballers who have consistency and longevity possess a real passion for the game. They need that at a young age when they can take that love of football and deepen it through discipline and dedication. The talented players willing to sacrifice everything are the ones who go on to become the likes of Michael Owen, Jamie Carragher and John Terry. This has always been my philosophy. I knew if I stayed true to it, the financial rewards would take care of themselves.

Everything changes when you're invited to train and travel with the first team. The moment you see your shirt number hanging on a dressing-room peg, all the innocence goes. The older players are judging you to see whether you're good enough to be in the set-up every single day.

When it was my turn seventeen years ago I learnt my lessons quickly. You give a ball away in training, or you turn your back in a game, and a player as experienced and hard as Paul Ince would come clattering down on you. He would give you an absolute roasting. But if you won the ball in a tackle or you hit a lovely pass then players as good as Incey, Robbie Fowler and Jamie Redknapp would be patting you on the back. It's sink-or-swim time when you come into a first-team dressing room. If you don't perform consistently you won't last very long. I recognized that straightaway but, for me, the best advice I ever received came from my dad.

When I got into the first team there were moments when I thought, 'I've done it. I've made it.' Dad got stuck into me. I appreciated his honesty, as hard as it sounded: 'You've done nothing yet,' Dad said. 'You've done absolutely fuck-all in the game. Everything you've done before this has gone. It's not important any more. If you want to stay with Liverpool, and you want to succeed, you've got to perform every single day. And it starts right now. You will only get out of the game what you put in.'

I'd never forgotten those wise words – and, even at the end, I tried to adopt that same approach. I had just six or, at best, seven matches left to play for Liverpool. It would be a perfect seven if we made it all the way to the FA Cup final. But I remembered then what Dad always told me: 'This is where it starts. Everything you've done before this has gone.'

On Monday, 13 April, six days before we played Aston Villa at Wembley in the FA Cup semi-final, I turned out for Liverpool under-18s. We played against Shrewsbury's under-18s at Melwood. It was important, after my ban, to play for ninety minutes. I handed the captain's armband to Trent Arnold. He seemed very shocked and he gave me a look as if to say: 'What are you doing?'

I made the gesture for a reason. It was my way of telling

Trent that I believed he could make it for Liverpool one day. I felt the same about Herbie Kane. I lined up alongside him in central midfield while Trent played at right back. They were playing a couple of age-groups up and they needed to fit in with the older boys. It was far stranger for me trying to play with kids between the ages of sixteen and eighteen.

I didn't want to look like a show-off, flying all over the place and wanting to be man of the match. I was a bit worried about stitching them up because I wasn't sure if they were ready for a Premier League tempo of passing. So I found it difficult to know how to approach the game. The opposition lads were also trying to impress and racing into me at a hundred miles an hour. I was caught a few times. But I got through the game without picking up an injury or flattening anyone. It was more difficult trying to adjust to the boys' level than playing a normal Premier League game.

I was happy when it was over. I shook the hands of all the Shrewsbury players once they'd had something to eat at Melwood. They were on a high being around some of Liverpool's first team squad, as Martin Skrtel and Fabio Borini had also played in the match.

They probably all knew that the next time I stepped out onto a football pitch it would be at Wembley that Sunday. I doubted if any of them would remember the 2006 FA Cup final. None of them would have been even ten back then. And if they had heard about the classic final between Liverpool and West Ham United it would have belonged to an ancient world to them. But, to me, it still felt like yesterday.

## *Millennium Stadium, Cardiff, Saturday, 13 May 2006*

There are days when the sun shines and you feel invincible. You are twenty-five years old and you feel incredible. This is such a day. Power, strength and belief surge through you. It seems as if the intensity of these feelings will never fade. If you weren't too young to appreciate it, such a day would seem almost heartbreakingly beautiful.

You feel perfect and, of course, it cannot last. But that's why such days are never wasted on a young footballer. When you're in that blinding place, feeling brilliant at twenty-five, you don't even think about it. You just accept it and lose yourself in the moment. It feels natural and true.

I had just ended the season as the Professional Footballers' Association's Player of the Year – and it meant a lot to have been voted as the best footballer in England by my peers in the Premier League. I had also been Liverpool's top scorer, with twenty-one goals before we arrived in Cardiff, as we finished third in the league. In the FA Cup we had beaten Manchester United, Birmingham City 7–0 in the quarters and Chelsea in the semi-final.

I had already won the FA Cup – as well as the League Cup, the UEFA Cup and the European Cup. I had scored a goal in the final of those last three competitions. I was ready to win another FA Cup winner's medal and score a goal to complete a historic set. I would then become the first English footballer to score a goal in each of those four cup finals. But I was more intent on lifting another trophy for Liverpool than carving out a place in history. I felt driven and serene – an unbeatable combination when you're chasing any kind of achievement.

There was happiness and pride too before the game. I sat on a wooden bench in a shiny dressing room and pulled on my red Liverpool socks. The names of my two little girls had been stitched into my boots. *Lilly Ella* stood out on the tongue of my left boot; *Lexie*, who was just four days old, on the tongue of the right boot. I felt like I was playing for them too, as small as they were, and a goal for each of my daughters would define a special day. Tying my laces, I felt capable of anything.

This would be the last FA Cup final to be played at the Millennium Stadium. There had been six in total, while the new Wembley was being built, and we'd won the first in 2000 when we'd burgled an Arsenal team who were much better than us on the day. That was the day of Michael Owen's brace at the very end of an afternoon when it seemed as if the cup was only going to Arsenal. We won 2–1. I was convinced we would beat another London team, West Ham, to provide Liverpool's supporters with another Millennium match to remember.

The stadium looked stunning on a glorious May afternoon. West Ham's fans were nearly as noisy and great as ours as they savoured what was for them a rare FA Cup final. Liverpool's supporters never seemed to tire of such occasions. In Rafa Benítez's second season they were also enjoying showing off their new grasp of Spanish. A huge banner hailed us as *Conquistadors* – which, as any good Scouser now knew, meant we were 'Conquerors'.

I was in a conquering kind of mood but I stayed polite as I led Prince William down the line of my teammates, introducing each player by his full name.

Nigel Reo-Coker, West Ham's captain, the officials and I all met in the centre circle. I spun the coin, caught it and slapped it down on top of my left hand. It was another way of showing that I felt in complete charge.

Reality then took hold of the game. Yossi Benayoun, who ran tirelessly all afternoon for West Ham, found Dean Ashton in the twenty-first minute. Ashton, whose career would be cut cruelly short by injury, released Lionel Scaloni with a lovely pass. Jamie Carragher saw the danger but he could only turn Scaloni's cross past Pepe Reina for an unfortunate own goal. We were 2–0 down just seven minutes later when Pepe spilled

Matthew Etherington's shot into the path of Ashton – who bundled it over the line.

I did not feel quite as invincible then as I had done half an hour earlier. Could I lose so badly on a day which had started with me feeling perfect? Less than a year earlier we had been 3–0 down against AC Milan in Istanbul. I drew on the reserves of strength I had gathered that night. I still believed.

In the thirty-second minute I called for a short pass. I had the ball and I moved into West Ham territory. I looked up, paused and took aim. I hit a forty-yard right-foot special. It landed exactly where I and Djibril Cissé wanted it. But Cissé still had to supply the finish – and he did it with a screaming volley as he fell. It had been an amazing hit. Cissé, with his zany patchwork-quilt haircut and yellow beard, pumped his arms and roared. We could not hear a word of what he was shouting but it might as well have been, *'Believe . . . believe . . . believe!'*

I believed. I remained focused. Nine minutes into the second half I got the goal that hauled us back to 2–2. I won the ball, tracked back and slipped it to Xabi Alonso, who found Peter Crouch. Climbing high, Crouchy used his 6-foot 7-inch frame and nodded it down towards me, as he had done on so many occasions. The ball bounced once and then again. It sat up, begging, and I lashed it home into the top corner with the kind of effortless power and technique you feel when you're twenty-five and indestructible.

The Liverpool fans behind the goal exploded in a massive starburst of red. I turned and ran. My left arm stretched out while my right hammered against the Liverpool crest on my chest. I waggled my tongue in delight. I might have felt touched by certainty before the game but, then, I was just touched in the head.

It was yet another example of the kind of goal I would have

imagined scoring back on Ironside Road. But it was real: the comic-book dream brought to life again. What a day! What a final!

I felt less enthused by the magic of the FA Cup when, in the sixty-fourth minute, Paul Konchesky, a future teammate of mine but an absolute West Ham nutter of a fan, came steaming in from left back. I chased him hard. Stretching out my leg, I was just about to block him when he produced a right old hammer of a strike. I'm still not sure if it was meant to be a cross or a shot but Konchesky the Hammer hit it with venom. From a long way out, it sailed over Reina's head. West Ham 3, Liverpool 2.

Injury-time approached as Cissé went down. Scaloni booted the ball into touch. It was a sporting gesture, but the game was almost over. We took the throw-in and, compelled to be as sporting, threw it back to Scaloni. He must have felt bewildered by all the honourable play because he hoofed it straight to me.

On the stroke of ninety minutes I controlled Scaloni's clearance. I slid it to the left, to John Arne Riise, just as the stadium announcer confirmed that there would be four minutes of added time. I heard him. You could not escape his booming voice, but I was stricken with cramp. Near the end of a long, hot afternoon, my legs were seizing up. But I still told myself I felt strong. I still felt unbeatable. Hobbling, but unbeatable.

Riise sent the ball curling back into the West Ham area. Fernando Morientes went up, looking for a Liverpool flick-on, but Danny Gabbidon won the challenge and headed clear. The ball bounced a long way from goal, once, then twice. Almost magnetically, the ball arced towards me. I was thirty-five yards away. I was too tired to take possession and set off on a surging run towards goal. Instinctively, I decided to hit it first time. I caught it on the rise, dregs of energy rippling down from my clenched right leg and my crashing boot into the flight of the ball.

I caught it like a dream. I followed its searing blur. I hit it so perfectly it was hard to track it in the air. My shot flew and flew. A few seconds stretched and then . . . *bang!*

The West Ham net billowed and shook in shock. I had to look again. Had I really just done that? *Goal!*

The Liverpool end exploded in a mass of firecracker red. 3–3. An injury-time equalizer – and the best goal of my career.

I was stunned, and tired, and my celebratory run was more restrained than it had been after my other goal. My teammates caught me, and I just smiled.

Riise, the great Ginge, took my face in his hands. His eyes looked as if they were going to pop out of his head in wonder. He was babbling words of amazement to me. I couldn't hear anything. I was still dazed and so, once Ginger let me go, I walked away and tapped the name on the back of my shirt. GERRARD.

It was my goal. I had done it. We were into extra time. The dream was still alive.

I can't remember much about the next exhausting thirty minutes apart from Pepe Reina's incredible save to deny Reo-Coker – and Marlon Harewood just missing the rebound. We went into a shoot-out and I felt no nerves. The same certainty and belief that had gripped me in the dressing room while I pulled on my Lilly Ella and Lexie boots still coursed through me. I still felt incredible. I knew we would win the cup.

Didi Hamman went first and scored. Sami Hyypiä missed our second spot kick but I and then Ginge both buried ours. Teddy Sheringham, at the age of forty, coolly slotted home his penalty for West Ham. But Bobby Zamora and Konchesky were denied by Pepe – our brilliant shot-stopper.

So it was 3–1 to Liverpool when Anton Ferdinand stepped up

for West Ham's fourth penalty. He had to score; but Pepe produced another great save. It was over. The FA Cup belonged to us.

West Ham had played magnificently but it was our day. It was my day. I'll always remember the way the West Ham fans rose to their feet to applaud Liverpool and me. Football might be cruel, but there is so much beauty too. I raised my hands to those West Ham supporters.

After I received my Man of the Match award, Prince William eventually handed me the trophy. I raised it high and Liverpool took off in tandem with the fireworks, fizzing and roaring, the players and our 35,000 fans up in the stands combining into one unbeatable party.

Only Rafa Benítez remained calm and sober. The ice man wouldn't melt in the fading sunshine.

Later that evening, at a party for the staff, players and our wives and girlfriends, I walked over to Rafa.

I was secretly hoping for a 'Well done, Stevie' but Rafa had moved on. He shook my hand and started talking in his familiar way: 'Next season we have to do better in the Premiership.'

I almost loved Rafa in that moment. His aim was my aim; my hope was his hope.

He didn't mention either of my goals or our performance as a team. Instead, he chided me gently, reminding me that he had set me a target of twenty-five goals at the start of the season.

After the cup-final pair I had come close but, as Rafa said, 'You never hit twenty-five. You missed the target by two.'

But then, incredibly, Rafa smiled. It was a compliment of a smile. There was almost the warmth of a tribute in that smile.

'Next season, boss,' I grinned back, 'I'll try again . . .'

Rafa and me, ice and fire, were maybe not so different after all. Even on one of our greatest days, and after an FA Cup final to cherish for ever, we both believed that Liverpool and I needed to improve. We were both consumed by the idea of winning the league title.

It never happened and, looking back now, I can see that I scaled my absolute shimmering peak that afternoon. Beyond even the goals and the assist, I produced a performance where everything fell into place for me. If I had to pick one game and say, 'Look, that's what I could once do on a football pitch,' I would choose that one: the FA Cup final of 13 May 2006.

Four days before the semi-final against Aston Villa at Wembley we gathered again at Anfield: 15 April was always the day we remembered another FA Cup semi-final.

Twenty-six years had passed since Liverpool met Nottingham Forest at Hillsborough. Twenty-six years, just like our ninety-six people, were gone for ever.

Every Hillsborough anniversary was riddled with pain. I found each one an ordeal. But I would never miss a service. The significance of the loss, and the fight for justice, are too immense not to be faced, and honoured.

Our family is just one of those united by grief and the need for truth. Margaret Aspinall, the chair of the Hillsborough Family Support Group, paid tribute to all of us and, also, to the supporters who had gone to Hillsborough and survived. 'A lot of the fans came home from Hillsborough feeling guilty,' Margaret said as she stood on the pitch and faced the Kop. 'Why they felt guilt, I will never know. The families owe a great debt to the fans, because without them coming home and giving their accounts we wouldn't be where we are today. So I thank them very much.'

The testimonies of those Hillsborough survivors were being heard at the inquest, which still had at least a year to run. As Margaret stressed, 'We will not see a job half done; we will make sure this job is done properly.'

Margaret said that, in April 1989, she had been a young woman, with a young family, including her eighteen-year-old son, James. If he had survived, James Aspinall would have been a man of forty-four who might also have been bound for Wembley next Sunday. With a wry little note in her voice, Margaret pointed out that she was now an old woman. She was a grandmother and she and everyone else were still fighting for justice.

'But it's coming,' Margaret said. 'It's coming . . .'

It took seven minutes to read out the names of everyone who had died. Seven long minutes when the silence was broken only by the echoes of the dead.

Sue Johnston, a passionate Liverpool fan and an actor loved across the city, read the lyrics to a Beatles song: 'In My Life'. Graham Stuart, a former Everton player, read from the Bible – as did John Aldridge. John was one of my heroes when I played football on Ironside Road. He had been a member of Kenny Dalglish's team at Hillsborough.

On the Kop I sat behind John and Kenny, Ian Rush and Robbie Fowler. I sat next to Lucas Leiva, a Brazilian who had been in Liverpool long enough to understand what the service meant to all of us. There was a shared pain which Lucas felt as a Liverpool player. Lucas made space for me to stand up near the end. I looked behind me and saw Phil Jagielka. Everton's captain was about to follow me down onto the pitch. We had been asked to release the ninety-six balloons that floated above Anfield each year on this date.

I agreed, because I was grateful that the Hillsborough Family Support Group no longer asked me to do a reading. I had done one a few years before, and I'd managed to hold it together, but I'd found it incredibly hard.

This would be my last tribute to the 96 as Liverpool captain. Phil and I walked out onto the field, and the crowd began to sing 'You'll Never Walk Alone'.

'When you walk through the storm, hold your head up high . . .'

Phil and I each held a giant plastic bag crammed full of red balloons. By the time we reached the centre circle the crowd was singing: 'At the end of the storm, is a golden sky . . .'

We opened the bags and the balloons broke free. They began to drift up into the sky, one by one, balloon after red balloon.

Phil's balloons moved quicker than mine. His bag emptied more easily. He stared up at the sky, watching his forty-eight balloons rising higher and higher. I took my time as I had at least ten more to set free. The last few stuck to the bottom of my bag. I shook them gently and, gradually, they came loose. I watched the last one escape. The wind caught it and carried it high.

Phil and I joined in the applause for those we had lost while we watched our balloons, floating further and further away, as the crowd sang on: 'Walk on through the wind, walk on through the rain, though your dreams be tossed and blown, walk on, walk on with hope in your heart . . .'

The hope felt very real until late on the afternoon of Sunday, 19 April 2015. A football fantasy had gripped me. If I could choose to play my last-ever game for Liverpool at the end of my seventeenth season as a first-teamer it would have to be either a Champions League or an FA Cup final. The European dream was never going to happen that year, but the FA Cup had been the aim from the moment we were drawn against AFC Wimbledon in the third round. It gathered pace in the fourth round, when I made my 700th appearance for Liverpool in a replay against Bolton Wanderers.

Even the luck of the draw seemed to look kindly on the magical idea of my thirty-fifth birthday being celebrated on

30 May with an FA Cup final. We beat Crystal Palace and Blackburn Rovers, needing another replay, before we avoided Arsenal in the semi-finals. Villa seemed much the easier option, struggling in the relegation zone and having recently changed managers. But Villa, under Tim Sherwood, were always going to be tricky opponents.

Our good fortune ebbed a little when, in the week of the game, any hopes of Daniel Sturridge being fit were ended. Lucas was also out, robbing us of some big-match experience. Both were big blows. Villa played a high line under Sherwood and I think Sturridge would have got behind and hurt them.

It turned out to be a strange day. Even when we went ahead through Coutinho after thirty minutes we seemed uncomfortable and listless. Perhaps some of the younger lads were lulled into a false sense of security by us being made such heavy favourites before the game. Brendan Rodgers likes his teams to be aggressive, to press high, show a lot of energy, pass the ball accurately at high tempo and use those attributes to control the game. But we failed in every aspect that afternoon. All of us did.

Villa equalized six minutes later through Christian Benteke and early in the second half Fabian Delph gave Villa the lead. Delph of all people. I couldn't understand why Liverpool had not signed Delph at the start of the season. We share an agent in Struan Marshall and I knew that Delph wanted to come to Liverpool. He wasn't after especially big money and he ticked so many boxes that are important to Liverpool. He had boundless energy, he was robust and ready to play week in, week out. Delph had just started to play for England and he had a winner's mentality. He was exactly the kind of player we needed and I passed on the message. But Liverpool never followed it up – and he punished us at Wembley with a man-of-the-match display.

I tried to rally myself and the team. With ten minutes left I thought I might have scored but Kieran Richardson cleared my header off the line. I then set up Balotelli with a long pass and he delivered. Balotelli scored but the goal was ruled offside. It had been the wrong decision – but the right result because Villa were simply better than us.

The birthday dream was over. The last big-game fantasy had gone. I would never play at Wembley again. I would never lift another trophy for Liverpool.

My disappointment felt as deep as it was bleak. All my Liverpool luck seemed to have run dry.

I had never believed that famous old Bill Shankly quote about football being more important than life or death. Six days later, just about recovered from the cup defeat, it seemed less appropriate than ever. My phone beeped with shocking news. Rio Ferdinand's wife, Rebecca, had died from breast cancer.

I was about to leave home and drive to Anfield for the second-last home game of my career. The music had been turned up loud and I'd felt that usual little buzz before a match. But that text changed my mood. I turned off the music as soon as I absorbed the news.

We were about to play Rio's club, Queens Park Rangers. Ever since the stamp against Manchester United I had resolved to try to find some kind of redemption. I had sat in the dressing room after being sent off and had promised myself that I would leave Liverpool with a last few uplifting memories in the form of goals and decisive moments.

I was never especially close to Rio during our careers but we had been England teammates for over ten years. We had shared a lot with England and we had always got on together. I respected him as both a great player and a good, intelligent man. But there was a small divide between us because we had been rivals for so long while he played for Manchester United and I was a proper red with Liverpool.

In the wake of both of our retirements, it's been a revelation to have spent quite a bit of time with Rio. We have a deeper bond now that we never quite shared when we were players.

We warmed up and other feelings surfaced. As I looked around Anfield I could not stop myself thinking that this would be the last normal game for me at home. I knew that my final appearance at home, against Crystal Palace, would be a struggle to contain the emotion as plans were already being made to give me a memorable send-off.

There was a different atmosphere as, before the game started, we all slipped on black armbands. I led the team out, carrying a huge bouquet of white lilies. Joey Barton, who is also from Huyton, accepted them on behalf of Rio, his QPR teammate.

I started the game poorly. My passing had little of its usual accuracy. I was even overhitting short passes as I struggled with my emotions. Nothing felt as it should.

We had lost our previous league game, against Hull, and were now in fifth place, ahead of Spurs only on goal difference. Some joker had even buzzed Anfield in a low-flying plane with a banner which said 'Rodgers Out Rafa In'.

I wasn't impressed – and, in my dark mood, I briefly wondered if Rafa had put someone up to the stunt.

At least we settled into a more familiar groove when, after seventeen minutes, I was booked by Martin Atkinson. I hadn't seen him since he'd sent me off for the stamp. At least we were consistent in never getting on. I thought I might as well start playing properly.

Two minutes later we were in front as Sterling and Lambert set up Coutinho. It was a sweet right-foot curler which Coutinho bent into the goal.

In the second half Sterling should really have made it

2–0 – while a deflection and a good save from Rob Green kept out me and Skrtcl. But any chance of a routine afternoon was ruined when QPR equalized. The pacey Leroy Fer had been a handful all afternoon and he volleyed home a Barton corner. 1–1 with seventeen minutes left.

Then, from a Henderson corner Skrtel was dragged down. Penalty.

The only doubt in my mind as I stepped up to take it, in front of the Kop, centred on the presence of Greeny in goal. I don't like taking penalties against keepers who know me well. I've taken hundreds against Greeny on England duty over the years so he knows all my moves. The key to taking a penalty is to make up your mind and stick to your decision. As Greeny danced about on his line I disobeyed my golden rule. I tried to mix things up by looking straight at him. I knew that he knew I liked to go left because it was my favourite side. So my new aim was to bluff him into thinking I'd go right and then reverse it. But Greeny double-bluffed me.

I went left. Greeny guessed correctly and went to his right. He turned it round the post for a corner. It had not been a good pen anyway because it was the perfect height for a keeper to save.

My head slumped. I could not believe it. Nothing seemed to work for me any more.

I grimaced, closed my eyes and tilted my head skywards. OK, calm down. How long to go?

I looked at the clock. Twelve minutes to make amends. Come on. I picked myself up. I felt less discouraged. Twelve minutes to score the winner.

Everything changed when Nedum Onuoha was sent off for a second yellow card. We began to overwhelm the ten men. Coutinho, a great little fighter, hit a scorcher. It was blocked by Richard Dunne. Corner. Coutinho to take it. Four minutes left.

I was alert now. I was twitching with intent. Big Bobby Zamora was marking me but I was ready to drop him and attack the near-post space. For a moment I thought about my duty as a holding midfielder. If QPR cleared then Fer could be away, at speed, on the counter. We could end up losing the game.

Stick or twist? 'I'm twisting,' I thought. 'I'm going in.'

Coutinho's delivery was perfect, dipping and zipping across the goal. I timed my run just right, bursting past Zamora and getting to the ball before Barton. Squashed tight between the two QPR men I climbed high. There was a good chance I'd get whacked in the face by someone's head but I didn't care. That ball was mine. I had timed my run to perfection. And my header was a beauty. It speared into the goal. No chance for Greeny. 2–1 Liverpool, Gerrard.

I knew it might be for the last time and so I ran along the edge of the Kop. I spread my arms wide, losing myself in that lovely, blissful feeling all over again as Anfield celebrated my goal. After all the recent hurt – from the stamp to Villa to my missed penalty eight minutes earlier – it was the best feeling in the world to score at the Kop end.

I hate all that badge-kissing stuff when it's done by some swanky new signing who's just got his new hundred-grand-a-week deal at a club where he knows he will stay for only a few seasons before his agent moves him on to something more lucrative. But I felt, after seventeen years, and my share of glory and heartbreak in the colours of Liverpool, that I deserved to kiss the badge. And so, as I ran to the corner flag, I lifted the crest of the Liver bird to my lips and kissed it.

By the time I stopped running everyone else had caught me. They jumped on top of me in the old routine.

There were so many of my teammates but they felt incredibly light amid my elation. Finally, I turned to salute the sea of red. The Kop rose again in waves of colour and noise.

In the last minute, in a touching gesture, Brendan gave me the signal. It was also a nod to Anfield to start saying goodbye to me. I heard them singing as I walked towards the touchline.

*Steve Gerrard, Gerrard / He'll pass the ball forty yards / He's big and he's fucking hard / Steve Gerrard, Gerrard . . .*

I stopped to fit the captain's band on to Jordan Henderson's upper arm and then, slowly, I spun around so I could look at all four corners of Anfield. I applauded everyone, to say thank you.

An hour later I was asked to do a BBC television interview for *Match of the Day*.

'Have you scored a better header?' I was asked.

I almost laughed, but I turned it into a little smile instead. 'Champions League final was all right, weren't it?'

'I forgot about that one,' the interviewer said, almost in embarrassment.

'I haven't,' I said.

José Mourinho held a press conference two days before my last-ever game at Stamford Bridge:

This is my time to honour a champion. It is my time to honour Steven Gerrard. It is with opponents like him that I am the manager that I am, because I learn with my players and I learn with my best opponents.

I learn with my players' problems, my players' doubts, my players' qualities and I learn with my best opponents, with the problems they give me – the way they make me think, the way they make me analyse them and studying the best way to play against them.

Steven Gerrard is for sure one of my favourite enemies – an enemy with all the good feeling I can express with that word in football. For sure, in England he is my dear enemy. For sure, he is the one that made me a better manager. To stop him or try and stop him has been very, very difficult.

I tried to bring him to Chelsea, I tried to bring him to Inter, I tried to bring him to Real Madrid but he was always a dear enemy. I want to honour him and I hope Stamford Bridge has the same feeling as I have – which is we need people like him as our opponents.

Mourinho was asked whether not managing me was one of his biggest regrets. It was too sweeping a question but he handled it kindly:

No, no. I am very happy that he didn't leave Liverpool. In the end I think he had an amazing career and such an amazing feeling with his people that he refused to play for other big clubs, he refused to play in other big leagues to play only for Liverpool.

I think this is a feeling that stays forever. Who knows? Maybe I will play against Steven as a Liverpool manager one day.

I was touched by José's words. But I knew that Chelsea's fans felt differently. I knew they would be out to mock me at every turn on Sunday, 10 May.

They also thought they were very witty. I was greeted by a mass of yellow warning cards. I could not miss them. One of the first I saw said *GERRARD* above a stick figure slipping. The words *Watch Your Step* were ringed in black. Another was meant to look like a yellow motorway sign. It said *Caution! Slip hazard*. It then had a stick figure slipping on his arse and, just to avoid any confusion, *STEVEN GERRARD* had been added.

They targeted me in the warm-ups and sang that tired old

slip song, again and again, while laughing and throwing 'wanker' gestures in my direction. I didn't react.

I was just as calm and expressionless when I led Liverpool out of the tunnel and into the spring sunshine. We formed a guard of honour for Chelsea. This was their first home game since becoming champions and it fell to me, of course, to have to lead the tributes to Chelsea.

As John Terry headed the procession of Chelsea players walking between our two lines of red I led the applause. They were a good team, Chelsea, and they had been by far the best side in the Premier League that season. I respected Mourinho, JT, Drogba and all their players.

JT had just won his eleventh major honour for Chelsea. I would have been close to him if I had joined Chelsea ten years earlier but, even amid the abuse and the guard of honour, I felt clean and good. There was not a moment of regret that I was in Liverpool red rather than Chelsea blue. I felt happy all over again that I had stayed true to Liverpool. Me and blue just don't work.

The song echoed around the ground most of the afternoon but I heard it clearest when, after just twenty-five seconds, Cesc Fàbregas cut down Sterling with a dangerous tackle. It was one of those challenges that could have deserved a straight red. The referee, Andre Marriner, reached for his pocket and waved the red at John Obi Mikel, who looked understandably confused. The Chelsea players were soon in conference with the ref. He called back Mikel and admitted his mistake. He turned to Fàbregas and showed him only a yellow card. It was a two-minute farce and it gave the Chelsea choirboys the chance to really belt it out, again and again.

*Steve Gerrard, Gerrard / He slipped on his fucking arse / He gave it to Demba Ba / Steve Gerrard, Gerrard . . .*

I showed no sign of hearing them; but I did.

We were a goal down after five minutes. JT nodded home one of his trademark set-piece goals.

The song started up again soon after the Chelsea celebrations. It made me more determined. Just before half-time Ivanović fouled Lallana near the corner flag. This was my chance. This was my moment.

Mikel was marking me closely but I danced forward and back and then just drifted away from him. He lost me and I was in space at the far post, as Jordan Henderson's free kick drifted in. I powered in a simple downward header. 1–1.

I turned away, showing not even a flicker of emotion or any attempt to celebrate. I didn't want to milk it in case we went on to lose.

We got the draw and I was happy we'd spoilt the Chelsea party, just a little. It was not like the way in which Mourinho and Chelsea had derailed our title train a year before – but it was something.

Brendan took me off with ten minutes left on the clock. He trusted the Chelsea fans, and he was right. As I walked off I noticed that the songs were silent. The whole ground, every section and corner of Stamford Bridge, rose as one. People were on their feet, and the standing ovation sounded suddenly genuine. I didn't give them too much back. I was not about to turn into a hypocrite. I was not about to start singing the praises of any Chelsea fan. No chance. As I said in my television interview after the game:

> I was more happy with the ovation from the Liverpool fans. The Chelsea fans showed respect for a couple of seconds for me but slaughtered me all game so I'm not going to get drawn into wishing the Chelsea fans well. It's nice of them to turn up for once today. A standing ovation from a stadium is always

nice but what's important to me is the Liverpool fans and they have been there since day one.

I was asked about Mourinho:

He is the best manager in the world for me. I'd have signed for him if I wasn't a Liverpool fan, if Liverpool weren't in my heart. He is the reason why my head was turned on a couple of occasions but he understood why I couldn't do it and it's because I love Liverpool. It always means more when you win for your people.

# 16. The Leaving of Liverpool

'I've been thinking seriously about your speech,' a friend wrote in a message to me at the start of the week marking my last appearance as a Liverpool player at Anfield. 'I think you should keep it along these lines.' A YouTube video link was embedded into the text and I wondered what my mate had decided I should say in those emotional moments when, after we had played Crystal Palace, I was handed the microphone. I was then expected to talk to 44,000 people, and millions more watching on television, so that I could show my gratitude for the past seventeen years of my life. I was supposed to say the words out loud without breaking down.

I'd told my closest friends about my fear that I would start crying when I had to admit that it was all over. We made a few good jokes about it; but they all understood how hard it would be for me to control my emotions. So I opened his link.

Leonardo DiCaprio's frame filled the small screen. His head was bowed. He looked defeated and desolate. A roomful of bankers, traders and office workers looked sadly at him. There was total silence. DiCaprio held the microphone to his lips but it seemed he had nothing to say.

Then, jerking his head up, he spoke quickly, but softly. 'You know what?'

He lowered the mic and looked at the crowd as if waiting for an answer. When there was none he lifted the microphone and said, huskily, 'I'm not leaving.'

Off camera you could hear muffled gasps and cries, and an incredulous '*What?*'

DiCaprio nodded, flared his nostrils and said, a little louder, 'I'm not leaving . . .'

People stared at him in confusion and then surprise. DiCaprio walked a few steps and then, suddenly, he shouted: '*I'm not fucking leaving!*'

The room erupted with joy and relief. It looked like a goal had just been scored as people jumped around and hugged each other. Middle-aged men bumped chests and screamed.

DiCaprio was not finished. His right hand gripped the mic while his left hand spun in a whirring motion as he yelled: 'The show goes on!'

Women hugged each other; male traders high-fived, whooped and hollered. DiCaprio kept shouting: 'They're gonna need a fucking wrecking ball to take me outta here! They're gonna have to send in the National Guard or a fucking SWAT team because I ain't goin' nowhere!'

The room exploded. It looked like the Kop going ballistic after another killer goal.

At home in little old Formby, still six weeks from leaving for America, I rocked with laughter. I could picture the scene being transported to Anfield. I could see myself looking forlorn and lost for words, too choked to say anything to the supporters I loved. And then, as the sun sank over the Kop, I'd say: 'You know what? I'm not leaving. I'm not fucking leaving . . . !'

The *Wolf of Wall Street* clip still played on my phone. DiCaprio was still giving it loads. He showed the finger and screamed: 'Fuck them!'

And then he began beating his chest and humming, occasionally breaking out into a monkey-like yelp. Slowly, the whole room started to copy him and, soon, everyone was beating their chest, while humming and squawking like an unstoppable troop of jungle gorillas.

I had my speech. Perfect. I could just imagine the stir I'd

cause when I yelled: 'They're gonna need a fucking wrecking ball to take me outta here!'

If I still found it possible to joke about my last game at Anfield, it was painful to read about the latest round of testimonies at the Hillsborough inquest. It was a shock that, in the very same week, evidence was being heard into the death of my cousin Jon-Paul Gilhooley. On Wednesday, 13 May, just three days before I said goodbye to Anfield, the inquest uncovered terrible details. This was the unending tragedy of Hillsborough, twenty-six years on.

## Anfield, Liverpool, Saturday, 16 May 2015

I was thankful I had my three girls with me in the tunnel at Anfield. Lilly, Lexie and Lourdes were dressed in matching cream-and-apricot outfits. I kissed each of my daughters in turn and then picked up Lourdes. Up ahead of us Jordan Henderson, captain elect, led Liverpool out into the soft evening sunshine at the end of a beautiful blue-skied day. It was 5.30 p.m.

Alex, as I expected, wanted to stay out of sight up in the stands with my mum and hers. She's worked as a model and is very confident when her photograph is taken. But there is still a shyness to her. She doesn't like being in the public eye or having her picture taken outside work or with her family. Alex is as shy as anyone I've known. She didn't want to suddenly step into my world of football.

But it felt essential to have the girls around me. I needed them to distract me from the threat of tears. If I had the girls I knew I would be strong. I would not let them see their dad cry.

Anfield was already singing about me: *Stevie Gerrard is our captain, Stevie Gerrard is a red; Stevie Gerrard plays for Liverpool, a Scouser born and bred.*

I got the signal. It was time. 'OK, girls,' I said. 'Let's go . . .'

Lilly and Lexie walked ahead. They led me and Lourdes down the stairs. They could see the sunlight ahead. Holding Lourdes with my right arm I stretched out my left hand. I touched the sign: *This Is Anfield.*

We paused again at the bottom, where we were asked to wait. 'Hold on, girls,' I said. The announcer was talking about me and I needed another diversion. I pointed straight ahead and told the girls we just needed to walk down the tunnel when we got the all-clear. I could still hear the words booming around Anfield.

'Having grown up as a Red and dreamed of playing in front of the Kop he went on to make 708 appearances, 502 in the Premier League, scoring 119 goals and winning almost all there was to win . . .'

I noticed that 'almost'. But it was true. I had almost won the league a year before.

The announcer continued: 'To those of you in the Kop and the Lower Centenary please raise your cards now and welcome your captain onto the pitch for his final game at Anfield. Ladies and gentlemen, the one and only . . . *Steven Gerrard!*'

We walked out of the tunnel and into the light. Liverpool and Crystal Palace's players were waiting for us. Up in the stands the outer edges of the Kop were framed in white. In the middle we had the old sea of red. My initials *SG* were highlighted in yellow – and between the *S* and the *G* the number 8 was in all white. Across the bottom of the Centenary Stand the word *CAPTAIN* had been spelt out in red card. The backdrop was made up of pure white card.

Palace were the visitors and so Lourdes and I veered towards the line of yellow shirts and pale blue shorts. All the Liverpool lads, and the Palace players facing them, were applauding me. Still holding Lourdes with my right arm I used my left hand to slap the open palm of each Palace man. By the time we reached the end, Anfield had burst into another old song.

*Steve Gerrard, Gerrard / He'll pass the ball forty yards / He's big and he's fucking hard / Steve Gerrard, Gerrard . . .*

Lourdes covered her ears – because of the din rather than the swearing. She looked at me and gave me an order: 'Turn the noise off, Daddy.'

I crouched down. 'I can't,' I said with a grin.

Lourdes normally runs me and she wasn't giving up. 'Tell them to be quiet,' she said. 'Tell them we're on the pitch now. Be quiet now.'

I might still have been Liverpool's captain for another eight days but my powers were limited. Lourdes didn't seem to mind. 'They've all come to see me,' she said, brightening.

'Yeah,' I smiled, 'you might be right.'

It was working. Little Lourdes made me want to laugh rather than cry. The girls and I formed a chain as we held hands. Lilly, Lexie, me and Lourdes. We walked towards the Kop and they began to sing 'You'll Never Walk Alone'.

It was almost too much for me. I stopped and went down on my haunches again. I already knew the answer but it was the best way to compose myself. I asked Lourdes if the singing was still too loud. 'Yes,' she said. She covered her ears again. Her big sisters were laughing and they also hunched down to be the same height as me and Lourdes. She runs them too. I felt better. We had a little laugh again while the Kop sang on.

I looked over at the soaring stand and saw some of the huge banners and flags.

*LIVERPOOL WAS MADE FOR ME & I WAS MADE FOR LIVERPOOL Thanks Stevie IT'S BEEN A PLEASURE LAD, Thanks Steven GERRARD Liverpool Legend 1998–2015*

## STEVEN GERRARD – ONE OF A KIND
## THANKS FOR THE MEMORIES STEVIE

It was almost a relief to turn away, hand over the girls and walk across to the officials and mascots for a photo. 'You'll Never Walk Alone' had just reached a shuddering crescendo.

'Walk on, walk on, with hope in your heart . . .'

I felt embarrassed at hogging the attention from my teammates and the Palace players. Thankfully we had a game of football to play.

It took a while but, after twenty-five minutes, having been outplayed by Palace, we could lose ourselves in the match. Raheem Sterling harried Martin Kelly. It was the kind of pressing we needed because Kelly's frantic crossfield pass went behind his fellow Palace defender Scott Dann. Adam Lallana made the most of the Palace fiasco. He raced away with the ball, swept into their area and drove it past Wayne Hennessey.

Adam ran and looked for me. He wanted to celebrate his goal with me even though I'd had nothing to do with its creation. We hugged happily, 1–0 ahead.

Yannick Bolasie had plagued us a year earlier when Palace came back from 3–0 down to shock us with three goals in nine minutes. He was as quick and threatening at Anfield and, just before half-time, he was brought down by Emre Can outside the box. Jason Puncheon nailed the free kick and levelled the scores.

The game slipped away in the second half. Wilfried Zaha came on and, after just twenty-two seconds, he scored. We were 2–1 down after an hour.

Once, it would have felt set up for me to stage a Hollywood finish. But I was drained after the season, and the month, and the week, and the day I'd had. I was also, really, on my way to Hollywood. I still couldn't quite believe it.

The old feelings returned. 'Come on,' I said. 'Let's go again.'

I wanted to win one last time at Anfield. I wanted to score once more in front of the Kop. It didn't work. I had a crack soon after Zaha's goal, and Wayne Hennessey saved it comfortably. There were fourteen minutes left when my free kick sailed over and into the red mass of Liverpool fans. When I hit another shot painfully wide, the Kop winced and then laughed. In good humour, they dragged out an old insult usually reserved for wayward away strikers:

*What the fuck, what the fuck, what the fucking hell was that?*

I gave the Kop the thumbs-up. They were right. That had been a terrible effort.

Then, of course, came the ninetieth-minute twist. Penalty.

Yeah, just my luck. A penalty to Palace. Glenn Murray took it, Simon Mignolet saved it; but Murray tucked away the rebound.

Liverpool 1, Crystal Palace 3. I minded, a lot, but Anfield was lost in a song. They were lost in my song. They sang it for the last three minutes of extra-time, without a break.

*Stevie Gerrard is our captain, Stevie Gerrard is a red; Stevie Gerrard plays for Liverpool, a Scouser born and bred.*

There were fifty seconds left, and still Anfield kept singing the same song. The sound became louder and louder. But maybe, just maybe, I had one last moment, here, at home.

We had a corner. I was all set to attack the near post space for the final time. But Palace were playing hard all the way, as expected. I had a little jostle for space with one of their defenders, Joel Ward, who was not about to give me an inch. He even put his hands on my chest as I tried to muscle past him.

Jordan Henderson swung in the corner – but it was easy for Kelly to head it away.

I knew it was over then. I followed the ball and kept running, as Anfield kept singing. The sound was incredible. It seemed as if 44,000 people were standing and applauding me. 40,000 of them, the Liverpool fans, my people in red, were singing, louder and louder, as the song resounded around Anfield.

*Stevie Gerrard is our captain, Stevie Gerrard is a red; Stevie Gerrard plays for Liverpool, a Scouser born and bred.*

It was all true; and I wanted to cry.

They clapped harder, and they sang more intently. I knew they were saying goodbye.

Hennessey took the last goal kick. He squirted it wide, out to Zaha, on the left. And then, before I could touch the ball again, the referee Jonathan Moss blew his whistle.

The game was over. My career at Anfield was over.

Jason Puncheon got to me first. He hugged me. And then he held my head in his hands and said some kind words I could hardly hear. Joe Ledley, another Palace player, was next in line to embrace me, followed by Dann and Ward and Kelly. I smiled at Martin Kelly. He had once been a red, like me.

My teammates followed, shaking my hand, giving me a squeeze, ruffling my hair. I wandered around, making sure I got to everyone. And then it was time for us to go back to the dressing room so I could pick up the girls. We would then all return for the final goodbye. Anfield kept on singing, so I would always remember:

*Stevie Gerrard is our captain, Stevie Gerrard is a red; Stevie Gerrard plays for Liverpool, a Scouser born and bred.*

Back inside I saw Alan Pardew, Palace's manager. He had transformed their season when he arrived from Newcastle. Pardew is a very good manager and, of course, we had shared that 2006 FA Cup final when he was in charge of West Ham and I was flying at my peak for Liverpool. We shook hands and said a few words.

I soon felt stronger again, back with the girls. They were

chatting away to me, and it felt normal again. I was just a dad in the end.

My teammates trooped past us again. The girls pointed and laughed. Every single member of the Liverpool squad wore the exact same shirt with number 8 and GERRARD on the back. Mario Balotelli inside a Gerrard shirt looked a pretty interesting combination. I grinned. Balotelli had said some lovely things about me, and written me an open letter. I appreciated it – but I still wished it had worked out for Mario and Liverpool. Instead, we'd all had a strange and difficult old season. Football, in the end, was like life. It could also be strange and difficult. They were both raw; they were both real.

Jordan Henderson held his own daughter as he led out his team of Gerrards. Anfield had broken out into a different chant: *Justice for the 96, justice for the 96, justice for the 96!*

Lourdes was playing with my hair when Brendan Rodgers came over to shake my hand. We were both still hurting over the loss. Palace had been great; we had been terrible. The girls, obviously, didn't care. I wasn't even sure if they knew the final score.

I rubbed my face and picked up Lourdes again. She was babbling away and then, suddenly, as if she had remembered something, my little girl looked up at me and said, 'I'm proud of you, Daddy'. I'm sure someone had said to her, 'Tell him you're proud of him.'

But the way she said it, and then put her arms around my neck, choked me up. I was thinking, 'I've got to go down those stairs and have a mic in my hand in another fifteen seconds. How am I going to do this?' I was ready to let go right there and then.

I'd forgotten all about channelling my inner Leonardo DiCaprio and screaming, *'I'm not fucking leaving!'* I was too busy giving myself strict instructions to hold it together.

Lilly and Lexie led us down the stairs again. This time I used my left arm to hold Lourdes. My right hand stretched up. One last time, I touched the sign: *This Is Anfield.*

We were made to wait at the bottom of the stairs as I was introduced again. I listened to the words: 'Our inspirational captain rose from the Kirkby Academy under Steve Heighway, Hugh McAuley and Dave Shannon to become one of the most complete footballers in world football. This man simply had it all. The growing influence of the treble season, Olympiakos, the Gerrard final against West Ham in 2006 and the big one, the night of our lives in 2005.'

Anfield cheered that reference to Istanbul. I was more pre-occupied with Lourdes. In the midst of this heartfelt tribute, she had stuck her finger into my ear. She was having a good old dig as if she might find something interesting. I let her get on with it. There's not much chance of getting a big head if one of your kids sticks a finger in your ear at the same time.

Unaware of my examination in the tunnel, Anfield heard: 'Words don't do justice to what this guy means to us . . . ladies and gentlemen, all good things come to an end. But his legacy lives on every day, as an inspiration to all the youngsters hop-ing to follow in his great footsteps. Ladies and gentlemen . . . your captain . . . *Steven Gerrard.*'

The roar made Lourdes look away from my ear. With Lilly and Lexie, we walked out onto the pitch again. Gérard Houl-lier, my favourite Liverpool manager, who gave me my start at Anfield, was waiting for me. He and Ian Ayre presented me with a golden number 8 on a plinth.

Soon, I had a microphone in my hand. 'I've been dreading this moment,' I said as I spoke to the whole of Anfield, 'and the reason is because I am going to miss it so much. I've loved every minute of it and I'm absolutely devastated I'll never play in front of these supporters again.'

The crowd cheered and applauded itself, rightly, and I was

asked if I was optimistic that the club could move on without me. 'If you go on today's performance there's every chance,' I said with a smile. There were a few groans of frustration with the question – because I knew the supporters were worried about the future after such a fitful season. But we had lost Luis Suárez, and Daniel Sturridge had missed most of the season. We had still reached two cup semi-finals, and we'd been close to going through against Chelsea in the League Cup. I was sure that if we'd have had Luis and Daniel we would have won a trophy and finished in the top four. Would the fans have been groaning at a question about the future then?

It was a strong reminder of the standards expected at Anfield, and the depth of ambition. But I had faith in Brendan Rodgers and my teammates, and I said as much:

> Listen, the club is in good hands. We've got fantastic owners and Ian Ayre under that and we've got a fantastic manager in Brendan. There is unbelievable potential in the squad. I'm sure there are going to be some new signings but I just look at the players in front of me, who I shared the dressing room with for many years. I absolutely love them to death and I wish them all the success in the future.

And then, to end my address, I was asked if I had any final words to say. I nodded and thanked the club and all the players and ex-players who had made me the footballer I had become. 'But I have to save my last thank you for the most important people at any football club – but these supporters stand out more than any. I've experienced . . .'

I had to stop at the start of that new sentence. The sound of the applause was too loud, the sound of my song was too much. I stood there and listened as it rang out again.

*Stevie Gerrard is our captain, Stevie Gerrard is a red; Stevie Gerrard plays for Liverpool, a Scouser born and bred.*

I lowered Lourdes to the ground and raised my left hand to the crowd. I wanted to cry, but I didn't. I paused and took a deep breath. 'Just before I go, and just before the tears come,' I said.

It was a relief to hear that my voice was clear. I'd avoided the crack-up. I'd avoided breaking down. I looked up and then gazed around the whole of Anfield before I said my last few words.

'I've played in front of most supporters in the world and let me tell you – you're the best. Thank you very much. All the best.'

I handed back the microphone and, together with the three girls, I began moving towards the Kop. I lifted my hand again as they began to sing, for me, one last time.

'When you walk, through the storm, hold your head up high . . .'

Lilly and Lexie skipped ahead of me. I scooped up Lourdes and put her on my shoulders. We kept moving towards the Kop, towards the fans, towards my people, to say a final goodbye.

A Saturday evening in Crewe, and I was shattered. I had just been through the two busiest weeks of my life. The build-up to the last home game against Palace, followed by my final week as a Liverpool player, had taken it out of me. I had one game left. Stoke away on a Sunday afternoon at the end of a disappointing season. It was not quite how I had planned my departure.

There had been so many goodbyes. I was going out for meals, holding press conferences and sorting out gifts – or receiving them. A few of the press boys, most of whom I had known my whole career, actually looked sad to see me go. I had snapped at them sometimes, maybe even bitten off one or two heads over the years, but we had been good to each other. Some people might think professional footballers and journalists are beyond the pale. We're all meant to be greedy footballers, they're all meant to be heartless sleaze-merchants. But it was different between me and the press. There was more honesty than bullshit, more decency than anything. At my last meeting with them they gave me a cake. It was very imaginative for a group of football people. They had arranged for a cake to be made which commemorated all my greatest games. I was genuinely touched.

I was also rushing around getting a shirt for every single person at the club, on the football side, so I could sign each with a personal message. I bought wine for all the other male staff, and flowers for all the girls at Liverpool. I don't think I'd ever been as popular as I was that last week at Melwood.

Liverpool FC TV had made a film about me. I had to give it the go-ahead and I felt the emotion surge through me again as I watched it late one night at home. My mum had been persuaded to be in it, and I was proud of her. I was also proud of my dad. And I admired him all over again for being so determined not to ride on the back of my success. He declined, politely, the chance to appear in the film. My dad said it should be about me, and not him.

My dad and my mum have shaped me. The best of me comes straight from them. Dad's a quiet man but he had talked quite a bit to me over the previous few days. He said: 'What a career. What loyalty. Look at your figures, your games and your trophies, and look at your send-off. Look at your people, look at your legacy. People don't want you to go, people want you back. Imagine how it would have felt if you'd have finished your career now at another club? You would have never got such a send-off, or such respect. You did great.'

We both knew how right I had been to turn down Chelsea

ten years earlier to stay at Liverpool. Dad had been a key figure in helping me keep my head straight, and my heart true. But Dad didn't need to shout about it. He knew that I knew. It was enough. Dad looked happy and proud.

At our swanky country hotel, on the outskirts of Crewe, a wedding was in full swing. But all the players were tucked away in their rooms. Some of them were already dreaming of their holidays. I had been told to pack a bag for four days. The boys were taking me away to say goodbye as a team – straight after the game against Stoke. They had arranged something special. While they had told Alex where we were going, and made sure she packed me the right sort of clothes, I was being purposely kept in the dark. I didn't have the heart to tell them that, then, feeling sad at the end, I wasn't really in the mood.

I had a whole evening to kill. My hamstring had been play-ing up and I'd just come back from treatment with the physios. I knew there was boxing on TV that night. I would watch the fight and, hopefully, drift off afterwards. I still had a couple of hours before I turned on the television and so I got back to doing a little more work on this book. I might have gone crazy if I'd not had something to focus on before my last-ever game in a Liverpool shirt.

I had spent a lot of time over the past few months thinking about the lows – the slip and the stamp, disappointment with England and Liverpool drifting down to sixth in the league table. I had almost shunned the highs. I only went back to the Olympiakos and West Ham games because they were so tied to disappointing recent matches in the Champions League, against Basel, and in the FA Cup, during that loss to Villa.

I had also written about Istanbul before. I had spoken about it again and again. I had seen the highlights over and over. Of course I still liked seeing them and I liked the feeling of watching myself lifting the cup. I liked the fact that Istanbul had done so much for the club and for Liverpool as a city.

But I also knew that the day after we played Stoke it would be exactly ten years since we won the Champions League in Istanbul. Ten years was enough. There had been DVDs and books and films and I had been involved in a lot of them. I had celebrated and milked it for ten years.

So I was actually relieved that on Monday, 25 May 2015, I would be with the boys at some unknown location. I would miss the tenth anniversary celebration of Istanbul which was being held at the Echo Arena in Liverpool. The current Liverpool squad is mostly new and fresh and young. A lot of them were babies, not even teenagers, when the Istanbul final was played. So they had no clue about the anniversary. I was glad. I've had enough tributes. I think the next time you'll see me at an Istanbul event will probably be in forty years, when it's the fiftieth anniversary. I'll be nice and old then – just a few days from turning seventy-five.

But, in Crewe, in the quiet of my hotel room, with no one wanting to tell me how great I had been that night, or making me watch the goals or the penalties all over again, I relaxed.

I began to think about AC Milan and Liverpool, about me and Maldini, about despair and elation, about all that Istanbul had meant to me. It was the pinnacle of my career, the best night of my life in a football shirt. Working away on these pages, the memories started to rise up again in a fresh way. They almost felt, as my career ended, that they belonged to me again.

It was amusing to remember the glaring contrast between Paolo Maldini, Milan's captain, and me. Paolo had the looks and the success. He was cool, he was suave, he was tanned, he had perfect white teeth. Maldini was also a brilliant footballer. He had already lifted the European Cup four times.

At the last press conference at the Ataturk Stadium, on the remote fringes of Istanbul, I felt a bit of a fraud sitting next to Maldini. What had I done compared with him? I almost felt uncomfortable getting my photograph taken alongside him. I was this twenty-four-year-old kid from Huyton, from number 10 Ironside Road. He was footballing royalty.

We stood up to shake hands. I looked into those flashing eyes. Maldini seemed unshakeably confident. But he was also polite. 'Good luck tomorrow,' he said in English.

My Italian let me down. 'Thanks,' I mumbled back in English. 'You too . . .'

Maldini looked like he had been born lucky – but what else could I say? I followed the lead of the King of Milan but, actually, I just wanted to say, 'Listen, Paolo, mate, you've already won this cup four times. Gizza go, please . . . let me lift it just this once.'

I then remembered a powerful truth. Liverpool had already won the European Cup four times. Milan had won it on six occasions. Only Milan and Real Madrid were more successful than Liverpool in Europe. We belonged on this stage. I belonged at this level.


## Ataturk Stadium, Istanbul, Wednesday, 25 May 2005

Rafa Benítez, the ice-cold tactical master, was the most reliable strategist I'd ever played under. But, for me, he made a blatant error even before we walked out to face the flares and fireworks, the colour and the clamour. I still can't quite get my head around it a decade later. Rafa played the wrong formation. He opted for a 4-4-1-1 formation and picked Harry Kewell and Ginge in wide positions, which meant we had only two in the middle. Didi Hamann missed out. Rafa wanted pace out wide and Luis to be creative between the lines as a number 10. But Harry was not 100 per cent fit. I was more worried that we had lost the steady anchor and vast experience of Didi – who showed no emotion when we all heard the shocking news that he was on the bench. It also left us playing 4-4-1-1 against the Milan diamond, where the quality of Pirlo, Clarence Seedorf and Kaká cut us to shreds.

After ten minutes it was obvious. We were being sliced open and totally struggling in central midfield, where two of us were always up against four Milan players. I was amazed that Rafa did not change the system after thirty minutes – but left it until half-time, when we were apparently dead and buried. Carra and I were trying to get the message around the team, and kept urging Luis García to help make up the numbers, but we were swept off our feet.

We were already a goal down as well. Maldini scored in the very first minute. Kaká won a free kick down the right. Pirlo lined up the delivery. They had worked out that we were sticking to zonal marking. Maldini ghosted into space, no one tracked him, and he volleyed home. 1–0 down after fifty seconds of my first European Cup final.

Kaká was phenomenal for the first forty-five minutes. He was electric. He was quicker running with the ball at his feet than I was without it. Kaká had a stride and a pace and a tempo that were difficult to match that night. Messi and Ronaldo are more ruthless now in terms of scoring goals and having a devastating impact on games, but Kaká was extraordinary in terms of his guile, class and running, like a very fast and unstoppable Rolls-Royce. He also had such vision, such touch. At the time he was probably one of the two best players in the world, alongside Ronaldinho.

We could have focused solely on Kaká; but then what do you do about Seedorf and Pirlo? We were outgunned and we just didn't have the protection we needed in the middle of the park. We needed at least two more bodies to blunt the cutting edge of that Milan diamond. Vladi Šmicer was on for the injured Kewell, which helped, but we were still rocking.

We tried desperately to settle down and make the tactical adjustments we needed. But, before the first half was over, we were losing 3–0. Hernán Crespo, on loan from Chelsea, got both to follow Maldini's opener. His second, and Milan's third, was sublime. I don't think any team in the world would have stopped that goal. Kaká made it with a stunning pass and Crespo's dink of a chip was out of this world. It was one of the best goals I've ever seen live on a pitch.

As we walked off at half-time Milan were, understandably, swaggering with confidence. You could just tell by Gennaro Gattuso's demeanour that he thought it was over. I remember seeing him wave to someone in the crowd. I felt ashamed, really. All I was thinking of then was, 'How do we get a bit of respect and pride back?' But deeper down in the bleaker corners of my head I was thinking, 'This could be a six–nil thrashing if we play like that second half.'

I knew Rafa would make changes. He always did. At first we were moaning and groaning in the dressing room but Rafa shut us down with icy calm. Steve Finnan was struggling with an injury. He wanted to stay on but Rafa was clear. 'Finnan off, Didi on. Three at the back. Didi next to Xabi. Very compact. Together, you two sort out Kaká. Gerrard, play forward, as a 10. Pirlo is not so mobile. Seedorf is slow too. You can close them down. Win the ball. You can get past them. Don't let your heads drop. You are playing for Liverpool. Don't let down the supporters.'

We could hear our fans. Even in the dressing room we could pick out 'You'll Never Walk Alone'. I wouldn't say our supporters sounded defiant or full of belief. It was more the sound of solidarity. They were saying to us: 'You have fucked it up but we're still there for you.' It lifted us, but it would be wrong to say that it made us believe in miracles.

In the second half Didi was key to our getting some kind of foothold in the match. He helped us regain a little control. Having that extra body in the middle allowed me to push further forward, as Rafa had instructed. We were more of a threat, and we were more stable in midfield.

They could have gone 4–0 up with a strong penalty shout. But we should have had a pen in the first half and that perhaps influenced the referee. Maybe he thought he owed us one.

The speed and tempo of Milan's passing and running dipped. They weren't closing us down or showing the same slick movement in attack. Milan took their foot off the gas. But it certainly wasn't until we got the first goal where I thought a tiny little bit, like Clive Tyldesley said on his match commentary, 'Hello.' Yeah. 'Oh . . . hello, it's 3–1 now. There's still time.'

Goals change matches and mine certainly changed this one. Rafa wanted me to play as a number 10 – but I didn't feel I could match Alessandro Nesta and Jaap Stam in terms of strength and physicality in the air. I decided to drop off them and try to get into the space either side of their holding midfielder. I was getting a bit of joy and John Arne Riise whipped in a cross – which was blocked. He got a second chance and I reached it. I nearly broke my neck getting to it because Ginge had smacked it hard and fast before Cafu could close him down. I was twelve yards out and I used the power of Ginge's cross to steer it over Dida, the Milan keeper. It was a relief to see it go in.

I ran hard towards the fans. I wanted them to lift us some more. My goal would help, but they could transform us. And they did. Their roar gave us more energy. I'd scored in the fifty-fourth minute and then two minutes later Šmicer added a second when Dida was slow in getting down and the ball trickled in. 3–2.

I made the run which led to our equalizer, our third goal in five minutes. It was the kind of move I'd made as a midfielder all my life. I was the third man running into the box and it's always difficult for a midfielder or a defender to pick you up when his attention is diverted by two other attackers. I went for the layoff. It was a little big, but I still think I would have got there. Next thing, I felt a click of my ankles. I went down. Penalty.

I had total confidence in Xabi Alonso. He had taken most of our penalties that season. He was calm, and a great striker of the ball.

Dida pushed the spot kick away but Xabi got him on the rebound. It was an incredibly skilful finish – to lift the ball up into the net with your left foot when their big six-foot-five keeper is rushing out for the second save. We were lost in the noise and the huddle. It turned into a bundle of bodies. There were so many of us you almost couldn't breathe. But we were so happy.

3–0 down after fifty-four minutes. 3–3 after fifty-nine.

After that goal I thought, 'Let's just get this to extra time and penalties.' Even though there was a lot of time left, and Milan were shell-shocked, we were shattered. If I could have done so, I would have taken penalties right there and then.

People now think that once I scored the first goal we battered Milan for more than an hour. But we didn't. We had to dig deep into all our reserves of desire and energy to keep them out. We all worked harder in that game than probably any other.

When Liverpool arranged for some kind tributes to me to be recorded in my final week in May 2015, Maldini said on the club website that he remembered me tackling every single

THE LEAVING OF LIVERPOOL

Milan player again and again. I might have done because I was completely knackered at the end of it. I ended up playing three positions in that match because, near the end, Rafa made me play right back so I could shackle Serginho. He was a Brazilian firecracker and it felt as if my whole body was shutting down with cramp as he came at me with ferocious pace. I had been throwing myself into tackles my whole life, from Ironside Road to Istanbul, and I think instinct took over. I tackled him every time he had the ball. But I was running on empty.

Carra was immense, blocking Shevchenko and Kaká. He was also struggling with cramp but Carra was indestructible. Djimi Traoré cleared off the line. No one ever mentions that any more. It's just been forgotten. But it happened. Jerzy Dudek also made his one-in-a-million save from Shevchenko. Someone was looking down on us that night. The luck was with us.

It was the longest penalty shoot-out of my life. I was due to take the decisive fifth penalty, if it got that far. But we had men with real courage that night. Didi Hamann scored our first with a broken toe. Djibril Cissé, who had broken his leg earlier in the season, scored our second. Serginho and Pirlo missed Milan's first two penalties. Jon Dahl Tomasson made it 2–1 and Riise changed his mind and his shot was saved. Ginge is usually a power merchant but he tried to be too precise. Kaká then scored. 2–2.

There was so much pressure on Vladi Šmicer. He was on his way out of the club. When he was left out of the team for our final home game of the season Vladi nearly strangled Rafa. But Vladi is such a pro he nailed his penalty. 3–2.

And then, in a moment I'll never forget, Jerzy psyched-out Shevchenko by staring at him, bouncing on his line and then moving a foot off it – seemingly for the hell of it. Shevchenko, a great player, shot weakly and straight down the middle. Jerzy saved it; and we all started screaming and running. There was no need for me to even take my penalty. We had won the Champions League. We were the kings of Europe.

We went as crazy as you would expect. We yelped, we shrieked, we laughed, we danced, we ran around like idiots. I look back now in amazement at some of our antics. Was that really me? Yes. I celebrated like I deserved to celebrate. Correct me if I'm wrong, but have you ever seen a better Champions League final? Every single one of Milan's players was either world class or very close to that exalted level. They were a better team than us but we beat them.

It was not just luck. The big moments in the second half went our way but, after we finally got back to the dressing room, I saw how much we had given. There were cuts everywhere, bruises, ice, bandages, sweat, dirt and plenty of tears. It looked like we had been to war. We had been through a brutal battle in the Ataturk; and, somehow, through will, skill and sheer bloody-mindedness, we had not only survived a 3–0 shellacking. We had won. We had won.

I celebrated for a week. It was a week of being on top of the world. I had been in the first team for seven years and I had grown up my whole life aware that, when you represent Liverpool, there is a pressure and responsibility to add to the great history of this club. It's almost unfair because there are so many more teams that are capable of competing now. The strength of football in Europe is so much deeper now than it was twenty or thirty years ago. But we did it. We won a fifth European Cup for Liverpool. It was such a blissful moment, but one of great relief as well. We had kept the flame alive.

When we got back to Liverpool and boarded the bus the volume of people waiting for us was unbelievable. The bus was shaking and it felt dangerous. But we didn't care. We felt invincible; and adored.

I had seen images of the Beatles on TV all through my

childhood. I often thought to myself: 'I wonder what that would be like?' The day of our Champions League homecoming told me. It was almost as if the Beatles had come back to Liverpool. We were the Beatles, for a week.

We had a party that night. The actor Jude Law, who I am a big fan of, was suddenly there. A few more faces arrived. I was too drunk to really notice them. I remember dancing on the seats until five in the morning. It was already light when we staggered out. I kept going. I kept partying.

Four days later, I sat in the house. I was a wreck. I was white as a ghost. I had red eyes. I looked drained but I was still on my Champions League high. I must have broken a few records for the amount of drink I poured into my body for four straight days. I could never do it now.

But I turned twenty-five on 30 May 2005. I was in my prime – on and off the pitch.

'Let's have another small party,' Gerrard the ghost thought. 'It's my birthday . . . and it wasn't a dream. We really did win the European Cup.'

My last-ever game for Liverpool, my 710th for the club, turned into more of a nightmare. An hour after the match against Stoke City at the Britannia Stadium on 24 May 2015, a friend texted me to ask what I'd made of a surreal afternoon. I answered him with one word:

Wow.

I might have had a slightly tight hamstring the night before the game, but it was fine during the match. We had no excuses. It was just a disaster. A catastrophe. Everything that could go wrong, did go wrong. There was no fight, no balls, no character, no passion. I couldn't believe I was in a Liverpool team.

We were 5–0 down at half-time. Yes – wow.

Emre Can tried to put his hand up during the break and take responsibility. I stopped him after a few words. Emre is some talent and I think he's going to be a great player for Liverpool. But he is a midfielder and he was playing out of position at right back against Stoke. A few of the others chipped in to make sure Emre didn't take sole blame. We were all at fault. The worst team performance of my Liverpool career was not down to Emre or any one player. It was a collective failure. Most of us looked like we were already on holiday. I also needed to take a big chunk of blame because I had dominated everyone's attention, again, during the build-up. But there was no excuse for the way we played.

I was stunned. Every time Stoke went forward it felt like they were going to score. It was diabolical. There were no mitigating circumstances.

The manager was disgusted. I felt for Brendan. He had plans to go and watch his son, Anton, in the League One play-off final at Wembley. I put myself in his shoes. Imagine if I was trying to shoot off after a game to see my kids in a dance show that meant so much to me – and my players let me down? I'd be gutted. And Brendan was rightly gutted by our appalling display.

From a selfish point of view, I didn't want something so humiliating to happen to me in my last game for Liverpool. But I have to live with it now.

We lost 6–1 in the end. I scored a goal, in the 70th minute. I didn't give up. The whole ground rose when my shot flew into the net for my last Liverpool goal. It was similar to the ovation I had received from the Chelsea and Crystal Palace fans. It was touching and respectful.

I was very emotional during my last four games in a Liverpool shirt. There was such an outpouring of goodwill and kindness to me. It was overwhelming at times; and deeply moving. Someone said to me, considering all my goodbyes, 'If

Carlsberg did farewells . . .' Yeah. They wouldn't have me kiss goodbye to my Liverpool career by being hammered 6–1 away to Stoke.

I knew that, straight after the game, we were going away as a squad. On the Friday, the night before we travelled to Crewe in preparation for Stoke on Sunday, I had felt low when I got into bed. I had a knot in my stomach at the thought I would never play at Anfield again. I was not in the mood for a holiday.

Sitting in the dressing room at the Britannia, slowly changing out of my Liverpool kit for the last time, I thought, 'Can we cancel it? It looks so bad to be going away after such a heavy defeat.' But I didn't want to ruin it for everyone else. By the time we got to the airport I began to understand the amount of work and planning behind the trip. The boys had gone to a lot of effort and we were off to Dubai for four days. I couldn't let them down. I had to park the result. But for the first twenty-four hours it was a subdued trip. No one said much on the flight. We were still in shock after the game five hours earlier.

On the Monday afternoon, taking it easy before I met up with the lads and went out for a meal, there was a knock on my hotel room door in Dubai. It was Lucas Leiva, one of my many good friends in the squad. Lucas asked if he could come in for a moment. 'I've got a little something for you,' he said.

'Of course,' I said. I was always happy to see Lucas.

He presented me with a silver salver. It was from him to me and he had written the words inscribed on the plate. 'I've been thinking about getting this done for a while,' Lucas said. I felt a lump in my throat as I read his message.

*We often hear the expression there will never be another.*
*In your case, my friend, it is most definitely the case.*
*A Captain, leader and a legend in every sense of the word.*

445

*Every moment I have spent on the pitch with you has been a privilege. The very best to you and your family with all your future endeavours – Lucas Leiva.*

I just about held it together while Lucas quietly watched me read his words. I thanked him and he smiled happily. We hugged it out.

But once he left, I was gone. There was no stopping my tears.

We all met up a few hours later in the hotel bar for drinks. I was happy again. I was in the mood for a night out with my mates. The first beer was going down easily when Jordan Henderson stood up. Everyone was suddenly very quiet as Jordan spoke. It was a good speech. It wasn't serious or heavy. It was just right. Jordan said the trip was to say thank you to me. He also said they had collected a series of messages from people who I had played with or against during my career. Jordan reached for an elegant leather-bound book. He said: 'We hope you like it, Stevie . . .' I could see how much effort had gone into it and I was blown away all over again. Each message had been copied out in beautifully crafted writing.

The first page was from Zinedine Zidane. It was amazing. I turned to others; and each one had written a personal message. The names and words blurred: Brendan Rodgers, Kenny Dalglish, Robbie Fowler, Steve McManaman, Danny Murphy, Lucas, Philippe Coutinho, Roy Hodgson, Jordan Henderson, Fernando Torres, Luis Suárez, Xabi Alonso, Kolo Touré, Joe Allen, Raheem Sterling, Jordan Ibe, Martin Skrtel, Sami Hyypiä, Ryan Babel, Mario Balotelli . . .

The list went on. Some of them made me smile instantly. Kolo, starting his message with his familiar 'Big Man' name for me; Mario saying 'Sorry my English' as his opening; Luis Suárez writing these words about me: 'For me you will always be a reference and, at club level, you are the best I have played with in my career as a person and a player. You are a legend Steven. Thank you.'

I looked at the lads in amusement. 'You must've got Luis to write that before he went to Barcelona,' I said. 'I'll be down to about twenty-fourth on the list now . . .'

After a while I had to stop reading. I didn't want to break down on a big night out. I told the boys I would read every single message later, on my own. It was time to leave the sentiment behind. It was time to have a party. We had another beer – and headed out into the night.

We went off in a big stretch Hummer. All twenty-five of us were in the Hummer and on the beers. My phone was on the music system. The music suddenly stopped as I had a call. Kolo Touré's name came up on the phone. I put Kolo on loudspeaker. He was phoning to apologize to me, the Big Man, for not being with us. He had a charity match in the Ivory Coast. We were chatting away but after a while I could hardly hear Kolo. The lads had all started singing the Kolo & Yaya song in his honour. They were still singing it after I said goodbye to Kolo and we got out of the Hummer and made our way to the restaurant. We had to go up an escalator and I went ahead so I could film the boys. They looked good singing and dancing together.

Next thing I know Mamadou Sakho grabbed my phone. I could have stayed out of it but, fuck it, I am the captain. I lead from the front. So I raced over to the front of the dancing and singing crew. I took charge. I got into it big time. Whenever we chanted *Kolo . . . Kolo, Kolo . . . Kolo, Kolo . . . Touré . . . !* the boys all went low, ducking down to near floor level. And then we went up, climbing high, reaching to the sky as we chanted *Yaya . . . Yaya, Yaya . . . Yaya, Yaya . . . Touré . . . !* And then I led them down low again for the next *Kolo . . . Kolo, Kolo . . . Kolo, Kolo . . . Touré . . . !* as I moved along in my own version of a West African dance.

A security guard grabbed my phone off Sakho. And then we had a full set as Sakho joined in and we chanted *Kolo . . . Kolo, Kolo . . . Kolo, Kolo . . . Touré . . . !* and *Yaya . . . Yaya, Yaya . . . Yaya, Yaya . . . Touré . . . !* The security guard filmed us on a hot, sticky and happy night in the United Arab Emirates. How else, but through football, my undying passion, could I have ended up here, feeling so blissfully crazy, singing in Dubai about two brothers from the Ivory Coast, one a teammate and the other an old rival from Manchester City?

When we got to the restaurant we had a group chat on Whats-App and I put the video up so everyone could see it. We surprised ourselves. Within twenty-four hours we had gone viral. One of the lads had sent it to a mate who had posted it on YouTube. It went bonkers. The England women's football team did the song and I had Sunday League sides sending me videos of their versions.

The girls back home were entertained. 'Daddy, what are you doing?' they asked, reasonably enough. 'That's not you.'

But it was me. Away from the pressure and the worry, the responsibility and the striving, the ambition and the heartache, I could also dance and chant: *Kolo . . . Kolo, Kolo . . . Kolo, Kolo . . . Touré . . . !* It felt as if my new life had just begun.

I was back home in Formby, in the property we were renting while between lives in Liverpool and LA. I had just five days left before Alex and I flew to Los Angeles on Saturday, 27 June 2015. The girls would join us soon, once school was out for the summer, and my mum and Alex's mum could bring them to America.

In the kitchen, on an ordinary Monday evening in Mersey-side, I had a little time to reflect. Brendan Rodgers and Liverpool were in the midst of a busy summer. Six new players had already been nailed down as certain transfers. I'd not had to text a single one to tell them that, in my opinion, they were about to make the move of their lives. The following footballers had already agreed to join Liverpool: Roberto Firmino, James Milner, Nathaniel Clyne, Danny Ings, Ádám Bogdán and Joe Gomez.

I was more surprised that there had been so much upheaval in the coaching team behind Brendan Rodgers. Changes needed to be made but I had not expected both Colin Pascoe and Mike Marsh, Brendan's assistants, to leave. I thought they would make a single change on the staff, having spoken to Brendan at length. He hadn't mentioned any individuals, but he told me he was looking to strengthen the team and his staff. Marshy obviously loves the club, and he had been there as a player. I was surprised he and Colin both went because neither had much responsibility within Brendan's set-up.

I could only think that Brendan wanted to freshen up his whole team. Colin and Marshy didn't do anything wrong or deserve the sack. It was just another example of football today. Was it brave or disloyal of Brendan? It was a tough question for me to answer. But I was surprised that the club, as a whole, had not mentioned the possibility to me before I signed for LA Galaxy.

I'm not saying I should have been offered the post of assistant manager or first-team coach because I am probably not ready for either role. But would it have hurt them to discuss it with me? Maybe I could have stayed on as a squad player while being groomed for the coaching staff? I think that would have been a sensible move with both Jamie Carragher and me. It would have given me an awful lot to think about because sitting here now, a week away from joining LA, I know I am still good enough to wear a Liverpool shirt. I know I could still contribute.

I know I've said I don't really want to be a squad player at Liverpool, but if combined with an offer of an eventual coaching position it would have given me an alternative to America. That experience would have been so important for me. I might have done a year or two – or more. I could have been a link from the staff to the players and, at the same time, I would have seen how training sessions and tactics are planned. I would have sat in on meetings with the staff and the owners. It would have been an unbelievable experience for me and, I believe, of value to the club. But Liverpool had other plans – which also made sense.

I can't quibble with the appointment of Pepijn Lijnders as one of Brendan's new assistants. I did my 'B' licence badges with Pepijn as he coached the under-16s and my favourite young players in Trent Arnold and Herbie Kane. Pepijn is a good coach and a decent man. He was great with me – and he was honest and gave me intelligent feedback after every session I did with him. He would soon be joined in Brendan's coaching team by Sean O'Driscoll and Gary McAllister, my former teammate and a man I respect hugely. Gary could have the same influence on Liverpool as a coach as he had when he joined us as an inspirational player in 2000.

The chance to play in America, meanwhile, is a great opportunity for me. Lexie walked into the kitchen to grab a drink and tell me that she and the girls were off for a bounce on the trampoline.

On a summer evening, I asked her a simple question. 'Are you looking forward to LA, Lexie?'

Her face lit up. 'Yeah,' she said.

It's going to be an adventure for me, Alex, Lilly, Lexie and Lourdes. While I'm away I will keep following English and European football closely. I will get up early in LA to watch every Liverpool game on TV and I will chart the progress of Luis Suárez at Barcelona, Fernando Torres at Atlético Madrid and Rafa Benítez at Real Madrid.

Luis and I keep in touch. I loved watching him and Barcelona win the Champions League. He knew all over again that we were right to have saved him from Arsenal – so he could join Barça. It was no surprise to me that Luis had done so well in his first season at Camp Nou and it felt like sweet vindication when he scored the crucial second goal in the Champions League final against Juventus. I knew Messi and Neymar would feel just as I had done with Suárez as a teammate. Luis Suárez might make the odd mistake, but he is a joy to play alongside.

I reached for the big book my Liverpool teammates had given to me in Dubai. I turned to read the message that Luis Suárez had written. I read the words written by Zinedine Zidane, and Kenny Dalglish and John Aldridge and Brendan Rodgers and Jordan Henderson and Lucas Leiva and everyone else.

What had my girls said when I led the Kolo and Yaya dance? 'What are you doing, Daddy? That's not you . . .'

But as I read the words about me, from people in football I respected, I felt both nostalgic and optimistic. I was the same person that Zidane saw. The same man that Dalglish and Suárez and Henderson knew. They were all part of my story. I was the boy from Ironside Road who won the Champions League and the FA Cup and the UEFA Cup and the League Cup – if not the Premier League. I had played 824 major football matches, 710 for Liverpool and 114 for England. I was about to complete the journey from the Bluebell Estate to Beverly Hills, from Huyton to Hollywood. But I knew that I would always belong to Liverpool. I had been with the same football club for twenty-seven years, and I had played for the first team for seventeen of them.

And suddenly, on that quiet Monday evening on Merseyside, I felt serene and calm. I shut the beautiful big book, full of kind words about me, and I thought of my dad. What did Dad always say when I was a kid? 'This is where it starts. Everything you've done before this has gone.'

At the age of thirty-five, life was not so simple. It was deeper. It was better. I could start again, but I would carry the past, and all I had done, the elation and the pain, wherever I went. It seemed clearer than ever to me.

The dark and the light, the joy and the hurt, the hope and the loss, cannot be parted. They belong together like the posts of an empty goal, in front of the Kop, at Anfield.

# Appendix: A Career in Numbers
### (compiled by Ged Rea)

Some Liverpool FC statistics:

## Penalties Converted

| Rank | Player | League | FA Cup | League Cup | Europe | Others | Total |
|------|--------|--------|--------|------------|--------|--------|-------|
| 1. | *Steven Gerrard* | *32* | *3* | *2* | *10* | *0* | *47* |
| 2. | Jan Molby | 30 | 2 | 7 | 1 | 2 | 42 |
| 3. | Phil Neal | 28 | 2 | 3 | 5 | 0 | 38 |
| 4. | Billy Liddell | 34 | 0 | 0 | 0 | 0 | 34 |
| 5. | Tommy Smith | 15 | 2 | 2 | 3 | 0 | 22 |
| 6. | Robbie Fowler | 14 | 1 | 3 | 2 | 0 | 20 |
| 7. | John Aldridge | 15 | 1 | 1 | 0 | 0 | 17 |
| =8. | Gordon Hodgson | 16 | 0 | 0 | 0 | 0 | 16 |
| =8. | Terry McDermott | 13 | 1 | 1 | 1 | 0 | 16 |
| 10. | Michael Owen | 11 | 1 | 1 | 0 | 0 | 13 |
| 11. | Kevin Keegan | 10 | 0 | 0 | 1 | 0 | 11 |
| 12. | John Barnes | 7 | 2 | 0 | 0 | 1 | 10 |

## Appearances as First-Team Captain

| Rank | Player | Total |
|------|--------|-------|
| 1. | *Steven Gerrard* | *470* |
| 2. | Ron Yeats | 417 |
| 3. | Emlyn Hughes | 337 |
| 4. | Alex Raisbeck | 267 |
| 5. | Donald McKinlay | 250 |
| 6. | Sami Hyypiä | 197 |
| 7. | Alan Hansen | 195 |

## *First-Team Appearances*

| Rank | Player | League | FA Cup | League Cup | Europe | Others | Total |
|------|--------|--------|--------|------------|--------|--------|-------|
| 1. | Ian Callaghan | 640 | 79 | 42 | 89 | 7 | 857 |
| 2. | Jamie Carragher | 508 | 40 | 35 | 150 | 4 | 737 |
| *3.* | *Steven Gerrard* | *504* | *42* | *30* | *130* | *4* | *710* |
| =4. | Ray Clemence | 470 | 54 | 55 | 80 | 6 | 665 |
| =4. | Emlyn Hughes | 474 | 62 | 46 | 79 | 4 | 665 |
| 6. | Ian Rush | 469 | 61 | 78 | 38 | 14 | 660 |
| 7. | Phil Neal | 455 | 45 | 66 | 74 | 9 | 650 |
| 8. | Tommy Smith | 467 | 52 | 30 | 85 | 4 | 638 |
| 9. | Bruce Grobbelaar | 440 | 62 | 70 | 38 | 18 | 628 |
| 10. | Alan Hansen | 434 | 58 | 68 | 46 | 14 | 620 |

## *Goals scored*

| Rank | Player | League | FA Cup | League Cup | Europe | Others | Total |
|------|--------|--------|--------|------------|--------|--------|-------|
| 1. | Ian Rush | 229 | 39 | 48 | 20 | 10 | 346 |
| 2. | Roger Hunt | 244 | 18 | 5 | 17 | 1 | 285 |
| 3. | Gordon Hodgson | 233 | 8 | – | – | – | 241 |
| 4. | Billy Liddell | 215 | 13 | – | – | – | 228 |
| *5.* | *Steven Gerrard* | *120* | *15* | *9* | *41* | *1* | *186* |
| 6. | Robbie Fowler | 128 | 12 | 29 | 14 | – | 183 |
| 7. | Kenny Dalglish | 118 | 13 | 27 | 11 | 3 | 172 |
| 8. | Michael Owen | 118 | 8 | 9 | 22 | 1 | 158 |
| 9. | Harry Chambers | 135 | 16 | – | – | – | 151 |
| 10. | Sam Raybould | 120 | 9 | – | – | – | 129 |
| 11. | Jack Parkinson | 123 | 5 | – | – | – | 128 |
| 12. | Dick Forshaw | 116 | 7 | – | – | – | 123 |
| 13. | Ian St John | 95 | 12 | 1 | 10 | – | 118 |
| 14. | Jack Balmer | 98 | 12 | – | – | – | 110 |
| 15. | John Barnes | 84 | 16 | 3 | 3 | 2 | 108 |
| 16. | Kevin Keegan | 68 | 14 | 6 | 12 | – | 100 |

# Acknowledgements

My family lived through every page of this book, the highs and lows, the ups and downs, in real life. And so the book also belongs to them because, without their constant love and support, I would not have achieved much as a person or a footballer. I owe a great deal to my wife Alex. She might not know much about football but she knows me better than anyone and so most thanks go to her for always supporting me and for being such an amazing wife and a fantastic mother to our three daughters.

While I still feel a little sad to not be playing for Liverpool any more, I've loved having the chance to spend so much more time with Alex and our wonderful girls – Lilly-Ella, Lexie and Lourdes. In America we're able to do things as a family that were simply not possible when I was captain of Liverpool. They make me laugh and they make me feel very happy. I'm pretty sure Lilly, Lexie and Lourdes will enjoy having an ordinary dad around them from now on.

My mum and dad have offered me incredible backing from the very start. They also instilled in me the values that mean most to me and which I hope I can pass on to my own children. Thanks to Mum and Dad for always being there for me – and for all the help and good advice they have given me for the past thirty-five years.

Paul, my older brother, is more than a friend. Our bond goes deeper and I have always been able to rely on him when I've needed him most. I'm also glad I made Paul, and Dad, happy by staying with Liverpool for my whole career in England.

I'm also very fortunate to have such a close-knit group of

trusted friends. I am just myself, and we always have a real laugh, when I'm with them. Thanks, as always, to them.

This book is also for the best fans in the world, those who support Liverpool FC, because without them I would never have been able to stay loyal to the same club. The support they gave me, and the amazing send-off they produced at the end, meant that I never regretted my decision to always remain at Liverpool. Liverpool's fans made me feel very lucky – as did all the faithful England supporters who followed the national team and me around the world. Without these proper fans, the game has little meaning.

Thank you to all the extraordinary people who belong to the Hillsborough Family Support Group. You have kept alive the memory of the 96. Justice, because of you, will eventually be won.

I would like to thank everyone at Liverpool FC – all my past managers, my former teammates, the coaches, medical team, office and administrative staff, the stewards and everyone else connected to the club at Anfield, the training ground at Melwood and the various Academies I've been part of on Merseyside. It says much about the club that I remain so close to so many people at Liverpool. I would love to return one day – in whatever capacity that Liverpool FC believe I can make a contribution.

In the meantime, I'm thrilled to have the chance to play Major League Soccer in America for LA Galaxy. Thank you to everyone at my new club for making me and my family feel so welcome.

My agent Struan Marshall has proved he's the best in the business and he's been at my side for almost my whole career. Thanks to Struan for all his advice and friendship.

This book came about after many discussions between Duncan Ross of the Wasserman Media Group and Daniel

ACKNOWLEDGEMENTS

Bunyard of Penguin Books. Dan and Duncan showed the persistence and enthusiasm we needed from the very start. I knew that Dan was serious when he tracked down a first edition copy of John Steinbeck's *Of Mice and Men* for me. Thanks to everyone at Penguin for their faith, passion and hard work on the book.

I also want to thank Chris Morgan, Liverpool's head of physiotherapy, for checking the sections which relate to my past injuries – and for all the help he and everyone else on Liverpool FC.'s medical team have given me over the years.

Paul Joyce of the *Daily Express* and I have known each other a long time. He interviewed me first in 1998 soon after I broke into the first team. Paul never let me down and I always trusted him completely. He was also a great ally to me and Don McRae when, working against a brutal deadline, Paul helped us so much with his memories and insights.

I told Don McRae I'd done my homework on him and his past books before we first met. And so I just about forgave him for being an Arsenal fan. We worked hard together on this book and, best of all, with so much emotion flying around as I prepared to leave Liverpool, we enjoyed writing it together. Thanks to Don for listening to my story, for recording it and piecing it all together. I also showed him what it means to be a proper Red . . . a Liverpool fan.

# Picture Permissions

## Inset 1

PA-2049076: Martin Rickett / PA Archive / PA Images
PA-6575773: Mike Egerton / EMPICS Sport
PA-297601: Mike Egerton / EMPICS Sport
PA-1304862: Fiona Hanson / PA Archive / PA Images
PA-362791: Adam Davy / EMPICS Sport
Getty 160842231: Michael Regan – The FA
PA-9303250: Nick Potts / PA Archive / PA Images
Getty 50970456: Ross Kinnaird
Getty 184702325: ADRIAN DENNIS
rexfeatures_1110007a: Andy Hooper / *Daily Mail* / REX

## Inset 2

PA-16164754: Kirsty Wigglesworth / AP / Press Association Images
PA-3309955: DAVE THOMPSON / AP / Press Association Images
rexfeatures_4198801a: Andy Hooper / Associated Newspapers / REX
PA-8139918: Peter Byrne / PA Archive / PA Images
rexfeatures_1076745a: Andy Hooper / *Daily Mail* / REX
Getty 52980325: Getty Images
PA-3491423: MATT DUNHAM / AP / Press Association Images
Getty 140080568: Pool
PA-18821856: Barrington Coombs / EMPICS Sport
Getty 96522060: PAUL ELLIS
PA-12377212: Peter Byrne / PA Archive / PA Images
PA-6786475: Peter Byrne / PA Archive / PA Images
rexfeatures_3716481am: Matt West / BPI / REX

## *Inset 3*

Getty 473623970: OLI SCARFF
PA-23026719: Peter Byrne / PA Wire / Press Association Images
PA-23097633: Peter Byrne / PA Wire / Press Association Images
rexfeatures_47855770: NSJsport / REX
PA-23106121: Dave Howarth / PA Wire/Press Association Images
rexfeatures_3716481am: Matt West / BPI / REX
Getty 480445168: Matthew Ashton – AMA
Getty 480467428: Matthew Ashton – AMA
PA-3437564: David Davies / PA Archive / PA Images
rexfeatures_983629h: Piers Allardyce / REX
Getty 97859096: AFP
Getty 97859082: AFP
Getty 50841242: Paul Barker
PA-8115071: Tim Hales / AP / Press Association Images

# Index